W9-BNO-998

Reconstructing 'Education'
through
Mindful Attention

Oren Ergas

Reconstructing 'Education' through Mindful Attention

Positioning the Mind at the Center of Curriculum and Pedagogy

Oren Ergas
Beit Berl Academic College and Hebrew University
Modi'in, Israel

ISBN 978-1-137-58781-7   ISBN 978-1-137-58782-4 (eBook)
DOI 10.1057/978-1-137-58782-4

Library of Congress Control Number: 2016954801

This Palgrave Macmillan imprint is published by Springer Nature
The registered company is Macmillan Publishers Ltd.
The registered company address is: The Campus, 4 Crinan Street, London, N1 9XW, United Kingdom

FOREWORD

What are the goals of a true education? Where is the focus of the heart and mind in the curriculum? And what is the basis on which we should develop educational curricula? In this engaging book, Oren Ergas deeply inquires into the requirements and practices for a truly educated person. In doing so, he lifts the veil of hidden assumptions that drive our current achievement-assessed model of curriculum and directs our thinking to a deeper set of postulates about the meaning of education. I should place 'education' in quotes, because Ergas takes us on an experiential journey into the deeper meaning of 'education' as a task of meaning-making that is profound, reflective, and insightful. In doing so, he reveals to the reader the central role of attention as the fundamental and basic building block for the development of awareness and discernment.

Drawing on the roots of Western Psychology as articulated by William James, modern philosophy of mind, the latest neuroscience, and the wisdom of contemplative practices, this tour de force of inner awareness takes the modern educator through a first-person, investigative journey into the nature of mind. In doing so, the book explores the inner curriculum, the nature of awareness, and its direct relation to compassion.

In a world obsessed with outer achievements and a blindness that prioritizes the acquiring of information over knowledge and virtue, Ergas asks the reader to take a deep look at the inner curriculum of self-knowledge and self-awareness that unfolds through the sharpening of attentional capacities. By turning attention to explore the mind and perception, Ergas leads us on a voyage into the nature of the mind and self-knowledge and positions the reader to consider the need to rebalance the concept of 'education' in which there is a new equilibrium between inner awareness and outer learning.

This book uncovers a deep void in current discussions of 'education'. It argues that a true education necessarily requires a focus on the nature of our own minds, how they operate, and how we can selectively attend to what is the core of being human. By doing so, the book not only brings the self into the realm of curriculum, but also seeks to enrich the learning of the 'external' curriculum of literature, math, science, social studies, and other subjects that are critical to success in the modern world.

By systematically and progressively deepening this inquiry into the inner curriculum of reflective thought and pure awareness, Ergas brings both the practice of mindfulness and the importance of social and emotional learning to the forefront of learning and pedagogy. While this book will be of interest to numerous audiences including those steeped in the philosophy, sociology, and psychology of education, pedagogy, and curriculum, Ergas focuses on all of us as learners, teachers, and individuals within a society. By taking the time to explore the nature of mind and awareness, readers will embark on a journey that will bring them to a deeper understanding of themselves and motivate them to create a 'true' education for their students, and for themselves.

Professor Mark Greenberg
Bennett Chair of Prevention Science
Pennsylvania State University

PREFACE

This book offers a different way of thinking, practicing, and researching 'education'. It will ask *you* to do something that you were probably never asked to do: to reconstruct the idea of 'education' based on a shared experiential journey into the embodied mind. Such idea may strike you as peculiar for usually you are not consulted with on such matters. 'Education', whether in its institutional form in 'schools', 'colleges', 'universities' or as a transmission of norms and culture based on informal 'social practice' and at home, existed long before you. Given this situation, there is that tacit feeling that it is more about how you fit in to its existing framework. But this book will radically challenge this 'natural order' of things. We're going to rethink this framework by turning to the source that had brought it about into the world – the mind. But, not just 'the' mind. Your mind and my own.

Regardless of how and where it takes place, 'education' is a 'mind-making process' as Eliot Eisner claimed. It is the way in which you are taught to see the world, live in it, and understand yourself as well. But there is something very fundamental that this book will seek to untangle in this process: 'education' shapes our minds, but in this process our minds are made to understand the form of 'education' itself. What I mean by this is that when you were a baby your parents pointed at a ball and said 'ball' a thousand times. Your brain-mind followed that act until somehow an automated habit was created – your brain-mind was 'made' to associate the word 'ball' with that round thing that bounces. The two became one. 'Education' is the same, only in a far more complex and subtle way. You were sent to institutions in which you did *this* and *that*, learned *this* and *that*, and throughout all those years it was as if a BIG mind called society was parenting you from above, pointing its finger at all those things in which you were engaged saying – '*this is education*'. An automated habit was created – your brain-mind was 'made' to associate the word 'education' with all *that*. The two became one.

This book will work our way back to separate 'education' from the mind. Indeed, 'education is a mind-making' process, but were there not minds there that made 'education' in the first place? It must then follow that those minds have stamped something of their nature on to this 'social endeavor'. That which we see *out there* as a collective 'social' creation must reflect tendencies of the human mind. This means that any problem we identify today in 'educational' theory and practice must somehow reflect problems in the nature of minds that brought this operation about. It is very likely that you have heard critique of 'society's' one-size fits all 'education', or you've read about school problems of violence, dropout, bullying, and substance abuse. Perhaps you've heard about 'curricular' problems concerned with 'not enough' math or science or too much of them at the expense of the arts and the deprivation of creativity. Maybe those problems are related to teacher burnout? Or, is it accountability or our rushing kindergarteners to begin their resume-building toward glamorous careers? Many of these observations are right on the mark, but could all these 'social' problems emerge without minds that think 'education' in certain ways, enact it, and become 'educated' by it?

Paradoxically, however, 'education' has mostly come to mean a 'mind-making process' that has very little to do with *your* mind – the mind that's reading *these words now*, living in *this* body *in here*, breathing, sensing, and emoting. How is it that 'curriculum' and 'pedagogy' have mostly become practices in which the mind is to attend to the world *out there* – the teachers'/lecturers' words, the PowerPoint presentations, the textbooks, the class discussions, the math, the history . . . yet the embodied life of this very mind itself is expelled from the game? Can an 'education' that hopes to 'make minds' and create the 'society' we want succeed without positioning that mind at the center of 'curriculum' and 'pedagogy'; without this mind's turning *in here* to examine its very own makings?

Do you realize how much of your conscious experience consists of the internal life of your embodied mind – your own thoughts, sensations, and emotions? Discoveries from the past decade of neuroscience demonstrate that healthy brains-minds spend close to half of their waking hours remembering the past, planning the future, worrying, regretting, thinking of social image, body-image, ruminating, fantasizing. Much of this domain has been associated with what has been aptly termed the brain's *default* mode network – a network into which the brain switches wittingly or unwittingly as a 'baseline' of sorts that undergirds our experience. We phase in and out of this baseline as we sit in a classroom or lecture hall, as we drive or walk to school, and as we engage in conversations with others. Research shows that this pervasive domain shapes our moods, well-being, and identity, and affects our behavior. Can something that takes place nearly half or our waking hours within our brains-minds-bodies not be of huge significance to the making of the mind – to 'education'?

Yet that is not how our minds have been made to understand 'education'. Much of that flux *in here*, which is pretty much *you*, is seen from 'social' eyes as 'noise' in the system. If it's there during a 'history lesson' we say that it in fact *interferes* with 'education' unless it is directly concerned with 'history'. This book boldly suggests that all this 'noise' is no less than the *other half of the curriculum*. While a teacher may be explaining a historical event, or reading a Shakespeare Sonnet a student may be miles away worrying about losing his friend, dreading the end of semester exams, wondering whether her overweight can be seen through her shirt...We tend to treat all this for what it *isn't* – it isn't 'history' or 'math' - rather than for what it *is* - alternative lessons that may be far more influential on who we are, who we will come to be, how we will behave with others, and the meaning we find in our lives (or not). This *inner curriculum* affects us moment after moment for better and for worse – but for some reason the mind that creates it along with the *subject matter* of these alternative lessons, have been expelled from the theory and practice of 'education'. Who is this mind that is 'educating' itself that we have somehow cast to the backyard of what we call 'education'?

Yet again, if we find ourselves blaming 'society' for having expelled our interiority from the 'curriculum' we are missing the point. 'Society' itself emerges from minds and as it appears, minds are capable of inventing an 'education' that expels their own presence from it. Part of the system that we've created 'educates' us to miss our own role in this. Our general approach of coping with the problems of 'education' is to look at their 'social' symptoms *out there* and attempt to 'fix' them *out there*. This book suggests that it may be time to forget about 'education' and focus on the mind *in here*. This by no means implies challenging the importance of math, history, science, literature, and reading skills. It is about challenging a blindness into which we are 'educating' ourselves – a blindness that initiates us in the idea that the 'subject matter' *out there* is somehow more important than the mind that studies it *in here*; that the mind is merely a means and not also an *end*. This mind – this *embodied* mind, which is mysteriously associated with the brain – is that with which we will have to live for our entire lives. It is that which governs the hand that is raised to hit or caress and the mouth that is opened to curse or to bless. *You* are the only one that has a privileged direct access to your mind as I have to my own. We are the only ones that can take responsibility for it. It seem like we need to engage in a far more rigorous study of this mind and what it brings to the 'curriculum' so that 'education' as a 'mind-making practice' will indeed tackle the problem at its source.

The ideas with which this book will engage you, are the result of an on-going endeavor that has begun more than 20 years ago as I started to tread what I initially thought of as a 'dual' path of 'education': a standard and familiar Academic path and a less standard one of studying my own embodied mind based on diverse contemplative practices. It took time to realize that these are two paths only in as far as they are seen from a mind that was 'educated' to understand 'education' in certain ways. At some point I began to question this entire 'social' construct that had instilled in me the idea that 'education' is something that 'society' *does to* the mind rather than a process that includes what this mind does to itself wittingly or unwittingly. We are educated by all those disciplines and skills taught at schools but we are also educated by our own minds and bodies at this very moment with every thought, sensation, and emotion many of which arise *in here* without our knowing why, or where they come from. From one moment to the next our sense of *agency, identity, knowing, being*, and *meaning* are shaped through our engagement with ourselves and with the world. It matters *not* whether the source of the making of our minds comes from the world *out there* or from *in here*. It matters far more whether we awaken ourselves to see this as we attempt to figure out who we are, who we want to be and how we may become of service to others.

It's been a long journey to bring these ideas into writing. Throughout these years aside from the articulation of these ideas in academic papers, the most 'educative' journey for me has been to teach them to my University students that grilled me with enough questions to send me refining them time and again. I'm hardly done refining and I suspect that this may be a state of being I shall have to learn to live with. The attempt to offer a structure to our *inner curriculum* and to reconstruct 'education' from the mind is bound to be cumbersome for it eventually results as an attempt to give structure to that which gives structure. I am hence sure that much of what will be offered here requires further work. Still, I think it is a journey worth taking in spite of imperfection. It is a journey that invites you personally to engage with your mind. The idea is simple: you study your mind. I'll study mine. Comparing our conclusions we might come to think quite differently about what our 'curriculum' ought to include and what kind of 'pedagogies' we want in schools and higher education institutions. With some help from neuroscience, psychological research, and philosophy, I think we can make headway in this endeavor of reconstructing 'education'. I realize that this may sound eclectic. Indeed it is. This book will speak to you and with you in many languages and voices. Some of its chapters will take you to empirical science, and others will apply evocative narratives, and phenomenology. I see no other way. Raise your eyes and look around you. All human made things have come from minds, and our inventiveness seems inexhaustible. The mind is infinite. Despite my very limited perspective that is grounded in my own mind, I will try to capture a fraction of this open terrain that 'education' to a great extent has been hiding from us.

Just as it is the case with my students at the university you might not agree with some (or many) of the claims that I will make. Many of them are way 'out there' compared to how we have come to understand 'education'. However, most of my students have substantially changed the way they see and practice 'education' as a consequence of spending time with these ideas. Many have come to understand that 'education' is something that the mind 'does' to itself wittingly or unwittingly just as much as it is something that 'society' 'does' to the mind. Most have come to take more responsibility for 'education' for they experienced clearly that our internal lives are an *inner curriculum* that unfolds with every passing moment whether we care to attend to it or not. Most have come to understand that a 'social curriculum' that initiates us in the norms, knowledge, and skills relevant to our epoch is crucial but without pedagogies that teach us to attend *in here now* deliberately it is half an 'education'. Half an 'education', creates problems that are half diagnosed and half solved. It is time to open the door of attention *inward*. Just as much as 'education' is a mind-making process, our mind can be an 'education'-making process. We hope to liberate our minds through 'education', but it is in fact 'education' that needs to be liberated. Only then can we return to 'society' with a difference.

***

I began writing this book as a visiting scholar of the Mind and Life Institute in the fall of 2014 in the midst of the inspiring sights of Amherst during foliage. It was there that the first part of the book was written and it was there that I was also able to enjoy the wisdom, kindness, and support of Arthur Zajonc (then head of the Institute) and Andrew Olendzki, as I discussed some of the ideas you are about to read with them. Following the time at Amherst, the rest of the writing went on as I phased in and out from other academic projects and teaching courses.

Behind every word in this book stands a chain of causality that is beyond my own understanding, but in some cases I can certainly put my finger on encounters and books that shaped my thinking in various ways. Some of the people I thank here never heard my name but their work has shaped my understanding significantly. I'll mention but a few of them with the clear omission of many due to scope and space. Iain McGilchrist's *The Master and His Emissary* opened my mind to articulate the idea of 'education' as shaping and being shaped by the mind, Tor Norretranders' *The User Illusion* taught me the utter limited position in which we stand in understanding experience, Daniel Siegel's *The Developing Mind* and Richard Davidson's *The Emotional Life of Your Brain* have both helped me articulate and understand the triad of brain, mind, and human relationships. Jon Kabat-Zinn's writings on mindfulness helped me articulate my ideas in communicable ways. I am utterly grateful to Mark Greenberg who agreed to write the foreword for this book. Thank you Mark for your friendship and for substantially affecting my thinking on the relations between 'education', social-emotional learning, and contemplative practice. Deep thanks to Sharon Todd, Robert Roeser, Ofra Mayseless and Jack Miller for the endorsements on the backcover of this book.

Though this book is by no means about wisdom-traditions in a literal sense, my readings of Buddhism, Taoism, and yoga and no less all those who taught me yoga, tai chi, mindfulness, and other types of meditation stand behind much of what I write. I am also thankful to my own mind-body that in moments of stillness overcomes its 'education' and enables me to see things from unexpected perspectives. I thank Philip Wexler who taught me to think like a sociologist, Hanan Alexander who taught me to think like a philosopher, and Samuel Scolnicov who taught me courage. I thank the contemplative academic community here in Israel for their support and wisdom: Ofra Mayseless, Nava Levit-Binnun, Asaf Federman, Amos Avisar, Eitan Chikli, Amir Freiman, Aviva Berkovich-Ohana, Nimrod Sheinman, Ricardo Tarrasch, Assaf Sati Elbar. I thank my students for their unabated critique and dedication, and for helping me make more sense. I thank Laura Aldridge and the production team at Palgrave Macmillan who've been so helpful throughout the process.

Deep thanks to Daniel Marom for reviewing parts of this book and proposing critical points, which substantially helped me understand what it is that I am trying to do here. Deep thanks to Judith Harel whose advising helped me march on with confidence. I thank my mother and father, my brother Yaron and my sister Shlomit. You have all been part of my own 'education'.

We unfold behind everything we do, but when we actually start noticing this unfolding as a 'curriculum', 'education' changes, the mind changes, life changes, 'society' changes. I know that from personal experience. On that note it is my wife Dganit and my children, Doron, Galia, and Noga that I need to thank most. I thank them both for enduring the non-compromising person that I am and for being there to awaken me from my own sleep-walking whenever I think that the problem isn't me.

Modi'in   Oren Ergas
October 2016

ACKNOWLEDGEMENTS

Oren Ergas wishes to thank the Mind and Life Institute (Amherst, MA, USA) for a visiting scholars' fellowship and MUDA Institute for Mindfulness, Science and Society, at IDC (Herzliya, Israel) for an additional fellowship that together provided partial funding for the writing of this book.

Contents

LIST OF FIGURES

LIST OF TABLES

Introduction: The Problem of Education Is 'Education'. Forget 'Education'. Study the Mind

The fact that 'education' has problems is hardly news to anyone, at least not if one reads the daily papers, raises children of his or her own, or simply recalls his or her own experiences of being educat*ed*. Diagnoses of these problems span the gamut. Some depict them in pedagogical, curricular, and/or organizational terms. Others see them as economic or social problems as they highlight inequality, bullying, dropout, substance abuse etc. It is not that I disagree with these observations. It is rather more of a feeling that something far more fundamental is missing from our view. It is not at all surprising that it is missing for I suspect that if I am doing my job properly as a writer then that something is missing from *your* view right now – *Your own embodied experience*. I've tricked you by becoming the agent of your attention. If your mind attends to these words, it cannot attend to itself. This is the story of 'education' in a nutshell. It is I believe the biggest problem we face – the expulsion of the mind from 'education'.

Missing from our diagnostics is the peculiar possibility: that the problem of education might be 'education'. We might have gotten stuck in how we understand 'education' as it relates to all those practices that we associate with it. That's why the word 'education' is going to appear in parentheses throughout the book just like many other terms like 'society', 'curriculum', 'pedagogy' that we have come to consider as if they are independent of the mind that perceives and constructs them.

There are numerous manifestations to the problem of education's being 'education'. The one we start with is that somehow much of what

© The Author(s) 2017
O. Ergas, *Reconstructing 'Education' through Mindful Attention*,
DOI 10.1057/978-1-137-58782-4_1

is happening in *your* mind has been expelled from the constructs of 'education', 'curriculum', and 'pedagogy'. Somehow we have come to think that math counts as subject matter whereas your fear or love of math does not; that 'education' is about 'society' *out there* and not about our embodied minds *in here* – our emotions, sensations, and by all means that internal narrative to which each one of us listens individually throughout our day. The 'education' we have constructed as a 'society' will tend to shape our view so that we see these internal domains as something that is marginal or in fact *interferes* with 'education'. This book will seek to convince you that *your* mind-body is the other half of the 'curriculum'.

This mind of *yours* is that through which you are perceiving *this* word based on your past experiences. Since these words are constantly changing, you're literally changing your mind with every word you are reading. You're not really *doing* that. It just happens. It will happen if you stop reading as well, for experience will be immediately 'filled' by other stimuli. Most of what is happening right now to enable experience is hidden from you. If you need a proof for that, then consider that your mind by all means includes the experience of your body that may be noted just for this moment because of 'hearing' its name, yet a moment ago it was cast to the background for your mind is also responsible for focusing your attention so that *this* word will take center stage.

That thing we call mind is mysteriously tied to a brain, and I will be speaking of both in some chapters of this book. I will mostly speak of the mind but in some chapters brain-language will help articulate the experience of the mind as I will follow psychologists and neuroscientists who clearly associate between the two. I'll argue in this book that whether you care to note this or not, your brain-mind is 'educated' at this very moment. *Right now* neurons are firing in your brain in ways that I hope are both familiar enough so as to enable the understanding of my words, but also novel enough to begin carving new patterns of neuronal firings based on which you will come to think differently about that thing we call 'education'. This process itself might count as 'education'; however, some might not view it that way, which leads us to another problem with 'education'. Some of our minds were 'educated' to think that 'education' is more of a *formal* process that takes place at 'schools', 'universities', and even at 'home' if you will. I argue that, if by 'education' we mean the shaping of our identity, agency, well-being, dispositions toward life, ethics, ways of being-knowing-acting in the world, and our ability to respond intelligently to life situations – and I think most would agree at least with some of these – then our brains-minds do not wait for an experience to be called a 'math lesson' in order to 'get' 'educated'. They are 'educated' here and now.

For those that are familiar with philosophers like John Dewey and Alfred North Whitehead, who viewed *all* life as education, such claim might not be considered to be novel. However, what *does* escape many is a more radical claim that I'll be making: your brain-mind-body does not care much whether the information it perceives arrives from what 'society' had thoughtfully placed in a textbook, what the teacher writes on the board/screen, what scientific research had validated, *or* whether it comes from *your* mind-body itself. The narrative that runs in your mind through-out your day (e.g., your worries, hopes, dreams, thoughts of your social-image, body-image), your emotional life, and your bodily sensations are all subject matter that forms an *inner curriculum*. This is regardless of how adequately this *inner curriculum* reflects reality *out there*, and regardless of what kind of state of mind you are in when you experience them. A child walking to school with the fear of being attacked by the school bully is 'educated' in fear as the bully waiting around the corner 'educates' himself in violence. Driving to work and worrying about being fired or planning your vacation is the subject matter created in *your* brain-mind that wittingly or unwittingly 'educates' your brain-mind then and there.

We are constantly 'educated' from within and from without, but the problem of 'education' is that we will hardly think that this is the case. Part of our 'education' has been to shape our minds to believe that 'education' is that thing that 'society' *does* to the mind, as it places the subject matter of various disciplines in front of it, and if a student's mind is preoccupied with his personal worries during a 'school-lesson' then the latter are in fact interfering with the occasion for which 'society' had gathered us. *I don't think so*. It might take quite a journey to convince you in this, but though such thoughts-emotions-sensation have not been 'willed' either by 'society' or even by *us*, they are not simply an 'attentional lapse' the consequence of which is 'missing science' or 'missing history' that the teacher is busy teaching. They are an alternative lesson. At times a good one, at others hardly so. Who governs this *inner curriculum* that simply arises in this mind? Is it indeed justified to consider it as part of the process of 'education'? Can we do something about this *inner curriculum*? Can we engage with our minds in an 'educative' way? These questions and others are discussed in this book at length. However, our initial task will be to awaken ourselves from the spell of an 'education' that has somehow hidden this *inner* terrain from our view. We will seek to diagnose what sustains this 'social system' in such a way that makes us believe that the math and history are more important than the mind that is shaped in the process of their learning. How is it that our public 'curricular-pedagogical' practice gives the impression that academic achievements are in some way more important than how we live with ourselves and with each other?

*

EDUCATION IS A MIND-MAKING PROCESS

"Education," as curriculum theorist Eliot Eisner claimed "is a mind-making process" (1993, p. 5). The meaning of this statement is that there are various ways of making meaning based on our experience and 'education' is no less than an initiation into a worldview that *specifies* and *habituates* those ways. That is, 'education' 'makes' minds see things in *certain* ways for better and/ or for worse. To use a metaphor that will appear later in the book – 'Education' can be likened to a process by which 'society' equips your mind and mine with a kaleidoscope through which we will come to see the world through certain settings. That kaleidoscope will determine the ways in which we will come to understand and participate in the 'social' world. Is there a problem there? – On the one hand *not at all*. There's a clear logic and desirability to this. We need to communicate and pragmatically organize our lives and we must then 'make' the 'mind' in some sense. Furthermore, the making of the mind is inevitable for this is how nature works: No matter how wisely thought and open our curricular and extra-curricular activities, they will always create patterns of automation and all learning and habits require such automation.

On the other hand there *is* a problem there. 'Education' as a mind-making process reaches far deeper, for it applies to the shaping of the mind to understand 'education' itself. 'Education' becomes a serious problem when it makes us blind to the fact that it is shaping our minds in very *particular* and *contingent* ways. Our current 'curriculum' and 'pedagogy' as I will argue, are initiating us into obliviousness to the *contingency* of the *specific* kaleidoscope with which we are equipped. I realize that I might be confusing you so to begin to scratch the surface of this problem I'll express this by paraphrasing the words of a contemporary curriculum theorist who wryly stated,

> Our eleventh graders have one difficult problem and a number of easy problems. The difficult problem concerns how to solve equations with two variables. The easy problems are how to handle the emotional turmoil when your father is dying of cancer, the fear of living with an alcoholic mother, or the horror of escaping the neighborhood bully waiting for you behind the corner. You see, our curriculum dedicates four hours per week to the hard problem in primary school, and five in high school. The other problems must be easy for they get one per week, or an occasional "intervention." (see Barak 2015, p. 172)

Barak's wry observation points to two problems of 'education'. The first is a *practical curricular problem* – students hardly ever get to discuss the problems that really trouble them in life. There's no time for that because they need to study math and history. This is a huge problem concerned with domains of the *inner curriculum*, which we will be exploring in the third part of the book. The second is a subtler yet more profound problem that concerns the *'educational' construct problem*. Our minds are shaped to believe that this is what 'education' *is* – a 'social' process that concerns things like math and history but not life-problems. This problem concerns the mind in the most direct way. It speaks to that famous Jamesean sentence: "compared to what we can be we are only half awake" (1907, p. 3). Our minds are initiated into mass habits that create 'education' as a *perpetuum mobile*. 'Education' becomes a mechanism that is sustained by an entire 'society' that walks 'half awake', which means equally *half asleep*.

'Education' as we have constructed it, shapes our minds in such a way that while we are busy gazing *out there* at the incredible versatility of the world and human genius, we cannot but become blind to the genius of the mind *in here* that is constantly feeding the kaleidoscope from within, shaping the image, which we see moment after moment *out there*. Every quadratic equation, historical date, literary piece, or geography of a distant terrain is a key to the world *out there* just as much as it is a key to the *inner curriculum* that unfolds in their learning. As Parker Palmer's (1983) book title depicts this, *we know as we are known*. But one realizes such profound idea only based on a reconstruction of 'education'; one that drives home the idea that we are shaped from within and from without based on the door of attention that is the gateway to our minds. It swings *out* just as much as it swings *in*, yet our minds were mistakenly shaped to associate 'education' far more with the former than with the latter.

You and I are born and initiated into a 'social narrative' that will create the feeling that *this narrative* reflects the way in which this world was made, and hence it has little to do with our own minds; as if 'education' was given to us on the eighth day of creation and now we need to cope with the consequences of an endeavor that is not really in our hands. Our general approach reflects a lack of understanding that whatever we consider to be problematic *out there* in the 'social world' must have somehow emerged from the *nature of our minds* that brought it about. Ignoring the mind as the other half of the 'curriculum', 'education' becomes a hall of mirrors in which 'society' educates the minds to mirror back its own ways of thinking and practicing 'education'. The theory constantly revalidates itself by minds that impose theory through practice. Very much following the analysis of critical pedagogues and grounded in Marx's 'social' analysis, 'education' becomes an initiation of the young in the image of the past – a *perpetuum mobile* sustained by mind and 'society'. It is a vicious cycle indeed, and attempting to diagnose a problem within such a self-justifying system means asking for trouble. Whether you gaze at 'society' that emerges from minds, or whether you gaze at the mind that was shaped in 'society's' image through 'education', you are bound to find yourself lost in a hall of mirrors. There may be a way of escape as I will propose. It involves stepping away from 'society' and 'mind' as we know them in order to complement (not substitute) our paths of knowing and being.

But first, a brief thought-experiment can demonstrate this 'hall of mirrors' formed through 'education'. It shows both the inevitability of this process and the problem that it creates. If you would somehow take a healthy baby that was born in the eleventh century, send it through a time-tunnel and raise and educate it in the twenty-first century, would this baby's mind 'catch up' with a millennium of human technology and knowledge to reflect the minds of adults today? Conversely, send a baby that was born today through a time-tunnel to be raised and educated in the eleventh century. Would the mind of that baby grow to reflect the ways of its era or would it reflect minds of a twenty-first century baby? – all this is highly speculative of course, but I think it is plausible to claim that 'education' will close the time-gap in both cases. Most minds will come to reflect the norms and ideas of their time and place through 'education' whether you think of it in its institutionalized or non-institutionalized and informal ways. If you want this in a slightly more realistic though unfortunate version, imagine a case in which an Argentinian and an Inuit baby become orphans at the day of their birth and are sent to adoption to France and Saudi Arabia respectively. How likely are these babies to grow into adults that reflect the societies and cultures of their origin? What this comes down to is that,

> 'education' as we constructed it is a mind-making process by which a mind is shaped to mirror the ways of its time and place for better and for worse. It is a path of roads taken that is automatically the exclusion of a myriad others that 'could have been'.

This tells us an incredible story about the mind that can be described based on two terms with which neuroscience has been busy in the past decade: *plasticity* and *pruning*.

> On the one hand, we have the incredible plasticity of a brain-mind that is born into the world and can be shaped in a myriad ways depending on the kind of 'education' it gets. On the other hand, the kind of 'education' we get prunes infinite options to the particularity and contingency that is reflected in who you come to be based on the fact that your 'society' at this moment in time believes in *this* and not in *that*. In due time *this* might become *that* and vice versa.

We might think that the sun revolves around the earth as was customary just a few hundreds of years ago, and we might live in a 'society' in which women do not have the right to vote. *Whichever the case the mind will be made through 'education'* to become blind to such contingencies. It will be made to view this as how the world *is*. Peculiarly, you and I might be sitting smugly right now thinking how wise we are now to have overcome those misconceptions about the sun, and no less about women's rights. The great fallacy in this may escape our view. Those living a hundred years from now might view both of us and our 'wise' contemporary 'society' with a similar kind of smugness that we experience now.

Education, Contingency, and Pruning

'Education' as a 'mind-making process' has shaped your mind to see the world in a way that is very similar to the way in which others around you see it and somewhat different than the way in which those living a few hundred miles to the East or South of you see it.[1] That shaping can include anything from the choice of disciplines that you find on an average students' timetable comprising of the public 'curriculum' at your home-town, the skills considered as necessary for contemporary life, as well as 'social' norms such as how one is to stand in line in the supermarket and when it is customary to go to college, get married, and have kids. All these are 'housed' within what Neil Postman (1995) called a 'narrative' – a broad belief system that provides context to our actions and gives them certain meanings. Some narratives are better than others but that is not the point I am making. The point is that *mutatis mutandis*,

> our mind can be shaped to see the world based on any narrative but all it gets is one. That is what I call contingency. However, contingency is not the problem. It becomes the problem when your mind is 'educated' to confuse it with necessity.

Norms such as having kids at the age of thirty or twenty, having one child, eight or none, the importance of mathematics and science or the preference of literature, the desirability of logical thinking over Romantic musings, the prestige of Harvard compared to some local college, the preference of becoming a lawyer rather than a carpenter, taking the transportation by engine cars rather than traveling in a chariot in the twenty-first century as taken for granted – these do not seem to be present in the mind that is born into the world. They are the product of 'education' that has built those meanings into that mind so that this 'educated' mind now sees things as they *ought* to be seen according to the narrative of *this* 'society'. The mind comes to see them as the way the world was made.

The point that I am making then is that our vocabulary of describing 'education' smacks of great optimism when we speak of it as a process of 'cultivation' and a 'bringing out' of potentialities (as the Latin *Educare* suggests). What we seem to miss is a different, perhaps more pessimistic perspective: 'education' very much follows the natural process that neuroscientists refer to as *pruning*. It is the sculpting of a brain-mind of a newborn that seems to be born with infinite potentials into the *person* that *you* are right now. It is not just the *positive* aspect of cultivation of certain ways of seeing, but by all means the *negative accent* of cutting off the many roads that could have been taken and were not. Truth be told, we are probably lucky to have cut off many of those roads, but the realization that things could have been different than they are *now* is crucial both to the kind of contemplative journey that this book hopes to offer you personally, and I believe to the very idea, practice, and research of 'education'.

Let us not forget what 'education' amounts to: we are in a business in which minds are attempting to determine how to form the process that makes them. Do we have enough 'inside information' about that mind that we are attempting to shape? Are we sure that students' timetables and school and higher education curricula as we know them constitute the best mind-making processes we can come up with? What makes us so sure that what we have now needs to be replicated? I seriously believe that exploring our minds as the other half of the 'curriculum' is an extremely fruitful path by which optimism will return to the starker image that I have begun to sketch. Once we become more aware of this pruning effect both at the 'social' level of our 'curricular' deliberations but also *at the level of how our own minds participate in the process of 'education'*, I think we will position ourselves in a far more knowledgeable place from which we will be able to engage in the task of reconstructing 'education'. The manifestation of the problem of education as 'education' in this case is that we have somehow managed to construct an incredibly thoughtful operation called 'education' that is to 'make minds' yet we never quite stop to directly examine the mind that this operation is to shape.

A reasonable objection to all the above may be that in its better cases, 'education' seeks to develop a critical consciousness in tune with the tradition of 'liberal education' and in more current manifestations of critical pedagogy (Freire 2007; Giroux 2011). Indeed you will find a very Socratic kind of approach in this book as it will constantly challenge the taken for granted. Furthermore, I am all for empowering students through the creation of a critical consciousness that 'educates' them to see 'social construction' at work as it creates inequality, gender-issues, marginalization of ethnical groups, violence, and several other problems that plague contemporary 'society'. But there's something far more basic at which I am pointing. It lies beyond philosophical and 'social' critique as we commonly practice them, for these too are 'traditions' that 'educate' the mind in certain ways that risk blinding it to its pruning. I am speaking of the last resort of *agency* from which this book will begin its methodical inquiry in the next chapter – the constructor of all *identities* that resides closer than our own eye – *Attention*. I think it's time to return to a place that we can all touch – *first person experience*, as it emerges from that to which we attend. It's time to reconstruct 'education' in a way that it will become more credible for right now even when it has to do with libertarian agendas (e.g., critical pedagogy) it seems to be too much about a thing we call 'society' as if such thing is independent of *your mind*, which perceives it *now* and is part of its makings. 'Education' and 'society' have conquered themselves a place of omniscience. Somewhat biblically stated, it's as if,

in the beginning there was 'education' then you and your mind came along.

'Education' is somewhat an invention of a BIG mind called 'society' that touches upon the surface of our individual minds, supposedly 'educating' us in a shared ethos of 'knowledge', skills, and norms, but leaving our interior untouched as if it has little to do with it. I see this phenomenon year after year as I meet my University students, teachers-to-be, that come to my courses during their Bachelor's or Master's programs. The first thing I ask them to do is define 'education' in two sentences. The common denominator of most of these definitions is that they all seem to emerge from that BIG mind – a 'social mind' that has come to own them. Contingent yet disguised as necessity, it hovers above the land of the living, assumes that omniscient point of view, and defines what all those subjects referred to as 'students' are to know and become. Hardly ever do I hear the word 'I' in these definitions suggesting that 'education' has something to do with an actual living person such as *you*, such as *me*. Rarely is the mind that defines 'education' included in the process that is eventually to shape it. Our 'educational' institutions across ages are pruning minds to fit the existing box of 'education'. It's 'education' that needs to be reconstructed to fit the open-ended territory of the mind.

> 'Education' is a mind-making process. But the mind is an 'education'-making process just as much. Our task is to awaken from our stuck-ness in the former, to position ourselves in the latter and balance between the two. Practically that means to turn to the mind from which all this is perceived and to which it is addressed.

This is what I attempt to do in my courses. This is what this book is about.

*

THE METHOD OF THIS BOOK

I am not arguing that 'we got everything wrong', but I do believe that we need a perspective that begins by acknowledging that the methods we use to assess and evaluate current public 'education' go hand in hand with how we think 'education'. Our methods prune our minds and shape them. Subscribing to Albert Einstein's famous aphorism – we can't expect to solve problems with the same kind of mind that brings them about. If we seriously want to learn something new, we need to embrace a novel way of understanding. If there is something fundamentally missing from our view then it is probable that 'educational' research as it is currently conducted will not discover it for that fundamental may be missing from our methodology as well.

Two methodological contexts arise from the above: the first stems from Thomas Kuhn's (1970) analysis of scientific progress. Every certain period various anomalies arise in different fields of scientific inquiry. These are not explained by means of the established theories and the consensual methods of inquiry known as the hegemonic *paradigm(s)*. Thus for example, Newtonian mechanics' failure to explain the ways in which subatomic particles move in space, was the bedrock over which the theory of quantum mechanics emerged thus substantially challenging our understandings of space and time. When paradigms fail to provide frameworks for inquiry that yield satisfactory explanations the only recourse is to reconstruct the fundamentals of the paradigms themselves. I believe this description is directly applicable to the discourse of 'education'; to the way(s) we think it, practice it, and study it. It seems to be yielding too many problems, or accused of not solving them properly. What I believe is necessary is coming at this entire business from a completely different angle, which brings me to the second context that flows directly from this kind of approach.[2]

The second context comes from an unexpected place and points to an unexpected discipline. It clicked in when I heard a TED (Technology, Entertainment, Design) interview with entrepreneur Elon Musk. Toward the end of this interview Musk was asked how is it that he keeps coming up with incredible ideas such as launching PayPal, initiating projects like the TESLA electric car, and building rockets that are to take us to outer space. This is what he answered:

> I do think there's a good framework for thinking. It is physics. You know, the sort of first principles reasoning...what I mean by that is, boil things down to their fundamental truths and reason up from there....Through most of our life, we get through life by reasoning by analogy, which essentially means copying what other people do with slight variations. And you have to do that. Otherwise, mentally, you wouldn't be able to get through the day. But when you want to do something new, you have to

apply the physics approach. Physics is really figuring out how to discover new things that are counterintuitive.[3]

Don't worry. We are not going to discuss electromagnetics nor quantum mechanics, but we are certainly going to examine the fundamentals over which an entire 'social' construction stands, and it can't but stand over minds that conceived it into being. Our method then is to boil down things to a bare minimum because that is how we will be able to tell the difference between contingency and necessity. It will tell us where exactly 'society' has made unexplained leaps that have become taken for granted within our construct of 'education'.

We can begin to apply this physics-approach right now as I explain this verb – 'construct'/'re-construct' – that's in the title of this book. This will further clarify the method. There are a number of meanings involved here:

First, 'education' is not some physical fundamental of nature such as mass or energy. It is more of a conglomerate that includes many different components such as 'curriculum', 'pedagogy', 'schooling' and many others. Each of these in turn can be broken further down in to elements such as 'learning', 'teaching', 'skills', 'knowledge', 'math', 'geography' etc. 'Education' is thus not a simple element but rather a *construction* of many components, and re-constructing 'education' will mean breaking it in to basic elements and rebuilding it from there.

Second, 'education' is not some God-given Truth and hardly a law of nature. It is a human creation that has taken its current shape based on human deliberations grounded in history, culture, environmental context etc. *We* constructed it. You might not feel personally responsible for this and I do not intend to blame you. What I mean is that the way in which 'education' is understood and practiced in your vicinity is only testimony to what it had evolved to become but it hardly has a status that is similar to the law of gravitation. It only means that this is what it had evolved to at this point and there is much contingency in it. What I am suggesting is that *we – not anyone else – are responsible* for re-constructing 'education' if our construct yields problems. Re-constructing is a *verb;* an injunction; a call to heed. By the end of this book you may ponder whether heeding the call to reconstruct 'education' is an 'educational' path in and of itself.

The third point goes to the heart of matter. When I speak of re-construction I am using a language that lends itself to the image of construction sites with bricks, cement, trucks, and so forth. You can think of it exactly in that way, yet with one slight change – think of your own mind as the construction site. We're going to be working directly with how the mind *sees* 'education'. That's not what we usually do when we attempt to solve 'educational' problems. Usually we tinker with the practices that are derived from existing conceptions of 'education' – we write new textbooks, improve teaching practice, change accountability policies etc. The course we take in this book reverses this conventional pattern. The idea is that we have been spending quite some time figuring out how to make our ideas about 'education' work *out there*. It's time to examine our internal kaleidoscope and its creation, which dyes the world *out there* (and *in here*) in accordance with the colors of its changing settings.

> Changes in how the mind sees things may very well change how this mind then engages with itself and with the world.

You will be right to ask: how will we ever overcome the fact that the minds that we bring to the study of 'education' have been made by 'education'? How can we reconstruct 'education' without falling right back into the very same existing construct when all we have for the task is our own mind that has already been made by 'education'? How can we escape time and place and embrace a synoptic view that will enable us the kind of freedom from which to reconstruct 'education' to suit the assumed infinite potential of the mind? What would be the way to break the vicious cycle in which we are caught?

Forget 'Education'. Forget 'Society'. Study the Mind

While we are interested in 'education', and in a just 'society', what I propose is that we forget about both for a while. If 'education' is a mind-making process then what we really need to explore is the mind and what is available to it. Once we understand what's available and necessary we may reconstruct 'education' anew and adopt new curricular domains and novel pedagogies. Conversely, we might think that what we currently have is the best of all goods, yet we will at least know that based on looking beyond our past habits of understanding and practicing 'education'.

Methodologically what we are seeking here is then to step away from an 'educated' state of mind, which is our habitual way of seeing things, to a state of mind that has not been pruned to prefer one way or another. Stepping away from our 'education' means asking: what experiences are available to a mind? We need to examine the mind with as little preconditions as possible, setting aside our wish to leap into determining what is right and what is wrong. We are seeking a mind in which all options are available; one that sets aside what it knows and returns to that place from which it could have been 'educated' to live life at other times, and other places, past or future.[4] We are then in search of the question: what kind of *universal* structure can we come up with that would mark the ballpark within which *any* kind of 'education' will take place?

The mind that I am speaking of is one that is grounded in *mindful attention* and contemplative inquiry. Mindfulness is no less than a discourse at this point. It runs the gamut from scientific research to wisdom traditions, and to popular culture. Important as these contexts are we are going to step away from them as well and focus on the fact that – as a *practice*, mindfulness involves turning our attention *inward* to explore our first-person experience – *our own embodied mind.*[5] We will not be discussing the practice or its outcomes here. We will simply attend to our first-person experience and garner data based on that. That is why you need not worry at all if you have no previous experience in mindfulness practice. In fact it might be an advantage, for you might come to the re-construction of 'education' with the exact state of mind that is required for such endeavor – a mind that is open to anything that unfolds and doesn't have too many expectations that are the product of its previous habituation. I will soon say more about *mindful attention*, but first I want to position both of us in the kind of attitude with which to engage in this journey. This involves two methodological shifts that re-establish our birth right to challenge the taken for granted-ness of how our minds were made by the process of 'education' and by 'society'. I call them: *reclaiming the mind from 'society' and 'education'* and *working from mind to 'education'*.

Reclaiming the Mind from 'Society' and 'Education'

The 'society' in which you happened to be born (as broad as you want to think of it) is far more contingent than your embodied experience. Returning to the above mentioned thought experiment – you could have probably been born anywhere else on the globe or even at another time. Your 'society' and 'education' in such case would be different, but it is hard to imagine that the basic structure of experience as it is perceived by your brain-mind-body would change. That is, whether the stork would drop you in Mexico or Ethiopia, in the twenty-first century or the ninth, whatever experiences you would undergo as you would be 'educated' in those respective 'societies', would probably still be experienced by you as sensations, emotions, and thoughts. The specific thoughts/emotions/ sensation you would experience would clearly change according to the external situation, but *not* these basic ways in which living beings such as you and I experience the world. So what I am establishing here is the,

> non-contingency of your embodied mind from which the contingency of 'society' and 'education' can be examined.

I realize that such position may send some readers moving restlessly in their chairs as it could sound 'egocentric'/'self-centered' to the point of questioning whether this is politically correct. If this is the case for you, I would encourage you to question *these* constructs in and of themselves. They might be coming from the 'educated' mind that we are supposed to leave behind us. Make no mistake. I am all for altruism, 'social'-engagement and the overcoming of self-centeredness as we colloquially understand these terms. I'm just less sure about what they mean. What *is* that 'self' around which things are centered? It sounds like something that's *in here* in this mind of mine? Do I know it well enough so as to be able *not* to act too 'selfishly'? What is the 'center' around which 'ego*centrism*' or 'self-centeredness' are formed? What exactly is the relationship between mind and 'self'? How does that flux of emotions/sensations/thoughts give rise to *identity* at all, and what in that flux is 'educated' when we speak of 'education'? Do you see what I mean? I think our 'social' talk about a kind, just, and equal 'society' in which people care about each other needs to be set aside for a while. I'm not sure we can be expected to overcome 'selfishness' without having a very clear embodied understanding of what it is, where it comes from and why in spite of our endless talk about overcoming it we find ourselves deeply entrenched in it. You might not suffer from this ailment, but I know *I* do, and I see others around me that may be suffering from that too. Could it be then, that moving *in* to explore this mind and this 'self' opens a way out of 'selfishness'?

The movement from 'society' and 'education' to mind is a movement into *your* own body *here* and *now*. It is an appeal to you to take charge of your own perspective, as well as a responsibility for everything that emerges from that place in which you dwell. It is an attempt to step away from the lure of the language into which we are initiated and to seriously probe what we mean by the words we use and by which we 'educate'. It's about mobilizing us form a view into which we seem to have 'educated' ourselves:

> that 'education' is something that only 'society' does to us, rather than something that I do to myself.

From Mind to 'Education'

The problem we face can be phrased in this way:

> The mind that is born in to the world is pruned to fit the size of 'education' and 'society'. We need to de-prune 'education' and 'society' so that they fit the size of the un-pruned mind.

In order to do this then we're going to forget about 'education' as we know it (e.g., 'schools', 'timetables', 'knowledge', 'skills'), *but* I *am* going to provide us with something to work with and against. I call this a 'place-holder' definition. It means a sentence that might sound 'nice' yet it is almost empty of meaning for the terms it uses can mean almost anything until they too, are defined. So I will ask you to agree with me at least to the following:

> 'Education' is a human endeavor the aim of which is to 'develop' human beings in light of a certain 'good'.[6]

Note that I am not saying what 'good' we are after nor what would be considered 'development' toward it. It does suggest, however, that 'education' has to do with human beings and that there is some kind of a progression involved in it. That's really all I will commit to at this point, and I hope that it is not too much to accept.

Just to demonstrate the power of such approach in poking holes in this construct of 'education' that we edify as a 'society', you can look at this definition and candidly ask one of those unasked peculiar questions:

What's the Problem?

'What's the problem that 'education' is trying to solve?' This might strike you as a bizarre question to ask but the kind of openness to which I am inviting you here, has no boundaries. Setting aside 'society' and embracing a perspective from the mind, I want to be as candid as possible here and suggest that maybe, just maybe, there *is* no problem.

Maybe 'education' is something that is some 'social' circular invention that created both the problems and the system that attempts to solve them. Maybe the whole thing can simply stop at least in its formal institutionalized form? Maybe it's just enough to grow up roaming the world based on what seems to be an innate curiosity as appears in a long history of radical educational ideas.[7] It does sound a little stressful to actually try this – or is it our minds that have become so used to 'educational systems' existence that such void will be too much for them to fathom?

What I am getting at is that the justification for the full-fledged operation called 'education' can't rely only on 'society'. It must be based on a tangible problem that is embodied and experienced in the human mind *now*. If we think we can motivate students by appealing to some future 'society' that lives in some transcendent world we don't stand a chance. 'Education' must mean something very concrete for *you* and for *me* otherwise the problems of 'education' will remain something that 'society' needs to care about, but not *me*.

> Working from the mind to 'education' means diagnosing whether there is a problem in the mind that warrants 'education', and what and who's 'good' 'education' is to serve. Ideally, it suggests that even if there was only one person in the world – you – it would still make sense for him to 'get educated'.

There *is* an 'educational' problem that exists *here* in this mind, and it needs our attention, but it will take a while until I will be able to convince you that this is the case.

Practically Speaking: First- and Third-Person Methods of Inquiry

The above two movements reposition us in *mindful attention* to which I promised to return. I am seeking to prepare you to accept your own responsibility in this business of reconstructing 'education', to motivate you to try things that this book will propose, but also to ensure that you remain the sovereign of your own mind. I am saying this because this book itself will attempt to shape your mind. It will try to convince you of its claims with every means possible within reason while at the same time expecting you *not* to accept anything it offers without personally engaging with its claims.

Practically, to make its case, this book will span the gamut of philosophy, neuroscience, psychology, evocative and biased narratives, as well as mindfulness practices, all of which are diverse ways of making an argument

(Philips 2014). I realize that this sounds eclectic. However, given that we're dealing with the mind – something that no-one has ever managed to fully grasp and this book will probably not change this situation – I suspect that we need all the ammunition we can get our hands on. Still there is a framework within which all the above can be positioned. It follows how I teach at the university: the combination of first and third person methods of inquiry within the context of a dialogical encounter. I will only briefly explain the idea here and count far more on your actual engagement with the book for its understanding.[8]

Third-person methods are those with which you might be familiar from most scientific research. In our case they will give us the (more) *objective* side of things as we rely on evidence-based research in psychology and neuroscience that ground their claims in questionnaires, quantitative data, brain-imaging (e.g., fMRI) and other consensual methodologies. Based on this approach we will seek to make more general claims about the mind. However, of all ways of conviction the strongest one is the one that makes you take your hand out of the fire without requiring the need for a doctor to tell you why that might be a good idea. Quixotic as it might sound that's what I am aiming at. Such conviction is usually not achieved by third-person methods but rather by first-person methods and even more so, when the two align with each other.

First-person methods send you exploring your own experience celebrating *subjectivity* as an indispensable source of data and validation. *This book makes no sense without them.* It will simply crumble back into the problem of 'education' that has been expelling this very idea from much of its research, theory, and practice. Your *particular* mind is where this begins and if you do not validate *general* claims made about mind*s* based on your experience, it leaves too much to be desired. If we do not send you to corroborate claims that are scientifically or philosophically grounded and leave them for you to accept or reject solely based on reading, we might as well stop right now. Don't let me reconstruct 'education' *for* you for in such case it is only my mind that's reclaimed in this business. I think you should be more interested in *your* mind and whether our minds have something in common; something that will later enable us to share visions about 'society' and 'education'.

Practically speaking, throughout the book you will be invited to try various self-experiments. These will include some brief contemplative practices but we will mostly rely on mindfulness. However, this book is not about mindfulness as much as it is about that which mindful attention enables when applied to the study of 'education'. Contemplative inquiry[9] is the broader name for what we will be doing here. It involves all practices that consist of the orienting of our attention to our own experience to consider the claims that apply to our own minds and the way in which we experience existence. They are all ways for you to assess the validity of both scientific and philosophical claims that are made in regards to your own mind and the reconstruction of 'education'.

Why do we need *both* first and third person methods? – because we're trying to establish a perspective that's both embodied, concrete, and valid for *you*, but at the same time it probably applies to anyone around you. We want to make a claim that is both about *the* mind as a *universal* and about *your* mind as *particular*.[10] The only mind to which either one of us has a privileged access is our own. The only mind from which 'education' can be reconstructed is our own. However, if you examine your mind and I examine mine and we then compare our versions and find similar results this can become the ground for shared agreement. We could have settled for that alone, but we do need more. That's where third-person methods come into the picture. Third-person methods are required for a number of reasons: first, they provide more objective tools that help ground our claims and generalize them. Second, as you will see, we are not always very competent in our ability to report about our first-person experience. Third, some things occur in our minds that we do not directly experience, but scientific experiments and philosophical arguments can unravel. Fourth, sometimes once science shows us the way through third-person methods we in fact are 'educated' to experience our first-person experience differently. So we need both first and third-person methods. At the same time as you may have noted the book is written as a dialogical encounter between the two of us, which is somewhat of a second person method that binds the two together. While you won't be able to share your thoughts with me in real time I am constantly trying to imagine your responses as I write. I will hardly capture most of them, but I'll rely on the responses I have heard from dozens of students and at least some of those responses might perhaps resemble your own.

THE STRUCTURE OF THIS BOOK AND HOW TO READ IT

I want to briefly explain the structure of this book and what each of its three parts hopes to accomplish. The first part of the book consists of two chapters that work directly with the 'physics' approach. Here we will not be concerned with any 'right way to educate', but rather with establishing fundamentals of experience that define the ballpark of *any* kind of 'education' one might envision. Chapter 2 begins with a mind boggling statement made by William James: "For the moment what we attend to is reality" (2007, p. 322). You'll be hearing it repeatedly throughout the book for it becomes the axis over which *you, me, she, and he*, as individuals, are positioned to reconstruct as well as practice 'education'. Based on the fundamental of attention as it is deployed from the mind, followed by its orientation in space and in time, the chapter develops the 'the matrix of mind'. This basic matrix provides us with what we need in order to convey a structure of how *a* mind experiences, and based on that – the kind of possibilities that open up for 'education' as a mind-making process.

Chapter 3 describes what seems to be a fundamental structure of 'education' as a process of *pruning* – a reduction of the mind from *universality* to *particularity*, to which we are mostly blind. This begins by moving *in here* to parse a clearer sense of our *identity* based on phenomenology, psychology, and mindful attention. We explore two senses of *identities: I* – a more *universal* embodied identity with which we are born, and *me* – a *particular* narrative-based identity into which we develop. We then move *out* to define 'society' and position the mind within and against it. Yet what in the mind connects mind and 'society'? – WE – a *universal* fundamental, which enables the formation of *particular* 'societies', and 'education'. Based on developmental psychology and phenomenology the chapter then describes the fundamental structure of 'education' in which an *unpruned I*-WE identity is *pruned* to a *me*-'society' identity based on a particular 'narrative'. Pruning is inevitable and indispensable, yet it also carries the root problem with which 'education' will have to struggle: a self-centeredness that is built into the very structure of attention to yield the 'illusion of omniscience' – a blindness to our own pruning that is reasserted unwittingly in moments of perception, and is mirrored at the 'social' level.

At the end of Part I we will be equipped with a powerful perspective that emerges from the mind and unravels the possible terrain of 'education'. Part II – also consisting of two chapters – applies this perspective toward a diagnosis and clear critique of how our contemporary 'curricular-pedagogical' approach shapes the mind. Chapter 4 examines 'curriculum' as it has been constructed based on the fundamental of 'knowledge'. From the position of mindful attention we arrive at the conclusion that 'knowledge' is what 'society' decides to call 'knowledge'. All 'knowledge' is eventually perceived by a mind but paradoxically our hegemonic construct of 'knowledge' has expelled the mind itself from that construct. I will argue that the deepest teachings we get lie in how our attention is 'educated' in space and time, and how we have come to see 'education' as a project that teaches that *here* and *now* are not the right time or place to be at. Chapter 5 delves to the heart of matter as it reveals how this teaching comes about based on the idea of meta-pedagogy – the deepest mind-making process of 'education' – a binary deliberation that is present within every moment in the classroom: *where* we are oriented to attend to: *out there* to the world, or *in here* to the mind. Meta-pedagogy reveals the nitty-gritty of our teaching practice as nullifying *me* and *I* from the 'curriculum' and entrenching the position that meaning exists *out there*.

Following the fundamentals established in Part I and the critique that Part II proposes, our problem results in a construct of 'education' that has gotten our attention stuck in space (*out there* without *in here*) and in time (*future* without *present*). The task of Part III is twofold: first, it will demonstrate how 'society' and the mind create a self-justifying system in which our own minds participate in getting our attention stuck and expelling ourselves from the 'curriculum'. Second, it will articulate the way out of stuck-ness by elaborating what is missing from our 'educational' menu – the possibility of an attention that is turned deliberately in space and time, toward the mind *in here*, and *to now*. It will methodically describe the *inner curriculum* based on phenomenology, psychology, neuroscience, and *mindful attention*. The four chapters of this part of the book include Chapter 6, which describes the ethics of the *inner curriculum* that stems from the fundamental work conducted in Part I and the critique of Part II, and Chapters 7–9 that are each dedicated to a domain within the *inner curriculum*. Chapter 7 examines *embodied perception* to reveal how in each and every moment our mind participates in the shaping of what it perceives. Whether it is a history lesson *out there*, a worried thought in here, or a sensation of pleasure, all are perceived by a brain-mind-body that 'educates' us by meeting that moment based on its past, reacting to it in the present and shaping our future identity, and sense of agency. Chapter 8 examines the *curriculum of me* – all those thoughts experienced *in here* along with their *embodied* effect on who we are and how we act. It is a 'curriculum' that emerges spontaneously through *mind-wandering* and more deliberately through *self-reflection* that to a great extent entrenches us in a false sense of *agency* and in resisting substantial changes in our *identity*. Chapter 9 delves into the *curriculum of I* that is based on a deliberate turning of attention *in here* based on a *reflective I* and a *contemplative I*. It is based on this chapter that I will argue that 'education' is a 'mind-making process' that creates a 'socially constructed mind' only if our attention remains stuck between a 'social narrative' and a 'narrative self'. Beyond narrative there is *I* – a core/minimal 'self' that can reclaim its agency over attention and is not bound by the 'social'. Contemplative practices constitute a curricular-pedagogical approach that unravels this possibility. It is here that we encounter the inner door of attention in which we learn a more authentic place of *agency* through which we can work directly with our identity at the moment of its shaping.

Chapter 10 – the concluding chapter of the book – turns to what usually comes at the beginning of academic books: a literature review and a location of this book within contemporary discourse. Here, I position this book in relation to the 'contemplative turn in "education"' that has been emerging since the turn of the millennium. I point both to how this book reflects its contemporary manifestations, but also how it pushes its envelope.

*

This book treads a thin line between science and life; between 'educational' research, theory, and *practice*. Frankly, I do not care much for that line. It is as real as what you make of it. The only things, which really concern me, are rigor, common sense, a sense of adventure and an awareness of our inherent fallibility, which means the clear understanding that we will do the best we can and we will still be wrong in many cases – all these qualities are found in living life just as much as they are found in science. Our concern in this book is not with Absolute Truth (though we will not complain if we find one). What I'm looking for is to convince *you*. You will find that this book is somewhat 'all over the place' in terms of the diversity of discourses it corresponds with, and the ways in which it speaks. In that sense, it is clear that some chapters will speak to you more than others, and some might in fact confuse you. I have chosen to speak in these different ways, because I believe that our minds are endless and open terrains, and one path will not do to open them further and to open 'education'. This book offers but those paths that I am capable of conveying at least to some degree. I suspect that if some of them do not work for you, others will; if not now then in the future. Think of this as a mind-opener. Not as an end but as a beginning.

One thing, however, is certain; in order to make many of the points of this book your help is unquestionably required. So here are a number of reasons for why engage with some of the weird experiments I will suggest in this book:

First, we are going to be dealing with concepts that will seem abstract, like attention, space, and time. Engaging in these experiments will ensure that they become as tangible as the breath you are breathing right now. This will substantially improve your ability to follow the claims made here, and will also make this far more fun and interactive; as somewhat of a conversation that we are having.

Second, this book is by no means a practical guide that will tell you what to do in a classroom or lecture hall. At times I bring examples of how I teach some of the topics discussed at universities. These might help you envision how this can be done if you are a teacher or lecturer, but most of all it is *your* engagement with the self-experiments offered here that will constitute a practical and experiential process that demonstrates how these ideas can become a practical curricular-pedagogical approach.

Third, and most importantly, these experiments will enable you to prove that I am dead wrong. If that is the case I seriously encourage you to write to me. If I'm still alive I'll either argue, or correct my mistakes. I do make them often, and there is no reason to believe that I somehow overcame that habit in this book.

That's about it for now. You will get the hang of our journey as we take it.

Notes

1. This is a paraphrasis of Neitzsche's critique of 'education' (Nietzsche 2014).
2. To a certain extent we are following a diagnosis that's been made forty years ago by Pinar and Grumet's in *Toward a Poor Curriculum* that has recently been republished: "We have gone just about as far as we can go in understanding the nature of education by focusing on the externals. It is not that the public world – curriculum, instruction, objectives – become unimportant; it is that to further comprehend their roles in the educational process we must take our eyes off them for a time, and begin a lengthy, systematic search of our inner experience" (2014, p. 4). Pinar and Grumet proposed a nuanced account of autobiographical inquiry that is integrated in to the 'curriculum'. The approach proposed here offers a more systematic exploration of the mind.
3. https://www.ted.com/talks/elon_musk_the_mind_behind_tesla_spacex_solarcity
4. Readers who are familiar with Shunryu Suzuki's (1999) writings will recognize this as the idea of a 'beginner's mind'.
5. Chaskalson (2014), Kabat-Zinn (2005), Young (2013), and Varela et al. (1991).

6. This connotes with Richard Peters's (1967) conception of 'worthwhileness', Neil Postman's (1995) conception of a narrative, and Hanan Alexander's (2001) conception of a 'vision of the good' as will be explored mostly in Part II of the book.

7. You will find them in Rousseau's *Emile,* in radical educational agendas such as Neill's (1960) *Summerhill,* and John Holt's (1995) *How children fail,* or in accounts of education in native traditions (Roderick and Merculieff 2013).

8. See Roth (2006), Varela and Shear (1999) and Varela et al. (1991) for more on this methodological framework. See also Kahneman's (2011) distinction between an inside and an outside view (chapter 23).

9. See Barbezat and Bergman (2014), Roth (2006), and Zajonc (2009).

10. This very much follows Thomas Nagel's (1986) idea of *A view from nowhere,* as well as conceptions of non-duality in light of East-Asian traditions (Loy 1988).

PART I

Fundamentals of Mind, Fundamentals of 'Education'

CHAPTER 2

Attention, Space, Time, and 'Education'

From within this mind-body things do not look quite the same as they do from out there.

It is hard to determine the first fundamental from which to derive all else. Faced with the thickness of experience it is as if you stand in front of a heap of yarn trying to pick a loose end, so that you can work your way slowly through the pile to the other end. It is quite pretentious to think that there are loose ends *at all*, or that the whole heap is necessarily made of one string rather than many. It does help to phrase questions in various ways until somehow the mind is lured toward a place that seems plausible.

Here's one such question:

What is that thing on which all experience depends; without which no 'education' exists?

Bizarre question indeed. It might help to begin with the fact that *your* mind must have something to do with that 'thing'. We have to assume that if we take your mind away, no experience will be left for you to ponder, nor will the probing of 'education', being 'educated', or 'educating' be possible. So we can begin with something like: 'everything depends on the *mind*'.[1] However, the mind is far too complex. We need to begin with something that is more basic and operative. Beginning with *your* mind then, let's ask ourselves

© The Author(s) 2017
O. Ergas, *Reconstructing 'Education' through Mindful Attention*,
DOI 10.1057/978-1-137-58782-4_2

individually: 'Thinking about this mind of mine, what is the fundamental on which my experience stands; such that if it is taken away
experience will be gone?'

I won't say there's one answer to this question. When I ask my students
the above question, some suggest, 'senses', 'awareness', or 'consciousness'. These are certainly possible answers; however, I have come to rely
on William James for a more concrete and operative answer:

For the moment what we attend to is reality. (2007, p. 322)

This sentence is like a mantra. It takes a while until our minds can wrap
themselves around it, and usually a moment later we are lost again. After I
present James's answer, I usually ask my students to say it to themselves in
first person – 'for the moment what I attend to is reality' to allow it to sink
in a little. You might want to try that.

*

Let's examine this for a moment. Consider your reading right now;
attending to this

WORD

I've just defined your reality based on your attention. I certainly do not
have control over the extent to which this has surprised you, intrigued
you, or bored you. But the word WORD stuck in the middle, probably
got your attention, just as much as **this** *word* captures it now. The life of
the student in the classroom is no different. His or her experience in
school is nothing but the concatenated moments in which s/he attends
to 'something'.

But what *is* attention? – this sounds like a basic, perhaps too basic,
question. Let's, however, not take anything for granted here. We want to
understand this mind that we are so busy 'educating'.

I am going to treat attention here almost mechanistically. It is a
condition without which there is no point of speaking of experience,
nor of 'education'. James defined it as, " . . . the taking possession by the
mind, in clear and vivid form, of one out of what seem several simultaneously possible objects or trains of thought" (2007, pp. 403–404).

So attention is that on which our minds depend in order to note, perceive, and know.[2]

There's a word that James didn't use above, but if you attend very closely, it might come to mind. From what James says, attention is a *selective* process. The importance of this claim runs as a thread throughout the book but for now I want to highlight that it speaks to two sides of one and the same coin that makes reality: The amount of information that can be attended to at any given moment on the one hand, and the implication of this as an 'educational' limitation, on the other hand.

The mind's attending to something is at the same time its not attending to another. There are different ways to think about this. One that we will develop and experiment with is the often used metaphor of the '*flashlight of attention*'. At any given moment there seem to be endless things that we can attend to, yet only those on which the flashlight of attention shines can enter what we conceive of as experience. Another way of thinking of this is that just as there is a certain bandwidth that limits the amount of information that gets to your computer through your network, there is also a limited bandwidth to our conscious experience (Nørretranders 1998). To give you a taste of this:

> For a moment raise your head from these words, look around you, and listen to the sounds you hear. Were all the things you now note there a moment ago while you were reading?

I am willing to bet that most were not, and let's be clear – the same applies to me, for the coffee mug in front of me, the birds, and the construction site that I am hearing right now seemed not to have existed when I wrote that paragraph. Now I experience them, because I attended to them deliberately, however, when I do so the paragraph above is *gone*.

At least in our day-to-day habitual way of perceiving, we are limited creatures that can only process bits of information in a linear fashion. So let's say this:

Your attention is selective, which means:

Your reality is selective.

Many described this in eloquent ways. Psychologist James Hans, claimed that, "the entire texture of our lives . . . is nothing more than the principles of selection that manifest themselves through the things we choose to note over the course of a lifetime" (1993, p. 40). More radically he concluded that, "attention is truly all we have and all we are ... " thus we can come to see our*selves* as, "nothing more or less than that to which we attend" (1993, p. 40). One of the founders of positive psychology, Mihalyi Csikszentmihalyi, echoed Hans's claims as he suggested that, learning to control the faculty of attention implies learning to control the quality of one's life (1991, p. 2).

*

From all that's been said so far, what can we say about 'education'? – First, if attention indeed is the fundamental that determines the reality of our lives, then an account of the construct of 'education' may well begin there as some have suggested before.[3] Second, for a moment I want you to reflect on the first-person perspective that this book introduces to the understanding of 'education'. That little trick played above with the word WORD, or my sending you to think of all those things that your attention had selected from your environment, invited *your* intimate engagement with *your mind*. Your attending to how you attend and to how your mind works is no other than a form of *mindfulness practice*.

Third and most important, I remind you (and myself) that *your attention precedes my words in terms of importance*. This is about distinguishing between that which is *contingent* and that which is not. This book happened to fall into your hands. You can think of it as a coincidence or as some causality working in your life, but one can imagine that things could have worked otherwise. Someone might have recommended another book, or this book might not have caught your eye at the library or on the internet. Had it not been for this book, your attention would have still been there, yet it would have been given to something else. Stated dramatically, what I am reiterating is that:

> *In the beginning there is your attention, all the rest is contingent.* And
> *In the beginning there is your attention, then we (re)construct 'education'.*

Despite this biblical way of putting things, I do not mean this as a 'religious' statement necessarily, although it can be interpreted that way if it is meaningful to *you*. I rather mean that 'society' might have worked us into a place in which we tend to think that 'education' precedes our personal existence. As if first there was 'knowledge' organized based on a 'curriculum' and only then came the individual that is to grasp it. I certainly do not reject human history or culture nor do I undermine their importance. I am merely grounding us in a fact:

> All of society's efforts to 'educate' will eventually be determined at their destination – your mind. Without your attention there is nothing; at least not for you.

*

Where Do We Stand?

Recall that 'placeholder' definition I proposed in Chapter 1:

> 'Education' is a human endeavor the aim of which is to 'develop' human beings in light of a certain 'good'.

We can actually advance with this an inch or two by saying that whatever 'good' 'education' is to serve, it will have to work with attention to get there. Thus, I propose the following two statements:

1. The foundation of any 'educational' practice is the orientation of attention.
2. Orienting attention means selecting content by which to define reality for the moment.

If you are a teacher teaching math or history, you attempt to define realities at the moments in which you teach. If you are a student, when your teacher/lecturer speaks, she is defining your reality. This might strike you as too dramatic a way of putting things. Reading James's instructions to teachers, shows that he was at least as serious as I am about this:

> [i]n teaching, you must simply work your pupil into such a state of interest in what you are going to teach him that every other object of attention is banished from his mind; then reveal it to him so impressively that he will remember the occasion to his dying day. (1983, p. 10)

A teacher attempts to orient students to attend to her words, and actions. If she is successful, then the content of her words defines the reality of her students for those moments. The fact that these very words might evoke a completely different *inner* experience for each student, is a core theme of this book, but we are building it one step at a time. Our first step has been to establish the first fundamental of mind and 'education': *Attention.*

*

ATTENTION IN SPACE

The trick we played with the word WORD earlier, gave you some taste of the methodology of this book that attempts to speak directly to and with your mind. Here, I am going to ask for a little more. The following is a self-experiment I conduct in many of my courses. It will take exactly three-minutes of your time, and I would really appreciate it if you try it because this will go a long way in making our next moves far more interesting and understandable. Try to just follow these instructions without expecting too much. Explanations will follow afterward:

> Please take out a piece of paper and a pen, set yourself comfortably on a chair and for the next three minutes, write down anything you attend to. As best you can avoid directing your attention to anything specific. Just let it go where it goes. Since we're not going to read your list out loud please don't censor anything. Write absolutely everything you note.

So get a pen and paper. Set a timer, and go for it.

*
*

I may be accused of naivety, but I'll assume we're back with a list of things that you attended to during three minutes. Here are the first few items on my own list:

Noise of fan,
Sensation in head

Breath
Sensation in chest
Noise from construction site outside
Noise from the kitchen
Thought: "I'm a little tired"...

As you can note, there's nothing here to write home about, but let's apply our mindful attention to this. What I want us to contemplate is whether we can sort the items on our lists into different categories. You can look at your list and consider this for a while before reading on. I can wait.

My students usually offer a number of possibilities. The one in which I am particularly interested that always comes up eventually, is the in/out categorization. Simply, some of the items on the list reflect things experienced *out there* (in the world so to speak) and some of them reflect things *in here* (in my mind-body). This will probably not surprise anyone. The observation that we can attend *out* to the world and we can attend *in* to ourselves, is as natural to us as breathing the air we breathe without being bothered to acknowledge such triviality. But there lays the crux of the matter. Those foundations that are most transparent become a platform that we tend to consider unworthy of further consideration. We tend to think that these can be set aside so we can move on to the more 'sophisticated business' of life. But this is actually where our lives fork out in a very certain direction without our even noticing that we have passed a junction in which more than one road can be taken.

There are certainly many other names that have been given to this in/out split (e.g., *in here/out there, me/not-me,* self/world, subject/object). Choosing the terms by which to describe this 'split' enables us to articulate nuances of diverse experiences we have. We'll be applying a number of possibilities so that each will allow us different ways for examining attention, mind, experience, and the reconstruction of 'education'. *In here/Out there* is the first characterization that I introduce because it is the most concrete:

> It is simply the indication of where in space we wittingly or unwittingly locate that which we perceive.

When you conducted the above experiment, whenever you heard a sound (e.g., a bird, the hum of the fan), if you did *not* reflect on it too much, you probably intuitively sensed it to arrive from outside you. If that sound came from your rumbling stomach, then you tacitly perceived it as arriving from *inside* you. *In here/out there* is a very literal spatial metaphor that mostly emerges from our sense of embodiment. Conventionally we see our bodies as marking the borderline between what we perceive as *in here* and what we perceive as *out there.*[4]

Some of this information may seem to you like a very complicated way of describing a simple day-to-day experience which is something you may not feel to be worth much ink. You are an expert in day-to-day experience, because experienc*ing* is what you have been doing for as long as you can remember. Soon, however, this triviality will become tricky so before we move further let's practice something here to establish ourselves in this *in here/out there* language that I am applying.

Read through the line below formed by the words 'Breathe, Breathe…'.

    Breathe,   *Breathe,*   *Breathe,*   *Breathe,*   *Breathe.*

Now read again, but each time you read 'Breathe', deliberately attend to your breath before you move on to the next 'Breathe'.

Now try to contemplate what you've just experienced. You may have noted that while reading your attention was *out there* over the written word, whereas while attending to the breath it was *in here*.

Now where does this lead us? – well, take our first fundamental – *attention* and combine it with the *in here/out there* distinction and what you get is *attention in space*:

"For the moment what we attend to is reality," and *there are only two loci in space to which we can attend: in here and out there.*

Remember that what we are trying to do here is get down to the most basic fundamentals of mind. Since 'educational' research, theory, and practice all depend on minds, and are addressed toward minds, any 'education' we shall construct will depend on these fundamentals.

An important note, however, is called for before moving on. Let's be clear about what kind of claims we are making here. Our claims are about what we experience, and not about some reality *as such*. In this sense, lets treat *in here/out there* as a *perceived* split. The fact that both of us probably experience it allows us to say something about how reality appears to our minds. Whether this split is 'really there' or not, is not something we can prove.[5] Following this reservation, please doubt every conclusion at which we arrive. For example, right now we can ask: are we missing anything? Can we attend to anything that is not *in here* nor *out there*?

If *you can*, then by all means explore this and improve the argument offered here. So far, the several hundreds of students with whom I've tried this never came up with other possibilities, therefore we will progress here as if there are none. For the benefit of the doubt we will add that we know of none; at least not within the kind of day-to-day consciousness with which most of us are familiar.

*

The Door of Attention

Now, again, all this might seem obvious. You may have known this all along, but maybe you never bothered to actually say it and really allow the profundity of this claim to settle in. In a moment we will see how this affects 'education', but first here's a poetic way of describing life based on the above observations:

> The fundamental of attention and its orientation in space proposes the possibility of considering attention as moving through a door. When the door opens one way, we get the view of the world, and when it opens the other way, we get the view of our inner experience.[6]

In, out, in, in, out, out, out, in, in, in, out. . . . Whatever it is you experience; whatever you are doing – swimming, talking on the phone, or sitting in the classroom studying Geography; whatever you are feeling or thinking – the structure of your experience is based on the fundamentals of attention and space. Reality comes to you through the door of attention that swings in and out constantly.

However, you might now want to question this image of the door. Does it really have to be either opened in or opened out? Can we not attend *in here* and *out there* simultaneously? – for a moment let's try the following short self-experiment to test this:

> Try to see whether you can read the following passage that is located *out there* on the page or screen, while simultaneously *feeling* your breath *in here*. Begin with breathing a few deep breaths, and then start reading. See what happens:
>
> > *Can*
> > you *a* tte **nd** to th *e* **b** *r* *e*ath and focus *on* wha T's written
> > he *re*
> > > simultaneously? –
> > Here. I'll even stop fooling around with the fonts, so you can test this in a more neutral situation.

What's your conclusion? Are you really attending *in here* and *out there* simultaneously, or is it a quick back and forth movement? We are basically asking whether so-called multi-tasking is possible, yet with our attention actually *there* in the diverse tasks performed in one and the same moment (rather than going on automatic pilot in one task, while performing the other task attentively). Sometimes my students insist that they can do both simultaneously, but upon seriously probing this they arrive at the conclusion that either their performance is highly compromised, or that it is indeed impossible to attend in *and* out at one and the same moment.[7]

ATTENTION IN SPACE: RECONSTRUCTING 'EDUCATION'

Now where does this lead us in terms of the reconstruction of 'education'? – first, let's locate the above in the day-to-day first person experience of 'school'. The 'educational experience' of a student in a classroom is the cumulative effect of moments attended to.

> Through the swinging door of attention, her reality will unfold, moment after moment, day in and day out, attending to this in here, attending to that out there, then this, that, that, this.

She will either attend to the teacher's words about quadratic equations *out there*, or perhaps feel like an idiot *in here* because she can't understand his explanation. She might attend to the teacher's reading of Hamlet out loud *out there*, or she might think *in here* how boring/marvelous Shakespeare is, or 'what a funny looking sweater the teacher's wearing today'. All this will be attended to by the mind. All this will happen in that institution called 'school' that we usually associate with 'education'.

We can now progress with the reconstruction of 'education' based on the above considerations of attention in space, combining them with what we've established earlier:

1. The foundation of any 'educational' practice is the orientation of attention.
2. Orienting attention means selecting content by which to define reality for the moment and *there are only two loci in space toward which we can orient attention to define reality – in here or out there.*

When speaking of 'education' as a *deliberate* 'social'-institutional act, no matter how we construct it we basically have two options:

a. Deliberately orient a student's attention *out there*.
b. Deliberately orient a student's attention *in here*.

Any 'education' we construct will be a practice that is based on a and b. It can combine the two orientations either in a balanced way in which students will be asked to attend in *and* out, or in a way that privileges one orientation over the other, up to a theoretical possibility in which one orientation will be so favored to the point of the exclusion of the other (i.e., an entire curriculum that asks students to attend *out there*).

You might start to get a feel for where this is all going, for this is exactly where for some reason as a 'society', we have arrived at (and I would say *educated ourselves in*) the idea that the practice of 'education' has mostly to do with 'a' – attending *out there*. Note my focus here: I'm not asking *what it is that we ask students to attend to* (i.e., curricular content), I am rather asking a far more basic question: *where in space* do we ask them to attend to. The former question is surely important but the latter is far more fundamental. However, we can't explore that yet. As mentioned in Chapter 1, 'education' as well as 'curriculum', which was just mentioned, are complex constructs. We need to explore basic fundamentals before we deal with complex constructs. Here comes another one – *you*.

*

The Birth of *Me* Through Attention in Space

So far we discussed attention in space by considering that when we attend to 'something' we very naturally perceive that something as located in space. It's either *in here* (e.g., thoughts, emotions, bodily sensations) or *out there* (e.g., sound of a car, sight of the school building, smell from the cafeteria). Yet, as mentioned earlier, there are various names to this perceived split, and *in here/out there* does leave something to be desired. Underlying *in here/out there* as a spatial experience there's a deeper psychological/existential flavor, which William James expressed in his eloquent way:

> One great splitting of the whole universe into two halves is made by each of us; and for each of us almost all of the interest attaches to one of the halves...we all call the two halves by the same names...those names are *'me'* and *'not-me'* respectively. (1984, p. 187, emphasis added)

I suspect that this statement matches your experience as well. This is a subtle and quite obvious spatial experience with which we travel that undergirds much of our day-to-day existence. Its content is like a statement that seems to undergird our experience:

> *It's me 'in here' and there's not-me, 'out there'.*

Those things to which (or other people to whom) we attend *out there*, we consider to be 'the world', and they are what James called *not-me* – the trees, houses, birds, and other human beings surrounding us. Those things to which we attend *in here* – our thoughts, sensations, feelings, emotions, premonitions, intuitions – we usually associate in diverse ways with what James called *me*.

Reflect for a moment on that self-experiment we conducted earlier: while making a list of what you attended to, I suggest that when you sensed a sound coming from *out there,* probably undergirding this classification, there was a *tacit* sense that the sound is *not* coming from *me.*

Now, if for a moment you just

> *Stop reading*
>   *and just listen to the first sound you hear....*

Where did that sound come from?

Now, ask yourself this question:

What is your relation to that place?

You will probably feel that the sound came from *out there* – a place, which you tacitly refer to as *not-me*. Conversely, if you experience a thought, you tacitly may feel: that's *me* thinking *in here*. The term I use – *tacit* – follows Michael Polanyi's (1958) observations as to the subtler aspects of our knowing. We do not explicitly bother to tell ourselves 'that's me'/'that's not-me' with every experience we attend to. It seems too redundant to even acknowledge, but if I stopped you for a moment and asked you what was the location of an object you've just attended to, setting aside some pathological conditions and altered states of mind, I doubt that you would ever answer that the noise of the bus came from your head, and the stomach ache came from outside you.

This obvious kind of experience would not seem much to bother with. However, as you may have detected, 'obvious' in this book is a synonym for something that has become automatic and automation also happens to be the very enemy of the kind of inquisitive approach proposed here. What we have here is the birth of *me* from attention in space. That's the person who's reading now with whom 'education' is supposedly concerned and as James claims – with which *you* are utterly concerned as well. We will have far more to say about *you* in the next chapter and especially in the third part of the book, but our task at this point is merely to establish fundamentals to work with. So far we have attention and space (*in here/out there*) which undergirds *me/not-me*. We need time before we can move further in to probe *me* in the next chapter. I actually mean that literally. We need to lay the fundamental of time because it has so much to do with the sense we have of who we are, and with our existence in space.

*

ATTENTION IN TIME

What I recommend now is to actually repeat the same experiment that we've conducted when we first discussed space, only now we will apply it differently. In my courses too, we repeat this same experiment and each time we repeat it, it leads us more deeply to deconstruct and reconstruct 'education' based on mindful attention.

> So again, set a timer to three minutes, and make a list of all things you attend to whether these are sounds, thoughts, smells, images, feelings, emotions, sensations. Do it nonchalantly, without any preference for certain objects. It's as if you are a passive observer that is asked to document your mind's attentional habits. You are like a non-participating observer in your own life.

> > Ok, here's my list this time:
> > *Stuffy nose*
> > *Hum of computer*
> > *Hum of computer*
> > *'This is boring'*
> > *Breath*
> > *Hum of computer*
> > *'Why am I constantly drawn to the hum of the computer?'*
> > *Stuffy nose*

I won't spell out the entire three minutes here. I hope yours were slightly more rewarding. At the same time, methodically it needs to be clear that the whole point of this self-experiment is to shift the way in which we attend to experience normally. For our purposes, it really isn't important at all whether the content to which we attended was rewarding or not. Far more important is the fact that the list you have depicts the direct relation between *attention and time*. This relationship was there all along. Recall James, 'for the *moment* what we attend to is reality'. What you have in your hands is no other than a documentation of three minutes that amount to *your reality* as it was garnered based on your attention. More profoundly stated these were not simply moments of attention, but rather moments of *mindful attention*. Our concern with *how* we attend more than what we attend to is a feature of mindfulness practice, known as non-judgmentalism or detachment. We are basically involved in a first person method of inquiry by which we garner 'research data' that enables us to propose fundamentals of mind that we then apply to the reconstruction of 'education'. Don't underestimate the list of benign experiences you came up with. Seriously examining it will show you that mindful attention holds a key to stepping outside of time as we normally experience it. The following might not be news for many have made the following claim, but it is important for our inquiry,

> time is not something we experience directly. It is a relationship we have with those things that are attended to in space.

For example, note that this experiment lasted *three minutes*, but at no point did we attend to 'minutes'. Surely, you may have wondered at some point when the experiment will end, or how much time had passed, but that's not really attending to 'time'. It is rather attending to a thought you had in your mind, with the word 'time' in it. 'Seconds', 'minutes', 'hours', or even 'days' are not 'objects' such as a 'table' or a 'computer'. We can neither see nor hear them as such. We do see the sun 'moving' (or rather, we believe that we see it moving) and notice the shifts between light and darkness from which we derive the concept of a 'day'. Or we might enter a classroom at 12:00 and see the hands of the clock moving until at 12:45 we hear the bell, but neither the hands of the clock nor the bell constitute 'time'. They are only *representations* of 'time' attended to *in space*.

Don't surmise from this that I am claiming that 'time' does not exist! It most certainly does; otherwise we wouldn't be discussing it and we wouldn't be running around so much so that we can be *on* time and meet deadlines. In these senses, time feels almost as real as the book you're holding or the chair on which you're sitting. Our point is not to build some imaginary world that's far removed from actual experience. It is rather to probe experience deeply based on a first-person approach so that we minimize the gap between what we have gotten used to saying *about* experience, and what we *actually* experience. This will go a long way toward distinguishing between what we *say* about 'education' compared to what it comes down to in practice in many cases.

So in regards to time, we need to make a mindful observation: time seems real, but it is not the simple act of attending that makes its realness. If you look at your list above, all you *really* have there is thoughts, sights, smells, emotions etc. none of which are an *object* that is 'time'. They are just discrete events that you experienced as a concatenation of moments of reality based on attention in space. 'Someone' in your mind is doing more than just attending to objects in space...is it that same *me* that we encountered above, who's reading time into that which is attended to?

*

Two Conceptions-Experiences of Attention in Time[8]

What seems to emerge here are two possible ways of conceiving-experiencing 'time'. One is that to which we are accustomed: 'When I finish high-school I want to go to college', 'Thank God this lesson is over', 'I can't be late again to school'. It's like a 'sea of time' within which life and 'education' seem to take place. The other is the concrete lived reality attended to through *mindful attention*. It's life in somewhat of a chopped present continuous – a series of events that happen *now*. Both of these are concrete yet in a very different sense. The first is as concrete as you would think of living life. Its concreteness has to do with your being fully immersed in *doing* things that all have something to do with the past and/or the future (e.g., you're at high school planning to go to college *in the future*, you're thinking of the boring lesson that just ended with relief, you are worrying about being late to a lesson).

The second option is the one you might have experienced while making your list above, and it might have felt quite bizarre. It is concrete because you certainly experienced those things that you listed, but it's far more as if you've stepped outside of that 'sea of time', and sat to watch the waves, in somewhat of a *being* mode. That is at least how some people experience it. It is like stepping away from past and future, not caring what will happen next and attending *now* to *now*; to reality as it is 'made'.

How would this help us understand 'education' and the mind? – If the mind has two ways of conceiving-experiencing time, then these are also two ways for conceiving-experiencing, studying, and eventually practicing 'education' in time. At this point I only characterize them, but the rest of the book builds on the following descriptions:

1. *The Horizontal Time Axis: Living the Movie*
Our conventional sense of time is this: There's our past (e.g., yesterday, a week ago, ten years ago) and we are constantly moving toward the future (e.g., ten minutes from now, next year, ten years from now). The above three minute-experiment has now become a chunk of your *past*, over which you might now reflect in the *present*, and through which you may now hope to understand how this past and present will lead into a *future* in which you will grasp the ideas I am presenting. We normally travel with this kind of view in which our life resembles *a movie* that begins when we are born and ends (at least based on our conventional understanding) when we die. Right now we are somewhere between those two extremes, hopefully closer to the beginning.

I was born here   I am here now   At some point this is going to end

Fig. 2.1 The horizontal time axis

It makes sense to call this *the horizontal time axis* because this is the kind of image I believe our minds create to depict it (Figure 2.1).

The insubstantiality of time stares right at us yet again. Why? – because we represent time by a line that is actually an image in space. The point to look at here is the arrow at the end. *We are always on the move.* The psychological-existential feel here is that we're *advancing* toward the future; as if we imagine it as a point in *space*.

Methodologically this conception-experience of time is where you will probably find nearly (if not) all of 'educational' research and theory. I will argue later that our minds are fully imbued with this disposition and this has a dramatic effect on 'educational' practice. I fully acknowledge that this is the natural state of day-to-day living as we know it. What concerns me is the price we pay for missing the *other* conception-experience of time, and our missing the reconstructed 'educational' theory, practice, and research that it opens. Here it comes:

2. The Discrete-Lived Moments of Now: Living the Frames
The three-minute experiment we conducted above offers a different take on time. Normally we divide our day into 'big chunks' to which we refer as morning, noon, evening etc., but the experiment above offered a higher definition 'image' of time. Time was broken down based on moments of attending to one content, then another, and another. Here we switch from 'living the movie', to 'living the frames'. If you've ever seen Charlie Chaplin movies, these were based on a technology that only allowed to film and project about 15 frames per second. You might remember that these movies did not give us that satisfying smooth illusion of actual reality. Chaplin moved on the screen jerkily until we raised the frame rate to around 25 to 30 frames per second as customary nowadays. Technology is an incredible invention that allows us to forget about the makings of the movie, and dive right in, feeling as if the movie conveys reality as such. Mindful attention throws a 'monkey wrench' in there and – excuse my French – somewhat 'poops the party'. It takes us out of the

movie, to explore the mechanism of how it functions. It takes us 'out of life' to examine the mind that is the source from which this entire 'thing' is *attended to*.

Life doesn't feel like discrete moments of time, but it does seem to be made out of them when we examine it based on mindful attention. This might have something to do with the well-known aphorism concerning the 'whole as greater than the parts'. Paradoxically delving deeply into this breaking down of time (or life) into discrete moments of attention, does not deprive life of anything but rather contributes to the mysteriousness of the whole. This may sound enigmatic at this point and will only be explained in Chapter 7, but our *embodied perception* is fundamentally grounded in our past experience. Eventually we will see that in a way, every moment embodies the entire horizontal time axis. The whole is in the parts as well.

The experiential feel of the *horizontal time axis* – of 'living the movie' – is that we are *advancing* to the future; swimming in that 'sea of time' toward a certain destination. Conversely, experiencing the discrete lived-moments gives us somewhat of the feel that we are standing still and *time/experience is coming at us*. Perhaps the meaning of time is lost. This is what happens when our object of experience is not grounded in our usual engagement with the world *out there*. We shift the orientation of attention so that our own perspective becomes the object of our study. We shift from attending to *what* we experience to attending to *how* we experience. This is not what we normally do in our day-to-day living. Usually we are immersed in our engagements with the world, and this immersion rules out our ability to attend to our own attention at the same time as Mihalyi Csikszentmihalyi described, "We cannot run, sing, and balance the checkbook simultaneously, because each one of these activities exhausts most of our capacity of attention" (1991, p. 28).

So if we create an image that contrasts the above *horizontal time axis* to reflect time as *discrete moments of attention* it might look something like this: (Figure 2.2)

Fig. 2.2   The discrete moments of attention

I want to list a number of reasons why I believe this mindful attention perspective can significantly contribute to the understanding and the reconstruction of 'education':

1. *'Education' has to do with experience, and experience has to do with perception.* Breaking down experience to its finer elements offers us a way of inquiry that is unavailable to us through a day-to-day habitual sense of time. It allows us to access our minds, that we seek to 'educate', and to explore what it is like to *experience* 'education'. This might go a long way toward improving 'educational' practice.

2. *Knowing the whole might not work without knowing the parts.* While I am not fond of thinking of life in mechanistic terms, I have learned to acknowledge the power of such approach. It can offer insights that are not available otherwise. An engineer would need to know how each part in a machine contributes to its functioning as a whole. On a similar vein, the claims that we make about 'education', about 'schooling', about what we are doing *in practice* should be examined both at the micro-level of this high-definition moment-by-moment image, and at the macro-level of the bird's eye view that is the sum of the parts.

   Furthermore, if you ever observed professional dancers, musicians, and athletes and marveled at their mastery, you might have felt that they were born geniuses. One can hardly argue with innate talent, but we tend to forget that mastery is usually the product of hours of breaking down wholes into parts. Any serious musician has to plough through hours of scales and arpeggios that might seem far remote from the mastery expressed years later in performance. Yet it is presumable that all this breaking down into bits and pieces is the way to what pianist Kenny Werner (1996) called 'effortless mastery'. I suspect that 'education' is the same. There will be much reward in looking at it through this higher definition, and working our way to mastery, whether we look at this as teachers, as parents, or as students.

3. *Lived concrete moments are essentially the only empirical data we have.* If we seriously want to examine the mind and 'education', then 'for the moment what we attend to is reality', and essentially, the only reality that's available to us for examination is the one we are attending to *right now*. Getting in touch with the raw moment-to-moment experiences that make our lives, may bring much rigor into our understanding of 'education' as a process that aspires to 'make the mind'.

The Necklace Allegory *and the Reconstruction of 'Education' in Time*

The following 'necklace allegory' came to my mind at some point. Keep this 'necklace' in mind (or on your neck) as you read this book. I will return to it often because it binds together many of the elements that were discussed in this chapter, including the two conceptions of time and the selective nature of attention:

> Let us consider life as a concatenation of discrete moments of experience. Such moments are unimaginably rich in content (e.g., background noise, a thought, a word uttered, a fleeting sensation). Let us think of every content-possibility as a bead, hence every discrete moment of experience offers numerous such beads. Just as a child stands against the splendor of a box filled with beads so does our mind stand against the richness of experience and selects from its content moment-by-moment. The necklace formed in this process is your life as it unfolds through the act of threading.[9]

This necklace allows us to consider *both* conceptions-experiences of time. When we think of the 'necklace' as a whole, we conceive-experience time as a continuous horizontal axis. But, you can also focus on one bead at a time as you did in our self-experiment earlier. When you do that you experience the *discrete moments of now* (Figure 2.3).

Just as the examination of attention and space provided us with three possible 'educational' orientations based on (a) *in here,* (b) *out there* and, (c) their combination, time grants us with the same structure of options. Intentionally or unintentionally 'educational' practice can be grounded in:

a. Orienting a student's attention to engage with the discrete moments of *now.*
b. Orienting a student's attention to engage with the horizontal time axis.

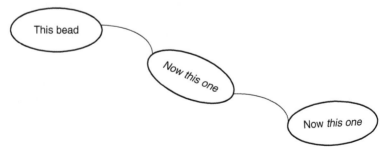

Fig. 2.3 The necklace allegory

Any 'education' we construct will be a practice that is based again on a and/or b. It can combine the two orientations either in a balanced way, or in a way that privileges one orientation over the other, up to a theoretical possibility in which one orientation will be so favored to the point of the exclusion of the other.

You have every right to demand an explanation for a question like – how on earth does this relate to 'school'? – I realize that the above is hardly a practical guideline for 'curriculum development'. Recall that what we are up to at this point is the establishment of basic building blocks over which *any* kind of 'education' can be constructed. That in fact means forgetting about 'education', and focusing on what a mind (like yours or mine) can experience. The following summary will help recap what we've accomplished.

*

Summary: The Matrix of Mind

Let's briefly review the fundamentals of mind that we have come up with in this chapter, and then see if they can be organized in some way:

1. Fundamental 1: *Attention* – for the moment what we attend to is reality, hence attention must feature in any (re)construction of 'education'.
2. Fundamental 2: *Space* – Attention can be oriented to one of two spatial arenas at any given moment:
   a. *In here* that we associate with *me* – our first-person experience of sensations, emotions, and thoughts as we experience them whether we are alone, or whether we are engaged with others. This will be substantially elaborated in the next chapter and in Chapter 8.
   b. *Out there* that we associate with *not-me* – all stimuli that we perceive, wittingly or unwittingly, as we attend to the world around us – sounds, smells, images, words, etc.
   Attention in space grants us with three options for 'education' when it is considered as a deliberate act:
      i. Orient a student to engage with *in here* to what he or she perceives as *me*
      ii. Orient a student to engage with *out there* to what is perceived as *not-me*
      iii. Combine a and b either in a balanced or an imbalanced way.

3. Fundamental 3: *Time* – We do not experience time directly. Our minds construct the idea of time based on that to which we attend. Two basic conceptions-experiences of time were described:

   a. The conventional horizontal time axis (i.e., the necklace/movie, the whole, or big chunks of it) based on which we normally organize our lives.

   b. The discrete-lived moments of now (i.e., the beads/frames, the parts) that we only start to consider when applying mindful attention that breaks down experience as we have done in this chapter.

   Attention in time grants us with three ways of constructing 'education' in time:

   i. Orient a student's attention based on the horizontal time axis.

   ii. Orient a student's attention based on discrete-lived moments of *now*.

   iii. Combine a and b either in a balanced or an imbalanced way.

Attention, space, and time are experienced *jointly*. Their breaking down as above is an analytical way of probing them; however, it makes sense to consider their joint experience based on a framework that binds them together. A possible way of doing this is the following matrix to which I will refer as *the matrix of mind*. It depicts the ways in which our minds *attend* to reality within *time* and *space* (Table 2.1).[10]

How will this table help us? – I have three answers to this:

1. Demarcation of the 'ball park' of 'education': Whether you choose to teach advanced math based on grouping the weaker students with the brighter ones; whether you take students on a

Table 2.1   The matrix of mind

Time \ Space	*Attending* in here	*Attending* out here
Attending to *now*	*for the moment what we attend to is reality*	
Attending to *then*		

field trip to study the archeology of ancient Rome; whether you allocate four hours per week to the teaching of rational thinking, or to practicing tai chi in the school yard; basically any curricular-pedagogical practice chosen by a teacher, a principal, a district etc. – all will require that students attend moment-by-moment *in here* or *out there*, and have their minds set on the horizontal time axis, or on this moment now. I am not saying yet that we understand what the latter statement means practically. It is only in Parts II and III of the book that this matrix will become more clearly grounded in practice.

2. A framework based on which any kind of 'educational' construct can be analyzed and/or critiqued. This is the task of Parts I and II of this book respectively.

3. A starting point from which to reconstruct 'education'. This is what Part III is about as it develops the *inner curriculum* and thus complements what I later refer to as the 'social curriculum'.

The matrix of mind can also help frame what we are doing in this book. Any 'education' we will think of can be constructed based on two main points of view as well as a third that combines them:

1. From *out there* to *in here*: This hearkens back to Chapter 1. Conventionally we feel that *in the beginning there was 'education' then came my own mind*. 'Education' has been here before *me*, and an 'entity' called 'society' *out there* has developed it. 'Education' is thus something that works from *out there* to shape *in here*.

2. From *in here* to *out there*: Reversing the above – *in the beginning there is attention then we (re)construct 'education'*. This is what we are introducing into the 'equation'. Here 'education' is not something that is 'done' *to* me, but rather something that I do from *in here*. Only in Chapter 9 will we see how this orients us from *in here* toward *out there* as we discuss ethics.

3. 'Education' can be constructed based on both orientations (with any degree of bias toward one of the poles).

As we will analyze later, option one has been eclipsing option two to the point that our minds were expelled from 'education'. This book heavily relies on reconstructing 'education' from *in here* in order to balance this situation. All this, however, needs much more fundamental work, for we need to get to know that 'being' called *me* that has been expelled from our 'educational' construct, and no less that 'entity' that might be responsible for that – 'society'. Let's dive in to *me* and then move back 'out' to 'society', to further build the fundamentals of mind and 'education'. These will then allow us to start looking at far more complex 'things' like 'knowledge', 'curriculum', and 'pedagogy' and how we have shaped them in ways that have expelled the mind from 'education'.

NOTES

1. This is no other than the Buddha's opening verse of *The Dhammapada*: 'All phenomena are preceded by the mind, issue forth from the mind, and consist of the mind.' (Translated in Wallace [1999, p. 176])
2. I am not claiming that what we know is limited to what we are aware of attending. James indeed claimed that, "[T]he sum total of our impressions never enters our experience" (1984, p. 227). Furthermore, Michael Polanyi (1958) proposed that 'we know more than we can tell'. My claim is that whatever it is that we *do* know can only be acknowledged as such, based on the fact that we attended to it.
3. This includes James (1983) and Ellen Langer (1997) about whom I will say much more in Chapter 9. See also Weil (1986) and Lewin (2014).
4. See Merleau-Ponty (1965) for a far more nuanced phenomenology of this domain, that I intentionally avoid here.
5. For the philosophers among you – I am attempting to stick with epistemology and avoid ontology as best I can.
6. This phrasing is inspired by the great Zen teacher Shunryu Suzuki (1999) who spoke in a similar way about the movement of breath in to our bodies, and then out. The conception of a 'view' follows neuroscientist Antonio Damasio's (2005) reference to the 'view' of the body in his discussion of Descartes' erroneous dualism.
7. Cognitive research and neuroscience reassert this. In fact attending *in* and *out* involves two different brain networks – the intrinsic and the extrinsic networks respectively (Golland et al. 2007). These two networks are antagonistic (i.e., when one is activated the activity in the other is reduced) (See also, Raichle et al. 2001).
8. There are actually more conceptions. A third one for example, is the *timeless* that is occasionally featured in this book as well, and has to do with the 'reflective/philosopher's *I*' (discussed in chapter 9) that works with abstractions such as Platonic forms.

9. If you are wondering 'who is doing the threading' or what exactly *is* the thread that binds these beads, I share your wonder. This book will not offer answers to questions that I cannot answer. It may, however, provide further paths by which to keep questioning and to seek answers.

10. It is important, however, to note that concepts such as 'flow' (Csikszentmihalyi 1991) and altered states of mind such as in meditative experiences (Berkovich-Ohana and Glikson 2014) challenge the rather rigid borderlines within this matrix.

CHAPTER 3

'Education' and the Pruning of the Mind

Who is that 'someone' that 'education' attempts to change, and whom is it that changes her/him/it?

Part of the task of reconstructing 'education' has to do with discerning between what is contingent and what is non-contingent. Contingency and non-contingency also have much to do with particularity and universality. Attention, space, and time that were examined in the previous chapter seem to be universal and non-contingent. You and I are identical, in the sense that our experience is fully dependent on these fundamentals. However, over these universal fundamentals, a completely unique and *particular* experience presents itself as *my* experience, which may be very different than yours.

Our particularity as individuals, is mounted over a universal scaffold.

Particular as we are, however, there is something in us that creates the possibility for shared living. We form 'societies' and our ability and *wish* to connect with each other and live together seems to be a universal fundamental of mind as well. Nevertheless, over this universality that enables us to live and form 'societies' we form *particular* 'societies' (e.g., French, Medieval European, Ecological, technological) that differ in their norms, institutions, laws, etc. 'Societies' thus develop a different 'narrative' based on which they 'educate' the mind. Thus,

the particularity of any 'society' is mounted over a universal scaffold.

© The Author(s) 2017
O. Ergas, *Reconstructing 'Education' through Mindful Attention*,
DOI 10.1057/978-1-137-58782-4_3

I call the process by which universality is reduced to particularity – the *pruning* of the mind. This chapter will suggest pruning as a fundamental structure of 'education', in which a *universal* mind is born into a 'society', which prunes it in accordance with its *particular* ways. As you may recall, part of this book's agenda is to diagnose more clearly what kind of problem 'education' seeks to solve. My argument all along is that, there must be some inherent problem within the mind, which warrants the huge 'social' operation called 'education'. The problem emerges given that the mind is pruned by 'society' from without; however, there is a process of pruning that occurs moment-by-moment from within the mind itself. It stems directly from the structure of attention. The source of self-centered-ness lies deep within how we attend through pruned minds at both the individual and the 'social' levels. Our journey here will begin by moving *in here* to further parse the *me/not-me* split and discover the thicker subjectivity that we are based on self-experimentation, phenomenology and psychology. Then we will move *out there* to explore the nature of 'society', the fundamental of mind that enables for its creation, as well as its becoming the primary agent of attention and 'education'.

I AND *ME*

It is time to return to James. Let's refresh our memory by recalling a statement that appeared in Chapter 2 and delve deeper:

> One great splitting of the whole universe into two halves is made by each of us; and for each of us almost all of the interest attaches to one of the halves...we all call the two halves by the same names...those names are *'me' and 'not-me'* respectively.... (1984, p. 187, italics mine)

Let's ground ourselves in this experientially for a moment. Try to follow the practices and the analysis I offer after each one. We will practice *mindfulness* in the same way that we've practiced it in the previous chapter, only this time we're not going to write anything.

> *Just take one minute, and note whatever it is that you are attending to that makes your reality.*

This time the question I want you to consider is:

> *What in me, allows me to intuitively accept James's claim that makes our experience such a binary – me/not-me?*

We attend to this, and to that, this, that, and tacitly sift this and that according to the places in space from which these stimuli 'arrive': *computer hum (out), noise from kitchen (out), pain in the knee (in), the thought: 'I have a meeting in an hour' (in).* We don't settle for *in/out* we actually tacitly know that every *in* implies *me* and every *out* implies *not-me.* Did it ever occur to us to ask (Figure 3.1):

> *Who (or what) is tacitly sifting our experience in this way? Who's creating the separation between in and out?*

There must be 'someone'/'something' *in here* that's responsible for distinguishing between that which is *in* and that which is *out.* The computer hum is a sound; the thought I hear in my mind is somewhat of an 'internal' sound, but as sounds, they do not contain the information that one is *out there-not-me* and the other is *in here-me.* Who (or what) is tagging them according to their location in space? A confusing yet perhaps appropriate way of phrasing my question is this:

> *Is there an other me in me that's telling me that the thought came from me and the computer hum didn't?*

I realize how peculiar (so as not to say esoteric) this question may sound, but it does suggest that *in here/out there, me/not-me* hardly exhausts the matter. Let me sharpen this: If *me* was thinking a thought, then while thinking, does

Fig. 3.1 Who's sifting/tagging/owning experience? the moon (out there, not-me), the thought (in here, me)

it also tag it as *in here*? Can it do both? Or maybe there's 'someone' *in here* that's more primary that only sifts experience while *me* is busy thinking? 'Someone' or 'something' *in here* is seems to be very observant. We can speculate that it functions based on some kind of an algorithm:

1. An experience of *this* is perceived (e.g., computer hum, thought)
2. *This* is located *in here* (in case of the thought) or *out there* (in case of the computer hum)
3. *This* is something that 'is' *me* (in case of the thought) or *not-me* (in case of the computer hum)

It's as if with every content we attend to we either claim *ownership* on the place of origin of experience or we don't. If it comes from *in here* we claim ownership and tacitly experience *me*, and if it doesn't, we don't; as we tacitly relate it to *not-me*. So we ask again:

> *Who's doing the sifting; the owning? Who's the one telling me that this thought in here came from me?*

If this feels too analytical and disembodied then if you don't mind close your eyes for one minute and try another version of mindfulness practice. Simply bring your attention to your breath:

> *Breathe,*
>> *Breathe,*
>>> *Breathe*

If you keep this up for a short while, you might identify something peculiar. Undergirding such experiment is a sense of a 'someone' who is attending, along with a 'something' that is attended to but *both seem to exist in* one *place that you normally think of as 'my body'* – me. However, I believe, that these 'two' *in here* do not quite feel the same. The 'someone' that's attending will feel more like an *agent* or a witness, and the 'something' attended to (the breath), will feel more like – a 'thing'; an object. Peculiarly, there seem to be two different entities in the locus in space that we call *in here* and they seem to be of a completely different ilk.

> *Try again. Close your eyes and focus on the breath.*

It almost feels as if the body that's *in here* becomes an object *out there*....

> *But does the body feel like the desktop or book you are looking at, which are all*
> *'really' out there?*
> *Not quite.*

If you are inexperienced in contemplative practices like many of my University students then all this may feel confusing. The mind is a peculiar thing, especially given that it 'comes with a body'. If experientially you find it hard to articulate your experience you may have to rely on my appeal to analytical thinking. I believe that reading on and experimenting you will hopefully agree with me that all the above amounts to this:

> there must be some kind of an additional internal (perceived) split in here. If I attend to a thought or sensation (both *in here*), then there must be some distinction between the one who attends and the thing attended to, despite the fact that this all seems to happen in one and the same body-mind. There's 'someone' noting, and there's that which 'it' notes in here. What shall we call this internal split?

The Sense of an Origin of Attention

In Chapter 2 I applied the flashlight metaphor to describe attention. It is like the beam of light that defines our conscious experience. No matter what you are conscious of, it is as if a beam of attention 'originates' from within you and 'shines' over an object to enable experience. I'm not claiming that you are creating or *causing* experience. You can think of it more in terms of the fundamentals of optics. Just as an actual flashlight can be viewed as the origin of a beam of light (not its cause), you can think of a *locus* from which attention shines as a necessary condition for experiencing a "bead" of experience (see 'necklace allegory' Chapter 2, p. 46). As I mentioned in the previous chapter I will treat attention at this point almost at a mechanistic level. If the light-switch is on, you experience something, if it's off, you don't.

When you attend to your breath in a mindful way, the *you* that's attending feels like the place from which attention 'shines'. This 'attending *you*' that you may think of as the *agent* – the one that you feel to be willing the actions within you – invites different names. Daniel Siegel (2010), applies the above flashlight metaphor, and refers to it as the 'hub' of a wheel from which attention is oriented. It feels somewhat like an 'inner self'; perhaps a 'core *here*'. No matter where we are, whether we are in motion or standing stationary, in Paris or in Seattle, at home or at work, we'll always say we're *here*. But normally when we say we're *here*, we refer to the location of our entire body. What I am saying now, is that there is a more intimate and less involved *here* that experiences the body itself. It is a *here* that feels more like an 'origin of attention' – the place within *me* from which attention 'shines'. Hence,

> Attention can be viewed as a beam of light that 'shines' from *here* over all else; which it *there*.

The implication of this is that when we engage our capability of *mindful attention* as we attempt to seriously probe *how* we experience, and not just *what* we experience, we may start to feel that even when we attend to thoughts or sensations *in here*, they too, begin to feel *peripheral*. The desktop/book you are looking at feels peripheral but peculiarly the breath can feel that way too. There's this feeling of dwelling in somewhat of a layered space; as if one is an onion. At our core lies the origin of attention, then comes the body (and what we experience within it – thoughts/ sensations/emotions), and then the *not-me* from which all those sounds/sights/smells 'arrive'.

> The 'you' that is tacitly felt to be attending feels like an innermost layer, while that to which attention is oriented feels outer, regardless of whether it is located in your body or outside it.[1]

Given these observations, the question is, what's the status of this *in here/ out there, me/not-me* split that was proposed in the previous chapter? – my suggestion is that it represents a coarse day-to-day dichotomy that doesn't capture the experience we have when mindfully engaging with our interiority. At the same time, even within our day to day coarse attention, we might feel this subtler internal split. Consider for example, banging into a chair. That first moment of attending to the pain is a moment of attention that shines from *here* over *a* leg. It is not yet *owned* and feels peripheral; almost exterior. Next, in an instant, the leg is owned as 'my leg' *in here; me – enters the picture*. Then, if you're like me, you'll blame someone *out there* saying 'who the hell put this chair over here'. *Here*, which in the first instant meant 'something'/'someone' that simply attends and does not yet own experience, becomes an extension of this origin of attention. It now includes your body, and your back in *me/not-me*. Next time you experience pain – pay very close attention to 'what just happened there' at that very instant (that would certainly count as a spontaneous mindfulness practice by the way). The bead-to-bead resolution of experience dissects the reality attended to and tells us a crucially important story about who we are, and how we perceive, as we'll elaborate in Chapter 7.

The above discussion took us deep inside to a place that might feel too removed from your day-to-day experience. I want to re-ground us in our task of reconstructing 'education'. What are we trying to do here? – we are trying to get a better sense of 'who' it is, that 'education' attempts to 'educate' and what are its/his/her problems that require 'education'? What develops in the process of 'education'? So, let's then move forward to ground the above in some operative fundamentals of mind.

From the 'Origin of Attention' to I-me

That primary *here;* that hub from which attention shines is, I suggest, a scaffold of experience. This 'locus' has been given diverse names by phenomenologists, psychologists, and is also fundamentally present within wisdom traditions. Entire books will not suffice to explore this discourse and you will have to forgive me for bypassing much of this. My aim is to come up with operative terms, which are grounded in experience or analytically assumed to exist, such that will allow us to progress in the reconstruction of 'education'. This entails reductionism right at the outset. What I offer in the following is a *reduced* version that is inspired mostly by James, phenomenologist Shaun Gallagher, and neuroscientist Antonio Damasio. I disclaim in advance that it is possible that neither of them would necessarily subscribe to the end result. Furthermore, reductionism means that the terms I'll come up with hardly exhaust the matter, and there will be contradictions here, only some of which may be resolved in Part III. Here's my proposal as well as my agenda on this:

> If your reading will create an incentive for *you* to engage with the *inner curriculum* described in part III, based on this proposal, and you find that the following is all wrong, then I would still consider this book to be a success.

So basically, we are now faced with an inner split that can appear once we turn attention *mindfully in here*. It is formed based on a subtle feeling of an attend*er* that shines the light on the one hand, and that over which the light shines on the other hand. Applying James's (2007) terms, I suggest referring to them as *I* and *me*.[2] They are both operational concepts for discussing the enigmatic (non)-'thing(s)' we call 'self'. Each reflects a very different *field* of experiences of our interiority. At this point, we're only going to depict their contours. The third part of the book opens them within the practice, theory, and study of the *inner curriculum*.

In this chapter I treat *I* as a primary, *non-conceptual* experience. As a rule, from now on, whenever I'll write an italic *I* in this book, I will be referring to this *I*-self. An I that is non-italicized refers to me as the writer.[3] What I call here *I* is what neuroscientist Antonio Damasio (2010) called the 'core self' and phenomenologist Shaun Gallagher (2000) called the 'minimal self'. As Gallagher claimed, "[E]ven if all of the unessential features of self are stripped away, we still have an intuition that there is a basic, immediate, or primitive 'something' that we are willing to call a self." This 'minimal self' is, "a consciousness of oneself as an immediate subject of experience...." (p. 15). This is that banging into a chair with a first instant in which you hardly even note what happened. In your daily living your explicit experience is hardly of this 'minimal self', and if you do know what I mean by the above example of banging into a chair, you usually hardly spend enough time in that 'experiential space' so as to acknowledge it or attribute any substantial meaning to it. Your day-to-day experience corresponds far more with the Jamesean *me* to which Damasio referred as the 'autobiographical self' and Gallagher called it a 'narrative self'. It is, "[A] more or less coherent self (or self-image) that is constituted with a past and a future in the various stories that we and others tell about ourselves" (p. 15). The only reason I am using all three names (i.e., *me*/narrative/autobiographical self), is to thicken the understanding of this experience. I treat all three as representing the very same sense of *day-to-day* 'self'. It is a 'narrative self' that is a full-fledged operation that you constantly hear and construct in your mind. We'll look at its construction in detail in Chapter 8 but basically *me* is your name, status, job, life story, memories, plans etc. Here's a glimpse at my own version of *me*:

> I am Oren, I am married, I am an academic, I grew up in . . . my kids are still asleep as I'm writing now. . . . I hope to finish this book by October, today is Saturday and the writing is going quite well. . . . I hope I can keep up the

pace. What happens if I don't? – oh, this reminds me that I have to contact the publisher because I'm going way over the word limit . . . and what about that paper I sent to that journal. . . .

Excuse the neurotic ending, but this is just to give you the utter prosaic nature of *me* in my own case. The thing is, 'my own case' is the *only* one I experience first-handedly and can report about. Each one of us has his own *me* to cope with. . . .

Looking at this from within the *matrix of mind* developed in Chapter 2 (p. 47): *I* and *me* are both sensed *in here* in space, *but* they can be directly associated with attention in time:

I is associated with the bead-to-bead discrete moments of perception. It is immediate, non-conceptualizing, non-elaborate, non-fixed, vigilant.

Me is the (creator/creation of the) necklace or movie mode – the interpreter, conceptualizer, elaborator, as well as the interpretation itself. (As you note I view it as both a 'someone' *and* the manifestations of its workings, but this will only be elaborated in Chapter 8.)

I is there tacitly attending-sensing, mostly unacknowledged unless deliberately probed, based on practices like mindfulness. *Me* talks this whole thing through, and automatically makes sense of it (wisely or not) and owns it as *my experience*.[4] *Me* translates the flow of experience, that might be interpreted in a myriad ways, into a lived particular story about experience. It can be viewed as a possible creator of the sense of the horizontal time axis. More dramatically and pointing ahead in the book *me is no less than a mind-making process. It prunes the mind based on a moment-to-moment process of perception and stamps those moments in the image of its particularity.*

I will leave that enigmatic sentence hanging for now, and reground us in the reconstruction of 'education'. We now have *two* spatial distinctions based on the examination of attention in space (and time). Each one of them comes with a psychological/existential sense of 'self':

1. *In here/out there*, which gives rise to *me/not-me* – *in/out* is the barest level of depicting experience in space based on the 'door of attention' that was described in Chapter 2 (p. 35).

   Undergirding *in here/out there*, there's a more existential/psychological tacit experience that I suspect instantaneously follows upon our day-to-day perception of a stimulus. That which is deemed *in* is also tagged as *me*, while the rest is tagged as *not-me*.

2. *Center/periphery* that gives rise to *I/me* – *Mindful attention* opens an inner split within us; as if opening a second-*internal* door of attention. Spatially we get the experience of a *center* from which attention shines. All that it shines *over* is experienced as peripheral (whether it is *in here* or *out there*). Based on this center/periphery experience, two tacit and distinct senses of 'selfhood' seem to become available: *I* ('minimal/core self') as the sense of a 'someone' *in here* that's *non-conceptual* and primary – *universal*. *Me* as an elaborate narrative/autobiographical 'self' experienced as those things attended to *in here* (e.g. thoughts, sensations) – *particular*.

Do not believe for a moment that the above settles the matter. We can certainly ask: Is the core 'self' the origin of attention? If so, then who is it *in here* that can *know* such a thing? Is there an *I* behind the *I*? Is it possible that attention is somewhat of a free agent that 'rents its services' to *I or* to *me* and thus we get a different experience according to the renter? These questions are here not only to invite your imagination, but also to say that I hardly cracked this matter, and there is also a limit to the complexity I believe is helpful for the endeavor that I have taken upon myself in this book. At this point we will leave these questions as they are. The third part of the book will bring more depth to this entire domain; however, many questions will remain unsolved. Take this as an invitation to continue where I leave things off. For the time being, let's ground these 'two' *identities* – *I* and *me* – based on examining how they emerge in us by a brief excursion to developmental psychology.

*

The Birth of I and me

It's been quite a while, that I've been cutting you some slack, but let's not get too lazy *out there*. We're back with self-experimentation:

> Close your eyes. Breathe intentionally a few breaths. Now try to recall a memory from the time you were a few months old, or even from around the time you were one or two years old.

How successful were you? – I surely can't remember a thing from that time. I have one image that I can vaguely recall of myself as a baby but

I am not even sure I fully trust its validity. It might be a picture I saw years later that I am recalling now. The thing is; this was a trick question. This phenomenon of not remembering early childhood has been referred to as 'childhood amnesia' (Tustin and Hayne 2010). Developmental psychologists have long asserted that we are not born with the 'autobiographical self' to which this question appeals (i.e., this *me* that is associated with memories of the past (as well as plans for the future)). Up to our second year of infancy, narrative, which we understand as dependent on language – is not a part of our internal life (Siegel 2012). You can't form a *me* (nor an autobiography) if you lack words as the building blocks from which it is constructed. During your first years as an infant you were certainly there attending to reality, but your reality was not encoded in narrative form, thus it yielded no narrative self. Metaphorically speaking, it could be stated that you lacked language as the 'software' that would enable you to store such information for later use. Continuing this computer metaphor, neuroscientists will tell you that you lacked the *hard*ware as well. Regions in your brain that are associated with autobiographical memory have not yet matured.[5] That means that, again, *me* was an impossibility at this point in your life. No brain 'real estate' in which to store autobiographical narrative-based memories, no language to encode experience – no *me*.

It follows that with the absence of *me* there may have also been an absence of *not-me* for the two are dialectical. The affirmation of *me* is automatically the negation *not-me* and vice versa. Once there's a border it creates *two* sides, yet with no language to create *me*, at least a narrative-made border, is not formed. Perhaps however, there *was* a more basic primordial *in here/out there* split that was perceived in a very primary non-conceptual form. The mind-body was there experiencing non-verbal sensations, but there may have been 'no one' *in here* to tell it that it is separate from those sounds and sights that it was hearing and seeing. So who *was* it attending there? perhaps a 'core/minimal self' – an embodied non-conceptualizing *I* with no *me* interpreter/interpretation. What may have been there is some sense of a shared space in which there was a more fluid dyad of I-world (Wilber 1981). So an *I* (core/minimal 'self') is there when we are born (and probably earlier) but *me* comes later; when narrative becomes possible. The mind with which we are born seems to be a more *universal* mind in which interpretation is not yet there to *particularize* experience and individualize how we see things. 'Education' as pruning is that which will move it from universality to particularization. Let's briefly develop this idea as it stems from neuroscience. Then we'll explore how the two agencies of *me* and 'society', will be involved in the pruning of the mind by introducing an additional fundamental.

*

'EDUCATION' AS *PRUNING:* A BRAIN-MIND PERSPECTIVE

'Education' has had a long-standing relationship with metaphors taken from the agricultural world. Commonly it has been associated with *cultivation*, and the 'bringing out' (the Latin for *Educare*) of potentialities. The metaphor of *pruning*, however, is less commonly used, nevertheless I believe it applies especially when we associate the mind with the brain. Explaining this natural development will go a long way as we later describe how 'society' prunes the mind through 'education' for *better*, but also for worse.

At every discrete moment of experience your brain is incredibly active whether you are resting or whether you are engaged in a deliberate task (Raichle et al. 2001). This activity takes place at the neuronal level. Millions of brain-cells are 'firing' neurotransmitters that are responsible for (or facilitate) the experience that you are having. Not even one of us experiences neurons directly. We can live our entire lives perfectly well without even knowing we have such things (or even a brain)…. But neuroscience will tell us a very interesting story about 'education' if we examine ourselves from this perspective.

From the brain's side of things, learning is a process by which neurons fire together to create a group of firings that are associated with a certain subject matter 'event' (e.g., the memory of a fact, a certain problem solving skill). Neurons that fire together *wire together* (Hebb 1949; Shatz 1992), and repetitive firings strengthen neuronal connection, to enable greater proficiency of recalling information (e.g., coming up with the capital city of Egypt as Cairo) and the execution of skills (e.g., multiplication, reading). *Synaptic (or axon) pruning* is the process by which, over time, the brain follows a 'natural selection' process. The more a certain combination of neurons fires to form a group and enhance the sophistication of a skill, the stronger and more robust it becomes. Conversely the less it fires the greater the chance for its *pruning* – its extinction (Craik and Bialystok 2006). What this comes down to is that,

> Learning is both the strengthening of efficient pathways, as well as the extinction of the lesser ones.

A baby that is born in to the world possesses close to a hundred billion neurons, with very little connections between them. It is a jungle of infinite possibilities ready for action. Neuroimaging shows the gradual development of a brain from this jungle of infinite potential to a far more specified system of connections that grows in complexity with time (Siegel 2012, pp. 195–202). This manifests two 'educational' processes at one and the same time:

(a) The strengthening of effective connections that will manifest in who we have become, *and*
(b) The pruning of roads not taken – all those things that we have yet to (or never will) become.

My interpretation of *pruning* builds on this neuroscientific conception; however, it moves beyond it to explore its 'educational' implications. If we briefly revisit our 'placeholder' definition of 'education' from Chapter 1 (p. 16):

> 'Education' is a human endeavor the aim of which is to 'develop' human beings in light of a certain 'good'.

Let's add to that:

> 'Education' begins with somewhat of a *universal* mind that is pruned to *particular* 'good(s)'. It is a mind-making process that develops certain potentialities and ways of knowing-being, *at the expense of others.*

connecting this with the above,

> *I*, as a universal fundamental, enables for the formation of many *me*s. The *me* into which you develop is one of many that might have been. It is the result of the pruning of a universal *I* into a particular *me*.

What we need to ask at this point is: Where does *me* come from? What happens to the baby we left above as an *I*, that evokes *me* within it? Who does that and what in the mind warrants this? So far we've spoken of *one* mind, but the fundamentals we have, do not seem to accommodate to the very basic constituent of 'education' as we know it – the encounter of *one* mind with other minds; with a 'society'. How does 'society' enter the picture?

*

THE FUNDAMENTAL OF WE

'Society' was here all along with us. It appeared in something very peculiar that I've been doing for some dozens of pages. I have been playing a dirty trick of reconstructing 'education' from the position of the mind, yet the only mind I can do such thing *from*, is my own. Nevertheless, I constantly come up with generalizations, every time I say 'we are like this' or 'we are like that'. In fact the entire case began with James's "for the moment what *we* attend to is reality". It makes sense to ask:

> What warrants a particular individual mind to make universal claims about other minds? It is as if the particular mind can see things from many (or all) perspectives in a way that enables it to make generalizations about other minds. The particular mind assumes omniscience and makes universal claims. As we will see this begins with attention too....

This WE – as the taken-for-granted ability to generalize; as the sense of sharing experience with others that are like me – is a fundamental that must be assumed as something that the mind brings to experience. Analytically stated WE implies at least two day-to-day beliefs that seem to be built into our most primary experience:

a) *Naïve realism* – The shared, tacit, and intuitive belief that objects and living beings out there are *real*.[6] You can certainly speculate about the 'nature of reality' and come up with the idea that all that exists are perceptions as Bishop Berkeley did in the eighteenth century; however, such contemplative ideas do not characterize raw day-to-day experience. We tend to treat that which is seen/heard/felt *out there* as *real*, and the way it is sensed *in here* reflects *things as such out there*.

b) *Theory of mind[7]* – This extends (a) to a higher level of sophistication. Not only do I consider those around me as *real,* their realness implies the intuitive belief that they experience life very similarly to the way I do. They have subjective lives, which are structured as mine – they think, sense, and emote. This means that there's a point in trying to communicate with others; that if I express ideas properly you will understand me.

Why is all this important for us? – because without these assumptions no 'society' would exist. We would never bother explaining ourselves to anyone, needless to say, *attempt to 'educate'.* WE is the basis for 'education' and for 'society'. Metaphorically speaking it is the virtual umbilical cord that is there connecting human beings and undergirding all acts of communication.[8] WE somewhat denies the possibility of considering the mind as if it is an enclave that is indeed fully separate from *out there.* How? – WE creates the space of *in between.* It's there right now, between you and me, on this very page that I am writing, and you are reading. It is that which is between teacher and student; between parent and child. It can also be a space that opens *in here* as we learn to turn attention actively as explored in Chapter 9, and as you have been doing based on various self-experiments. Most importantly for us,

> WE as a universal fundamental enables for the formation of all potential 'societies'. However, the one (or more) with which we associate ourselves is one of many, hence it reflects the pruning of a universal WE into a particular 'narrative' by which 'society' 'educates'.

Again, a thick statement. Let's see what this means by defining what 'society' *is.*

*

'SOCIETY'

'Society' in the Matrix of Mind

Following the previous chapter, I'm going to suggest an explanation of what 'society' is, based on the fundamentals of attention, space, and time. After all 'society' itself must depend on a mind that attends to it, (even if that mind is also part of its makings). Let's first spell this out analytically and then relate these points directly to *I-me*, WE, and 'education' as pruning: 'Society' exists in space as follows[9]:

1. *In here* – 'Society' can be viewed as a nexus of ideas, norms, rules of conduct, manners, morals, and ethics, all of which govern human interactions. All these amount to *a belief system that 'lives' in the minds of individuals expressed in their embodiment and actions.* It is experienced at the depth of your embodied-sensed-emoted first-person experience, and dramatically shapes your meaning-making processes as we will examine in Chapter 7. Your blushing when flattered, your palpitation rising before asking a question in the lecture-hall, the experience of fear before an exam – all these are responses of your embodied mind that reflect just how much 'society' is alive in the cells of your body as you develop to react to social cues.

2. *Out there* – 'Society' comprises of the physical institutions and human interactions perceived as *out there*. Schools and higher education institutions, banks, hospitals, houses of representatives, generally – all human-made physical structures – are places in which 'social' ideas that live in our minds, are *practiced*.

'Society' appears in *time* as follows:

1. *In the horizontal time axis* – 'Society' as experienced *in here* and *out there* is the result of a historical past and a practiced present, which will lead to a future.

2. In the discrete moments of *now* – 'Society' exists in every concept you use. It is there in all your thoughts, for 'society' has planted language in your mind through 'education', and language is the tool through which *me* interprets the world as well as itself.

'Society' Is a BIG Embodied Mind with a 'Narrative'

If you look closely at the above you will find that 'society' is very much like you. That should not surprise you because,

> *minds make 'society' and that which minds make must reflect their nature. 'Society', I suggest, is a BIG mind.*[10]

As a BIG mind, 'society' has an *identity* that's similarly structured to the human mind. Most importantly it is a BIG 'narrative self', which shapes 'education'.[11] To explain this I turn to Neil Postman's (1995) *The End of Education*. As you read on, ask yourself whether the description of 'society' as a 'narrative' is not very much a description of your own 'narrative self' – the person you refer to when you say "*me*".

Postman claimed that 'education' must have some 'narrative' that provides it with meaning and purpose. He defined a 'narrative' as a story, "that tells of origins and envisions a future, a story that constructs ideals, prescribes rules of conduct, provides a source of authority, and above all, gives a sense of continuity and purpose" (1995, pp. 5–6). A 'narrative' entail beliefs about what is right and what is wrong, who and what counts (and who and what doesn't), as well as what one needs to be, know and/or do in order to become one who counts (although sometimes a 'narrative' in fact entails resistance to such 'social' mobility (e.g. Feudal Medieval Europe)).

A 'society' does not necessarily have *one* cohesive narrative. Diverse narratives can exist within one and the same 'society'. Each narrative proposes different and sometimes conflicting beliefs (e.g., the belief in equality vs. a capitalist market, the cultivation of patriotism vs. cosmopolitanism). Postman clearly showed that some narratives are far more compelling and 'educative' than others, but we will set that aside for now. What matters for us at this point, is first, that narratives 'educate' us whether we are aware of it or not and they surround us. Second, WE represents a *universal* that enables the mind to accommodate to *any* narrative, yet we are pruned into the *particularity* of seeing the world through the narrative of *this* 'society' in which we are 'educated'.

So first, a 'narrative' is expressed *everywhere*: in 'schools', in the media, through technology and in all human interactions in which we are involved or to which we bear witness. A 'narrative' will be carried *in here* within our embodied minds everywhere we go, and *out there* as we will see human-made buildings around us and we will wittingly or unwittingly enact our 'narrative'-based beliefs within them. As social psychologists show we act differently because we are in a dinner party, at school, in a bank, or conversing with a friend, all of which reflect that we constantly adjust ourselves to 'social' settings whether we are aware of these shifts or not. If our children do not do that, we teach them to do that (e.g. recall how you hushed them recently when they made too much noise in public). 'Social narrative' is a substantial part of the reality we attend to *out there* and *in here*, and part of what shapes the way in which we attend, act, and think. What this amounts to is that,

> once 'society' is there, visions of 'good' (e.g., what is best to have, to be, to do) are there *in* the minds that make 'society' and in the way in which these minds manifest through the embodied enactment of such ideas. 'Good and Bad' are all around us in the air we breathe.

Which leads to:

> Once 'society' is there, whether we say the word or not and whether we intend it or not – 'education' as a process of human development toward particular 'goods' is there. We are 'educated' by our mere existence in company with others.

The second point toward which I am moving is by no means concerned with overcoming this. This I believe is a *non*-contingent built in structure of 'education' as we know it. However, this non-contingent process can occur in a myriad ways each of which *is* contingent. This is where the problem of education becomes 'education', and this is where this book's agenda becomes more explicit:

> A mind that is born into this world seems to be an open terrain. If the experiences it gets, follow a 'social narrative' that has become a routine, that mind will be made to fit the past, not the present, nor the future. It will know not what, nor who, nor why, it is and for whom it exists. If the experiences it gets will not turn that mind to explore itself and the processes that make it and prune it, it will become part of a mass that has entrusted its life in the hands of a BIG mind. 'Society' supposedly 'educates' yet can only do so based on its generic, non-specific, contingent, and impersonal narrative. It comes from not-me and conquers me having no idea that I-WE exist.

There are several ideas concerned with pruning that need much more elaboration. I will mostly focus on three in this chapter: the pruning of a *universal* WE to a *particular* 'society', the pruning of a *universal I* to a *particular me*, and the blindness into which pruning can lead. In the following, I'll develop these themes beginning with revisiting the baby we left *me*-less above. We'll examine how its WE is pruned to and by 'society' based on the medium of *narrative* to gives birth to *me* as its *narrative* self. This continues to depict a fundamental structure of 'education', which applies, I believe, regardless of the quality of the 'social narrative' that guides it (even if some 'narratives' are definitely better than others). Based on the following, the second part of the book, will demonstrate and critique our *particular* 'narrative' as it reflects this movement.

*

The Birth of WE and the Appropriation of 'Education' by Out There

Consider what normally happens during the first years of our life. Think of your parents or other caregivers who were around you. (If relevant, reflect on yourself as a caregiver). What do we do with infants? Wittingly or unwittingly, our acts are oriented toward making them members of *our* group. Beyond feeding babies and tending to basic needs, the whole thrust of mother/father-child relationship is communication as established in attachment theory research (Ainsworth 1979; Cassidy and Shaver 1999). Any form of communication with a baby whether in gibberish or in actual language, whether by handing a bottle or changing a diaper, invokes WE. It creates an *ex*change; a space of *in-between*, which bridges *me* and *not-me, me* and *you*. That space creates the WE-ness that is the foundation of *any* 'society'.

Healthy human beings are born with this WE potentiality that will basically enable them to accommodate to *any* 'society'. This fundamental is reasserted with every moment in which a baby's and a caregiver's beams of attention intersect, as minds *relate* to each other. Whenever a one-day old baby cries and is responded to with food, the wheels of WE begin to role. Whenever a mother guesses a smile on her one-month-old baby's face, smiles back, and says *'you are smiling'*, WE is further enhanced. Whenever I draw my seven-months-old son's attention by pointing a finger at a cloud and saying *'cloud'*, WE is further established. All this is our tacit initiation into the assumptions of WE: the realness of the sides communicating and the empirical proof of the reasonability of communication.

Clearly the interactions between infant and caregiver can be nurturing or damaging, and different kinds of attachment relationships will form as a consequence (Siegel 2012), but again I want to point to something more dramatic and deeper that tacitly happens here:

> Our utter dependency on *out there* as babies to fulfill survival needs means that a mind that is born as a more *universal I*, is dependent on a particular

'society' (reflected in a particular parent and environment), which must leap in and become the agent of 'education'; the agent of attention in space. Our existence as non-contingent depends on contingency from the moment we are born.

The fundamental of *I* seems to come 'hard-wired' to WE. Both are implicit universals in our very nature. Both point to quite an infinite potentiality of who we might become as *individuals* and the infinite potentiality of 'societies' to which the mind can accommodate. *But* we are born into *particular* circumstances; most notably to a *particular* 'society',

> It is here in which – for better and for worse – the mind begins to undergo 'education' as a process of pruning – from universality to particularity. 'Education' is contingent at its outset.

Throughout the rest of the chapter, I'll elaborate this based on two 'educational' processes that will further ground us in this fundamental structure of 'education' as pruning: Language and narrative as the vehicles of 'society', *me,* and 'education' *and,* 'education' and the habituation of attention. We'll be moving *in here* and *out there* to emulate the effect of the 'hall of mirrors' that 'society' and mind create through 'education' as pruning.

Language as the Vehicle of 'Society'

Here's another self-experiment to get us going:

> Close your eyes, take a couple of breaths to relax yourself. Now for a few moments just listen to the sounds you hear around you. Do this for say, a minute.

Now try to reflect on this experience by answering the following questions: if you heard a sound (e.g., bird singing), did you automatically label it (e.g., 'bird'), or did you attend to the sound without labeling it? Perhaps you had a sense of the sound and the label as distinct from each other? If you heard the dishwasher from the kitchen, did you acknowledge a labeling of 'dishwasher'?

I realize that it may not at all occur to you to ask such questions, and that they might sound puzzling. The intention behind this experiment is to retrace what I suspect would have been your experience during your first months in this world as you were not yet that *me* that you feel yourself to be, but rather an *I*. Not even one of us can guess exactly what goes on in the mind of a newborn, but it would be safe to suggest that the experience one has in the first months is *non-conceptual*. The term 'conceptual' refers here to our mind's creation of a meaningful relation between an object and its label (i.e., the table and the word 'table'). I argue that this is *not* your experience as a one month-old infant. An infant would probably attend to a bird sound but know not that it *is* a bird. As an infant you might perhaps attend to this W o R *d* yet it would carry no meaning beyond its graphic shape. You would smell *something* but know not that it is milk or even that there is a *something* associated with that smell. This kind of existence may be associated with the *I*/core/minimal self.

When I introduce experiments such as the above, which can evoke these primary experiences in my courses,[12] some students need a number of trials and some work of explaining on my behalf before they can access and/or realize this primary and non-conceptual experience. Beyond a difficulty to concentrate on sounds, without thoughts intruding and luring attention away, I believe there's an additional profound difficulty involved here. Undergirding the WE that 'society' 'brings out' in us we are also taught a dramatic meta-lesson:

> We are trained from day one to label the world based on language as our basic means for communication. Without anyone mentioning this to us we learn that labeling the world is desirable and effective.

Early in our life the moon had little to do with the word 'moon' for us, and the idea that a word can represent a 'thing' was probably completely beyond our reach. What I am proposing is that,

> Sensations are first nature. Language and labeling begin as second nature, yet become so efficient so as to mask our first nature.[13] Applying our terms: *I* is first nature, *me* becomes our second nature, which masks *I*.

We were born 'hard-wired' to acquire language. Healthy brains develop to provide us with the hardware that enables lingual communication, *but our life began without it*. It takes an infant quite some months before he or she can arrive at the act of expressing sensations in words. What's important for us, is that once this discovery is made, its power becomes obvious and the desirability of language-based-communication becomes apparent. A baby discovers that *saying* 'milk'/'bottle'/'cold'/'pacifier', etc. as an expression of a need seems to move things far quicker in the proper direction, rather than 'just' crying as a general act of communication, which a caregiver struggles to decipher so that she can attend to a baby's needs. As Michael Fishbane puts is, "[E]ach successful communication imprints trust in the power of words . . . " (2008, p. 17). This is clearly no logical conscious 'conclusion' on behalf of a baby. It seems far more an evolutionary matter of trial and error, by which the success of saying 'bottle' and getting a 'bottle', hardwires the generic conditioning toward entrenching a preference for words.

> Slowly but surely, words become more powerful than things because they have the potential to move things in space according to our needs. *Language becomes the expression of agency.*

This shift from an *I* to a *me*, which becomes a full-fledged narrative is a gradual process. It transforms the way we are in the world.[14] It moves us from an attention that is attuned to non-conceptual, embodied-sensed experience, which is associated far more with a *universal* bead-to-bead *now*, to an attention that is taken by labeling, making-meaning, *interpreting, particularizing*. It is the difference between living the experience, and living the description of the experience in retrospect. It may also have to do with the distinction between *feeling* others as a 'warmer' quality as opposed to *understanding* others as a 'colder' quality. I can feel an other's suffering or joy, or I can label it by the words 'suffering' or 'joy'. What we usually hope for has more to do with the former, which implies that I will actually be motivated to aid the suffering and share the joy as I communicate with an actual human *being* rather than only *understand* the words that she expresses.

Word by word the world that appeared to the *I* as a sensed world, is conquered by *me*-concepts. With every word that conquers the world the building blocks for the 'narrative self' are provided and are taken to be a far more articulate, useful, and communicable vehicle that overtakes the core self. *Me* gradually conquers *I*.

Where does *me* emerge from? – from an *I* that attends from the mind's side, and form 'society' that *particularizes* a world *as such* based on language (as a general communicative vehicle), and on 'narrative' as a *particular* worldview of *this particular* 'society'. WE is the intermediator that enables this. 'Education', very broadly, is this process.

The mind is pruned through two processes here:

(1) From non-conceptual experience through *I* to a conceptualizing *me*.
(2) From the potentiality for life in any 'society' and the development of any *me* based on that, to the *particularity* of *this* 'narrative' that creates *this me*-'society'.

The question is: is there a problem here, and if there is, where does it lie? My argument has little to do with rejecting the validity or value of language. This entire book builds on the power of language. The argument is that,

> The gradual takeover of *me*-'society' over *I*-WE becomes our limited identity, that confuses the contingency and particularity of a pruned mind with the non-contingency and the universality of an unpruned mind. It transforms 'education' into dogma.

Let's see how this happens.

'Society' as the Pruning of WE

'Society' as 'narrative' and *me* as 'narrative self', share at least two things in common:

a) They are *particular* expressions of the *universals* of WE and I respectively, which makes them both *contingent*.[15]
b) They are blind to (a). That is, they tend to think of themselves as non-contingent.

How does this work? – I've pointed to this earlier at the individual level as I argued that *I* is universal, but *me* is the expression of *my* particular interpretation of experience that differs from yours. WE-'society' is simply an extension of the same idea. WE is a universal fundamental of our minds that enables us to learn to live a shared life of some kind within a group. It is the structure based on which our minds are initiated into the *particularity* and *contingency* of *our* 'society'. The 'society' in which we live, is a particular expression of *certain* norms that are optional and contingent. Look around you and you will see that different norms apply in Argentina compared to Iran or the Philippines (and probably change from one region to another within each and every country). The latter three 'societies' are *particular* possibilities that all emerge based on the *universal* fundamental of WE.

WE represents a starting point of a mind that can be 'socialized' into pretty much any kind of narrative. Narratives can be extremely horrible (e.g., Nazism), but WE enables the mind to accommodate to them regardless. *You* could have grown in an Alaskan terrain among the Inuit to live in the wilderness in a culture in which very few words are exchanged (Roderick and Merculieff 2013); you could have been raised in pre-WWII East-Germany, or in Nineteenth century London. There is contingency in the fact that you are who you are right now; your mind could have certainly developed otherwise had the consequences been different.[16] The *me* that you are, as will be explored in Chapter 8, is reflected in a myriad *contingent* ways: in certainty in things like having to go to college right after high school, equating success with certain amounts of money, the need for kids to learn the ABC prior to kindergarten – it matters not whether these beliefs apply to you or not. If you don't hold these, you still hold others. They are always brain-mind pathways taken, at the expense of others that were *not*. They are also the product of your WE pruned to a great extent by the 'society' in which you live.

The circumstances by which *your* 'society' had evolved into its specific form based on its specific history, have pruned your mind to be as specific as it is now for better *and* for worse. It was based on choosing to teach you *this* but not *that* or *that* but not *this*, to favor democracy over totalitarianism or vice versa, to prefer monogamy over bigamy, to be a Christian or an Atheist or resist both. What this comes down to is that:

Pruning is inevitable.

The argument here is not about overcoming pruning. It is a non-contingent process that seems to be part of the deal of being human. It is also not some advocacy of nihilism or relativism. There is a highly ethical stance here that will be developed in Chapters 6 and 9. For now, this is about the fact that,

'education' as we constructed it entails a pruning of 'education' itself. It blinds the mind to the process of pruning.

Blindness, as we soon see, paradoxically creates a sense of omniscience, certitude, and self-centeredness in which we come to confuse *me* with *I* and WE with 'society'. We come to believe that our minds indeed provide us with the image of the world *as such*. How does this happen? There are only two places to search for answers . . . *in here* and *out there*. We'll do both. First we come full circle to the beginning of the chapter in which the spatial *center/periphery* that gives rise to *I/me* was discussed, then we'll revisit that infant and further deepen our understanding of its initiation into *me*-'society'. My moving *in* and *out* may be confusing you. It is my attempt to overcome the hall of mirrors of mind and 'society' in which we are caught. I hope, however, that the important point will eventually come across as you read on and into the next chapters – *nothing exists in 'society' out there that is not a mirror image of the mind in here*.

*

THE ILLUSION OF OMNISCIENCE

There is something utterly subtle but deeply profound that lurks behind the phenomenological observations we've made above when we distinguished between *I* and *me*. It is, I believe, an inherent problem that's built in to the very structure of our moment-to-moment perception *here* and *now*. The problem is a tacit interpretation – the domain of *me* – that is attached to every bead of experience. That *center/periphery* structure of attention, creates the sense that I stand at the center of a solar system as if I am *a* sun; in fact *the* sun, around which everything else revolves. One of the best expressions of this idea, was offered by psychologist Julian Janes:

> Consciousness is a much smaller part of our mental life than we are conscious of, because we cannot be conscious of what we are not conscious of. How simple that is to say; how difficult to appreciate! It is like asking a flashlight in a dark room to search around for something that does not have any light shining upon it. The flashlight, since there is light in whatever direction it turns, would have to conclude that there is light everywhere. And so consciousness can seem to pervade all mentality when actually it does not. (1976, p. 23)

Janes speaks of consciousness, while I speak of this sensed 'origin of attention', but the flashlight metaphor still holds. It takes us to a two-layered utter blindness that is fundamental to our perception and existence:

1. *Blind-spots due to the limits of the beam of attention*: This is a significant yet less profound level. As mentioned in Chapter 2, we are blind to a huge amount of data that either enters our system beneath our awareness or does not enter it at all as far as we know. Pointing the flashlight in one direction implies missing that which remains in the dark. At this level, if you study math now, you can't experience your personal thoughts at the same time, and vice versa.

2. *Blindness to our own blindness:* This is the more profound problem. Numerous experiments effectively show that we really believe we see reality *as such* despite the fact that we can miss huge portions of day-to-day experience (Chabris and Simons 2010). I argue that:

> The great paradox of all is that blindness to blindness, is like a dual negation. It creates the illusion of omniscience. We are by no means omniscient, but built into the very structure of our experience is the illusory belief that we are.

Despite the fact that what we attend to is only *one* possible perspective on *this* moment, our *most immediate* sense is that it is the *only* available perspective. The only reason we have for this tacit feeling is that the image we get every moment never includes all that remains outside it by definition. It's the tautologeous nature of how *me* – our habitual inter-preter – interprets what it sees that gets us:

> Blindness 1 gives us: *we don't know what we don't know.*
> Blindness 2 gives us: *we don't know that we don't know.*

The profundity of this, however, should be articulated because this is not just about missing a certain object in space due to our looking in another direction. The far more dramatic and by all means, 'educationally'-relevant, issue, is that this applies *to missing another human being's point of view on things,* and traveling the world with the attribution of omniscience and certainty to *my* point of view. This is not something that *I* does; it is a characteristic of *me* that *owns experience and is fully identified with its own point of view.* Our attachment to *our* point of view is manifested in all those moments in which we get furious because someone else doesn't think the way we do. Traveling in the world with the illusion of omniscience, it is as if a constant whisper accompanies our every perception:

> for the moment what I attend to *is reality*, so if that guy doesn't see *reality* just as I see it, then something must be wrong with him. Had he attended to reality properly (as I do), then he would see reality *as such* just like me. He would then reach the same conclusions about the situation and would not be arguing about something that is so obvious.

Undergirding many human conflicts, regardless of their specific circumstances, is this tacit sense that is reaffirmed with every object that re-asserts our illusion of omniscience. Built into the very structure of attention is the experience of *me's* self-centered-ness – an *identification* and *ownership* of 'the way I see the world' that feels far more real than the way you see it. I'm right, you're wrong.

Of course, we are *taught* to look at things from other perspectives, but the fact that we need to be *taught* such thing only proves that it is by no means our first nature. Reminding ourselves that others around us are 'projecting the flashlight of attention from another point in space', and hence think differently, is *not* necessarily our first instinct. It is a *secondary* rationalization and by all means part of what 'education' in most cases hopes to develop within the context of empathy and compassion.[17]

We may certainly ponder why things work this way? – One explanation suggests that it is exactly thanks to this mechanism that we stay alive. Being fully convinced that what we see reflects reality *as such* is the foundation for survival (Hoffman 2008). We are better off mistakenly believing that there is a snake in the bush when there isn't a million times, rather than mistakenly believing that there isn't a snake when there is, even once (Hanson and Mendius 2009). It is as if our survival depends on creating the illusion of omniscience that entrenches us in being attached to our own views.

Thinking the reconstruction of 'education' directly here,

> given such circumstances, perhaps we do not need to be that surprised that empathy, understanding the other, compassion, altruism, do not come easy to us. It may require a willful effort that trains one to overcome a tacit habituation that takes place moment after moment beneath our awareness.

While this will be articulated more elaborately in Chapter 6 and in the concluding chapter, I suspect that what we are struggling with far more than getting children and youth to learn math and history, is how we are to live with each other; how *you* and I develop healthy relationships, avoid harming each other, and in fact help each other thrive. I am not arguing that we can either teach math *or* 'educate' in kindness and compassion. I think we can do both, but I believe that a reconstruction of 'education' requires that we face who we are and how we are constructed every moment through attention. The above suggests that there is an inherent self-centeredness built into our every moment of attending to reality that seems to work *against* 'educational' ideals that many of us hold. Our *own* minds carry the seeds of the problem. They provide us with the illusion of omniscience and *necessity* whereas in fact there is a built-in blindness and *contingency* in the image we get every moment. The image I get from the door of attention as beads are intercepted by *me*, is different than the one that you get from yours, as 'your' *me* stamps them with *your* interpretation. It is only if I learn to detach myself from this illusion of *necessity* and omniscience that the wall between us, can begin to dissolve.[18]

The 'social narrative' prunes I into me 'narrative self'

Look at this

Word

If you and I understand this word similarly, this expresses 'society' then and there.[19] How so? – Meanings of words are never isolated from 'social context' when they are learned as our native language. As an infant/child while you learn words you cannot but automatically absorb the undercurrent of the belief systems of those that use them. The initiation into language is never an initiation into a mere labeling of objects. It always comes with the molding of the *Universal* WE into the specificity of *this* 'social' narrative, based on which *me* creates its 'narrative self'. As infants, in the first years of our lives we acquire a '*mother* tongue'. However, in this acquisition process grammar and syntax are hardly as important as the *ideas* that glue us as a *specific* 'society' that believes *this* and not *that*, prefers *this* 'knowledge' and not *that*. Learning to speak English/ Mandarin/French, is undergirded by a more profound process. The essence of our becoming connected to a group through the medium of language is primarily our becoming competent in understanding this group's *ways of living together* – the grasping of a *particular* 'social narrative'. As infants we attend to the individuals in our group as they move in space, make gestures to each other, collaborate, argue, like, dislike, *do* things together. *You attend to all this from day one* through primary senses. You do not yet have that *me-interpreter-pruner* in you so you hear the spoken language more like music that accompanies a theatre show. Your mind is initiated into 'social' meaning that was there long before you arrived to this scene. Gradually and quite miraculously you develop competency in applying language as a *tool* through which you can join in. But the learning of this tool always comes mounted over 'social' usage that shaped its meaning. The building blocks of narrative by which *me* will develop thus come fully imbued with the 'social'.

The point I am making is that 'society' and *me* are made of the same fabric. We will see much more of this when we discuss *me* as a process of mind-wandering and *self-reflection* in Chapter 8, but overall, based on the fundamental of WE, you are initiated into *this* 'society'. Despite the universality of WE that can serve as a home for *all* 'societies' you come to believe that *my* 'society' sees the world as it was created. The very same self-centeredness built into *me's* interpretation of 'the origin of attention', appears in our initiation into 'society's' BIG mind from our infancy. We are fooled by our own game for the BIG mind too *knows only what it knows*. Both 'society' and *me* mistake optics with causality, *particularity* with *universality, specificity* with *generality, contingency* with *necessity*, 'society' with WE, *me* with *I*.

Some pages ago, I argued that 'society' exists *here* and *now* with every word spoken. So indeed, 'society' lurks behind every bead of experience thread based on the medium of language imbued with 'social' context. Whether you speak French or Mahrati is not as important as the fact that the acquisition of French is but *one* possibility of which your mind is capable, that rides over the acquisition of very *specific, particular, contingent* ideas of right/wrong, worthy/unworthy, meaningful/meaningless, which are associated with a French- or a Mahrati- speaking *particular* 'society'.

> Our minds-bodies are shaped by the habituation of attention based on a natural and inevitable process. It is a 'social' process of 'education' by which WE-I are pruned to me-'society'.

A huge problem emerges when part of the pruning process includes the pruning of 'education' itself so that our minds are made to fully believe that its ways convey the world *as such*. 'Society' and *me* easily become automatic habits that edify each other as a hall of mirrors; a self-justifying system; a *perpetuum mobile*.

The Habituation of Attention at the Social and Individual Level

What we have then seems to be a system that we can never escape. A 'world' formed by the 'social' through language and narrative, which molds the mind into a specific contingent 'social' context, geography, and time-period. It is a mind that loses sight of its original *unpruned* state that lies in its past, which might still be here at this very moment, within that pre-'educated' *I*-WE.

'Society', just like *me*, flourishes on the bedrock of narrative. The 'social' narrative breeds the 'narrative self' to form somewhat of a closed system. The 'education' we construct based on 'society' shapes *me* to see the world through the eyes of a BIG mind that is in charge of meaning-making based on language.

There's an inevitable meta-habituation at play here in which the mind is inevitably pruned to fit the contingency of its time and place through the 'social narrative'. It is a progression in which our brains-minds-bodies are 'educated' by the very instinctual needs with which we are born. As we suck in the first drops of milk from *out there* based on our instinctual will to survive, our minds cannot but develop a habit of dependency by which we orient attention *out there*. We sip in the 'social' into the cells of our body with every word exchanged with us and depend on it for physical and mental nourishment. Even our individuality is then expressed based on the building blocks of 'social' language. This must somehow play out at the 'social' level in the kinds of institutions that are created by brains-minds-bodies that have thus developed. They will be fully biased toward the 'social' as they prune each other to the point at which the 'social' world will lose its utter contingency and becomes the world *as such* – a *perpetuum mobile* governed by the habituation of a past. No one expresses this better than James:

> Habit is thus the enormous fly-wheel of society, its most precious conserva-tive agent. It alone is what keeps us all within the bounds of ordinance, and saves the children of fortune from the envious uprisings of the poor. It alone prevents the hardest and most repulsive walks of life from being deserted by those brought up to tread therein. It keeps the fisherman and the deck-hand at sea through the winter; it holds the miner in his darkness, and nails the countryman to his log cabin and his lonely farm through all the months of snow; it protects us from invasion by the natives of the desert and the frozen zone. It dooms us all to fight out the battle of life upon the lines of our

nurture or our early choice, and to make the best of a pursuit that disagrees, because there is no other for which we are fitted, and it is too late to begin again. (2007, p. 121)[20]

Is this our destiny?

I don't think so. This self-justifying system is not sealed. New ideas appear in the 'world' all the time. They appear in spite of this process, because there's "more than *me* that meets the *I*". Novelty comes from that mind as it engages with *in here* and *out there*, yet we are taken by *what* comes out of it far more than *where it comes out from* and *how*. The mind itself occasionally resists the very 'social' regime that it had invented. However, it can do so far more deliberately. Attention can be taught to be turned *in here* toward a reclaiming of *I* and WE, in a process of de-pruning that embraces the important indispensable aspects of pruning yet, 'educates' the mind out of blindness to its blindness.

If 'education' is a human endeavor that is aimed at 'developing' human beings in light of a certain 'good', it is only once the mind is taught to see beyond its particularity that the 'good' can be fully examined. Such universality, cannot but require our turning *in here* to *I*-WE.

SUMMARY: RE-GROUNDING OURSELVES IN THE RECONSTRUCTION OF 'EDUCATION'

In this chapter we further developed the fundamentals of mind based on the matrix of mind. This led to a thicker understanding of our identity as individuals within 'society':

- *In here/out there* is a perceived spatial split by which our identity as *me* is perceived as split from the world that is *not-me*.
- *Center/periphery* is an *internal* perceived split that emerges based on mindful attention and the sense of an origin of attention within. It creates the experience of *I* as a minimal non-conceptualizing self that observes *me*, which is a conceptualizing-interpreting narrative self.
- The fundamental of WE is an integral part of the mind. It must be assumed as that which enables us to communicate and to form 'societies'.

- 'Society' is a manifestation of minds hence can be characterized based on the matrix of mind:
  - It is a BIG mind, with a BIG narrative, and a BIG attentional flashlight.
  - It exists *in here* within our minds as beliefs, norms, ways of conduct, and embodied reactions to 'social' cues.
  - It exists *out there* as institutions in their physical form and in the ways of being that are enacted in them.
  - It exists over the *horizontal time axis* as the past based on which 'society's' narrative has formed, its present enactment, and the future to which it leads.
  - It exists *now* in the ways in which the mind *prunes* this moment based on language and interpretation into which it has been initiated through 'education'.
- The structure of attention in space yields the *illusion of omniscience* and our inherent sense of self-centeredness at the individual and 'social' levels:
  - We are blind to that which does not enter our conscious experience: we don't know what we do not attend.
  - We are blind to our blindness: we don't know that we don't know.
- *Pruning* is a process by which experience is reduced from an impregnated *universal* one, which lends itself to infinite interpretations, to *my particular* experience *now*. 'Education' is not only the cultivation of potentialities but also the *pruning* of possibilities that occurs in multiple levels of which we focused on these two:
  - From without: 'society' is a *particular* expression of WE, hence for better or for worse, *my* mind is pruned from its potential to be initiated into *any* 'narrative' – to *this* 'narrative' of *this particular* 'society'.
  - From within: *I* observes an experience that can be interpreted in a myriad ways, yet *me* transforms it into *my* experience in every moment of perception. This will be clarified in Chapter 8.
- Natural development is a process by which we are 'educated' from *I*-WE to *me*-'society'.

I am quite sure that you have several questions troubling you at this point. At least some of them will be answered in the following chapters. To wrap up this chapter I want to briefly position what we've done here in relation to the task of reconstructing 'education':

1. Fundamentals: in Chapter 2 we came up with the *universal* fundamentals of attention, space, and time. Here we added *I, me,* WE, and 'society', to these. By now you see that I associate universality (*I,* WE) with non-contingency, and particularity (*me*-'society') with contingency. All this fundamental work will pay off as we move next to Part II to examine where as a 'society', we have confused contingency with necessity and where 'education' can be liberated.

2. Exploring where is our problem? Recall that biblical statement: *In the beginning there was attention then we reconstruct 'education'.* As this chapter showed, there is something in our experience that makes the stark facticity of our self-centered-ness into a necessary starting point for understanding 'education' and its greatest task. It is a starting point that acknowledges the very non-ideal position that mind-'society'-'education' face *now*, rather than a starting point that leaps in to ideation that proposes what we *might* become in the future. There is absolutely nothing wrong with hopes, dreams, and visions. We need them too, but we must have a good idea about where we stand right *now*. Whichever the case,

> Our minds are integral parts of the problems of 'education'. We must address those problems both *out there* where they manifest, which is where we have been accustomed to attempt to solve them, but also *in here* at the place from which they arise – our own personal embodied experience – the mind's side of the 'curriculum'.

The feeling one gets when observing children and youth in schools is that our biggest 'educational' problem has to do with being able to solve quadratic equations, reading and writing, knowing history and so forth. Those are certainly important, but hardly as important as how we live within our own embodied minds and with each other. What we refer to as self-centeredness (or egocentrism, selfishness) is that which stands in the way to a compassionate world. Compassion does not arise in places in which one is addicted to one's own way of seeing things. Becoming compassionate requires an 'education' that disentangles us from the habituation of attention; from what seems to be a pruning that takes place at diverse levels: from *out there* as 'society' prunes WE to yield *me* and from within as *me prunes I* through interpretation.

Equipped with the matrix of mind and the additional fundamentals offered in this chapter we are now in a position to move into more familiar constructs of 'education' – 'curriculum' and 'pedagogy'. Part II that is now coming up will both construct these fundamentals but also apply our diagnostical tools toward an analysis of the *particular* constructs that we have developed. It'll be an interesting journey that will reveal how our 'educational' construct seems to send us away from exploring our own mind, while blinding us to this process, which essentially means that 'education' is neither about *me* nor about *I*. The mind seems to have written itself out of the story of 'education' it had conceived.

NOTES

1. I set aside various experiences in which *in here/out there* merge as in Csikszentmihalyi's (1991) 'flow' and in altered states of mind (see Berkovich-Ohana and Glicksohn 2014).
2. In effect James (2007) split the *me*-self into three: material, social, & spiritual.
3. In this chapter *I* connotes with the *contemplative I* and *not* with the *reflective I*. Both are developed in Chapter 9.
4. This dual conception of the 'self' is becoming grounded in neuroscience. This begins with a coarse left/right hemisphere dichotomy that is too colloquially understood these days yet some accounts depict it with great rigor (McGilchrist 2009). It continues with more elaborate distinctions that clearly demarcate brain regions/networks associated with language, interpretation, mind-wandering, and the 'narrative self' (e.g., medial regions, default mode network) as opposed to regions that are involved in non-conceptual primary perception (e.g., higher level regulatory regions, insula). (See, Ataria et al. 2015; Berkovich-Ohana and Glicksohn 2014).
5. This includes the medial temporal lobe, areas of the hippocampus, prefrontal regions of the brain, orbitofrontal cortex (Siegel 2012, p. 70).
6. See Searle (2015) for a far more nuanced description.
7. Saxe and Baron-Cohen (2007).
8. In neuroscientific and psychological terms all brain networks with which we are born, which provide us with the capacity to communicate and develop relationships, might be considered as the 'hardware' behind this WE.
9. This can be linked to Marx's 'superstructure' and 'base', but there are some differences that I will not explore here.
10. The other reason that this is unsurprising is that, I just laid the matrix of mind over 'society', and surprise, surprise 'society' fit to it like a glove. *Frameworks of inquiry tend to define their end product.*
11. It may very well have a BIG core 'self' but we will not develop this here.

12. Berkovich-Ohana and Glicksohn (2014).

13. As usual James will be the person to say it better: "Where the body is is 'here'; when the body acts is 'now'; what the body touches is 'this'; all other things are 'there' and 'then' and 'that'." (James 1976, p. 33).

14. In McGilchrist's (2009) analysis the shift from the *I* to *me* is associated with the left-brain's gradual takeover of the right-brain. Research shows the first years' primacy of right-brain activity gradually yielding to the left-brain that is characterized by the experience of conceptualizing the world, and making *use* of it.

15. To be sure, however, *I*, WE, *me*, 'society', are *all* fundamentals of mind. The former two are universal the latter two particular.

16. Science now tells us that genetics and environment work in tandem every step of the way, so genes do not sabotage this argument (Kaufer and Francis 2011).

17. What I refer to as *the illusion of omniscience* is described by Daniel Kahneman (2011) as the feature of our intuitive, non-controlled process of perception (which is the functioning of 'system 1'). It yields the naive disposition that he calls WYSIATI: "what you see is all there is".

18. I do not develop this here but rest assured that 'society a' vs. 'society b' is but an expression of the same problem yet in an extended form, as WE becomes the center/periphery and *my* 'society' becomes right*er* than yours.

19. I am fully willing to accept Witgensttein's (1953) conception of 'language games' in this respect, rather than suggest that there is a clearly articulated meaning to the word 'word'. This does not affect the argument in any way.

20. This grim description reverberates through diverse perspective such as, Weber's prophecy of the 'iron-cage' in which rationalization and bureaucratization take over *charisma*; McGilchrist's (2009) depiction of the brain's left hemisphere's takeover of the right hemisphere as a gradual process that has accelerated during the Enlightenment and modernity, and Turkle's (2012) analysis of technology's taking over our capacity for caring for each other.

PART II

The Expulsion of Mind from 'Education': A Diagnosis of the Current 'Educational' Construct

CHAPTER 4

'Knowledge' and the 'Curriculum' in Time and Space

If a copy of Hamlet fell from the sky in a forest and no-one was there, would it still be meaningful?

The task of this chapter and the next one, is to apply the matrix of mind we've developed in Chapter 2, toward an analysis of two constructs that make 'educational' theory and practice as we have constructed them: 'curriculum' and 'pedagogy'. 'Curriculum', which will be the focus of this chapter, has been constructed as the institutionalization of 'social narrative'. It is an expression of the kind of 'beads' that 'society' expects to thread with the hope that I will come to appreciate the beauty and worthwhileness of the 'necklace', which is formed in the process (see Chapter 2, p. 46). It is an expression of constructing 'education' from 'society's' side of things. We have come to understand it as concerned with Biology, Math, History, Literature, Geography, and so forth, but far less with the interior experience of their learning. You and I might attend to a 'Biology problem' at a time called *now*, and agree about its content seen *out there* in space. Internally, however, the experience we each have, may be utterly different. You might feel highly alert and enthusiastic, and I am terrified for I'm clueless about Biology, I happen to detest the teacher, and I'm far more interested in the girl sitting ahead that I've been planning to approach for weeks. These are two very distinct understandings of the process of 'education'. On the one hand there is attention, space, and time as a *universal* scaffold, which provides us with the shared 'Biology problem' *out there*, yet on the other hand

© The Author(s) 2017
O. Ergas, *Reconstructing 'Education' through Mindful Attention*,
DOI 10.1057/978-1-137-58782-4_4

there's the particular experience of the 'Biology problem' *in here* – in our individual embodied minds – which manifests in its lived *particular* experience *now*. This chapter will explore the way in which the construct of 'curriculum' associates our understanding of 'education' with the former and not with the latter. It is the manifestation of an attention that has gotten stuck mostly in one field within *the matrix of mind* (see Chapter 2, p. 47) – *out there* and over *the horizontal time axis*. Ignoring the possibility of *here* and *now*.

'Curriculum' however, is a complex phenomenon. We will first need to examine a more basic fundamental that serves as its building-block – 'knowledge'. The first part of the chapter will thus take us to a critical reflection on how we have come to understand 'knowledge'. You may recall that part of our work of reconstruction is to retrace our steps and diagnose where contingency has entered our 'educational' considerations – especially the places in which contingency appears as necessity in disguise. We will seek to place the finger on where this occurred in the case of 'knowledge' based on self-experimentation, sociological, and philosophical analysis, and grounded in our fundamentals of attention, space, and time. Then we will explore the deepest teachings into which our minds are pruned by the construct of the public 'curriculum', and based on the matrix of mind.

*

'KNOWLEDGE'

The Contingency of 'Knowledge' as the Vehicle of 'Education'

The basic 'placeholder' definition I offered in Chapter 1 (p. 16), proposed that 'education' is oriented toward a certain 'good'. Setting aside the *specific* 'good' proposed, and the question of 'who thinks this good is "good"?', there needs to be some kind of a *vehicle* by which this process can lead to the aims toward which it is geared. Confining this to 'educational' institutions with which we are familiar, such as 'schools' and higher 'education' institutions, we can think of it this way:

> If a student begins his 'educational' journey at a time and place we call A, and by the end of the journey we hope that he will arrive at B, with B being

'better' in some sense, then our question is, what name shall we give the vehicle that takes him or her from A to B? If you are of the analytical kind here's a mathematical way of putting this:

$$A + X = B$$

What is X?

If B is a place at which we arrive based on natural development, then 'education' as a *deliberate* effort on 'society's' behalf, is not required, for in such case it adds nothing we do not naturally grow in to. So what kind of change is a change that merits the term 'an educational change'? What is that thing that brings it about? What, other than the passing of time and natural development is added to the mind here, or characterizes its shaping?[1]

First, let me suggest that whatever name we give this 'thing', it must be thought of as another fundamental of 'education', for as we see, without it, the very idea of 'education' becomes either impossible or redundant. You can reflect on this on your own for a moment, but you've probably gathered from the title of this section that the name I'll deploy for this vehicle is unoriginal. As a 'society', we have become quite accustomed to referring to this vehicle as 'knowledge'. In fact, one of the most fundamental questions that has been guiding the development of the field of curriculum theory, appears as the title of Herbert Spencer's (1860) essay that was published over a hundred and fifty years ago: 'what knowledge is of most worth?' – no doubt there's a very reasonable ring to this question. But as usual, even here there's contingency that ought to be noted. I'll make three observations that challenge 'knowledge' as such vehicle:

First, 'why 'knowledge'?' – The fact that establishing 'education' and the 'curriculum' over 'knowledge' is somewhat second nature to us does not make it the only way to construct 'education'. We could have thought of 'creativity', 'wonder', 'awe', 'inspiration', 'wisdom', 'love', or other vehicles for the curriculum. These ideas were certainly there in Ancient Greece, in Romanticism, and appear in contemporary times as well (Robinson 2009; Zajonc 2009). It is quite reasonable to ask, 'now what kind of a curriculum can we develop if "love" is its vehicle?'. Just thinking wildly here, maybe in a 'schooling' system that teaches such 'curriculum', throughout their day, children and youth will engage in conducting acts of love and kindness to themselves and their environment and 'knowledge' (if we would think in such terms at all) would be some 'side-effect' of whatever they do? My argument here is thus not about the validity of 'knowledge' as a productive vehicle for the 'curriculum' as much as it is about our minds that have been pruned to take it for granted as a necessity, which leads us to the second point:

Consider that once I utter the term 'knowledge' there is all likelihood that you have certain ideas about what I mean by it. In fact, the above paragraphs were written as if the term 'knowledge' has little to do with 'awe', 'wonder', or 'love'. This tells you that contingency may appear not only in the choice of 'knowledge' as the vehicle for the 'curriculum', but also in *how we have constructed its meaning*. As you can see I am suspending the term 'knowledge' as well and the re-construction path we will take in this chapter will have much to do with questioning this 'social'-construct.

A third thing that might occur to us is the kind of pretentious position that is assumed when we go about asking questions like 'what knowledge is of most worth?' Can someone actually *know* what knowledge is of most worth when constructing a public 'curriculum'?!? Claims made about this matter, if not substantially confined are based on a false assumption,

That we stand over some omniscient vantage point that allows us to:
1. Choose the best of all possible 'knowledge'.
2. Know that this 'knowledge' will be of most worth to *all* of us
3. Know that this 'knowledge' is always good.

The thing is of course, that none of these are valid assumptions. Our lack of omniscience prevents us from knowing what is best, that the best is best for all and that the best is always best(est). We engage in conversation with the hope of arriving at conclusions that are better than the ones at which we arrive individually, but the cumulative effect of adding limited perspectives is not likely to yield omniscience. The question 'what knowledge is of most worth?' is clearly a 'modernist' question, and much critique has been cast on the over-optimistic geist of that era. But, the previous chapter did demonstrate where this might come from. The mind suffers from the illusion of omniscience. 'Society' cannot but reflect the tendencies of minds for minds are the stuff of its makings, and hence our ways of thinking, research, and practice of 'education' will reflect such tendencies.

To sum the above, I am arguing that the choice of going with 'knowledge' as a fundamental of 'education' is *optional*. It is a useful and productive one, but not the only one, nor necessarily the best. That how-ever, should not yield despair, for what we *are* capable of doing, is actually following in the footsteps of those that preceded us in constructing the *meaning* of 'knowledge'. By so doing we'll try to figure out where and how contingency has entered our image of 'education' and somehow disguised itself as necessity. Once we find that place, and identify it as a place where other possibilities have been overlooked, this would be the place to which we will orient our spotlights to chart new 'educational' terrains.

*

The Contingency in the 'Knowledge of Most Worth'

So far, I've been doing much of the work on this. It's time to engage you more directly in active reconstruction. If I asked *you* this traditional question:

> *'What is the knowledge of most worth?'* and more concretely *'what do students really need to learn at school?'*
> What would *you* answer?

I don't know what *your* answer is, but as others have noted, answers to such 'curricular' concerns tend to revolve around: allocating more school time to sciences or rather to humanities, initiating students in to 'the great books', improving technological literacy, cultural, and art literacy, preparation for job-market skills, etc.[2] As you can see, I've just bundled content that might represent *very* diverse opinions about what schools ought to teach as the 'knowledge of most worth'. What most readers (or most of my students at least) will *not* notice is something that takes us right back to the matrix of mind; most specifically to the fundamentals of attention in space:

> By the time we got caught up in diverse *content* issues we have already answered a question that escaped our reasoning. That question is not '*What* knowledge is of most worth' but rather: '*Where* knowledge of most worth is found?'.

This might sound like a peculiar question. But I am asking the question quite literally: Where is 'knowledge' in *space*? – is it *in here*, in this body-mind of mine (e.g., sensations, thoughts) or *out there*, in *not-me* (e.g. historical facts, textbooks)? Or perhaps in both? – It might take a moment to understand what I am asking here at all, so please read on. Basically, I am saying that,

> built into our understanding of 'education' and 'curriculum' is the belief that 'knowledge of most worth' (and perhaps 'knowledge' as such) exists *out there* not *in here*. 'Knowledge' is more of an 'entity' that can be mobilized over the horizontal axis than 'something' that might have anything to do with our minds-bodies *here now*.

You might be puzzled by this way of putting things as you wonder, how can we possibly think of emotions/sensations *in here* in the same way in which we think of 'WW II' for example?' You may also complain that I asked a trick question when I sent you thinking about the 'knowledge' of most worth without offering *in here* as an option. This would actually strengthen my point.

> Our failing to note that the option is there, is the best way to expose the default state into which our minds were 'educated' by 'society'. 'Education' and the 'knowledge' with which it is associated, have been constructed in our minds in such a way that leaves most of what goes on in our minds-bodies-hearts as residing outside of the game.

Let's get more concrete here with another very short self-experiment; almost identical to the one we conducted in Chapter 2, only now you will not be writing down anything:

> Please set a clock; this time for two minutes. Sit comfortably, and just note what your attention is drawn to during these two minutes. As best you can don't dwell on anything particular. Just make a mental note of any experience you have by mentally labeling it. If it's a thought – mentally say 'thought', if it is a bodily sensation, mentally say 'sensation', if it's a sound from out there, say 'sound/noise'. Don't worry about how accurate your labeling is.
> Set a clock,
> Try it.

The question I want to ask following these two minutes of practicing yet another form of mindfulness practice[3] is:

> *Would you consider any of the experiences you had during these two minutes as 'knowledge'?*

Most of my students, and I suspect, most readers, will hardly think so. If you indeed labeled your 'beads of experience', these may not have amounted to more than 'sensation' (e.g., an itch in the hand), 'noise' (e.g., the neighbor's baby crying), 'thought' (e.g., 'what's this book up to now'). We don't normally consider the latter as resembling what 'educational' institutions take to be 'knowledge'; things like: '2 × 2 = 4', 'the French Revolution began in 1789', or the skill of critical thinking that we are applying right now.

The question that lurks behind what we are discussing is an ancient and familiar one: 'what is knowledge *at all*?'. There are many ways to discuss this question, such as to examine the endless philosophical literature on this matter, but,

that's exactly what we need to avoid.

Trust me, I have nothing against Plato, Descartes, Kant, and other towering figures as well as East-Asian philosophers that may teach us a thing or two about 'knowledge'. I actually owe them a great deal for shaping my own mind in various ways. However, turning to them we will already be manifesting our belief that 'knowledge' resides *out there*; that others have the answers and we *in here* do not. What we need is in fact to liberate ourselves from what others have been thinking about 'knowledge', for you have to understand the vicious circularity over which this whole business stands:

'Knowledge' ends up to be what 'society' had determined to be 'knowledge', and the 'curriculum' flows directly from there.

While Kant is known for his Copernican revolution, in which he clearly showed that the 'laws of nature' that scientists 'discover' and are deemed as 'knowledge', are not really 'laws of nature', but rather the laws of how the mind (and more specifically *reason*) conceptualizes nature, I think that his substantial message never quite sunk in. Don't worry if you are not familiar with Kant. The message is that,

Knowledge has no nature, but the one given to it by us. Who's 'us'? – 'society'. Who's 'society'? – interacting minds.

When it comes down to 'knowledge', what counts as 'knowledge'? what is the 'knowledge of most worth'? – This is where contingency, choice, deliberation, and selection come in to the picture.

> 'Knowledge', as a concept, eventually depends on itself, for to label something as 'knowledge' must imply that one 'knows that it is knowledge'.

The mind is not born into the world with principles that establish what 'knowledge' *is* and what counts as knowledge. It is initiated into those principles. How? – through 'education'. If 'society' limits 'knowledge' the mind inevitably follows to limit itself. 'Knowledge' boils down to what human minds decide to accept as such. By accepting something as 'knowledge' we build in *meaning* into how we define the term and based on this process we then teach and 'educate'.

Yet if we recall our not-so-ideal perspective on matters such as 'knowledge of most worth', we can clearly entertain ourselves with the option that we got it wrong with how we defined 'knowledge'. How so? – well, think about it, if my thoughts, sensations, and emotions experienced *now* are not to be viewed as 'knowledge' then their status must be somehow inferior, and they will not belong in 'education'.

> It is very peculiar how the mind that knows expels its embodied experience from 'knowledge'. It's as if it does not trust itself…

The *mind*, mysteriously related to the *body* (and do question whether these are two at all), is where *your* life and *mine* take place. Can we seriously treat that which we attend to within them as anything less than *knowing* our own being and existence? – My point is not to refute what we have gathered so far by means of conventional conceptions of 'knowledge' within science for example, nor am I claiming that teaching math or geography is a bad idea. We have developed a very useful system that works for many purposes. My point is to expose what might not be working in our best interest. Limiting 'knowledge' we limit 'education' hence we limit the mind. Let's examine this more analytically.

The Reduction of 'Knowledge' and the Pruning of Mind

Return to the above self-experiment. In fact repeat it if you will. Sit for two minutes, simply attending to your experience and labeling it based on broad categories: thought, sensation, emotion, sound, smell . . .

Most people would *not* consider the items attended to during two minutes spent practicing mindfulness to be worthy of the term 'knowledge'. It may be safe to assume that at this point, if we extend this mindfulness experience to ten minutes or an hour (hard as it may seem some people actually do that) that might not make a big difference. The important question to ask here is this:

> What does *not* considering these as 'knowledge' tell us about how we understand the 'nature of knowledge'?

Or asked otherwise:

> What prevents us from thinking of the sound that comes to you right now, or a sensation in your body, as 'knowledge'?'

Here is a *non*-exhaustive list of reasons for why most would *not* consider those discrete moments of mindful attention to be 'knowledge':

1. They are too simple/too primary, hence they are negligible.
2. They don't seem useful in any way.
3. They are not true/false. They simply are.
4. They don't seem to appear within a context that provides them with meaning.
5. They don't seem to be incremental pieces of information that can be accumulated into a meaningful construct.
6. Some of them are non-conceptual. Their *just* sensations.
7. They don't seem to be something that you can (or should care to) teach to someone else.

If you reverse these characteristics you will get a clear picture of the way our mind has been 'educated' to conceive of 'knowledge'. This applies to school or University 'curricular knowledge' that appears in the form of 'disciplines' and most notably to the ways by which 'knowledge' earns such status – scientific research methods. Generally, we would call something 'knowledge' if at least some authoritarian figures (e.g., philosophers, scientists) and/or institutions (e.g., ministries of education, schools, Academia) deem some of the following categories as applying to it: importance, utility, falsifiability, appears within a context that provides meaning (e.g., certain discipline, social context), lends itself to the accumulation of a cohesive 'body of knowledge' by connecting between one 'piece' of information and another, builds in sophistication by creating such connections and enabling us to learn more, expressability in language or numbers, teachability. Not all criteria apply in all cases, but many do. Examine a school discipline and you will always find that there is some justification for its presence in the 'curriculum' that has to do with an association between the discipline and some of these meanings that we associate with the term 'knowledge'. Nevertheless, there are competing arguments about 'what knowledge is of most worth'; thus advocates of meaning will perhaps highlight arts and literature and debunk utility; advocates of utility might emphasize science, technology and math and debunk the arts and so forth.

None of these arguments are important for our purposes. Quite the contrary, it is the contingency involved in any of these preferences, which in fact strengthens my argument. There is absolutely nothing in the specific 'knowledge' that we speak of that makes it 'of more worth' or of 'little worth'. That is why there are disagreements. The preferences are all superimposed by 'society' and the mind over 'things' like 'literature', 'math', 'chemistry' or 'civic studies'. These are all no more than possible dispositions of the mind toward those things that have ended up in our 'curriculum'. My argument is not concerned with advocating relativism, but rather with contingency. Contingency begins prior to relativism; in the choice of what will count as 'knowledge' at all. *The matrix of mind* can come to our aid here as we articulate how we have come to understand the 'nature' of 'knowledge':

1. In terms of *space* – 'knowledge' belongs to the world *out there,* those things that are *not-me.*
2. In terms of *time* – 'knowledge' belongs to the *timeless.* 'Knowledge' is more of a 'thing' that was created by others in the past, but once created/discovered, it can be mobilized to the future, hence we are studying it *now* (I wonder if that is why we ended up with the term 'subject *matter'?*). In fact in our system we also make sure that you 'get' the 'knowledge' as others before you have gotten it. You are tested to prove that. Conversely, whatever you are thinking *now*; whatever sensation you are experiencing *in here* at this moment – an emotion or the breath that you are

breathing right now – these have little to do with the occasion for which we have gathered called 'education'.

Reconstructing 'Education'. A Brief Recap Before Moving Forward

So far we pointed to two loci of contingency in the construct of 'knowledge':

1. The contingency *of* 'knowledge' as the vehicle of 'education', and
2. The contingency *in* the construction of 'knowledge' as having to do with *out there* and not *in here,* and how it becomes the ground for 'curricular' considerations.

We might ask: 'What's the alternative?' At this point, just theoretically speaking, there is no reason why we should expel embodied experience – *being here now* – from 'knowledge'.[4] What if we considered extending our construct of 'knowledge' in space and time in the following way:

1. In terms of *space* – 'Knowledge', can just as much be defined as that which one experiences *in here*. Not just the 'Biology problem' *out there*, but also my fear, enthusiasm – the sensed-lived experience of it *in here*.
2. In terms of *time* – 'knowledge', can just as much include the experience of 'know*ing*'. It's not just the 'Biology problem' that has been taught in the past and can be taught in the future, but rather the experience of its learning *now* by *me* (or in fact *I* as we will see).

However, we need to understand why an alternative is required *at all.* Maybe we are fine just as things are? – As we now turn to analyze the 'curriculum' that builds on the construct of 'knowledge', based on the matrix of mind, we will see that our minds are pruned by it in ways that hardly work in our best interests neither as individuals nor as a 'society'. We need the *inner curriculum* for we are paying a huge price if our attention remains stuck in *out there* and over *the horizontal time axis*.

*

'Curriculum'

The 'curriculum' can be analyzed based on the matrix of mind beginning with exploring the etymology of the term. In Latin it stands for 'a running, a course, a career'. It comes from the word *currere* which means 'to run'. In this sense its image immediately captures time and space. A very slim and more conventional definition that I will soon flesh out suggests that the 'curriculum' is,

> *The structuring of 'knowledge' over the horizontal time axis, based on 'social deliberation'.*

Interestingly, the 'curriculum' has been constructed as a third person phenomenon – it is designed from *out there* by the 'social' BIG MIND that tells us when and where to run, but *we* – the first person living beings who are to actually do the running, have not been included in its image. Peculiarly we understand 'curriculum' as a course of a race that is independent of the runner. It is about the 'knowledge' and far less about the 'knower' or the 'know*ing*'; about 'society' not about *me*. This is what I mean by saying that we have effectively expelled the mind from 'education'. In the following we will diagnose and elaborate this problem (or problems). We will do so by exploring why and how the 'curriculum' is a 'mind-maker' and what's 'society's' role in this. All this of course will have to do with our fundamentals: attention, space, and time, or simply, with *the matrix of mind* as the ballpark of 'education'.

*

The 'Curriculum' as a Mind-Maker: 'Society's' BIG MIND at Work

Broadly, I argue that the foundations of the construct of the 'curriculum' are the place where we can expose how 'society' shapes the mind within the possibilities of the matrix of mind. This is the paradigm through which our minds will come to see themselves and the world and consider their own place in 'education'. This doesn't happen just in 'school', because our minds enact their 'education' in attention, space, and time anywhere we go. However, school will be the setting for exemplifying how it works. They are institutions that externalize our belief systems in ways that can be examined based on the matrix of mind.

The relation between the 'curriculum' and the mind has been established by many. Notably, Basil Bernstein (1971) referred to it as a 'mind-altering device'. Eliot Eisner, followed in his footsteps and claimed that it is a 'mind-making process'. What made these scholars make such strong statements? – Eisner explained, "What we teach...is a means for altering the ways in which students think" (1988, p. 19). Later he added, "what schools allow children to think about shapes, in ways perhaps more significant than we realize, the kind of minds they come to own. Education...is a mind making process" (1993, p. 5). I think that this claim should be accentuated:

> the deepest teachings we get arrive at our minds as an unnoticed indoctrination that occurs beneath awareness. We cannot help but be subject to it for usually the entire system has long become blind to these teachings' subtle existence. The system itself marches in a terrain that it had itself created with the self-conviction that the creation represents things as such. It shapes minds to see it through its eyes. While our eyes are caught in external things such as more math, more technology etc. that's not where the 'curriculum' practices its most significant existential-psychological impact. It's how we relate to space and time that we should probe to find the aspects of the 'curriculum' as a mind-maker.

The incredible impact of the 'curriculum' as a mind-maker, comes into view once we recall our first fundamental – *attention,* and the nature of (deliberate) 'education' as a practice by which we seek to orient attention to a *certain* domain. The 'curriculum' basically represents what *we* as a 'society' have come to appreciate as 'knowledge'. It is a locus of 'worthwhileness' by definition (Peters 1967, p. 19). Recall the kind of questions that guided curriculum theorists when they engaged in choosing what students need to know; questions like 'what knowledge is of most worth?'. The 'social' process of asking this question leads to a sifting process at the end of which the world becomes a *divided world*. At one side there are the things that are meaningful and valuable, at the other – those that are lesser. At one side you get 'knowledge'; at the other, it's either lesser 'knowledge' or things that are not considered to be 'knowledge' at all.

What this comes down to is that:

The curriculum is a locus of choice – It's the end product of a 'social' process of selection.

This might ring a bell if you recall Chapters 2 and 3. Attention was depicted as a flashlight of our conscious experience that constantly selects stimuli as our minds and bodies are bombarded by a myriad of possibilities in each and every moment. The mind is itself a 'curriculum deliberator' (and I did make an enigmatic statement about *me as a mind-making process* in Chapter 3). We will examine these ideas in Part III. At this point we are formalizing 'society's' role in this scheme that I discussed within the framework of our natural development in Chapter 3. What I am arguing is that 'society' can be viewed as *A BIG MIND* THAT FUNCTIONS AS THIS BOOK IS FUNCTIONING ON YOUR MIND RIGHT NOW. IT TELLS YOU WHERE TO ATTEND.

I think you got my point so we can go back to lowercase. Basically, I am arguing this:

> Just as your attention serves as 'the flashlight of your consciousness', you can think of 'society' itself as a 'big attentional flashlight'. It is this big flashlight that insistently points your attention to where knowledge of most worth is to be found. The difference between your flashlight of attention and 'society's' flashlight, is that 'society's' beam of light carries an incredible conviction and force with it compared to which your own mind dwarfens. When this 'social' flashlight is enforced in school by means of the 'curriculum', it usually comes with an authority that manifests in a system of punishment and reward. It is enacted based on how well your personal flashlight of attention originating in your mind follows the one 'society' has 'in MIND'.

This might sound totalitarian. Well it *is*, but do not think of this as some planned and neatly worked-out 'conspiracy' on behalf of 'society'. It is inevitable for two reasons:

1. The mind itself brings the feature of being willing to submit itself to the 'social' based on its utter dependency on *out there* as we've seen in Chapter 3. 'Society' builds its safe abode within *you* from day one.
2. 'Society' establishes the validity of selecting 'the knowledge of most worth' based on what Joseph Schwab (1969) called 'curricular deliberation' – a process that builds the credibility of the 'educational narrative'. In other words, wise people are engaged in constantly rethinking and developing the 'curriculum', hence there is always the sense that *someone out there* is taking care of 'education'. From a 'social perspective' this sounds reasonable and healthy. The only

problem is that this only reasserts the fact that *you* are excluded from the game. The mind *here* and *now* is made by deliberations made by others; its own story left untold. *Its own agency within attention is left to atrophy* as we will explore in Chapter 9.

*

The Three Curricula that All Schools Teach

A good way to explain why the 'curriculum' leads to this 'totalitarian' 'scheme' follows a framework that Eisner (1994) offered for understanding the nature of 'curricular' deliberations. This appears in his seminal *The Educational Imagination* in a chapter called "The three curricula that all schools teach". It is also a good framework for rehearsing the idea of 'education as pruning' described in Chapter 3.

According to Eisner, there is no way we can avoid teaching the following three 'curricula':

1. *The explicit curriculum* – when people speak of 'curriculum' this is what they will usually mean. It entails the most apparent manifestations of a 'curriculum' that were deliberately selected out of a wealth of possibilities. It's what you will see on a typical public school timetable (e.g., math, sciences, history, geography). It's the foreground of what we normally think of as happening in schools. It's where the flashlight of 'society's BIG mind' shines, so that students' minds will orient themselves in that direction, and *not* in another.

2. *The implicit curriculum* – this has also become known as 'the hidden curriculum' (Apple 2013; Giroux 2011). This 'curriculum' is *not* spelled out. It consists of how 'knowledge' and behaviors are presented and enacted in school life. It appears in how textbooks are written (e.g., choice of words and examples, political correctness, choosing this historical period/event and not another), punishment and reward systems in schools, the structure of the school day (e.g., preferences within a student's timetable, giving prime-time to this discipline and not another), the preference of sciences over arts and a myriad other issues. We learn this *implicit* 'curriculum' by living school life as we wittingly or unwittingly become 'educated' by means of all that is *not* explicitly taught. This is hidden from us most of the time but we learn it nevertheless.

3. *The null curriculum* – is composed of all those disciplines and ways of thinking that are *not* in the public curriculum at all (e.g., archeology, economics). As Eisner rightly argued, "what schools do not teach is at least as important as what they do teach" (1994, p. 97). Not having archeology in a child's 'curriculum' suggests that it is unimportant, marginal, and perhaps even "has nothing to do with 'education'".

There is no way around these three curricula for once you have limited time, you will have to choose what goes in to a students' day and what doesn't. What you choose is deemed 'knowledge' and is attributed 'meaning' and 'worthwhileness'. It becomes an integral part of the educational 'good', that I will soon elaborate as *the promise* of 'education'. Once you teach it there are various other things that will 'happen' in school and university that will give rise to the *implicit* curriculum. Whatever the explicit and implicit curriculum will not include, will yield the *null* curriculum. In this book we are mobilizing our own mind from the *null* curriculum to the *explicit curriculum*. At this point we are mostly exposing the process of its nullification, whereas in Part III we will position the mind at the center of curriculum and pedagogy as we explore the subject matter of the *inner curriculum*.

*

'CURRICULUM' IN SPACE

A Phenomenological Perspective

A powerful way to show how the current construct of the public 'curriculum' shapes the mind's conception of what counts as 'knowledge', what is 'educational' and what isn't, is to begin with *space*. We'll look at a very concrete example and apply the methodology of our two conceptions-experiences of time: looking at the beads of 'curriculum' thread moment-by-moment, and looking at the necklace that is its end-result. Based on this we will locate how the 'curriculum' relates to the matrix of mind.

a) Here's the 'bead-to-bead' micro-level:

Imagine Ruth. She's a tenth grader, and she's now sittings and attending to the teacher's explanation of why WWI began. Her eye spots her best friend's new cell phone sticking out of her bag. She notices that little grip of envy in her stomach, then a thought crosses her mind about how her friend always gets the best things. The teacher notices her distant gaze and calls her back to planet earth. It's WWI again. For a few moments Ruth's attention is taken to a different time. It's 1914. Franz Ferdinand, the archduke of Austria-Hungary is assassinated. The teacher points to the map and gives the students an orientation of the different alliances in Europe at the evening of WWI. Yet, at some point Ruth is called by a fellow student. She wants her to pass a note to John who's sitting next to her. She passes the note, and wonders what's written in it. Are they going to invite her to the party that she heard that they are organizing? Last time they didn't . . .

If we made a list of the 'beads' of attention that made Ruth's reality during these moments as you did with your own experience earlier, we could list them as follows:

1. History of WWI
2. Her best friend's new cell phone
3. A little grip of envy felt in the stomach
4. A thought about her best friend
5. The teacher that spotted her wandering and asked her to re-attend
6. WWI again. . . .
7. A note passed
8. A thought. . . .

There are two points I would like to make here:

First, a methodological point. Note the grounding effect that emerges when we climb down from that tree we call 'education', or 'schooling' and actually attend to the bead-to-bead process of attention that makes *reality* from the perspective of the embodied mind. Looking at it this way, are we willing to call all this 'a history lesson'? Children and youth spend endless hours in schools, but their presence there says little about what they actually experience. Reality exists at the place where attention is oriented, and Ruth here, attends to far more than what our definitions of 'education' and our understanding of 'school' tend to disclose.

On that note, you may certainly question the validity of Ruth's story, which may give the impression that she's far more distracted than the average student. It is only in the third part of the book that I methodically explain what's happening there in Ruth's mind (and brain) that very much happens to you as well, but just to give you a sneak peek ahead, empirical assessments suggest that our minds wander to thoughts that have little to do with our present task between a third to a half of our waking hours (Kane et al. 2007; Killingsworth and Gilbert 2010). This phenomenon, referred to as mind-wandering is now widely studied revealing mostly negative but also some positive effects on our well-being, identity, and actions as we will explore in detail when we get to the *curriculum of me* in Chapter 8.

Second, a normative argument. The point of the matter for us is this – the life of the mind *in here* is too pervasive, influential, and life-determining. It cannot be treated as if it is a world apart from the 'curriculum'. It is simply the other side of the coin to which the BIG MIND cannot shine its flashlight of attention, *but you certainly can*. As we will see contemplative practices can be viewed as pedagogies, which teach us to turn the flashlight of attention *inward* and explore the ways in which our minds produce an *inner curriculum* that shapes us.

Leaving the mind outside of the 'curriculum' suggests that right *now* the words that you are reading in this book are more important than the effect that they have on your mind and body. It's as if this book is more real than your own breath and experience; as if the book has the final say, rather than the way you interpret it, which essentially is all that exists for you. For a moment just think of Ruth, myself, and by all means – *yourself.* What do you think affected and shaped our lives more? Was it WWI, quadratic equations, and Macbeth or all that flux of thoughts, worries, social interactions, hopes, and dreams, that may have had something (but not much) to do with the subject matter of the 'curriculum'? I am well aware that no one can answer such question with full confidence. I present it to you more as a means to plot a route into your mind; to acknowledge the importance of its inner life. Our minds-bodies have a story to tell. There is an entire curriculum there that we have been nullifying. If you are there then it's there right now as well, in your every sensation, thought, and emotion that arise in you as you read *these words.*

b) Looking at this from the 'necklace' – the macro-level:

From the perspective of 'society' that has ardently worked to edify a 'curriculum' and place it at the foreground of 'education', all this background that's occurring in Ruth's mind, is no more than noise. It is not what curriculum planners have in mind for Ruth's 'education'. Nevertheless, if we extend this kind of experience as it goes on for years, and think of the *necklace* that's formed in this process, what we come up with, is a far thicker image. Some of the beads will clearly have to do with the 'social' side of the 'curriculum' (e.g., WWI), but many of them will be of an entirely different realm.

If one will actually reflect back and narrate the part of the necklace that corresponds with 'high-school' years, or another period, that narrative may very well sound like this one that describes my own:

> I remember myself sitting long hours in the class as a high-school student. I was a pretty good student, but there were certainly times in which other things than the physics and history spoken *out there* by the teacher, were on my mind. Things like whether my biceps were impressive enough to draw the attention of the girl I was after. Things like making sure people around me knew that I was tough and bright enough by exercising my cynicism over whoever seemed unable to respond, as I remained oblivious to my own cruelty. Things like being jealous of other boys that always seemed to have what I didn't, nicer shoes, cloth, or blond hair. Things like asking what the hell is all this 'life' about, if much of the time it didn't seem that much of an invention.

Both Ruth's case and my own narrative work to lure you to the backyard of the 'curriculum'; to that which supposedly happens in the 'background', while the 'worthy knowledge' occurs in the 'foreground' of our 'social' thinking and practicing 'curriculum' *out there*. We normally consider the 'curriculum' as having to do with everything but those things that I tried to highlight here – the internal life of our mind, which has *not* been given the title 'knowledge'. Our minds go to that background quite often as we shall see. Why do we think that this does not have an 'educational' effect on who we are? This is not about debunking the value of studying history, it is about elevating that *inner curriculum* so that we become aware of how our minds are constantly shaping themselves.

This phenomenological excursion of the view from within, based on the beads on the one hand and the necklace on the other, demonstrates the way we have come to understand, practice and construct the 'curriculum'. The lesson is clear: 'curriculum' is that which we see on the board and in the textbooks, it's 'knowledge' – something that can be mobilized, tested, articulated, used. It is very much the opposite of our living, pulsating, emoting minds, and bodies. In the following I present this in an analytical way.

An Analytical Perspective

From the perspective of attention in space we can attend to one of two arenas at any given moment: Either things perceived as *out there* (*not-me*) or things *in here (me)*. If you think of a student in the classroom this corresponds with two possibilities – that each in turn entails two domains:

(1) Stimuli perceived from *out there* that is, from *not-me*. This is the 'socially deliberated curriculum' and it will appear in two forms following Eisner's conception (p. 105):

(1a) The explicit curriculum: words uttered by the teacher, formulas on the board, sentences in the workbook etc. It is what 'society' thinks of as *knowledge of most worth* or at least that which ought to be taught in schools.

(1b) The implicit curriculum: all those unintentional or non-declared lessons learned in school.

Whichever the case, generally speaking, both of these will require attending to *out there*.

(2) Stimuli that arises *in here* within *me*. What are these? – thoughts, feelings, emotions, sensations that I experience whenever my attention is oriented wittingly or unwittingly *in here*. There are two possibilities here as well:

(2a) Thoughts/emotions/sensations that are associated with the explicit (or even implicit) curriculum (e.g., thought about a math problem discussed in the classroom) or,

(2b) Thoughts/emotions/sensations that will be completely personal as in the narratives above. That is, having no clear relation with what 'society' deemed 'knowledge of most worth' (e.g., thoughts about my biceps).

The conservative understanding of 'education' and the 'curriculum' will include domains 1a and 2a. Critical pedagogues have been emphasizing the inclusion of domain 1b, *but hardly anyone considers the domain of 2b*, which as mentioned, may occupy close to half of our waking hours.

If I think *in here* about the math problem presented to me, we would probably count that as the 'curriculum', whereas if the teacher speaks 'math' *out there*, while the beads threaded on my personal necklace are to do with my self-image and other *personal* issues that concern *me* – those would count as interfering with the 'curriculum'. It's a waste of precious time.

> Considered from the perspective of the 'necklace allegory', it is as if there is only one desirable necklace to be thread in the business of 'education'. It contains those beads that 'society' has selected for you, him, her and me.

Broadly speaking, we have constructed a 'curriculum' that has to do with *out there*. Either you are to attend to *out there* directly, or you are to think *in here* (in your mind) about things *out there*. Following Eisner, however, there's a deeper teaching that is in the *null* curriculum that stems from our analysis of the taken for granted answer to the question: 'what knowledge of most worth?' answered by 'knowledge' of the 'world' *out there*. There is the null curriculum of missing disciplines/professions such as agriculture, or stock-market trading that most schools don't teach. But if we think that adding or substituting 'disciplines' to a high school student's timetable will somehow save us, we only reflect how caught up 'in our act' we are. There are numerous reasons to study Economics, Archeology, and other 'missing' subjects, but they are to a great extent 'more of the same'. The problem is not 'missing' disciplines *out there*, but rather missing our own mind *in here*. It's *us* that have been nullified.

My claim here has little to do with 'child-centered approaches' that hold that a six or twelve year old can make a sound claim whether there's a need to study history at all. Only one who actually knows history can determine whether there is worth in it, and usually one who knows, finds that there *is* (assuming he knows other things well enough to compare it with). Hence the argument here is hardly about doing away with studying the 'world'. This is about targeting our minds as they were shaped by our 'social curriculum' to believe that the mind itself has little to offer on its own accord. This is about escaping the vicious cycle of creating *your* mind in the image of ready-made 'curriculum deliberations' that prune it to see things as if this is how the world was made, and not how *we* made it, and how it is seen *now* based on this 'made' mind. We, as a 'society', are incarcerating ourselves by attending to a monolithic construct of a 'curriculum' that gazes only to *there*. Paradoxically the way out is by positioning this very mind at the center of curriculum and pedagogy and that is done by incorporating the null options within the matrix of mind – *in here, now*. This means incorporating contemplative practices the essence of which is to make the person that is *I-me* explicit to myself; to understand what makes me tick? What is my mind up to when it thinks/emotes/senses in the ways it does? How can I be of service to myself and to others? How much are my actions an expression of a *real agency* within me? *Who am I, how do I find meaning, and how do I help you do the same?* – All questions that will be explored in Part III.

What we have at this point, is an explanation of the circular reasoning behind the 'curriculum's' establishment as a construct that sends us to attend to *out there* in space. It stems naturally from 'knowledge' as we have constructed it as a 'society', but it is also clearly grounded in a deep tendency of minds to nurture themselves physically and mentally based on how we develop from infancy, as developed in Chapter 3. But there is more to explore here in order to deepen our understanding of the price paid for a 'curriculum' that nullifies *here* and *now*. It emerges when we expose the deep teachings of the 'curriculum' as a construct of time.

'CURRICULUM' AND TIME

The previous section showed that our contemporary construct of the 'curriculum' fixates students *out there* (*not-me*) and nullifies *in here* (*I-me*). But here we'll see that it also fixates their attention on the horizontal time axis and nullifies *now*. The critique that I will propose has nothing to do with the reasonability of curriculum planning and design. It has to do with the way this structure makes the mind swim in the sea of time toward an unreachable destination called 'the future', while nullifying the concreteness of *now*. Basically I argue, that the 'curriculum', which we constructed, initiates us into an 'out of body' experience. It bifurcates mind from body by constantly sending the mind to attend to the future while the body cannot but live and breathe here and now. To begin to present this let's further explore the thing that the 'curriculum' *is*, as I ground this in the analysis of the 'social narrative' that was offered in Chapter 3 (p. 68).

'Curriculum' as a 'Social Normative Map'

Following our analysis of 'society' as grounded in 'narrative', the 'curriculum', I suggest, is eventually the higher-order structure in which one finds society's ideas about 'development' and its conception of what is considered 'better' or 'good'. It represents the way 'society' sees you developing according to the norm. If you adopt this way of thinking (and as we saw in Chapter 3, you cannot *but* adopt it given our natural development at least up to a certain age), it becomes the yardstick by which you will measure your life. 'Schools' and 'higher education' are institutions into which 'society' had built formidable meaning. That meaning does not only comprise of the worthiness of 'knowledge'. It also comprises of *the promise* that 'education' embodies, which is captured in the trajectory of the 'course of the race', the 'curriculum'. It tells you individually that if you will walk the distance something 'good' awaits you, for the 'curriculum' is not *just* some arbitrary 'social deliberative' process:

> *Its trajectory reveals the 'educational' promise for those who walk the path.*

The thing to which I want to draw attention, is that no matter how well-researched, well-thought, well-intended the 'curriculum' that we develop and teach, the way we think of it results as a 'normative *temporal* map'. This map represents our ability to mentally travel in time (a feature of our minds that will be explored in Chapter 8) rather than in space, and it has a clear destination called 'the good' (whether this 'good' is ethical living, social progress, self-actualization, academic achievements, or any other).

Setting aside the actual 'knowledge' to be acquired, our *temporal* 'map' looks somewhat like this (Figure 4.1).

Locations/destinations on this map correspond with age and age corresponds with an appropriate 'knowledge' level. It is thus a topography of *normative* 'social' decisions, which determine the 'knowledge of most worth' that is to be known at certain ages. Basically:

> It is a map that tells you where you are now, where you are going next, and when you are supposed to get there. Most importantly this map tells you whether you are in (or out) of sync with 'society's' clock.

preK   K1   K2...................K12........BA........MA.......   **The 'good'**

Fig. 4.1   The curriculum as a 'normative map'

If you are in fourth grade, your level of reading should correspond with this temporal destination. If you get too out of sync that is an indication of a problem. It can work both ways; being 'ahead', or being 'behind'. Children that want to move ahead, are in many cases discouraged from doing so. While clearly derogatory if we use Deresiewicz's (2014) image of 'excellent sheep', 'society' has a hard time shepherding the herd when some of the sheep graze 'knowledge' too far ahead. The bigger concern however, are the children who are behind as we later see. There are a number of highly problematic issues that arise when we seriously examine the kind of relationship with time into which we are initiated. In the following, I develop this based on three fundamental issues: (1) the metaphysical error: *Now* is not the time to be at, (2) 'education' is about '*society*' not about *me*, and (3) the discrepancy between the 'social' promise and embodied experience.

1. The Metaphysical Error: Now Is Not the Time to Be At

Applying our temporal methodology that moves from the 'necklace' to the beads, you can take any chunk on the above map and expand it to get a higher resolution of time (paralleling the scaling up of a topographical map). In our case you get a more specific representation of subject matter, skills, and 'knowledge of most worth', say by looking at a math curriculum during K1 (Figure 4.2).

While we are at it, let's zoom in further into a specific math lesson (Figure 4.3).

Time   **K1** Sept, Oct, Nov., Dec., Jan.........................**K2** **The 'good'**

Subject matter   Addition (1 to 10), (10 to 20)..Subtraction......

Fig. 4.2 Higher resolution (1) of 'social curriculum' as a normative map

Time 12:00   12:10   12:20   12:45 **The 'good'**

Subject matter Page 25 (in the work book)..page (28–30 if you got there...)

Fig. 4.3 Higher resolution (2) of 'social curriculum' as a normative map

Fig. 4.4   Higher resolution (3) of 'social curriculum' as a normative map

And why stop there? (Figure 4.4).

What am I suggesting here? – I am suggesting that there's something built into the structure of the 'curriculum', which we constructed, that dooms us to suffering. We are basically initiated into the idea that *now* is never good enough.

> Now is a means for getting to the next moment that will get us closer to the 'good'. Once we 'arrive' at the next moment, the situation never quite changes for it is similarly understood as a means to get to yet a loftier moment in time at which we can never actually arrive.

I am well aware that challenges and goals are utterly important and I do not believe we are born in to this world to remain idle. My intention is to point to a deep sense of lack (that I elaborate in Chapter 8 as 'the insufficiency of now') into which the 'curriculum's' stuck-ness over the *horizontal time axis* prunes the mind. It is a metaphysical error that has severe ethical-psychological-existential consequences. It looks somewhat like this (Figure 4.5).

At any given moment an 'educational' institution places a normative map in your hand that carries a tacit injunction:

1. *You are here now*
2. *Do you see that point in the distance (that place that's 'then' and 'there')?*
3. *That's the place to which you need to be going.*

Why? – *Because 'knowledge of most worth' is found then and there.*

Fig. 4.5   The metaphysical error of a 'curriculum' grounded solely in the horizontal time axis

The 'good' exists in the future. If we run fast enough *now* we shall arrive at a time that is *then*. Well, we can't really do that, can we? If the future is always presented as better, then this must apply at the level of discrete moments of attention as well. That is, *this* moment is inferior compared to the *next* by definition. How 'good' can a life be if this becomes its ethos?

At least two critical responses can be proposed to these arguments: first, there may be an interpretation here, that the 'good' is yet to come which can possibly introduce optimism in to this, but as we will see in a moment, when the 'good' is represented in arriving at 'social' destinations (e.g., graduation, passing the bar exam) it may more likely produce a sense of meaninglessness. Satisfaction that is based on achieving is important, but the fact of the matter is, that even those destinations at which one arrives upon 'covering the ground' indicated by the 'social normative map', do not always bring such experience. Demonstrated in first person, the following quandaries may be representative of such cases:

> "How is it that I am a second year Law student at *Harvard!* but I need a Prozac to keep my sanity?". "How is it that I've just passed the bar exam, yet I can't find a job or conversely, I feel more like a slave as a Law intern?". "How is it that now that I graduated/finished my PhD/became a partner at a prestigious firm/made tenure at the University/opened my own business, the promise of the 'curriculum' – that 'good' – still escapes me?"

A second critique would challenge us with the question: what is the alternative way of looking at this? This is the subject of Part III so the following will clearly be left hanging, but here's something to think about (Figure 4.6).

What's the mind's side of the 'curriculum' at this moment? What is the story of *my* experience of the math, the history, the literature, the

Fig. 4.6   The possibility of a curriculum of here now. What's the mind's side of the curriculum at this moment?

conversation I am having, the food I am eating, the anger I feel? What is it telling me about who I am, and where I am going?

2. 'Education' Is About 'Society' Not About Me

Since we have fully externalized the 'curriculum' as something to be attended to *out there* in space as we have seen above, our entire sense of what it means to 'develop' to a 'better' place – is itself externalized. Concretely depicted, consider that a child at school cannot but get the sense that Math 4 is better than Math 3, and that Grammar 7 is lesser than Grammar 9; that those that are stuck in page 27 are behind, and those that are on page 85 are advanced. (Of course 'behind' is more like 'slow', or 'dumb'). At the 'social' level he is clearly right. He may know more math or grammar, and this is presumably good. But two questions trouble me:

First, did this student struggle with the problems and in fact develop through the challenge, or did he effortlessly cruise through those pages, which implies he might not have learned a thing? From the 'social' side of things the question seems unimportant. Accountability and standardization do *not* tell this story for they are more about the broader picture of 'society's' march over the 'normative map'.

Second, did this student ever question whether math is meaningful to *him*, or has meaning become something that he understands to be a part of math, which has nothing to do with his own mind? Perhaps his mind is shaped to find the meaning *not* in the math, but rather in a general 'marching in sync with 'society's' clock' and preferably being just a tad ahead so as not to be 'behind'?

We are 'educated' to believe that 'development' means marching the 'social *normative* map' and covering *visible* destinations that 'society' had positioned over it. The first person experience of attending to *this* moment from *your* mind *in here*, to in fact find meaning in what one does, has very little to do with the 'curriculum' as a normative map. *'Education' becomes a mass production. It is about 'society' not really about you.* But what kind of a 'society' will this become? – Just imagine for a moment what would happen if this kind of 'curriculum' will actually work. We will get a mass of 'students' the minds of whom will all have been pruned in the image of a BIG mind. They will know all the 'knowledge of most worth' and idolize it rather than question its worth and refute it or rediscover it through their own minds. They will become 'house-keepers' of 'education' rather than its architects who will enrich 'society' after having examined their *inwardness* and discovered their own gift of worthiness that they will contribute to the world.

Again! The reasonability of the destinations over the map we have constructed is not questioned at all here. I fully agree that learning to read, for example, is a huge accomplishment that opens one's world to a myriad satisfying paths; that appreciating Pythagoras's theorem can be an esthetic experience; that learning Chemistry can open us to the marvels of our 'world' as well as to inspiring stories such as Mendeleev's discovery of the periodic table. The *problem* is not in the 'knowledge' itself. It is in how our minds are shaped to see 'knowledge' as having some kind of value that is to be cashed in the future and not *now*; it is thinking that anything 'good' can be experienced in a mythological place at which we cannot arrive; it is losing touch with our bodies – the organs of our experience – that are always *here* and *now*, yet our 'curriculum' invites the mind to depart from them for we are busy getting to the future; it is also 'educating' ourselves to measure our worth by subscribing to standards that have little to do with *this* moment as it is experience in our embodiment, but rather with how well we are doing *compared to others around us*.

3. The Clash Between 'Social Narrative' and Embodied Experience
The above two points lead to the third, which has to do with the way in which the 'curricular' image of the 'good' that's projected at us from *out there*, shapes our minds so that we measure our experience *in here* against it, and struggle with the promise of 'education'. We supposedly 'arrive' in these normative temporal 'social' destinations yet our experience simply might have little to do with the kind of image that we get from *out there*.

This can be presented by overlaying two kinds of charts: one that follows the embodied beads of experience *in here* as the 'subjective good' laid over the other, which is the horizontal time axis that is represented in the 'curriculum's' promise as the 'objective good' (Figure 4.7).

By no means should you treat this chart literally. It is a metaphor to play with, but broadly the linear continuous line represents the image of the 'curriculum' and its promise. It is a line that somehow 'sits' there at the back of one's mind as the 'course of the race' progresses to the future 'good' that will reward the runner with whatever it is that schools, teachers, policy makers promise for walking the distance. Inconsequentially it is continuous to correspond with the rather isomorphic understanding that we have of this disembodied non-lived horizontal time axis.

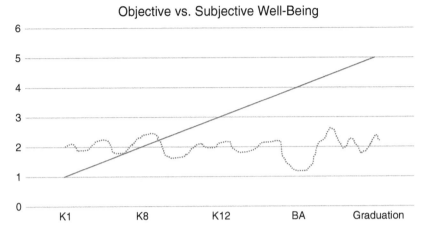

Fig. 4.7   The linear line represents the horizontal time axis and the promise of 'education'. The dotted line represents bead-to-bead embodied experience of subjective well-being

The neatness of linear lines appears in two places alone – on charts like this, or in a 'Greek' world, either within Euclidean geometry or within Plato's 'perfect' forms. Conversely, the lived side of the 'curriculum' – the place *from* which it is experienced, is an embodied mind. If it were possible to sample the actual well-being one experiences while 'running' the curriculum (as we will somewhat do in Chapter 8 when examining the *curriculum of me*), it is more likely to look like the dotted line – A series of mental states in which I experience life in a very subjective and idiosyncratic way.

My experience is clearly affected by 'society' *out there* and the 'curricular good', but as we shall see far more is going on *in here* in my brain-mind-body-heart that determines my reality. The 'education', which we constructed has very little to do with the dotted line. As a 'social' construct it is about the continuous horizontal time axis. But *I* live in this body-mind to which the door of attention opens and a flux of thoughts, sensations, and emotions of which 'society' has little clue, are brought into *my* view. All these are part of a far broader 'curriculum' within which 'society's' plan is but *one* aspect. The third part of the book will examine how the 'social' image of the future 'good' intersects with this mind-body *here* and *now* to form a far more impregnated 'curricular' *moment*, one that is far more attuned with life, and includes *you* in it.

The critique I propose reorients our understanding of 'development' and 'good' from an attention that has been pruned so that it is stuck on the horizontal time axis, thus the status of my embodied experience is diminished, to an attention that is educated toward the additional perspective of the discrete beads of attention *in here*. This is about balancing the two, not about a complete reversal of our orientation. It is about nesting the 'social curriculum' in meaning and meaning is something that the mind must give in order for it to stand on its feet as we shall see in the next chapter.

SUMMARY: CONTINGENCY AND NECESSITY IN THE MAKINGS OF THE 'CURRICULUM'

- The 'curriculum' as we constructed it is a way of structuring 'knowledge' over the *horizontal time axis*.
- The nature of 'knowledge' must depend on 'knowing' what 'knowledge' is, which means, 'society' decides what it is.
- We have come to understand 'knowledge' as mostly independent of the mind and existing *out there*.
- The 'curriculum' results as a 'social' practice that initiates us into a 'world' while expelling the mind that is to study it, from 'education'.
- The 'curriculum' carries the promise of the 'good' which entails a twofold contingency by which we are pruning the mind:
  - We come to believe that the *particular* 'social normative map' we get represents the objective and *universal* state of things in the world. While each 'society' will craft a 'good' according to its history and culture, the map you'll get is the one that corresponds with *your* 'society' and despite the fact that a hundred miles from where you live the situation might be different (not necessarily better), from day one you will be initiated into *this* map and not another. Eventually you may come to accept its contingency as the way things *are*.
  - As a 'society' we treat the 'student's' existence as contingent for we attach meaning, worthwhileness, and 'goodness' to objects and ideas *out there* such as 'Chemistry' or 'Science', 'finishing fourth grade' or earning a Master's degree, as if 'goodness' is an inherent characteristic of their color or shape, that is independent of the disposition of the mind that attends to them. We seem to

create a fixed world in which things have their cash value attached to them independent of the mind's preferences.

Following the matrix of mind, the exploration of 'curriculum' and 'knowledge', has yielded several insights as to some of the problems we have in 'education'. However, the expulsion of the mind is to be explored at the bead-to-bead level within *pedagogical practice* as the emissary of curricular practice. Practice embodies theory. Mind is made by both. This is where we turn next.

NOTES

1. Do consider the option that the question is posed incorrectly. Maybe 'education' is actually a process of subtraction. Perhaps it's more like $A - X = B$? Thinking of Socrates for example, (or even Postman (1995)) one might certainly think of the 'educational' process as one of getting rid of wrong ideas more than of acquiring the right ones.
2. Bloom (1987), Eisner (1994) and Postman (1995).
3. This version is associated with the twentieth century Burmese Buddhist monk, Mahasi Sayadaw.
4. Some philosophers like Arthur Schopenhauer (1966) indeed suggested that our internal sense of embodiment grants us with a unique type of knowing that is both intimate and draws us closer to the realm of things as such.

CHAPTER 5

Pedagogy and Meta-pedagogy

What is the mechanism that traps 'education' and makes it a self-justifying system?

'Curriculum' is a construct that lends itself more easily to thinking 'education' within the horizontal time axis. 'Curriculum' design is basically the art of charting a temporal map of 'knowledge of most worth'. This might give the impression that it is a rather distant and merely 'theoretical' endeavor, which in itself tends to mean that it is somehow less influential. There are two reasons why this is an utterly false idea. First, thinking 'curriculum' and making choices about what students will learn is *practice* – one in which a BIG 'social' mind works to define *what* is to be attended to, to make reality, *when* it is to be attended to, and as I constantly reiterate – *where* in space ought we attend (*in here* or *out there*). Second, 'curricular' deliberations are embodied in teachers' thinking and classroom practice. Students are hardly ever made aware of the thought processes behind the 'curriculum' they learn. They receive the 'final' product, *but they receive it imbued with a 'social narrative'* that the designers' minds wittingly or unwittingly planted in it. Hence, students' minds are shaped directly by all the premises that undergird the theory and the practice. The previous chapter dealt with these premises, but it is time to look at the way in which minds are made by the construct of 'education' as a student *practically* engages with the 'curriculum' – as beads are thread over the necklace of his or her life through the nitty-gritty of classroom/lecture-hall *practice – through pedagogy; through attention.*

© The Author(s) 2017
O. Ergas, *Reconstructing 'Education' through Mindful Attention,*
DOI 10.1057/978-1-137-58782-4_5

Think of *yourself* as a student:

> As you went to school as a child no-one told you what 'education' *is*.
> By engaging *out there* in the *practices* that were all housed in 'school' that
> was 'socially' associated with the idea of 'education', with all those children
> and youth around you similarly engaged, the meaning of 'education' was
> constructed *in here* in such a formidable way, that when you grew up and
> engaged in the reading of a book called *Reconstructing 'education' through
> mindful attention*, you read that book based on a mind that already 'knows'
> what 'education' *is*.

It is based on *pedagogy* that we are 'educated' in the nature of 'education'.
It is based on *practice* that our minds are pruned from a *universal* state in
which all human forms of 'education' were potentially possible, to the
understanding of 'education' in a *particular* way, concomitantly with a
blindness to the *contingency* of this situation. This chapter will describe
how the pedagogical choice of *where we ought to attend* becomes the place
where 'education' got stuck, and the prices that we pay for this stuck-ness.
It is a lesson that is taught with every bead thread in a classroom, which
becomes a 'social habit' in which we learn to search for meaning everywhere but *in here*.

*

META-PEDAGOGY, ATTENTION, AND THE
EXPULSION OF THE MIND

Teachers have much to do with the 'curriculum'. Their work entails
translating it as a set of ideas into a living teaching that interacts with a
learner. From the teacher's perspective, 'curriculum', as we understand it,
concerns *what* to teach and *when* to teach it. My claim here will be that the
most important aspect of 'education' begins with examining not *what,* nor
when we choose to teach something. It is far more in a very particular
aspect of *how* we teach. It is here at which 'curriculum' and 'pedagogy' are
unified, for we are speaking again about *where* students are asked to attend
to in *space*, yet now directly based on the *practical* perspective. To make
these points I begin with a distinction that I propose between pedagogy,
and what I call *meta-pedagogy*.

Pedagogy consists of all methods a teacher applies for teaching certain subject matter: frontal lecturing, class discussion, power-point presentations, group work, problem posing, project-based learning, watching videos, having children come up with questions, writing on the board, working in a workbook, etc.[1] It is an important domain, but I don't think that this is our biggest problem. Big changes occur when foundations are moved. We need to look at all the above pedagogies from the perspective of the fundamentals of attention, space, and time if we wish to come up with something that is not 'more of the same'.

What I want to explore is *meta-pedagogy – a pedagogical principle that undergirds all pedagogies whatsoever*. This will be a certain aspect of *how* one teaches that is always present whether a teacher is aware of it or not. Being all-pervasive meta-pedagogy is the core of 'educational practice' because it becomes a continuous teaching that undergirds everything a teacher does in a classroom. As you might guess, here, this will be based on the three fundamentals of attention, space, and time and their implications to 'knowledge'. Reviewing what has already come up from the previous chapters:

> Every moment of teaching requires the orienting of a student's attention. From the perspective of the student's mind, there can only be two places in space to which attention can be oriented – in here (to me) or out there (to not-me).

It can be stated in this more elaborate way:

> All moments of teaching carry an implicit or an explicit meta-pedagogical injunction: 'attend out there' or 'attend in here'.

No one needs to spell out a meta-pedagogical injunction. It rides over anything done in a classroom and no pedagogy can do without it – for 'education' is orienting attention. My words right now embody this injunction. You might not heed it; nevertheless, I'm calling you to attend *out there*, where *these words* are perceived by you to exist.

Conversely, if I ask you to attend to your breath *in here. And please do...*

> *Breathe....*
> > *Breathe....*

I just asked you to attend *in here*. I didn't say this explicitly, but it was implicit in my appeal to your body – that's the only place in which you would normally feel that *your* breath exists. By so doing, even for an instant, you were not *out there*, but rather *in here*. I am not yet saying anything about the merits of attending *in here*. At this point, we are back to exploring what is possible, or what is available to our mind. Only based on choice between available options can we justify any further deliberation as to an 'educational good'.

Meta-pedagogy is engrained in the most negligible occurrences in a classroom. We need not search for it merely in the actual teaching of subject matter. It matters not if this is a history, math, bible, or any other lesson. Everything a teacher does rides over the orientation of the door of attention. The teacher's entrance to the classroom is a meta-pedagogy that asks the student to attend *out there*. His or her writing on the board tells me as a student to attend to *out there*. Similarly, the sound of a teacher's voice asks me to attend to *out there*. Much of the subject matter taught at school requires a meta-pedagogy that orients attention *out there*, and clearly one will have a hard time learning historical facts without attending *out there* to a text, screen, or teacher, as possible sources from which to learn them.

We've spoken about how our 'curriculum' thinking has expelled the mind from 'education', but here we are going to see this imbalance at the bead-to-bead level of classroom practice. It is here that our monolithic meta-pedagogy – attend *out there* – drives home the deepest teaching of our construct of 'education' as an implicit teaching that is hardly ever questioned. I want to expose the ramifications of this simple, so subtle and transparent act, that is the foundation of the moment to moment of school life. There are two ways in which meta-pedagogy is practiced in school:

1. The *implicit* injunction that undergirds everything that goes on in school – attend *out there* or attend *in here*, yet only if that's to serve the purpose of thinking about *out there*.
2. The *explicit* injunction to attend *out there* whenever you seem to succumb to daydreaming or some self-absorbed state that appears to the teacher as a hindrance to the activity conceived as 'curriculum-relevant'.

There is however also the fundamental psychological mechanism known as 'operant conditioning' to which our brains take like bees to honey that ensures that we will keep attending *out there*: Attending *out there* gets rewarded, attending *in here*, if not for pondering the questions that are presented from *out there* (i.e., from 'society's' side) is either ignored, or met by an explicit meta-pedagogical reprimand: 'Sarah, are you with us?', 'John, will you bring yourself back to the lesson?'.

The utter simplicity here escapes the eye and blinds us to the incredible power of the habituation of the mind. Here lies the nitty-gritty of how we expel ourselves from 'education'. An analysis of the implicit and explicit injunction and our psychological conditioning will show us:

1. How 'education' earned its meaning as a process by which 'knowledge of most worth' became detached from the knower.
2. How our 'curricular-pedagogical' approach became one in which attending *in here* for extended periods of time and deliberately, would seem out of place within the construct of 'education'.
3. How the problem of education becomes 'education', since the monolithic meta-pedagogy over which we have constructed it becomes a *perpetuum mobile*; a self-justifying reproductive system that recreates the future in the image of the past, and prunes the mind to think that this is how the world was made.

In the following I describe these three gradually.

Who's 'Education' About?

The implicit and explicit injunctions are elaborated first through this narrative of a boy named Tommy – a child at a public school that probably could have been you. I'll be the voice of the narrator depicting somewhat of Tommy's personal 'necklace' thread by his moments of attention as he grows up:

Tommy is a nine-year-old boy. His parents send him to a place called 'school' in which he is told that he is receiving his 'education'. All the children around him seem to be doing the same thing, so 'school' and getting 'educated' seem to be important things, given that this goes on for years, day in and day out.

At school they mostly attend to things out there. They learn geography and math, literature and history; they listen to the teacher, and engage in class discussion. Sometimes they are asked to think, but the things they are asked to think about usually have to do with those things out there written on the board and in the workbooks. Whenever the teacher spots Tommy daydreaming or somehow engaged in his inner-world- in his personal thoughts – she usually asks him 'Tommy are you with us?' or 'Tommy, are you paying attention?'

Now, Tommy might have actually been paying attention, but not to what the teacher, and 'school' view as the things one ought to attend to at this point of the day. Those things are saved for 'recess' or for one's leisure time. Tommy is quick to learn. He's just like any other boy. He likes to be appreciated, so he resolves to attend to the teacher's words out there – the place in which math, history and all those things that are called 'education' are going on. All those personal issues that run in his mind; all those ideas he has about the history they learn seem to intervene with the purpose for which they have gathered them in this place called 'school'.

Years of such practice teach Tommy that his body and mind are not a place one ought to attend to seriously. Here and now seem to be the wrong place and time to be at. Gradually but surely a tacit quite startling realization dawns on Tommy. He never quite says this nor does anyone else, but it turns out that:

"'Education' is not really about me."

It might be the case that after some more years Tommy becomes so well-practiced in attending to not-me that he never becomes quite quiet enough to hear his own mind asking: "well, if 'education' is not about me, then who is it for?"

When I offer this narrative to my university students some feel at first that it is exaggerated. Others become impatient as they ask what exactly am I getting at with all this *in here* business? Am I suggesting that school would become a place in which children spend their days day-dreaming? At this point I will only answer briefly with the following two points:

First, try to remember that I am saying nothing about the value of studying the 'world' *out there*. What I *am* attempting to describe is what happens to someone who goes through an 'educational' system that tells him day in and day out that *in here* is not a place to be at. I am pointing to the way in which we make 'education' into a practice of disembodiment for our bodies can live nowhere *but* in the present threading bead after bead *now*, yet we are constantly asked to *mind* those things that are not present in us, and concern only the world that is of *not-me* – the 'social curriculum and narrative' that *I* am to become.

Second, rest assured, what I am developing is not some soft 'child-centered' orientation that assumes naïvely that if we just let the children 'be', all will be well. My aim here is to explain how meta-pedagogy constitutes the mechanism that has gotten us in trouble. So, patience is required here, for only in the third part of the book will we get to *in here*. Furthermore, there we will see that there is nothing simple about it, and we will deepen the understanding developed in Chapter 3; namely, that this 'social practice' is an expression of the natural development of the individual mind. Nothing exists in 'society' that has not emerged from the mind as the constructor of the 'social curriculum'. Cryptically put at this point, *our individual minds, in and of themselves, do a great job of expelling us from exploring our own minds.*

For now, let's look at how this psychological operant conditioning works. How our attention gets stuck in space and time to prune our minds in the form of 'education' and create a 'social' self-justifying system.

META-PEDAGOGY AS THE CONSTRUCTOR OF THE 'SOCIAL CURRICULUM'

Richard Peters (1967) claimed that 'Education' "has worthwhileness built into it" (p. 19). In the previous chapter we saw that such meaning is built into it right at the outset because 'worthwhileness' is the criteria based on which 'society' chooses what 'knowledge' to include in the 'curriculum'. What I want to focus on here, is how this appears in *practice*. How we shape the mind of the young to mirror the 'social narrative'.

Children or youth have little idea of 'curricular deliberations'. Such 'social' practice precedes their entrance to school. A student is initiated into it in a very different way. It is a tacit assumption that runs as a current throughout his childhood and on. He is sent to 'school' where he is 'educated', day after day, year after year. Anyone within this system cannot but attach importance to it, and create the associative link between 'school', 'education', 'meaning', and 'good' – the alternative is too unhappy to even consider. *Why would everyone be doing this? Why would my parents be sending me day in and day out to this place, had it not been a worthwhile endeavor?* Could we actually have gone through all these years of 'education' without assuming that our going to 'school', college, or university is meaningful? – Actually we could, and perhaps we spent quite some of our time wondering 'what am I doing here?' as some confess.

Nevertheless, something was working to keep us going even if we were those kind that tended to ask such questions. *What is that something? – I suspect that our monolithic meta-pedagogy works to disempower us here.*

While we are caught up in the diversity of disciplines we might find on the 'social curriculum' (e.g., History, Math, Science) as we think students are learning a variety of lessons; while we seemingly move between class discussion, frontal teaching, group learning, workbook writing.... at the meta-pedagogical level there are only two lessons that we can learn:

> *Attend in here/Attend out there. This meta-pedagogical mechanism is so powerful because it is a binary. Only two lessons are possible and one of them is taught every moment. Its teaching automatically nullifies the other for that moment.*

At the mechanistic level of attention, 'curricular-pedagogical practice' is a constant lesson that tells us that *out there* is more important than *in here*. There are three huge prices we pay here: First the reinforcement of *out there* comes at the expense of *in here* and depletes it of meaning. Second, this lesson cannot but teach us to attribute more meaning to that which others around us are doing. Third, it perpetuates the form of 'education'.

Since we are concomitantly taught not to consider what goes on in our bodies and minds as 'worthy knowledge', we become fully dependent on 'society' to provide us with meaning. If at some point I sit in a lesson and experience the subject matter to be meaningless (which I suspect is not that uncommon), the very thought that others around me are doing the same feels almost as an appropriate motivation to keep at it. No less, I might in fact get the feeling that I am missing on something here: 'this must have some meaning, and if I'm not seeing it then the problem must be with *me*'. Some plow on obliviously. Others – the more optimistic kind – persevere based on the famous *promise* that there's something better that awaits in the next lesson or in the future, hence meaning might at some point emerge. Broadly however, the repeated meta-pedagogy that has sent us away from dwelling *in here* – the place at which resistance to *out there* might be examined, studied, critiqued, built, and acted upon – serves as a very powerful mechanism that effectively erodes the merit of our inner world, and subjects us to trust what we attend to *out there* at the expense of what we experience *in here*.

I am not saying that we need to act immediately at the moment in which we experience a university lesson or another activity as meaningless.

Studying our constantly changing mental states and moods and cultivating discernment as to the unfolding of experience *in here* is in fact something we must do in order for our actions to transcend caprice. Yet, this kind of *inner curriculum* that is described in Part III is not present in our construct of 'education'.

Not only are we *not* educated in making meaning of this internal life based on practices that deliberately cultivate self-understanding, but in fact, our interiority is considered to be a place that needs to be kept at bay, so that it does not interfere with the real business of 'education' that has to do with *not-me*.[2] If a student suffers from what might be termed 'psychological problems' he will probably be sent for consultation, in which he will be encouraged to speak out that which troubles him *in here*. Such issues might very well be disturbing and make it difficult for this student to learn. Yet, the sense that 'society' gives one within our current construct of 'education', is that these issues derail one from the 'proper' course of 'education'. They need to be ventilated and cleared out so that one can realign oneself with being initiated into *out there* 'education'. Handling this inner-domain is thus deemed an extra-curricular therapeutic issue, not an 'educational' one. The aim eventually is to get the student 'back on track', so these issues troubling him from within, will stop interfering with what 'society' is trying to accomplish here. Getting 'back on track' is that 'ideal state' in which this student renews his membership in a 'society' that attends *out there*, and whatever arises in him *in here* either remains non-disruptive, or if it *is* disruptive, he becomes accomplished in keeping it at bay.

The core lesson one gets as the moment-to-moment practice of 'education' takes place, as the door of attention swings in and out, is this:

> As long as in here concerns matters that are not essential to the 'social curriculum', either wait with it until school-day ends, or if you really have to, we'll figure it out together so it won't bother you as we go about with the real business of 'education'.

We don't spell these lessons out literally. They are built into the system and are practiced moment after moment based on meta-pedagogy. The image they create is that those things that occur *in here*, that are not directly related to the public worthwhile curriculum, constitute an inferior domain of life.

META-PEDAGOGY AS THE CONSTRUCTOR
OF 'EDUCATION'S' FORM

Imagine yourself walking through the corridor of a public high-school. You pass the tenth graders' first class and you see them engaged in a discussion about the American Civil war, you walk further to the next class, and you see them studying the structure of the atom. When you reach the third class you see them sitting silently with their eyes closed, and they are instructed to observe the sensations in their bodies. They sit still like this for ten minutes as the teacher herself guides them in this 'body-scan'. They just attend to their sensations, from their toes to their heads. What would you think as you walk by this class?

It is highly probable that you would pass the first two classes on 'automatic pilot', but the third class might very well perplex you: The sight of these closed-eyed students, and the silence would invoke a cognitive dissonance. Even if you've heard of things like 'mindfulness', and/or meditation, the sight of that third class would travel in your brain, your hippocampus will remind you that you are at 'school', hence 'education' and 'knowledge' are involved. The activity that you see *out there* will most likely conflate with the construct of 'education' that's in your mind.

Just like we identify a table in an instant because there is some kind of a representation of tables in our minds that is based on hundreds of tables we've seen in our lives, at some point the *form* of 'education' is constructed in our minds as well. 'Education' is a concept, a construct, and a highly complex one, nevertheless it becomes a 'thing' that we can implicitly or explicitly identify. We learn to associate 'education' with very certain activities in which we ourselves engaged and based on which we acquired the 'knowledge of most worth'.

Like the Mobius strip there's a circularity here that looks inescapable. We are the ones who determined what that 'knowledge' is, and we are the ones who determined what are the practices that yield its acquisition. We do not tend to rethink the 'knowledge' *in here* when things don't work. We try to adjust the practices *out there*. We reconstruct the pedagogy *out there* where the symptoms of our minds appear; however, the problem may well lie in how our minds have come to believe that they are not the theoretical source of what they see *out there* in practice.

Through the habituation of our construct of 'education' the possibilities of attending *in here* deliberately and for extended periods of time become out of place in our 'curriculum'. What would such activities look like? – writing a journal, practicing yoga or meditation, mindfulness, tai chi, Feldenkrais technique, guided visualization, walking silently in nature. These and others are known in our times as contemplative practices and are located within the discourse of contemplative education, which we will encounter in Chapter 10 that concludes the book. At this point, I only bring them as examples for activities that seem to jar against the constructs of 'curriculum', 'pedagogy', 'education', and 'knowledge' as the constructs have been shaped in our minds. As Dewey (1958) claimed we have habits of thinking just as much as we have physical habits. As I phrase this, the way in which we think about 'education' is *also* a habit:

> It is as if concepts are like windows constructed in our minds through which we gaze at the world *out there*. When we look from our mind through the window of 'educational practices' we will see children and youth doing endless things but hardly any (so as not to say none) will include a deep reflection as to who they are? Who they would like to be? What makes them feel the way they do? Where do their thoughts come from? Why do they have scary thoughts sometimes? How can they cope with embarrassment, shame, fear? How can they feel happier?

Pure 'educational' *practice* had constructed our understanding of 'educational theory', and that theory now expels our own being from the view. The practice was made of the simple act of going to 'school' and being told that this thing that we are doing *now*, studying math, history, geography etc. by attending *out there* or thinking about *out there* is 'education'. *This is how it is done.* As a child enters school he does not merely study the various disciplines and diverse skills. He learns what is the *form* of that which is called 'education'. What it is, what it isn't, and mostly how it is practiced, and what it means to be an 'educated person' in his or her society. If the core lesson habituates my attention *out there* as an individual and expels *me* from the curriculum, the lesson that is eventually learned is *conformity and stagnation*. The interesting thing is that there is much talk about teaching creativity, entrepreneurship, and inventiveness but the only possible place from which these might come to the world – the mind – is left to attend to that which is already there and present. The mind will clearly need some input from the world *out there*, but what about its own input? Such input can in fact be demonstrated if we recall that very virtual tour through school corridors above.

If the activity in the third class would have indeed surprised you, then the basis for the surprise would stem from the way *your* mind functions. That is because a full-fledged 'educational theory' lives there. It is 'society' that placed it there, so that now every time you come to 'school' you gaze at it through the frame of a window that is based on your past. Hence your thoughts might be: 'wait a minute? What are they doing? We're at 'school' aren't we? Is this what they call 'education' these days?'... all this would occur in an instant. You would possibly experience another chain of thoughts such as: 'oh, this looks far more refreshing then what the other classes are doing... why didn't they have this back in my school days?'

No matter what kind of thoughts you would experience, what begins to emerge is that our minds are protagonists both as they are the locus from which attention emerges, but also since they participate actively in the process of our perception *and the specific makings of our reality*. The fact that 'society' sends us gazing *out there* based on the monolithic meta-pedagogy we have constructed, does not imply that things are not happening *in here* simultaneously – things that may need to be included in our understanding of 'curriculum', 'pedagogy', 'education', and 'knowledge'. However, in public education this is rarely something that a student will learn. Such things can only be learned by attending to the locus in which they occur: our first-person experience *–in here*.

> This means that the re-construction of 'education' will have to incorporate a reversed meta-pedagogy in our understanding of the 'curriculum'; one in which we will suddenly see ourselves in the 'knowledge' that is to be gained by 'education'; one in which our own mind will be acknowledged as creating meaning.

Just to further drive home the point and to bind this with the previous chapter, one of the reasons that some might have serious difficulty in wrapping their minds around the possibility that practices such as meditation, yoga or tai chi, can be associated with 'education' is that they seem to be so different from learning about the Civil war, or solving mathematical equations. One of the ways that a mind will try to work around that is to suggest that, these meditating students probably engaged in some relaxation technique *so that* they can focus better on the Civil War afterwards. That is indeed one of the more common ways to think of the current uses of mindfulness practice in schools these days as we will see in the concluding chapter of the book. There is absolutely nothing wrong with that aside from the fact that in such case, you elevated *in here* slightly to the status of a domain that might serve the acquisition of 'knowledge' *out there*. Thus these practices do not yield 'knowledge' in and of itself. They are more of a scaffolding activity for the actual 'education' that will take place *afterward*. Yet, the idea of considering that observing sensations, or the breath, or cultivating a mental state such as compassion will constitute a 'curriculum' seems to conflate with what we were educated to think of as 'knowledge'. It may have to do with our understanding of 'education' as having to do solely with *doing*, with getting somewhere, achieving something and becoming someone – *running the course of the race to that time called then that is never now; to that place called there that is never here.* How about *here* counts as being somewhere? How about the achievement of simply breathing and feeling that for this moment that is 'good' too?–

These are difficult ideas to grapple with. They are wrenches in the *perpetuum mobile* of 'education'. I am not recommending their implementation as *the* new agenda of a reconstructed 'education'. I am speaking of balance. We do need to move in the world, do things, and engage with the external world, experiment, fumble, and fall. If you were a parent of one of those teenagers in that meditating classroom, you would have every right to ask the teacher why is your child doing whatever it is that the class was doing, and not doing what the other classes were doing. The teacher would be obliged to explain this. The third part of the book will explain how that very activity described above would represent a reconstruction of 'education' that is both more appropriate and far more loyal to the fundamentals of experience *when combined* with our more common views of the 'curriculum' that are here critiqued mostly for we rely *solely* on them.

Meta-pedagogy as 'Education' in Meaning

The practice of fixing attention *out there* creates a vicious cycle for it is a '"society"-reverberating feedback loop'; a mechanism through which the construct of 'education' self-justifies itself as a social practice of meaning – as *the way to educate*. Missing from our understanding is that,

> the two possible lessons taught by meta-pedagogy are core-lessons that establish the hierarchy of authority and agency over our lives. Who shall we be heeding as the voice of meaning – out there, in here? Or both?

Meta-pedagogy is the crux of 'education's' work with attention.

Every moment in the classroom either reinforces *in here* or *out there*. The more we lean towards attending *out there*, the more our reality is defined by that which we find *out there* to which we are taught to attribute worthiness and meaning.

Social habits become the habits of our own minds. We are 'educated' to see the world through the ways in which 'society' habituates our attention. As John Dewey proposed – habits that become fixed are, "ruts, routine ways, with loss of freshness, open-mindedness, and originality. The fixity of such habits means that they have a hold upon us, instead of our having a free hold upon things" (1997a, p. 16). If our attention, as that which defines reality becomes fixed, *reality becomes fixed* – and the possibility of its rectifying in case of problems becomes fixed. The more our attention is habituated *out there* the more this becomes the place in which meaning and worth is considered to be found. What needs to be clearly spelled out here, is the all-pervading nature of meta-pedagogy as 'education in meaning':

If you habituate a child to attend *out there*, based on a meta-pedagogy that does not orient him *in here* to explore his own mind-body, then don't expect him to find meaning only in that 'knowledge of most worth' that the 'curriculum' represents (e.g., sciences, humanities). While he is taught that they are worthy, he is concomitantly taught that that which is worthy exists *out there*. That which is *out there* is not just 'knowledge', it is also money, real estate, and fancy jobs in the better cases and substance abuse in the worst ones. These will be the things that this child or youth will grow to look for, after years of attending *out there*, for such imbalanced practice inevitably erodes the status of *in here*.

There is nothing wrong with making money, or having nice cars. The problem has to do with organizing our lives around the principle that these things in themselves bring meaning to our lives, which cannot but be the result of a meta-pedagogy that initiates us in the idea that meaning lies *out there*. The world *out there* is perceived by us as a world of objects as opposed to the world *in here* that we tend to view as inhabited by 'things' of another nature – thoughts, sensations, emotions. If we are instructed to attend *out there* – even if that which we attend to in school is 'knowledge' and not money, or real-estate – we end up with a worldview that attributes more meaning to the world of objects, than to the world of those abstract substance-less 'things' experienced in (and perhaps as) our minds-bodies from one moment to the next.

We certainly like to discuss meaning, and meaningful learning, yet, just like the question of 'knowledge' presented earlier, not enough do we consider the question 'where meaning exists'? Is it in the thing attended to, or in the mind of the attend*er*? Or is there some co-dependence there? Does meaning exist *in* the 'knowledge of most worth' or was it in fact, 'social' practice that introduced worthwhileness and meaning into it, and hence created an image of a subject matter that actually embodies meaning independent of a learner? It is quite weird to speak of meaning without mentioning that there is someone there who attributes and makes meaning. Some of our most difficult 'educational' problems arise from the way in which our meta-pedagogy initiates students into a misconception of the idea of meaning itself.

> What does it mean to experience something as meaningful? How is meaning created? How are 'meaning' in life and finding 'meaning' right *now* related to each other? What's the difference between the 'meaning' of a word, and the meaning of life? I am only raising these questions to explain somewhat what I mean by questioning 'meaning' and to invoke a meta-pedagogical turn within you so that you search for the meaning of 'meaning' *in here*. If you allow these questions to echo within you before reading on, your mind-body will become a pedagogical space in which your *inner curriculum* will begin to unfold.

Broadly I want to suggest that meaning is an experience that arises *in here* based on an encounter with something that was presented from *out there* or from *in here*. Yet, without the embodied experience it brings to one *in here* there is hardly any sense in speaking about it. Meaning is by no means a property of any subject matter we place in the 'curriculum' even if 'society' had thoughtfully positioned it there. If it were an absolute property of an object, we would all be seeing the object and seeing meaning in it. This applies just the same to curricular subject matter like Hamlet, and WWII or to new cars and real estate. It is only 'society' not the mind that placed the label 'this is meaningful' over them. The mind that is not made to see itself as a meaning-attribut*er*, is a mind that has been pruned by 'society's' BIG mind. It is a mind that has lost its original freedom and it may well rob others of this freedom as it enacts its 'educated' dogmatism in the world.

This understanding of 'meaning' is in most cases, *not* what one learns in school. The whole idea of the 'curriculum' as depicted in Chapter 4, and as practiced based on *out there* meta-pedagogy, is the subjecting of the student's flashlight of attention to the locus selected by the flashlight of 'social attention'. As a 'society', we have established the meaning of 'meaning' as a 'social' practice and left out the first-person perspective from which any meaningful experience whatsoever can be lived in actuality, and acknowledged as such. Meta-pedagogy in its current practice has hardly anything to do with attending *in here* and finding how subject matter *out there* resonates *in here*. Once the subject matter has been deemed meaningful by 'society', it is almost taken for granted, as a property of the subject matter in and of itself. Students are thus initiated into a 'world' that has meaning that exists there regardless of whether it is attended to by them or not – *as if in the beginning there was 'education', then you came along to be initiated in to it.* Taken to a hypothetical Zen-like level this results in a very weird idea – the 'world' is meaningful even if there is no actual mind that attends to it. The 'social' construct of 'education' becomes one in which students are compelled to find meaning *out there,* and if they don't, *then something must be wrong in here.* I argue that,

> the most 'education' can do is invite students to see what 'society' has found meaningful, but meaning can never be forced, and part of 'education' is to ensure a clear distinction between what 'society' found meaningful, and the student's sovereignty over his or her own self as meaning-maker.

This does not mean that we are initiating students into disrespect for 'society', nor does it make everything relative. It only means that now 'society' respects the individuals without which it has no existence, and it becomes a very different 'society' – one that will be far more self-critical of its ways, and led not (or perhaps less) by blind habit. As will be developed in the third part of the book however, this approach can only be based on a 'curriculum' that turns us inward so that we in fact become knowledgeable as to what meaning is, and we become far more clear on *what kind of agency can we depend on when we attribute meaning.*

*

RECONSTRUCTING 'EDUCATION' THROUGH META-PEDAGOGY

Approaching the end of this chapter, which also ends parts II of the book, let's remind ourselves of Chapter 2 in which we considered the options that attention in space creates for 'education'. We listed three but now we have a better sense of what they mean:

a. 'Education' can work to orient students' attention *out there*. If we go for this it implies a meta-curriculum that suggests that 'knowing the not-me (thy world)' is the knowledge of most worth. More subtly it should be claimed however, that the meta-pedagogy itself can certainly ask students to attend *in here* – but the purpose of so doing would be to think of *out there*.

b. 'Education' can work to orient students' attention *in here*. If we go for this it implies a meta-curriculum that suggests that 'know thyself' is the knowledge of most worth. More subtly, consider that knowing ourselves does not necessitate a meta-pedagogy that turns only *in here*. Rather, we can certainly attend *out there*; however, our goal would be mostly to examine how we experience *out there, in here*. In other words, Hamlet or Math would be viewed as ways of enriching the experience of myself and knowing myself.

c. 'Education' can work to combine both modes 'a' and 'b'. This would reflect a meta-curriculum that proposes 'know thyself', and 'know thyworld'. knowledge of most worth exists in both. The meta-pedagogy here will thus combine the above two perspectives.

If you trace every moment in a classroom and make a list of the meta-pedagogical injunction that undergirds the teacher's pedagogy, you will get an image of a meta-curriculum. The more moments spent attending *out there* the more it is a meta-curriculum of *know thy world and leave yourself out of it*. The more moments are spent attending *in here* you will get *know thyself and leave the world out of it*. At this point our public meta-pedagogy is substantially located in the former meta-curriculum. This is no other than the ethos of objectivity that education had adopted from the natural sciences and the era of positivism as many argued (Eisner 1996; Palmer 1983). With this practice we are shaping the individual in the image of 'society' – we are appropriating *me* by the *not me*.

From the social third-person 'bird's eye view' from which we have come to think 'education', *you* and *I* collapse into identical twins called 'a student' – an 'entity' that doesn't exist in reality. This is that so-called one-size-fit all standard toward which we – as a 'society' – tend to orient 'education'. Our 'education' addresses the 'student' but there is no 'student' to be found – only *you, him, her, I – who attend from in here –* full-fledged living beings with minds, bodies, souls, spirits that constitute an *inner curriculum*, which has been expelled from 'education'. Our monolithic meta-pedagogy that sends us *out there* for meaning, creates an illusion of a shared *public* 'education'. Yet, it is a shared alienation of an 'education' that supposedly belongs to everyone, but in effect is owned by no one. It might work for 'society', but not for the actual living beings – *you* and *I* – who make 'societies'. We gather ourselves in 'schools' and higher 'education' institutions around meaningful 'knowledge' that we position *out there*, without ensuring that this meaning is reasserted moment-by-moment from within the individual *in here-ness* of our embodied minds-hearts.

This hegemony of attending *out there* thus creates both alienation between us and within each one of us as our interiority is deprived of its inherent meaning. The price we then pay is that students who come to 'school' with minds that are far broader in potential then the pruned 'curriculum' they get, will become the adults that will do the same to their own kids, through the vicious cycle of 'education'. There is no conspiracy here; only a sleepy consequence of personal routines, fixed habits, and a fixed attention entrenched through 'social' habit. The problem of education is 'education' for we have constructed it as a meaning-making process in which minds that are shaped by it are blinded to their pruning.

Young minds are pruned in the image of 'education' that comes from a past. By the time they become capable of reconstructing 'education', such reconstruction remains no more than rudimentary if the mind is not liberated from the 'social' mirroring effect. Our only recourse is to make 'education' into a process that includes pedagogies that de-prune that mind. For that however, we need a balancing meta-pedagogical turn that sends us to explore the *inner curriculum. If attention is where we got stuck, that is the place that holds the key to our liberation.*

*

Summary of Parts I and II: The Matrix of Meta-curriculum and Meta-pedagogy

The aims of the first part of the book were to establish the fundamentals of mind based on which any 'education' can be established, and to conceptualize the basic structure of how we understand this construct. This began with the fundamentals of attention, space, and time, and their positioning within the context of 'self' and 'society'. The aim of Part II was to examine more complex fundamentals of 'education', namely 'knowledge', 'curriculum', and 'pedagogy' based on the fundamentals of mind, and then to apply them toward diagnosing problems of our current construct of 'education'.

I can imagine that reading the first part of the book with little clue about what I mean by engaging *in here* deliberately is an unsettling experience. However, I hope that we are more ready to do so now. Before that, I'd like to propose an operative framework that will enable us to think and practice 'curriculum' based on our journey so far.

The Matrix of Meta-pedagogy and Meta-curriculum

The model I offer depicts the interdependence of *meta-curriculum* and *meta-pedagogy* (Table 5.1). *Meta-pedagogy* is indicated by the concatenation of moments of a students' attention that is either oriented to attend to *out there* or to *in here*. *Meta-curriculum* is the overall orientation or aim for which this *meta-pedagogy* is deployed – either study *in here* (know thy 'self') or study *out there* (know thy 'world'). At this broad level that combines the bead-to-bead level of meta-pedagogy and the horizontal time axis of the meta-curricular level, a matrix of four categories emerges.

Table 5.1 The matrix of meta-curriculum and meta-pedagogy

Meta-Curriculum / Meta-pedagogy	know thyself	Know thy world
Attend *in*	Attend *in* - know self	Attend *in* - know world
Attend *out*	Attend *out* - know self	Attend *out* - know world

Some of the boxes in Table 5.1 are more trivial than others, but the following briefly exemplifies the four possibilities that are presented here:

a) Attend *out there* to the world in order to know thy world (e.g., read a historical book, look at the map of England, listen to the teacher or the classroom discussion).

b) Attend *in here* to your thoughts/sensations/emotions in order to know thy world (e.g., reflect on the historical book, think about the geography of England, come up with a response to the teacher's question about the former)

c) Attend *in here* in order to know thy 'self' (e.g., write a journal, meditate, attend to the sensation of the breath)

d) Attend *out there* in order to know thy 'self' (e.g., read a historical book in order to reflect on the personal meaning of the events, look at the map of England and envision what it would be like for *you* to live there).

What I attempted to show in the previous chapters is that our 'social curriculum' tends to focus on a and b (and mostly reducing b to disembodied *thinking* as we will see). The *inner curriculum* that will be described in Part III brings in c and d. 'Education' I believe, ought to be about all four.

*

While we've walked quite a journey so far, I must inform you that there is much more to do. The main issue that I mentioned repeatedly is that whatever problems we diagnose and find *out there* must have something to do with the brains-minds-bodies-hearts that identify them and create them from *in here*. There's no way around this. We must see our minds as part of the problem. We must also be somewhat optimistic about the possibility that diagnosing the sources of these problems, may lead us to more responsible and appropriate solutions.

The following summarizes the first two parts of the book concisely. It might help to return to this summary here and there whenever the thread becomes lost for I somehow fail to communicate with you:

1. Rather than examine 'education' from 'society's' perspective that tends to ignore the mind as the source of ideas and practices, it makes sense to retrace our steps and examine fundamental structures of experience to explore 'what is available' to the mind.

2. The fundamentals of attention, space, and time can be seen as the foundations of any kind of 'education' we shall construct. Anything beyond them brings contingency and choice into life and education.

3. The sifting between that which seems to be fixed and that which is contingent is a good place to examine where we made 'educational' deliberations that are not necessarily obvious.

4. *In here* is a rich experience in which there are at least two fields of identity to explore:

   a. *I* – a core 'self' that attends to raw experience at a bead-to-bead level and non-conceptually.

   b. *me* – a narrative 'self' that creates the horizontal time axis through an interpretation of *I*, and builds a stable identity.

   c. Attention might be like a free agent that rents its service to either of these fields.

5. WE is the fundamental based on which shared living, the creation of 'society', and 'education' become possible. It enables the space of in-between that allows us to establish relationships.

6. 'Society' can be likened to a BIG mind that resembles *me*. Both are somewhat of an embodied narrative, that dwells in the horizontal time axis.

7. Pruning is a process that reduces universality to particularity.

8. '"Education" as pruning' entails at least the following two processes:

   a. A *particular* 'society' prunes the mind from WE (that could have lent itself to *any* 'society') to *this* 'society's' *particular* narrative.

   b. *me* prunes *I* from an interpretation-less non-conceptual experience to a 'society'-based *particular* narrative self.

9. The illusion of omniscience:

   a. Is inherent in the experience of attention that shines from *here* over all else and creates a two-layered blindness:

      i. We don't know what we don't know.

      ii. We don't know *that* we don't know.

   b. Is a feature of the individual mind as well as of 'society'

   c. Is a mechanism that establishes 'society'-*me as* a self-justifying system that is closed within its narrative and replicates the past.

10. The construct of 'knowledge' is where contingency enters the game. 'Knowledge' has no nature but the one that human beings have

attributed to it. *It is what we decide it is.* Change our conception of 'knowledge' and you might begin to change 'education'.

11. Though attention, space, and time warrant diverse experiences, we have constructed 'knowledge' based mostly on 'things' that are *out there* not *in here* and can be moved in time over the *horizontal* time axis.

12. The 'curriculum' as currently constructed:
    a. Is designed through a 'social' process of deliberation. It can be viewed as a 'social' BIG mind's proposal of those things that are worthwhile to which *you* and I ought to attend.
    b. Is a 'normative temporal map' created by 'society'. Its destination is the 'good' and it proposes a promise. If you walk the distance you will arrive at the 'good'.
    c. Is an expectation builder. It instills the tacit idea that 'life' is supposed to get better somewhat linearly, yet our embodied subjective well-being fluctuates independently depending on our interpretation of our bead-to-bead experience.
    d. Initiates us into the horizontal time axis and *out there*. The overall lesson we learn is that: *here* is not as good as *there*, and *now* is not as good as *then* (the future). It thus becomes a teaching of bifurcation of body and mind, for the body is always here, yet our minds are sent to the future.

13. Meta-pedagogy is:
    a. The nucleus of 'curricular' practice. Every moment of teaching in the classroom always teaches one of two lessons: attend *out there* or attend *in here*. The teaching of one nullifies the other for that moment.
    b. The accumulation of moments of our current meta-pedagogy teaches a meta-curriculum: *out there is where meaning is to be found*. This leads to these two lessons:
        i. Objects (subject matter or material objects) are more important than my inner experience.
        ii. What others do *out there* becomes a compass that tells me what is desirable.
    c. There are great reasons to study the 'world' and 'society's' 'curriculum' yet our meta-pedagogy's one-sidedness results as a teaching that:
        • Expels the mind from the 'curriculum'.

- Shapes the mind to understand the *form* of 'education' as consisting of practices that send us attending *out there*.
- Creates the self-perpetuating reproductive nature of 'education' as the problem of 'education'.

Yet again, let us not forget – our individual minds seem to be drawn to these very curriculum and meta-pedagogy. After all minds created this curriculum and this meta-pedagogy hence they cannot but find themselves in their makings. It is time to point our fingers to our own mind and take responsibility. *You and I are responsible too. We need to start looking in here to examine our role in our own expulsion from 'education' and position the mind at the center of curriculum and pedagogy.*

NOTES

1. This will include the domain of 'didactics' that can be seen as a more technical aspect within pedagogy.
2. Hargreaves's (2003) research on the nullifying of emotions from the classroom is but one compelling example.

PART III

The *Inner Curriculum*: Positioning the Mind at the Center of Curriculum and Pedagogy

CHAPTER 6

The Ethics of the *Inner Curriculum*

Life is experienced as all that we attend to whether it is experienced as emerging from *in here* or from *out there*. All of these experiences are part of our unfolding, to which I refer as the 'curriculum of life'. The 'curriculum of life' includes the 'social curriculum' and the *inner curriculum*. The 'social curriculum' is both the planned and deliberate 'curriculum' that 'society' constructs and in light of which it 'educates' in its institutions, as well as the informal 'social' interactions to which we are witness and in which we engage. The *inner curriculum*, which is the focus of this part of the book, emerges once the customary meta-pedagogy and meta-curriculum of our 'social curriculum', as described in Part II, *are reversed*. Once we attend *in here* to deliberately or spontaneously with an appreciation of our minds-bodies as loci through which, as Parker Palmer (1983) claimed, *we know as we are known*.

The *inner curriculum* is far more dynamic, broad, and inclusive than what usually goes under the term 'curriculum'. But it is this 'curriculum' and its location within the 'curriculum of life' that is there present moment after moment if we care to attend to it. It is this *inner curriculum* that is imbued with the 'social' with which we need to learn to live, and within which we hope to thrive, give to ourselves, and give to others.

This chapter establishes an ethical stance that undergirds such all-inclusive understanding of the 'curriculum' in which *in here* and *out there* are to be eventually integrated. In this book I do not speak much about their integration as much as I am mobilizing the *inner curriculum* from its unjust nullification from the 'social curriculum', to an explicit presence within the

© The Author(s) 2017   149
O. Ergas, *Reconstructing 'Education' through Mindful Attention*,
DOI 10.1057/978-1-137-58782-4_6

construct of 'curriculum' as such. Followed by this chapter that speaks of the broad intention and disposition of this approach, Chapters 7, 8, and 9 will each be dedicated to a specific domain within the *inner curriculum* based on the fundamentals developed in Part I of the book. These will include:

1. *Embodied perception* – The mind's moment-to-moment threading of beads of experience.
2. *me* – The 'narrative self' as the necklace that constitutes the horizontal time axis of my embodied life.
3. *I* – The contemplative curriculum that opens spontaneously or methodically based on contemplative embodied engagement and practice.

*

BRAIN-MIND-BODY IN THE JUSTIFICATION FOR THE 'CURRICULUM OF LIFE' AND THE *INNER CURRICULUM*

What warrants this approach to a 'curriculum of life' that suggests that *every bead* is to be viewed as part of 'education'? – The previous parts of the book that reconstructed the fundamentals of 'education' based on the mind, and applied them toward a critique of our current construct of 'education', are certainly something to build on. However, I want to also point to the original and *un*original aspects of this suggestions, in order to shed some light on the mind with which we are dealing.

First, accounts of 'education' that lend themselves to the concept of a 'curriculum of life' have certainly been proposed before this book. John Dewey (1997a) argued that 'education is life', and Alfred North Whitehead claimed that, "there is only one subject matter to education and that is life in all its manifestations" (1967, p. 10). Furthermore some have certainly offered influential accounts that inform our engagement with *in here* within curriculum theory (Huebner 1999; Miller 2013; Pinar and Grumet 2014), educational psychology (Kegan 1982), and teacher education (Korthagen et al. 2012; Palmer 1998). The inclusive approach proposed here to the 'curriculum' is thus certainly not novel. However, I do not think that enough has been done to depict this 'curricular' terrain as methodically as we are about to explore it, and grounded in the interdisciplinary approach that I believe is required when positioning the mind at the center of 'curriculum' and 'pedagogy'.

I said many things about the mind throughout the previous chapters, but here we are going to get more deeply intimate with this 'thing' that we have and are, that makes 'education' and is made by it. Mind as I use the term,

> is that which thinks deliberately or that in which thoughts arise non-delib-erately. It is that which can attend to stimuli that arrive from *out there* (the world), as well as to stimuli that arise *in here* (within the mind-body itself). It is that which processes all these stimuli and that which reacts and/or responds to them. It is that which attends to experience based on its past, changes as a consequence of the engagement with the present, which leads to its changed future. It shapes experience and is shaped by it constantly.[1]

Whether we are aware of it or not, the mind is the examining locus from which our lives are conducted wisely or unwisely and it is related directly to the brain. The question of how the two reflect each other is known as the 'hard' problem that I set aside.[2] I will be pragmatically relying on this relation between mind and brain following contemporary neuroscience and psychology and will often thus speak of brain-mind/mind-brain. This approach is useful for understanding and grounding some of the concepts I explain. Note, that very often I will also say brain-mind-*body (and even heart)* or *embodied mind*; all of which are intended to remind us of the impossibility of considering 'education' and experience without addressing the crucial role of our bodies and hearts in this as we will see in the following chapters.

The complexity with which we are dealing here is beyond articulation. Basically this book reflects a mind that tries to understand itself yet its own gaze changes what it sees, and what it sees changes its gaze. Given this situation all theories about a mind and its *inner curriculum* need to be taken with a grain of salt, especially when they become etched in *words* that tend to freeze them, whereas the mind, as mentioned above, is changing in *you* at this very moment. When we bring this to the field of 'education' that attempts to make minds, our theories can become hindrances. As wise and as helpful as our theories may be (including the current one if you will think it to be so), we quite easily confuse the map for the territory, and come to believe that the world was made in the image of our language and concepts. Such conceptual maps are especially problematic when they depict experience based on categories such as mind vs. body, cognition vs. affect, brain vs. mind, thoughts vs. sensations – all those notorious dualisms, that apply also to 'education' vs. 'schooling', 'knowledge of most worth' vs. 'knowledge of less worth'. I too, have been applying a dualistic language to communicate my ideas, but there is something that I believe must not be forgotten, which cannot be overstated. It is fundamental to the understanding of the reconstruction of 'education', and the view of an all-inclusive 'curriculum of *life*':

> our brains-minds-bodies-hearts don't 'sit there' waiting to become 'educated' only in those times at which we are situated in a place that 'society' had categorized as an 'educational institution'. We are constantly 'educated' whether we are aware of it or not. Sometimes in fact changes that we would be willing to call 'worthy educational changes' (e.g., in character, moral behavior, dispositions toward oneself and the world) will occur outside these 'social' institutions and perhaps despite of them.

There is substantial naivety involved in thinking that the 'social curriculum' and its subject matter *out there* somehow settle the matter of 'education'. Some might think for example that the mind is keeping its emotional life at bay just because we are now studying science or math in the classroom, as if our brain will compartmentalize its prefrontal cortex while sending the limbic regions on recess upon demand. Most neuroscientists will assure you that the brain simply doesn't work that way.[3] The brain can be seen as an 'entity' that is quite oblivious to the kind of language by which it is described. It knows not of its left and right hemisphere, and it couldn't care less about what name we will give the locus in which long-term memory is stored. *It simply functions.* Our language allows us to name those functions, yet most people can live their entire life, rely perfectly well on long-term memory, completely oblivious to the fact that such a 'thing' as a 'hippocampus' may play a fundamental role in its formation.

The language we use can thus trap us in misunderstandings, for the theories we adopt prune the mind to see the world like *this* at the expense of like *that*. At the same time, even *that* might be wrong, and then again, the error may be necessary for opening a new *this*. As we will see the mind tends more to regularities that are necessary for day-to-day living, and it takes quite a project of de-educating, and de-pruning it so that it can see things with fresh*er* eyes. Hence, I argue that,

> A 'curriculum of life' is necessary, because just like the brain, our mind can be seen as oblivious to the theories we create as a 'society'. It will be shaped by 'knowledge of most worth' as well as by an itch in the toe, worrying about tomorrow, reading the newspaper or speaking with a friend on the phone.

Everything must be taken into account within 'education' if by 'education' we mean broadly: acquiring 'knowledge' about the 'world', and about 'who I am', how I act, becoming a responsible agent that seeks to act with benevolence and kindness to another person, cares about his or her environment, learns to live with him or herself as well as with others, is a contributing citizen, performs well academically,... and all other 'good' things we like to associate with the construct of 'education'.

The reconstructed 'curriculum' that I propose includes every bead of experience attended to by the mind regardless of its origin (*out there* or *in here*), regardless of its content and regardless of the setting in which that bead is perceived ('social' or personal, institutional or informal). It also includes both conceptions-experiences of *time:* the horizontal time axis as well as the bead-to-bead perspective of *now*.[4] It is a 'curriculum' that positions the mind, and the *body* with which it arrives, at its center.

Loyal to my creed, before I conclude this section that sought to justify the all-inclusive approach to the 'curriculum', I want to pull the rug from underneath the above, or at least blur the image I depicted, if by any chance it became too smugly clear:

Is there something beyond this brain-mind-body-heart?

For all I know, everything I write can actually be emerging from something/ somewhere that is beyond them; call it soul, spirit, God, Brahman, Tao, or by any other name. Those who do not believe in this possibility may very well go with the above depiction of the mind, and those who do may interpret the term mind as including or connected/related to that beyond. There's no sense in quarreling about this and I have no intention of trying to convince you whether one view is better than the other. I leave this for you to determine if you feel that it is necessary to decide at all.

*

The Difference Between the 'Social Curriculum' and the Inner Curriculum

There is a substantial difference in the nature of the two sides of a *'curriculum of life'*. There's the 'social curriculum' that Part II took pains to examine, and there's *your* mind as its other side. The 'social curriculum' could be seen as the third-person side of things. It is conceptualized and practiced by 'society' as an *it* into which you as a student are initiated. Conversely, the *inner curriculum* is the first-person lived experience to which only you have access. As we saw in Chapters 2 and 3, however, it is actually 'society' that is more contingent then the presence of *your* mind. Whatever 'society' deliberates to position in front of your mind as a 'curriculum' can change. The facticity of *your* experiencing it and the fact that you will experience it *in a particular way*, is what we want to examine here as *non*-contingent.

The fundamental difference between the subject matter of the 'social curriculum' in many of its common conceptions, and that of the *inner curriculum*, is that the former is usually planned, seen publically, has a very clear aim, is communicable and transferable, aspires to efficiency, and is constructed methodically. It is a product of past planning that we aspire to implement and take to the future. It is by all means the product of the horizontal time axis.[5]

The *inner curriculum* has different modalities, some of which are the exact opposite of the 'social curriculum'. As a non-deliberate spontaneous unfolding, it is unplanned, seen only by me (or you), its aim is unclear, it is not fully communicable nor transferable, it knows not of efficiency, and its method just like its subject matter unfolds one moment after the other. Other modalities, some of which will be explored in the subsequent chapters, locate it as a planned and deliberate activity, which can consist of practices such as reflection, mindfulness, deep listening, tai chi, yoga, journaling, and several other contemplative practices. The pedagogy in this sense is planned yet the results are not always fully predictable, for the mind both leads the way here, and is led by it. There will be more to say about this later.

Let's first give you a taste of what this *inner curriculum* looks like when it results as the *opposite* of the 'social curriculum'. We're going to do the very same thing we've done a number of times already. That in itself says something crucially important about the pedagogical approach to this *inner curriculum*. It's by no means fancy. The mind is fancy enough. You can only see that if you stop luring it *out there*. So pedagogically speaking:

> Having an arsenal of pedagogical tricks is a great asset, but here your arsenal broadens when your mind starts finding infinite possibilities in a pedagogy that is supposedly the same.[6]

So here's mindfulness practice in the open-attention version again, yet leading in new directions:

> Set a clock for two minutes and just allow anything to come to your attention without initiating or willing anything specific. Just attend to your mind-body in any way you see fit, and note whatever you note.

If you tried the above, you've just experienced the exact opposite of what the 'social curriculum' is in most of its renditions. Similar to the analysis of 'knowledge' offered in Chapter 4, these two minutes were unplanned, experienced only by you, did not have a clear aim (aside from perhaps experiencing the opposite of a 'curriculum' that has a clear aim), probably some of the content it contained was non-communicable and non-transferable (you probably can't remember much of what happened and some of it cannot be articulated at all), there's nothing efficient about it, and it is not methodical (at least when method is associated with some linear and clear plan).

For some people such experience results as outrageous. I know all about that because I used to feel that way, and sometimes I still do. There may be this feeling of not being able to stand such aimlessness. We want to get to the point. That is completely understandable. At the same time, it brings to the fore the way we are constantly habituating ourselves into the rat race of running after our own tails – or better said having our minds throw bones to the future and treating our present-grounded bodies as the dogs that are to fetch them. The mind, whether following 'social' ideas or on its own accord, constantly comes up with the infinite possibilities of how things will be better once we get to a *there* and *then* while all there is is *here now*. Thus when I engage my university students with this practice, usually their mind immediately seeks a plausible explanation for this activity, which some of them view as 'leading nowhere'. Truth be told it's not exactly leading nowhere. It simply isn't leading to the *there* that we are so accustomed to associate with the 'good'.

> Where it leads depends to a great extent on the kind of 'social narrative' within which it is nested, the rhetoric based on which it is presented, and the mind that you bring to the practice.

This point will be discussed in the chapter that concludes the book. Here, however I do not focus on the place to which the *inner curriculum* leads, but rather on what our experience of *here* and *now* tells us. This is about examining the locus from which our 'social curriculum' emerges every moment – *here now* – a time and place that is usually left unconsidered.

For a moment, reflect on what it means *not* to be able to dwell *in here* for those few moments in that 'aimless' practice (and if you did not feel it was 'aimless' try extending it to ten minutes, an hour or more):

1. It means that habitually, I have to be on my way to somewhere better constantly. That is, the ethos of the 'social curriculum' along with its promise of being on the move and getting somewhere *lives in my own mind*. When I present my mind with something that does not comply with this ethos, my mind seems to reject that.

2. It means that we have come to respect experience only based on 'our terms'. We feel that this moment right now as it is experienced from *in here* is worthless, unless there's something 'worthwhile' with which to fill it. Some beads of content are 'worthwhile', while others are not. The question I ask brings the foundations of 'curriculum' thinking discussed in Chapter 4 into *your* mind: how does my brain-mind-body determine 'what beads are of most worth'? How does my mind decide what to attend to to make reality? Is it the 'social narrative' in which our 'narrative self' is invested as Chapter 3 describes? Is it the reward system in our brain? Chapters 6 and 7 will probe these questions, but for now there seems to be a realization that's profound and quite frightening beneath all this:

being alone with myself is unfulfilling.

Most would not be willing to articulate it this way, but could it be that:

I am empty of meaning as long as I don't do something; that I have to justify my existence somehow.

Those questions of 'meaning' discussed in Chapter 5 are re-invoked: How will I determine what is meaningful? Who will be the agent of meaning – 'society', *me, I*? Is that agent *in here, out there*, or in both locations? This also sends us to rethink that 'school corridor' stroll, which we took in Chapter 5 (p. 132). Perhaps the 'social curriculum' practice in which we were 'educated' has pruned our mind to consider only certain activities and experiences as meaningful and worthwhile. Some of these activities are definitely helpful, but they hardly exhaust all possible meaningful paths of which our mind is capable. To begin with, this experience of just being here and now that exposes some inherent restlessness, shows that we have an urge to 'keep going'. This happens regardless of how convinced we are of the direction in which we are headed. Indeed a sense of meaninglessness is pervasive in our society as many have analyzed.[7] We may need to extend the concept of a 'curriculum' as a planned 'course of a race' based on which we run toward a clear (perhaps too clear) destinations –

> To a curriculum in which we stop running, and in fact let things unfold as a series of moments that reveal themselves as we attend to them. We do not know where they will lead, hence our best policy is to attend to them with our fullness, for that is the only reality to which we can concretely respond. If we make the best of this moment, and do that with the next, it makes sense to assume that the future will take care of itself. So this is a curriculum that attributes incredible meaning to where we are now and not only to where we are going.

This is far vaguer than the planned 'social curriculum', but at some point, we have to admit that the sense of certitude that is associated with our planned 'curriculum' and all the 'good' that we attribute to it is somewhat bogus. It is a 'social' construct that sells a story to the individual who then struggles as s/he asks: 'why doesn't *my life* correspond with this 'social' BIG narrative; where is my promised land?' as discussed in Chapter 4. The answer is simple. It is a story for the mass but not for *you* as an individual. If we get caught solely in 'society's' narrative as *me* becomes its mirror, we are bound to depart from the present as which our bodies dwell. The *inner curriculum* remains with this body that is walking *now;* the place from which our minds can constantly receive the grounding in what we are doing *now*.[8]

The 'curriculum' as we've constructed it, is a handy solution. It dissuades us from that feeling that *I am empty of meaning*. Every moment of teaching in the classroom as we think of it, is there to serve the next moment in which *more* of the 'good' that 'society' plans for the student will supposedly be achieved. We hop (or rather 'are hopped') on the bus that takes us to the future, hence we do not have to face incertitude as long as we are on it. This works to some extent, but I suspect that it does, because when you are on the move you can't focus on that void *in here*.

> *You can thus comfortably renounce your responsibility for making meaning;*
> *'society' does that for you.*

As seems to be the case, there's a price to pay for this kind of life –
it becomes the life of John Doe, not *yours*.

> Look at it any way you like. Sooner or later either, your running will get you
> to the question 'what and whom is this life about?', or the question itself will
> chase after you and reveal itself when you stop for a moment just to catch
> your breath.

THE ETHICS OF THE *INNER CURRICULUM*: EVERY BEAD IS LIFE

The *inner curriculum* faces the void. By facing it we may discover that it is
not a void at all, only a new curricular terrain that takes some getting used
to. We set aside the delicate curricular-pedagogical approach that is
required for skillfully approaching this terrain that is discussed in some
places in the next chapters. Here I focus on what it means to engage in such
'curriculum'. It means a witting or unwitting robust shift in our view of
what counts as 'knowledge'-'meaning'-'worthwhileness' – *'education'*.
It stands on different foundations that suggest that all moments attended
to receive the benefit of the doubt and are deemed *worthwhile*. The beads
on our necklace can be of different colors and shape, *but they are all beads.*

> They all share the fact that they are placeholders of life; moments of atten-
> tion that make reality and at the same time they make *you*.

Note, that at no point did I say that this is all fun and games. It is what it is,
which at times might feel quite lousy and meaningless – (or is it again the
mind that sees it as such?). What I propose here is separating between two
different levels: The bead as a *universal* 'placeholder', and the content that
makes it a *particular* bead. Again and again this is about distinguishing
universality from particularity, contingency from necessity, the pruned
mind from the unpruned mind. This is the difference between a moment
of attention, and the specific content that this moment brings. The former
is the universal scaffold of experience and the latter is the specific content
of the experience that is mounted over this scaffold.[9] The former is
non-contingent; the latter *is*. That is, you might experience a pleasurable

ice-cream cone, or a stroll in the park, or you might experience a failure in an exam, or being fired from your job. These are *possible contents* that could have been other. What could not have been other is the facticity of their being moments in your life. Facing them as such is part of the ethical stance of the *inner curriculum*.

'Curriculum' as conceptualized here is all pervading. It's there whether we like it or not. It is the stream of beads flowing that we attend to with varying degrees of awaken-ness. It shapes us as we shape it. It also includes a myriad stimuli of which we are unaware, which are still there affecting us in diverse ways, because when we attend to one thing it does not mean that we capture all that there is *nor that we are affected only by that to which we attend.*

Deliberate engagement with this *inner curriculum* cannot, and probably should not, be practiced at all times. When we deliberately study math as part of the 'social curriculum', we will have to focus on the math *out there* and on thinking about the math *in here.* When we simply flow into a conversation and forget ourselves in the act, we will not (and probably should not) be there to engage with the *inner curriculum*. That does not mean that when we do so it is *not* continuing behind the scenes, and that we are not shaped and affected by that which goes unnoticed. It most certainly *does* continue, but you are not there with it to attend to its unfolding, and even if you are, you are never in a position to fully understand, nor are you in a position to choose exactly what will affect you and to what extent. The *inner curriculum* thus calls you to both embrace its existence, yet know that you remain limited in your ability to fully grasp it, and work with it.

This is a very different stance toward the idea of the 'curriculum'. It can indeed be considered as the opposite of that to which we are accustomed. Technically speaking an A student in our public 'social curriculum' has somewhat 'figured it all out'. He has 'command' over 'education'. He's tethered it. The question asked here, is whether it is not 'society' and the A that had tethered *him* or *her*. Following Dwayne Huebner (1999, p. 403), it is only when we meet the world, fumble and "fall on our behinds", that the broader all-inclusive 'curriculum of life' will 'educate' us out of smugness and teach us, that the game played is far broader than what we have been so far taught.

The above could be read as a disenchanting statement about the naivety of the 'social curriculum' we have constructed or as a re-enchantment of life. It could be read as spiritual reverence of the kind you might find in various wisdom traditions. But it can also be considered as a secular ethical approach that stems from phenomenology, pragmatism, and even neuroscience if you will; simply an acknowledgement of the fact that we are here and to some extent we can choose what to make of it. It is less important which kind of interpretation works for you, but if you choose to accept this approach, then it suggests that:

> all moments are 'created' equal based on the fundamentals of attention, space, and time, regardless of the content they bring, and regardless of the neat categories we come to lay over them based on our 'social normative map' or based on our own individual idiosyncrasy. If we commit to this, then this starting point is always an a priori ethical stance by which we accept a primary absolute meaning and worthwhileness of any bead of experience.

The actual content that is attended to, and the way in which we attend to it that shapes the content, is secondary and contingent. It is hence less reliable as a source for appreciating life. In this sense, feeling that *I am empty of meaning* or that this moment now is 'useless', 'aimless' etc. is a secondary and contingent feeling. It is a possible experience out of infinite other possibilities that could have been mounted over *this* bead *here now*. It hardly means that it should be ignored; however, when such feeling of meaninglessness arises, the ethics of the *inner curriculum* suggest that we got caught in the secondary level. Acknowledging the sense of meaninglessness as part of the game, is making meaninglessness itself, full of meaning, and hence it hearkens back to the primary level.

*

Is There a Trajectory or Promise in This Inner Curriculum?

There is a paradox between the idea of 'education' and 'curriculum' that the placeholder definition offered in Chapter 1 (p. 16) nests in the idea of 'development', and this grounding that I offer in *this* moment of attention. The question is what is the promise of the *inner curriculum*? what is the 'good' toward which we develop? This question will be taken more elaborately in Chapter 9, but for now I will state, that there is certainly a developmental trajectory involved here, yet one that is very different than the one proposed by the 'social curriculum'. Paradoxically, the development in this case is the *growing* commitment to the *present* moment. It is a growing sense of integration between mind and body, knowing and being, self and other. A sense of being at home in life; within this body, this mind, this phenomenology of existence that you and I both share regardless of the *particular* 'societies' and contexts into which we happened to be born.

At the same time this trajectory proposes instability, for it is established over the state of mind-body that I experience *here now*, which is in flux. When that integration and feeling at home is sensed, it is sensed *here and now*, which is 'good' for that moment, yet carries no promise for the future for the next moment is yet to unfold. What does this feeling at home consist of? – an understanding of life, gratitude, humility, full acceptance, *love*. It is not an either/or experience, but rather a spectrum of possible experiences that run between utter pruning, specificity, and particularity that is caught in *this* interpretation of this moment, and the vastness of an un- or de-pruned universal mind. We are always somewhere over that spectrum but we stand a better chance of experiencing the latter orientation if we start to seriously probe the game in which we are being played and within which we are players. It's only such 'education' that might gradually create an opening to this feeling of being more at home in this life, traveling with a sense that this has meaning, that I have a place here alongside you, that both of us have something to give each other. That *this* is what this is about.

Rather than think that what is offered here is some 'navel-gazing curriculum', one needs to realize that this 'curriculum' is not an escape from anything. In fact setting our eyes on the 'social curriculum' along with the taken-for granted-ness of the disciplines so neatly placed in it, is a form of 'social navel gazing' that serves as a comfortable escape from the human condition of incertitude. Engaging with the *inner curriculum* nests the whole construct of 'curriculum' as we know it, along with the disciplinary knowledge we appreciate, and the learning skills we want, within a greater meaning of life that is sensed from *here and now* and includes your mind-body in it. It is a perspective of standing in the midst of life within an instable environment that is in constant flux that arrives at a mind that is itself a system that is in constant flux, and seeking balance from one moment to the next within this incertitude.

The trajectory and promise of the 'curriculum' that's offered here can only be an acknowledgement of *past* moments in which I realize, that for some time now, I've been feeling more at home in life. Yet, again, this retrospect yields no guarantees as to the next moment, which will require the very special care and attention that the previous ones required. Practicing this *inner curriculum* there is a chance that a growing confidence in one's ability to face life with more serenity and joy will have gradually become a more stable trait.

If the 'social curriculum' (intentionally or unintentionally) feeds our tendency to *arrive* at a certain destination and get there quickly, the *inner curriculum*, is a constraint that insists that we have an eye on where our minds-bodies are *now*, and that we will not lose sight of them as our locus of meaning. We won't be able to do this all the time, and there will be times in which we in fact will have to forget that our life needs constant work, nevertheless this orientation is required, for otherwise we will simply keep running away from ourselves and into trouble.

*

This talk, however, may have given the impression that we have gotten caught up in ideation. So it is time to recall our bodies and test the above ideas for a moment; allow them to sink into our cells. My recommendation is trying those two minutes of open attention again, but this time perhaps with the *intention* set in mind toward treating all the content of the beads to be experienced as *contingent*. Their content just 'happens to be' *this* or that, but it rides over the more important and meaningful aspect in them that has to do with their bare non-contingent existence, which automatically implies *your* bare existence as the attend*er* and perhaps a mere atten*tion:*

> Take two minutes. Just attend. If you get caught in a thought of aimlessness, just remember that aimlessness is itself a content that can be considered secondary compared to the fact that you just had an experience that 'happened to be' aimlessness. That just might make it aimful.

It is by no means easy to accept this idea, nor to withstand such practice. But this *inner curriculum* is not about offering something easy. In fact, it is probably far more challenging than studying chemistry or math that have already been deemed meaningful by 'society'; a meaning that you are simply called to accept. Here, however, the 'curriculum' constantly turns responsibility back on *you*; on *me*. It stems from the raw and inescapable facticity of the mind *in here* as the locus of all my perceptions, and the source from which all my thoughts, speech, action, behavior, and character emanate.

Your turning *in here* is an acknowledgment that *Wherever you go there you are*, as world-renowned mindfulness leader Jon Kabat-Zinn's (1994) book title proposes. Externally we can run away, but internally there's no place but *here*. We turn *in here* to acknowledge that no matter what challenge we encounter *out there* eventually it's *me* that's experiencing it, and since my experience is a reality that I am naturally very concerned with, I need to make sense of it, and work with it to the best of my ability. As I take care of myself, as we will see in Chapter 9, I'm taking care of you as well. It's not about ignoring 'society', only about repositioning it in space and time, to acknowledge its presence and in fact take care of it, from a mind that returns to it with a difference.

*

How Do We Progress From Here?

The plan now, is to discuss the *inner curriculum* by dedicating three chapters to domains within it, that have been *nullified* from 'education' as we have come to practice and understand it in public settings. The three are: *embodied perception, me,* and *I.* The idea is to render these three more intelligible, so that the visionary aspects of this book will become more practical. This does not entail the provision of clear recipes for their implementation. However, I do describe various ways in which I introduce some of these ideas to students along with continuing the self-experimental approach that runs as a thread throughout the book. I generally believe that all I can do is inspire with these ideas and examples. You can't teach an *inner curriculum*. You can only describe its features, the pedagogies by which it can be accessed deliberately, as well as typical subject matter that unfolds once one engages in it. You can inspire people to take that journey and accompany them, but all the rest is first-person experience – that one thing that *cannot* be taught. However, if you think of bringing such ideas to a classroom, a lecture hall, or even to your home, you will be required to deeply engage with yourself in order for it to be meaningfully taught to your students or to your children. Otherwise, it becomes another form of an *out there* curriculum in which *you* become too much of a subject matter, blocking the view of your student's from seeing their own interiority.

Just to prime your mind for what's coming in terms of subject matter and methodology, in the following I briefly characterize each of the three domains of the *inner curriculum*, which are discussed in the subsequent chapters:

1. The *curriculum of embodied perception* is the theoretical and experiential first-person understanding of the mechanisms of moment-to-moment perception. This takes us back to Chapters 2 and 5 to provide an understanding of the discrete moments that make up experience and 'education'. This process is made of beads that are thread throughout your life. There's a micro-process within each of these beads that needs to be articulated. The whole is in the parts, but this can only be seen, when looking through a magnifying glass on each bead. Your brain-mind is a 'curriculum deliberator' that selects beads constantly. It also comes to every bead thread (whether it comes from *in here* or *out there*) as an 'internal embodied pedagogue' that places a kaleidoscopic setting of its past and hence shapes what you (the student) see as you see it, whether you are aware of this or not. This domain of the *inner curriculum* focusses on this kaleidoscope's workings, and on *how* the process of perception as it stems from our past shapes the content that makes who we are. Here you will see why focusing on parts, does not reduce experience, but rather shows the grandeur of its thickness.

2. The *curriculum of me* is the theoretical and experiential first-person subject matter of our 'narrative self' that creates the *inner curriculum* as a day-to-day horizontal time axis. It includes *me* as the sense of an agent that's narrat*ing*, as the narrative itself (the subject matter), and *me* as the one *in here* being shaped by this internal *unwitting* 'internal schooling'. Of all three, it is the most similar to the 'social' curriculum for it was born from the 'social'. However, here it is not 'society' that's creating the incentive to *get there to the future* but rather the brain-mind's remarkable ability to travel in time (i.e., think about the future, remember the past) and *me's* inherent sense of the *insufficiency of now*. This domain is the locus of our day-to-day sense of identity and agency. It is also that which is most resistant to change for it is the level of our automated habit. It proposes both the gift of

being able to perform in the world, and the predicament of blindness to pruning. It is the very stumbling block that stands in the way of 'education', for *me* likes to be *me*, and likes to school itself in who it already is.

3. he *curriculum of I* is the theoretical and experiential first-person subject 'matter' of *I*. This is the deliberate or spontaneous contemplative engagement that enables me to detach from a habitual *me*, experience *embodied perception*, and de-prune the mind. This *I* has two modes: a) the 'philosopher's/reflective *I*' that runs as a thread from Plato to Descartes and Kant, and is pervasive in 'educational' discourse within Dewey, Schon, and others' conceptions of *reflective practice*. We will examine it *but* also show why it is utterly *limited* and why the *inner curriculum* must include b) the *'contemplative I'* that can take us to the place from which even the certainty of language is surrendered, hence the mind unravels itself to itself, and re-opens 'education' to resist its blindness to pruning. This chapter is thus an '*I*-opener', as it will describe the depth of a deliberate 'educative' engagement with ourselves, the idea of 'good' that is associated with it, and how this idea of 'good' may be seen as transgressing the idea of 'social-construction'.

There is a fluid movement between all three domains, and the distinction offered here is by no means something that one should care to have in mind constantly. It is one out of different structured ways to articulate types of engagements with the *inner curriculum*, corresponding with different pedagogies, needs, and intentions. We need not think that one domain is better than the other, nor that our engagement in one domain does not affect the others. This framework is also not necessarily exhaustive, and I'm in no position to claim that it is the best way of depicting domains of our internal life. It follows the foundations developed in the first part of the book so it works well in that sense and it does work well in my courses.

A Word on Methodology

It is in fact because of the fluidity and complexity of our internal life, that I feel that we need some kind of structure to make the *inner curriculum* more understandable. It is because of this too, that I recruit evidence based science to make some of the arguments. The next chapters will thus follow this structure for each of the three curricula:

1. Articulating the curricular domain.
2. Backing it with science (in Chapters 7 and 8 but not in 9), phenomenology, and first-person perspective (with self-experiments when possible).
3. Making a case for its inclusion as an integral part of an 'all-inclusive curriculum of life'.

NOTES

1. The sources for this understanding are diverse, and include Damasio (2005), McGilchrist (2009), Siegel (2012), and several others.
2. Perhaps they are not two at all, but rather two modes of engagement of the brain-mind with itself. See Chalmers (1996), Hoffman (2008), and McGilchrist (2009) for interesting perspectives on this matter.
3. Damasio (2005), Davidson (2012), McGilchrist (2009), and Siegel (2012).
4. As well as others that are not discussed in this book, such as the timeless.
5. This does not mean that teaching practice is necessarily a technical, non-spontaneous endeavor. There are certainly distinctions between the 'implemented curriculum' and the 'planned curriculum'. I am here referring more to the 'curriculum' as it appears in our statements about what is done in schools and higher education institutions.
6. I owe this idea to Mick Goodrick (1987). This genius guitar Master describes this idea when discussing jazz improvisation – it's not how many fancy chords one knows but rather how many utilizations one comes up with for one and the same chord.
7. See for example Turkle's (2012) analysis of technology's role in this.
8. This does not exclude the possibility of practices such as visualization that use the imaginative power of our minds to envision a different reality. There are nuances to this that I do not elaborate here.
9. Such conceptions follow both East-Asian wisdom traditions such as the Vedantic Atman/Brahman as well as Schopenhauer's (1966) depiction of this idea.

CHAPTER 7

The *Curriculum of Embodied Perception*

The brain is not just a tool for grappling with the world. It's what brings the world about.

McGilchrist 2009, p. 19

The fact that our attention seems to be very much preoccupied with what goes on *out there*, does not imply neither that nothing goes on *in here* at the same time, nor that that which we attend to *out there*, is the most important and worthwhile possibility at each moment. The need to respond to life situations in real time and focus on external tasks, does not leave much room for us to reflect on or become mindful of *how* we attend. This chapter points the flashlight of attention over this inner domain. We will be breaking down the process of perception. This means shifting our focus from the *content* of the bead of experience, to the act of its threading and examining *how* that content appears in the mind to affect how it is experienced. As I will suggest an integral part of our *inner curriculum* entails the 'mind as pedagogue' – the way it teaches that which it attends to, to itself.

How we perceive includes the process of threading of beads that our day-to-day attention is usually too coarse to capture. It includes the kind of brains-minds-bodies' that we bring to the moment from the past. They become like a kaleidoscopic setting through which we attend. The kaleidoscope constantly changes to shape the particular experience that we get; however, it tends to get stuck on certain past configurations. The mind creates this moment's teaching, based on that which it attends to, and itself.

© The Author(s) 2017
O. Ergas, *Reconstructing 'Education' through Mindful Attention*,
DOI 10.1057/978-1-137-58782-4_7

Studying this curricular domain opens a theme that will become more significant in the next chapters – *agency* – where does it begin and where does it end? If for the moment what we attend to is reality – we may want to ask *how does my mind decide what to attend to?* From the perspective of the BIG 'social mind', the 'social curriculum' is the 'hottest show in town', but students often choose to attend to other things...how do their brains-minds-bodies select what to attend to make their reality for that moment? Exploring these questions, we will continue our quest to examine what is contingent and what is not? What can 'education' affect in us and how do attention, space, and time feature in this? In this chapter we will examine the scaffolds of this *universal* process, whereas in the next, we will examine how our *identity* is *particularly* shaped by the *curriculum of me*.

So what exactly is the curricular content of the curriculum of *embodied perception?* – At the very instant at which something is attended to at least two things happen *in here – in our brain-mind-body*: one concerns the 'mechanics of cognition' – that which allows for that something to be cognized; the other concerns our reaction/response to that which is cognized. I argue that the experiential understanding of this process is an integral part of 'curriculum' and 'education'. Why? – Because once the math on the board is there, we can say that its presence is now a non-contingent fact. But this is hardly the place to look at, in order to understand how 35 different students experience 'education' as they all attend to that *same* math on the board. Each of them arrives at that moment shaped by a particular past and perceives this math's content, based on a *different* and *particular* state of being. This results as 35 'educational' experiences that were molded based on an *internal* pedagogy about which the teacher has very little clue. Each of these minds *teaches* its owner a curriculum that is based on its past, is affected by the present, and will affect the future as a consequence.

We tend to get stuck on the 'math' *out there*, yet as many report, years later much of it is forgotten. But there's far more there that's left that is not related to numbers. It is not the math, but rather the states of being *I* experienced every time I studied math that make it completely different than what *you* made of it while sitting next to me during the same lessons. I am not saying that one remembers exactly all those emotions and feelings one had while studying, just as one does not remember many details of the content learned. I am saying that you were shaped by them fundamentally to become who you are, despite the fact that you think that you were 'just' studying math.

I am making two very strong claims here that will require examining:

a. A fact of life: Wittingly or unwittingly we shape the content that we attend to for we are hardly some passive mirror that just stands there reflecting reality *out there.*
b. An 'educative' implication and motivation: By learning and experiencing how *embodied perception* unfolds, we eventually might learn something about working directly with the mind, rather than being governed fully by a process about which we are clueless.

The second point opens a profound 'educational' agenda. Understanding how my own mind shapes my experience, may help me change the way I experience. This is exactly what Mihalyi Csikszentmihalyi argued:

> There are two main strategies we can adopt to improve the quality of life. The first is to try making external conditions match our goals. The second is to change how we experience conditions to make them fit our goals better... Neither of these practices is effective when used alone. (1991, p. 43)[1]

The 'social curriculum' is fully immersed in the first strategy. I suggest that as part of the *inner curriculum* we incorporate the second one, which must imply a meta-pedagogical turning of attention to *in here.* Just as our knowledge of the structure of the atom resulted in our ability to control chemical processes, so too the understanding of our own moment-by-moment process of perception might help us have more control over our experience. What we are doing here is shifting the axis of where the 'action' of 'education' actually takes place. We are positioning the mind at the center of 'curriculum' and 'pedagogy'. If we get to know that inner terrain in which things are determined, we will know far more not only about *what* we perceive, but also about *why* we perceive it the way we do. Knowing the 'rules' that govern the *inner curriculum* will put us in charge of our 'education' and our lives, and grant us far more choice.

The language of this chapter meanders between the banks of cognitive theory, and curriculum theory. It thus moves between science and more personal narratives that will exemplify how I teach *embodied perception.* We will begin by exposing mechanisms that undergird perception by which I will gradually mobilize us from our somewhat 'cold cognitive' focus on content, to the 'warm affective' *state of being* that undergirds perception, which shapes us constantly beneath our awareness. We will then explore how our brains engage in curricular deliberation by selecting what to attend to, how our *bodies* become the organs of our perception, and how our past is involved in this process, creating tendencies that are enacted in the present and affect the future. From this more *universal* and somewhat *impersonal* perspective of the curriculum of embodied perception, we will then be ready to move into Chapter 8 in which we will explore the *curriculum of me*.

*

THE BRAIN-MIND AS THE AGENT OF 'CURRICULUM' DELIBERATION: A COARSER RESOLUTION OF PERCEPTION

The Mind as a 'Cold' Pedagogue

The description of the mechanisms of our perception will be based mostly on psychology and cognitive theory. There will be nothing original in these descriptions. The importance of the following lies in the articulation of why these mechanisms must be viewed as part of an 'all-inclusive curriculum', and how they apply to 'educational' theory, practice, and research in terms of the *inner curriculum*. I explain these mechanisms moving between a broader perspective on perception and examples that ground them in 'educational' practice.

At the very basic level of cognition beyond which we will quickly move, James argued that, "[W]hilst part of what we perceive comes through our senses from the object before us, another part always comes out of our own head" (2007, p. 747). I wish he would trade the word 'head' with embodied mind, which I believe would articulate *his* intention better, but for now let's agree that you cannot cognize the number 8 on the classroom board or on your desktop, without your *memory* of the shape of 8 and its association with the word and the meaning of 'eight', which comes out 'of your own head'. However, we usually think of 'memory' in terms of actively recalling past events. Cognitive scientists refer to this latter meaning of 'memory' as 'episodic memory', which is part of our *explicit memory*. This kind of memory locates it in the *horizontal time axis* that we discussed in Chapter 2 and will have more to do with the *curriculum of me* in the next chapter. What we are speaking of here is quite different. Our ability to cognize the 8 is associated with a different kind of memory called *implicit memory* (Schacter 1987). This kind of 'remembering' becomes second nature to you, since you've practiced it so often. The thousands of times you saw an '8' as a toddler and child created *automation*. Such automation is a necessity of life, for it is fundamental to learning, *and it happens without our awareness.*[2] You were taught to read eights and these words as well, but that does not explain in any way *how* reading actually occurs, and saying that much of this 'just happens beneath awareness' is saying that we do not have an embodied first-person experience of this. However, we infer that such unaware process must somehow support our reading.

What is my point? – I am deepening my claim that our mind-brain is a *pedagogue*. It attends to the content *out there*, and constantly reconstructs these *l e tter s* in real time, to make them decipherable and meaningful. Your mind intervenes to render these words intelligible so that they can become a *teaching*. It could be a negligible teaching or even a wrong one, nevertheless even at this almost 'technical' level we have to think of our mind as a teacher that decodes these signs that we once did not know, and now can't *un*know. Try *not* to read this word – Apple. I bet you couldn't.

Thus to begin with, there is this level of 'computational' functioning of your brain, that constantly works 'behind the scenes' to allow you to attend to a sign 'x' *out there* by recalling its meaning from *in here*.[3]

*

States of Being as the 'Warm' Kaleidoscopic Setting of the Mind as Pedagogue

Interesting as the above 'computational' level may be, it results as somewhat of a 'cold' processing that might fool you and disguise the deeper aspects involved in real-time perception. We tend to focus on this 'knowing' part of things, while there's a state of *being* undergirding it, that supports it, *shapes* it, *and is shaped by it*. Explaining this begins again at a coarser level. While you are at it reading these lines, you may note some emotion that is present as part of your first person experience. Perhaps it is not a full-fledged emotion of happiness, fear, or envy, nevertheless, the following two categories that cognitive and neuro scientists use, may well apply to it[4]:

1. Arousal: Colloquially, a certain level of energy that could run anywhere between *very low* (e.g., being tired) to *very high* (e.g., highly

alert as when having had to stir left so as not to crash into a car that's just crossed your lane).

2. Valence: A certain appraisal of your embodied mental state that can run anywhere between *negative* (e.g., horrible) and *positive* (e.g., elating).

Arousal and valence are part of your *state of being*[5] at any given moment. If you are alive, then at any given moment you are somewhere over these two spectrums. The arousal component manifests in your biology in the most basic functioning of your body (e.g., blood-pressure, temperature), hence it lends itself to what is considered to be very reliable scientific data. A peak in your pulse signals that you are aroused; however, this could be the consequence of a negative emotion (e.g., the house is on fire and you are terrified), or a positive one (e.g., receiving the news that you've won the lottery). I clearly can't fight loss of sleep with this book, but if I managed to get you so focused on *these words* that you lost a sense of your *body* for these moments, then there was an appropriate level of arousal that allowed alertness, which enabled you to read full-speed ahead and understand all of this. If not, then drowsiness, boredom, and other low arousal-negative valence states *commanded* the reading process.

Why use this rather strong word – 'Commanded'? – Because while your brain was cognizing these words and doing all that 'computational' work of implicit memory, unwittingly, the whole experience of reading this *content* carried an additional meaning – one of a tired and drowsy mind. Any student in the classroom is commanded by these states of arousal and valence. This is not something one can do without. It is a constant component of first-person experience at any given moment. You will note it when your attention deliberately or non-deliberately turns to it and reveals it to be part of your reality. Whether you'll note it or not (and there can be different levels of noting it) it will shape your experience regardless.

Along and in full interdependence with arousal and valence, your state of being is fully affected by 'what is on your mind'. That which is attended to is selected from *out there*. It could be Bible studies or social studies as possible subject matter for learning. At the same time *in here* the mind of a student may be preoccupied with settling down from a fight during recess, looking forward to spending time with Daddy who's now living apart from Mommy, being concerned about a friend who hasn't showed up for school after feeling very low yesterday or any other possible thought. In addition this student's perception is affected by several other things such as liking/disliking the teacher's shirt, enjoying the April sun, or feeling down because of a dark February winter.

All these preoccupations along with the arousal and valence that come with them, affect our minds-bodies at this very moment and shape how we attend, the meanings we'll make, and most notably how we shall act and behave. They are changing kaleidoscopic settings through which each one of us attends. It adds its own shadings that will enwrap the bead spoken by the teacher as it is perceived. It will no longer be 'just math' for math will have been *infused* by the content of the *inner curriculum* to become *my experience of this moment of math*.

What we will be getting at is this,

> If you hate math, it's not just the numbers. If you hate history it may have less to do with Napoleon. If you love chemistry it may have less to do with chemical formulas, and if you love literature it's not just Shakespeare. While all these may be the expression of the things to which you were introduced *out there* as the 'social curriculum', what you actually like, love, dislike or hate, is also the states of mind/body that you experienced in here as a consequence of being introduced to the subject matter. They were encoded in your memory along with your experience of the specific teacher that taught them, the smells in the classroom, the sounds and sights that you saw, the posture of your body, and the wandering thoughts you had while things went on *out there*. All these were appraised and tagged by your brain. They lay there dormant as sediments that leap into here-now in a mysterious process that infuses your present, with odors smelled twenty years ago, the sense of terror of a shouting science teacher, the kindness of another, the exhilarating palpitations of love to a girl sitting next to you, which were entwined with the words of Wordsworth read outload by the teacher...The whole is in the parts....

What we've done so far, is only an initial parsing of the *state of being* that undergirds *knowing*. It is there all the time, and we can certainly bring it from the background to the foreground to make it *explicit*, based on practices that turn us to explore our embodiment mindfully (Ergas 2013, 2014). However, our construct of 'education' has not lent itself to considering this domain of experience as 'curricular knowledge' as demonstrated in Chapter 4. We think of it perhaps as just 'all that stuff' that supports or interferes with the 'social curriculum'. It is in fact necessary to forget our *state of being* so that we can allocate all our attentional resources to studying history or math. However, this tacit strata is somewhat that which gives the color to a black-and-white experience, and it is a substantial factor in the makings of our sense of identity, agency, character, and behavior. Our attention, however, tends to get stuck *out there* and our 'social curriculum' exacerbates this tendency, hence we are blind to the *inner curriculum in here* that quietly shapes who we are.

*

The Brain-Mind as a Curricular Agent and Its 'Educational' Idea of the 'Good'

As I now open a new paragraph, something is happening in your brain-mind, whether you are aware of it or not. That something is far more than the implicit memory that enables you to decode *these words* in an instant. It has more to do with arousal and valence and appears constantly as a question that lurks behind the reading:

should I continue reading now or not?

If you fill your mind with this thought alone, you won't be able to do anything else, and certainly not to keep on reading, but a point will come at which you will decide to put this book aside. It could be your own initiative, or some demand imposed on you by your wife, kids, a meeting you need to get to or other. Whichever the case – your brain-mind is constantly appraising and reappraising the value-meaning-importance-necessity-worth of the activity in which you are engaged. *Your brain-mind is engaged in 'curriculum deliberation'.*

At any given moment, millions of stimuli can reach the skin, the eyes, the ears, the tongue, and the nose from the environment, a myriad possible thoughts may arise in your mind, and your brain is constantly in touch with the internal functioning of your body. I'm sure for example that you weren't aware of your right hand pinky at this instant (and now that I mention it, that might have changed). That does not mean however, that your brain is not receiving input from it. It just means that it does not 'consider' it to be top priority at this moment, hence it doesn't allow it to come to the surface of awareness. A student in a classroom is faced with this exact situation. Her brain is censoring a myriad stimuli appraised as irrelevant, hence they do not enter awareness. Only a fraction of 'content beads' are left based on the brain's *not vetoing* them. They result as the relevant ones. This is *a selective process* and my italicizing these words should ring a bell if you recall Chapter 4 in which we discussed the 'social curriculum' as a 'social' selection process. What I am saying is this:

> Whatever 'society' "thinks" is important and worthwhile has its place, but the brain-mind of a student eventually determines whether it shall enter conscious awareness through attention or whether it will not. From the perspective of 'society' it should be thought of as a secondary curriculum-constructor reacting and responding in its own ways to that which 'society' presents to it. From your first-person perspective and the vantage point of life-long learning, our brain-mind does that all the time, choosing, selecting, bead after bead, moment after moment, making reality. How does my brain-mind-body determine what is worth attention and what isn't? What kind of curriculum deliberation is going on *in here now?*

Do not underestimate the power of our brain-mind to shape itself by determining what it selects to attend to out of experience. The brain-mind works in tandem with 'society' to determine what enters the mind through attention in space and how it is attended to. We literally 'educate' ourselves every moment. *We'd better understand how.*

Let's first look at this generally and then we'll 'go back to school' to look at it in the context of a classroom:

> The brain as a complex system of neuronal circuits requires some way of determining which firings are useful, neutral, or harmful. Without such an appraisal mechanism, all stimuli would be evaluated as equally important. The organism would not be able to organize its behavior, to accomplish tasks that allowed it to survive, or to pass on its traits. (Siegel 2012, p. 162)[6]

Our problem – as Tor Norretranders (1998) very effectively shows – has less to do with *what to attend to* and far more with, how to censor and sift all this data and remain with that which is most relevant and *worthwhile*. What we are asking here is: *what is the brain-mind-body's criteria for determining what is 'good', 'best', 'worthwhile'?* You may recall Chapter 4 in which we said that there are several problems with making such curricular deliberations: how does 'society' know in advance what is *the* 'good'? What *is* 'good' at all? How can we know what 'good' is 'best', and will also be 'good' in the future? The brain-mind-body faces the very 'curricular' question that 'society' faces concerning 'what knowledge is of most worth' every single moment. Much of what goes on in our brains-minds has to do with censoring endless alternatives to what we are doing, while choosing the one to which we commit. At this very moment, you can choose to go on reading, set the book aside, go make a coffee, call someone, watch TV, think about life, go for a walk, walk your dog...all these and a million other options are all possible at the level of awareness or beneath it, which brings us again to *pruning*:

> The next moment of our life is potentially infinite yet the brain-mind prunes it down to that one particular moment that we get. How is the choosing conducted?
>   A deeper question lurks behind this – who is the agent that works to orient my attention and thus define my reality at this moment? That agent will determine 'education' for it will place a bead of content to make reality now.

The question of free will is clearly begged here. Given that no one has solved this mystery don't hold it against me if I will not provide a 'final' answer. This chapter and the next two offer different ways for considering an answer to this question. We begin here by consulting the theory of evolution. We don't have to stick with it, nor do I believe that it settles the matter. But there is clearly much to learn based on it. It can tell you why you may be still reading now, and when you might stop. It will also offer some insight into the battle over attention that goes on between a teacher, representing 'society' and a high-school student's brain-mind-body representing 'nature' in a classroom situation.

*

Evolution as the Brain's Curricular Agenda

From the perspective of the theory of evolution and its association with the brain, at a very gross level, there appear to be three criteria that determine where attention will go based on real-time perception, at any given moment. The basic principle follows a painfully simple algorithm of either avoiding or approaching stimuli and there's no coincidence in the order in which these two appear. Evolution is about *survive* and reproduce, hence threats are given priority over satisfaction. A little more detailed analysis will give us three candidates for the selective process of attention in space and time. They are demonstrated here in the following hierarchical order: survival, salience, and satisfaction (or pleasure). I describe the phenomenology of each followed by a brief mentioning of the most relevant brain networks/regions associated with them:

1. *Survival*: The first sign of threat (physical or psychological, real or imagined, as discussed in Chapter 8), will immediately call your attention to assess the danger. Even the most thrilling teacher will not be able to ensure that students attend to her words if the school is on fire. Similarly, you will immediately drop this book if you even imagine you heard a burglar breaking in to your house.[7]

   According to MacLean's (1990) model of the Triune brain, survival will be primarily associated with our Reptilian brain; the most primitive and ancient part of our brain that equips us with the fundamental strategies of survival – fight, flight, or freeze responses. Normally, these will override any activity in which we are engaged and all attentional resources will be allocated to protecting ourselves. A *perceived* sign of danger can create the famous 'stress response' that will prepare our bodies for protective action (Hanson and Mendius 2009). The situation doesn't have to be 'really' dangerous, but only individually perceived that way.[8] This will be central to the *curriculum of me* that has much to do with creating bogus dangers during mind wandering, and conditioning us to an 'education' in a non-concrete reality.

2. *Salience*: Whatever breaks a routine, may lure the mind even if for an instant. Clearly this is also a subcategory of survival, for sudden danger is salient; however, here this applies to non-threatening situations as well. Sitting in that same lesson with a thrilling teacher, you will find that stimuli such as a sudden cheer from the schoolyard or an occasional cough from the student next to you will not wait for permission to enter your reality. While such stimuli may be of very little interest in and of themselves, they break routine, and your brain seems to be very willing to be interrupted by them. It is as if "for the moment what we attend to is *conscious* reality", but underneath this *conscious* reality, 'someone' is watching a broader reality and is ready to take charge. This indeed may be a feature of our survival instinct, as our brains have evolved to protect us by remaining vigilant to all that happens around us. Some people very easily return to their task, hardly noticing the interference, but others, especially those diagnosed with ADD/ADHD may have substantial trouble in this respect.

The salience network works both through bottom-up processing in which stimuli are filtered based on their perceptual features, and as a higher order function that is responsible for focusing the 'flashlight of attention' (Menon 2015, p. 597). We may be highly focused on a certain activity, however, if someone says our name out loud many of us will quickly respond, as if we were constantly ready to be called (known as the "cocktail party effect" (Wood and Cowan 1995)).

3. *Satisfaction*: We approach what we take to be satisfying and avoid that which is taken to be a source of suffering and pain. This is where our sense of *agency* might come in to play far more than with the foundations of survival and salience. Pleasure can be interpreted narrowly as responding to earthly desires *or* as the recruitment of our will for the postponing of our wish for a quick reward, in favor of long-term goals that we view as worthier.

If you sit as a student in a boring lesson, you don't feel that you can just leave the classroom, so your mind will constantly search for something more satisfying to do. This can be daydreaming, talking to your neighbor, sending her a note, reading under the table, etc.. Conversely, you may fear that if you keep doing this, you might flunk this class. You might then try to re-attend to the lesson despite your appraising it as unsatisfying (whether it is the subject matter itself, the way it is taught, or both). This will still have to do with satisfaction – however, one that has to do with your long-term motivation, and one that is based on deliberation.

Satisfaction has to do primarily with the reward system (associated also with levels of dopamine; the neurotransmitter that is related with pleasure). Again, a very primitive function, however, the ability to resist the impulse to satisfy short-term desires is associated with the more august executive functions that are related to our prefrontal cortex (Davidson 2012, pp. 80–85). Thus here, some stimulus will be perceived, creating a sense of arousal and desire toward it (e.g., a phone call from a friend offering you to go for a beer). Your brain will tell you 'this sounds nice, let's go for it', and while noting that, almost at the same instant another part of your brain will say 'this is not the time, there's that test coming up in a week'. This moment of deliberation, is a moment of discernment that is based on deliberate reflection discussed in the next chapters. It is no other than the human experience of life; a constant choice. In William James's words it boils down to this: " ... the whole drama of the voluntary life hinges on the amount of attention, slightly more or slightly less, which rival motor ideas may receive" (1984, p. 247).

It's all about what one will do with one's attention; how good one gets in choosing the right things to attend to, and by so doing censoring less desirable and/or harmful alternatives.

From the student's side, there is a brain-mind-body that is responsible for determining what is most important right now. 'Someone' in there is constantly *choosing what to attend to.* A teacher may well try to lure a student's mind to attend to the subject matter yet all teachers know that this is easier said than done; especially if you are expected to interest a hormone driven teenager in the American civil war when a high-school cheerleader is sitting next to him. What will make attention go either way? Who's responsible for that choice? The teacher? the student? both? The teacher may do her job quite well. However, she is up against nature itself – a primitive reward system. It may be quite difficult to lure a brain thus inclined, when your ammunition is a 'social curriculum' that at this point can only offer the conquest of Virginia. So what's it going to be? The reward system of the brain will send attention no doubt to the cheerleader, and the mind will follow along with it to a fantasy land departed from the present. But then perhaps the fear of flunking 'history' may serve as an inhibition, alerting the brain to prioritize the American civil war.

> Someone/something *in here* will have to choose what to attend to. Will it be an ancient Reptilian brain or a more august prefrontal cortex that is thought to be responsible for our ability to withstand instant gratification, regulate our emotions, and prioritize our long-term goals?

The above only begins to elaborate a point made in Chapter 2:

> 'Education' is determined by how we orient attention.

But, it may justly be suggested that,

> 'Education' is the site in which several agencies fight for the orientation of attention. Some of them emerge from *out there*; some from *in here*. The winner takes it all for that moment.

Our habitual perspective probes this from 'society's' side of things. Conversely, we began to explore the brain-mind's side of things as we ask: *who* governs attention and based on what principles? According to Norretranders (1998, p. 143) roughly summing all the sensorial inputs to the body (and leaving out available thoughts) there are about 11,000,000 bits of information available to our conscious awareness every second. Assessments as to how many we are actually conscious of vary between 7 to 40. As you can see, it is rather marginal whether we go with the minimal or the maximal assessment. Someone in our brain-mind-body is reducing all this – *pruning* wholeness into beads through a radical selection process. There's a curriculum *planner-designer* in us ferrying beads of content to create what we experience. These internal deliberations are determined substantially and then shaped by a *state of being* over which these beads are thread.

> A teacher in a classroom is not merely teaching a 'social curriculum'. She may be viewed as fighting with or against a brain-mind-body in a battle over attention that results as the 'curriculum'.

Our exploration so far offered the evolutionary perspective that introduces some very primary principles of internal 'curricular' deliberations, but it is of course far more complex than that. Evolution has much to do with our *bodies*. It also has much to do with how the past shapes the present.

*

EMBODIED-PERCEPTION: THE FINER RESOLUTION OF BEAD-PERCEPTION

Let's get even more intimate with *one* bead of experience. In the following I propose what I have gathered from diverse sources, to be a basic structure of a *present*-moment of perception of one bead. Later we will build on this to examine how our *past* is involved in this process, and how past and present condition the future. Note, that the mechanism described is not something that most people will experience (or care to bother with) during day-to-day life, unless they have practiced contemplative practices (especially if these are body-based, like postural yoga and mindfulness). I do not build on such experience here but rather offer what I believe to be a plausible description of these processes. As in the case of my depiction of *I/me* in Chapter 3, this ought to be viewed as an operative framework that is to be examined, and there are ways to do so as I'll demonstrate.

The chain of events that leads to our becoming aware of a bead of experience (at least when it runs on automatic pilot) seems to work as follows:

> At the first phase of emotional response, initial orientation lets the organism 'know' that it should pay attention to something important. The second phase, elaborative appraisal and arousal, gives the stimulus the value of good or bad. Good things should be sought; bad things should be avoided. *Value systems in the brain function by shaping states of arousal.* (Siegel 2012, p. 162)[9]

This scheme somewhat depicts Siegel's description (Figure 7.1).

Importantly, the first two phases are usually not part of our day-to-day experience. Much of the time our aware life happens at the third phase:

> We run much of our lives based on deliberations of which we have little clue: an interpretation and (re)action that are the result of a primary sifting process followed by a very primitive embodied mechanism.

There is much to question here, which I skip here. My entire explanation of this process will focus on two aspects that I view as fundamental to the reconstruction of 'education': the dramatic role of the body in perception, and the fact that all perception is self-perception. Most importantly I want to show that the *curriculum of embodied perception* is about making us aware of these lessons to which we are mostly blind.

Extreme situations provide the most obvious examples for the above. William James made a peculiar claim in this context: we don't run from a bear because we are afraid; we run because we experience heightened palpitation, heat, hollowness of stomach – basically, arousal and valence of a fearful body – and only in the aftermath we perceive our own

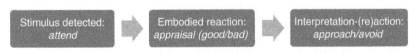

Fig. 7.1 Basic structure of present moment perception

embodied state and say that 'this was fear'. We don't say 'I'm afraid maybe it's best to run' and then run (2007, p. 1065).[10] Even more peculiar is the application of James's observation to crying and sadness. We are sad because we cry rather than vice versa. The fundamental, counterintuitive, and dramatic lesson that needs to be spelled out here is that:

> Perception is self-perception. We react to our *embodied appraisal* of that to which we attend, far more than to that to which we attend 'as such'. However, we are blind to the fact that this is the case.

The following will demonstrate this by a description of how I teach this in lectures at the university. I don't necessarily recommend this pedagogical approach. It is somewhat brutal, but it will take us quite far in understanding what kind of lessons can be learned at this level of the *inner curriculum*.[11]

I warn my students in advance that we are going to be studying about the mechanism of perception and its relation to 'education' and that at some point I am going to surprise them. After checking with them that no one suffers from any heart condition, at some point during the lesson, I suddenly *S H O U T*. Sure enough students' embodied reactions are very easy to detect. I then immediately say that the experiment is over and I won't be doing such thing again. Then, we turn to reflect over this dramatic 'bead' I've just provided them with:

> "What was the most obvious aspect in your experience?" I ask. Answers vary, but most revolve around the experience of embodied sensations: "heat in the stomach", "peak in the pulse", "a holding of the breath" and several other bodily symptoms.[12] What are these? – They seem to be the signs of a reptilian brain that has triggered the sympathetic nervous system inducing a stress response that prepares the body for fighting, fleeing, or freezing. This is the survival instinct that gives us that "first phase of emotional arousal" (Figure 7.1) in Siegel's terms. This occurs before we can even understand what just happened. It is only *later* that we might come up with the label "fear", "terror", "attack", "anger", "insult".
>
> I suggest to the students, "I assume that you don't like these sensations even one little bit" and receive clear nods of consent. "My question is: 'What don't you like here – my shouting, the sensations evoked by my shouting, or both? . . . What do you hate more – is it *me*, as the one shouting, the shout itself, or your body's response to all of this?"

For some this is a puzzling question. They never thought that you could actually separate these different aspects of the experience. But with this pedagogical "trick", we can very clearly make such distinction. We can't make too broad a generalization here as to perception as such, because the case of this fear-inducing shout is too extreme, but it is quite clear that at least *this* kind of stimulus brings about a real-time perceptional process that follows these phases:

1. A stimulus is detected – the shout.
2. My body seems to be the first to react with sensations over which I have no control.
3. A very primitive sense tells me whether this is something to approach or avoid. That is, my brain appraises the situation based on my embodied reaction.
4. Only in retrospect do I construct 'what just happened' – a shout, my body reacted, fear.
5. Conclusion: I don't like this. . . . this lecturer is *nuts*...

The question is – what am I eventually reacting/responding to? Is it the 'shout' *out there*, or my embodied reaction to it? – Three possibilities emerge:

1. I react to the 'shout' *out there* and *not* to my embodied reaction.
2. I react to the sensation in my body and the appraisal that came next.
3. I react to both.

Option 1 is unlikely. A 'shout' will lose its meaning if I do not become *really* scared of it. The whole point of it is that it has an effect on me. It is an effect that I can truly *feel* and not just 'think about'. Option 2 follows upon James, in suggesting that we first run from the bear because of the embodied stress response, so I must be reacting to my *embodied perception in here*, to that which occurred *out there*. but still – there was a bear (or a shout) *out there* that invoked this response. Without it, there would be no reaction. Option 3 then must be more appropriate.

So far so good, but there are two issues here: one concerns our blindness to our own process of perception; the other is the result of that – much of our life is hardly based on option 3. It actually follows *option 1* – the least plausible one and *that is a first-class 'educational' concern as we now turn to examine.*

*

THE 'EDUCATIONAL' IMPLICATION OF EMBODIED PERCEPTION AT THE LEVEL OF REAL-TIME PERCEPTION

Let's look at the blindness toward our own perceptional process. Option 3 carries with it the heavy assumption that we explored in Chapter 3 when we explored 'the illusion of omniscience' (p. 77): *I can trust my perception.* There has to be 'someone/something' *in here* believing both that there's a bear (or a shout) *out there*, and that this stress I'm feeling is *real* and requires addressing. If I do not trust either one of these, then there is no case for being afraid, running away, fighting etc. The question is:

> Do we seriously believe that there's actually someone or something *in here* that has time to do all this thinking, believing, and choosing what is the best way to respond to the situation? – hardly.

What I am getting at hearkens back to the primary-ness of sensations. At least in these stress situations *agency* follows the action. We don't deliberate. We act. The body reacts, and we claim *ownership* over it only in retrospect. But let's not miss the profound lesson that we are taught in these cases. As always – it's grounded in attention:

Our attention is stuck *out there*, hence we are blind to the fact that it is primarily our own body to which we are reacting. We are basically attempting to get rid of the *state of being* that has been invoked by our brains-minds-bodies as a consequence of their momentous interpretation of the situation. 'halting the breath', 'palpitation', 'perspiration' *in here* – all are extremely unsettling. We are trying to restore a stable state of being. Thus I argue that,

> we perceive ourselves perceiving the world and act quickly based on our inner curriculum and pedagogy. However, we are hardly aware that this is how things work. We think we react to *out there*, yet we are really reacting to our bodies *in here*. Given the coarseness of our attention and its stuck-ness *out there* such realization cannot be brought into awareness.

As Iain McGilchrist suggests this is about questioning, "what it is that we come to have a relationship with" (2009, p. 5). As I put it:

> Attention, mind, space – they constantly fool us into thinking that our primary relationship is with the world *out there*, whereas that is only secondary to our relationship with ourselves.

Yet, the profundity of 'education' needs to be spelled out more literally here. My students hear the shout, dislike it, *which in turn leads to disliking me as the shout-er.* They are blind to the fact that disliking *me* is secondary to disliking their unpleasant embodied reaction to the *shout.* The lesson this boils down to is:

> *Hating out there* is in fact *hating in here*
> *Hating you* is in fact *hating me*

It may follow that,

> *Loving you* is in fact *loving me*[13]

There's a profound 'educational' lesson here, that has to do with the scope of the responsibility one takes over one's life. If I argue with you and end up disliking *you* with no acknowledgement of the role of my own *embodied perception* in this, then my experience *in here* (e.g., my life satisfaction, happiness, well-being) depends fully on what the 'world' *out there does* to *me.* However, if I come to know my brain-mind-body as substantially (if not fully) affecting my *interpretation* of things experienced, then my experience *in here*, depends on how *I* see things, and on *what this mind of mine does to the world with every bead perceived.*

Before we move on, I want to briefly consider some implications of these profound lessons that the *inner curriculum* domain of *embodied perception* might contribute to 'education' writ large.

*

Some Implications for the Re-construction of 'Education'

1. Teaching us that all perception is self-perception might go a long way in shaping how I behave in this world; an ideal to which probably all robust 'educational' agendas aspire. Having my attention fixed on math and science, may yield the teaching of math and science but hardly the understanding of our lives as we experience them through our minds as pedagogues; through the *inner curriculum* of our embodied perception.

If we can somehow teach a child in an age-appropriate way, to observe that his rage is a bodily reaction; that his hand raised to hit the other is primarily a reaction to his own body rather than to the other child, he may become slightly more aware of what is actually happening here. He may begin to see how we lose control over situations as externally we seem to be battling the world, while in effect, we are seeking redemption from our embodied reactions. If a teacher becomes agitated by a student who keeps barging in with questions in the middle of her sentences, she may become more aware that the agitation is *in here* as much as it is *out there*. It is safe to assume that if she sees her own perception in the process, and responds in a measured way, rather than reacts by sending this student out of the classroom, she may teach this student something about regulating impulses through her own example.

As will be discussed in more detail in Chapter 10, it is only recently that this aspect of the *inner curriculum* has come to the fore based on the concepts of emotional regulation, mindfulness, and the discourse of social-emotional learning (Durlak et al. 2015; Schonert-Reichl and Roeser, 2016). Emotional regulation is my ability to understand what is happening *in here* experientially as well as conceptually, and my ability to work within this internal domain to meet myself and the world with a *state of being* that is beneficial and appropriate to the situation (Siegel 2012). Generally, schools seem to treat emotional regulation and the idea of a *state of being* writ large, as somewhat of a 'given', but hardly as a curricular domain that requires teaching. Emotion regulation is more likely to be discussed when it gets in the way of the 'real business' of 'education', which we have been 'educated' to believe as consisting of the 'social curriculum'. *Embodied perception* as discussed so far, suggests that it is a part of the *inner curriculum*; that this is a determining factor of who we are, how we act, in the classroom, in the lecture-hall, and outside them.

2. We may have cornered ourselves into a system that works exactly against transformative lessons learned by engaging with *embodied perception*: from the perspective of the theory of evolution our reptilian brain is there to protect us, and there are good reasons to fight/flight or freeze in cases of danger, while forgetting completely that there is anything important in attending *in here now*. However, the 'educational' system that we have constructed may be forcing us into this mode that engages our reptilian side that is by no means capable of examining *in here*. I hardly argue with the need to teach math and history, but consider that the choice to teach them is 'society's' choice, not the students'. Very skilled teachers can lure students' attention almost to anything, but if that skill is

not there (which is not uncommon), what can we rely upon to ensure a brain-mind's attention that is governed by survival, salience, and reward? – *fear* is the #1 candidate. Scare students of the consequences of *not* learning and at least some of their brains may engage in the survival mode, sending them to do their assignments. You can also reward them in various ways. All in all however, punishment and reward may become the deeper teaching. This way of engaging this primitive system of our brains, is bound to lure us further away from getting in touch with the *inner curriculum* to examine the 'educational' lesson of: how we are constructed moment-by-moment through the curriculum of *embodied perception*.

Conceptually, a curriculum of embodied perception then has to do with two interrelated aspects of 'education':

1. Knowing the 'rules of the game': understanding how we attend and perceive and how this shapes the reality that we experience.
2. 'Playing the game': knowing the rules may grant us more freedom in 'education' – 'educating' who we are, and who we shall become.

This is about attention, space, and time, and how we apply ourselves to our own attention as the faculty based on which any 'curriculum' unfolds and is reacted/responded to. This is about *agency*, and our ability to capture the moments of perception as they come and see not only *what* we see, but also *how* we see, and *why* we see it that way. It is about de-pruning the mind out of a blindness that seems to be inherent in our brains-minds survival mechanism that protects us on the one hand, yet may stand in the way of our individual thriving and our compassionate 'social' engagement, on the other hand.

Practically, it seems that we have two ways of functioning[14]:

(a) React automatically based on *embodied perception* (which as we shall see later, reinforces that habit) *or*
(b) Respond in a novel way based on an attention that has somehow managed to stumble on an alternative, which had not appeared before the automated mind.

In this chapter we are only laying the grounds for this based on *embodied perception*. The following chapters will in fact relate these two options to the *curriculum of me* and the *curriculum of I*, respectively.

So far, we've seen how perception works in real-time at a broad somewhat *universal* level. The 'educational' implications have only begun to emerge, but we are moving in to draw more of these implications as they relate directly to *you*. This has to do with showing that survival, salience, and reward are there behind the scenes, but our past is far thicker than that, and it is there with us every moment. As McGilchrist expressed this eloquently:

> When we look at our embodied selves, we look back into the past. But that past is no more dead than we are. The past is something we perform every living day, here and now. (2009, p. 8)

In the following we explore this aspect of the curriculum of embodied perception and ground the discussion more explicitly in 'education' and teaching.

*

The Past in the Present and the Conditioning of the Future

Hearing the 'shout', looking at the math on the board, at the textbook, or the notebook, focusing on the teacher's teaching – all *out there* - without looking at *this* mind that perceives them all, will yield a very inconclusive story about 'education' – about how we become who we are; about what will eventually make us become the *agents* that choose wisely rather than poorly.

One can assume that there are great differences in how students in my lecture respond to the 'shout'. They each arrive at this moment with a brain-mind-body, which was shaped by genes and experience throughout their past, as well as with a *present state of being* (i.e., arousal-valence, 'what's on their mind at the moment of the shouting'). Their past has a lot to do with *how* each one of them experiences the non-contingent variable in this case – the 'shout' *out there* – as it encounters their brain-mind-body as the contingent variable in such experiment. A student who's been shouted at a lot in life may be more immune to such act, or conversely more sensitive to it. A student who's just had a nice sip of coffee will arrive with a state of being that is different than the state of being experienced by a student who is absorbed in Facebook covering his face by the screen of his laptop. Basically, I am saying that,

> our entire autobiography; our childhood and our recent experiences come with us to this moment of attention to shape the reality seen now. The horizontal time axis is here and now. The necklace is in there in each bead. Even the future is here now.

Our past conditions the present because that which was experienced a moment ago or years ago, can leave an imprint that will send us searching for more of it, or rather seeking to avoid it. Whether this is about instant gratifications such as chocolate, a great learning experience or a horrible one, the brain-mind-body *remembers*, and projects its preferences into the future. It searches for more of what it already likes and hopes to avoid those experiences that it doesn't. This brain that is rooted in its own autobiography, also orchestrates our present levels of arousal and valence, which fluctuate throughout our day based on our interpretations of our experiences. The distant and recent past arrive to constitute our present *state of being*. We hope that this *state of being* will stop us from having more chocolate once our body's had those three extra bars and said *enough* despite our engrained sweet-tooth.

As Siegel (2012) claims, "*memory is the way past events affect future function*" (p. 46, emphasis in original). We've discussed the rather 'cold-cognitive' computational aspects of this as in recalling that 8 is 'eight' known as *implicit memory*. Here, however, we are speaking of how my past eights condition the one that I see now on the board in a deeper way. Let's try this with a short self-experiment: Reflect for a moment on your high school years. What comes to mind?

It is more likely that you will recall events that created substantial impact.

> That time when you skipped class and was caught by the principal . . . the time you excelled in a physics exam . . . the time in which your friend was shamed by other students and you didn't do anything to prevent it . . . those times in which you read your 'homework' out of an empty notebook . . .

All these incidences left a trace based on *embodied perception* and created the sense that 'this was meaningful'. Siegel (2012) argues that, "[E]motions are what create meaning in our lives, whether we are aware of them or not" (p. 161).[15] Whether the teacher said something is meaningful or not, or whether it is 'socially' consensual 'worthwhile knowledge' (e.g., the history of Rome), the level of arousal in your body has the final word on this. It tells you whether this is worth remembering or not. It is our *idiosyncratic* emotional state that tags something as meaningful, not the content *out there*.[16] The 'social curriculum' is given meaning by the appraisal system in our embodied brains-minds.

Our minds are pedagogues through which this moment is taught based on a particular past.

Clearly, a teacher and the way she teaches as well as her own *state of being*, will affect this process, yet the student's mind has the final word. 'Education' has far more to do with *how* a present moment is delivered between and within minds – their *states of being* – than with the particular content delivered (e.g., Chemistry, social studies). Furthermore, how you perceive this moment *now*, will affect how similar events will be perceived by you in the future. Briefly put: at the moment I sense a stimulus (e.g., the number 8, a shout, a sensation of hunger) several other things happen in my brain-mind-body. While my attention is *out there*, *in here* past experiences with this stimulus are tacitly evoked beneath my awareness, and it is based on them that an *automatic embodied reaction* informs (or dis-informs) how I will react to it.

Poetically put, every stimulus that enters attention evokes a shift in the kaleidoscope that our mind places as a filter through which the present bead is seen. Some stimuli like the wall in front of you, or the sound of children playing outside may result as insignificant. Your brain-mind-body probably inhibits many of them from entering awareness. But some stimuli are far thicker, for our past has infused them with individual meaning. The past thickens my first-person experience of this situation, and to a great extent defines *what* I attend to and *how* I attend to it. Yet my span of attention is utterly limited hence I will hardly be aware of most of what constructs this moment.

The artwork behind the mind's crafting may somehow be designed to conceal this mind's workings from its owner. Perhaps 'education' is about taking us beyond this 'natural' tendency?

A PEDAGOGICAL EXAMPLE:
THE RECURSIVE NATURE OF OUR BRAIN-MIND

As I did in the previous section of this chapter, I want to ground these ideas in a pedagogical example. This example demonstrates how the *inner curriculum* can be spontaneously incorporated in how we teach. But it also begins to point to how *embodied perception* may well get our kaleidoscope stuck on a certain setting that prunes the mind in to *recursivity* – seeing the present as it was shaped in the past, which amounts to seeing the past; not the present.

> A month ago, during a course I teach on curriculum design in college, I gave my students an exercise in which they had to plan a unit for an 8th grade history curriculum. Before even mentioning what historical period we will be working on, at the first mentioning of the word 'history' the expression on my students' faces disclosed their 'history of studying history'. I saw faces that were testimony to years of a 'social curriculum' that seemed to have been taught based on an over-preoccupation with *its* side of things and little care for the *particular* minds to which it was taught. I saw students for whom the word 'history' evoked the memory of lists of dates and battles vaguely recalled entwined with *states of being* of boredom over which the former were mounted as they were thread laboriously bead after bead.

As the brain-mind hears the word 'history', it is not just the implicit memory of its meaning that is evoked. It is rather a thick re-presentation of 'history' that follows all those moments better or worse, spent throughout our school years, the books we've read (or were supposed to, but didn't), the teachers we had, the boredom, the interest, the smells and tastes and our slouching bodies as we sat there in school for hours on end. Witnessing my students' faces (some of whom may actually teach history in the future), I saw that I risk the replication and further entrenchment of an unsatisfying past if I do not make them aware of how their past has just emerged in the present. At that moment, this lesson was not about 'curriculum design' any more. It was about accessing these students' *states of being now* over which 'curriculum design' and 'history' were to be taught. I clearly cannot fight hundreds of past hours that shaped my students re-presentation of 'history', but I *can* try to make them aware of *embodied perception* at work, and attempt to access the current *state of being* over which anything we will be doing next, will be mounted. I set aside the 'social curricular plan' I had, in favor of a few reflective questions.

Your faces are telling me a story about 'history' right now...What is that story? The word 'boredom' came across quite clearly. 'But what makes history boring? is history really boring?' – Some blamed the teachers that taught them. Others blamed the specific topics taught that they deemed as irrelevant to our times. 'It is clear that these may affect our experience with history, but what is boredom? And where is boredom experienced?'

As always, these questions puzzle them. Though they have experienced many hours of boredom, many of them never thought of it as something that can or ought to be further probed – after all, probing boredom sounds boring. 'But if boredom is something that *you* experience, perhaps *you* have something to do with it too?' I told them. How is it that the student next to me may have actually been interested in what I found to be boring? It suggests to me that there are experiences of 'history' that may be initiated by the teacher, but they are determined by the mind that attends to reality through its private kaleidoscope. Once it places boredom as the kaleidoscopic state of mind through which the French Revolution is studied, the teaching becomes a few dates, something about Robespierre and the Bastille, along with a brain that tags them with the label 'boredom'. The more this happens the more I get used to this association. Boredom becomes a far more pervasive lesson than the diversity of dates and events learned. It gets to a point at which at the first mentioning of 'history', my mind is primed to meet this bead with its past, and make my future match the image.

In neuroscientific terms this follows Donald Hebb's claim that was briefly mentioned in Chapter 3 (p. 64), "[T]he general idea is an old one, that any two cells or systems of cells that are repeatedly active in the same time will tend to become 'associated', so that activity in one facilitates activity in the other" (1949, p. 70). More popularly this idea was summed by Carla Shatz's (1992) statement: 'cells that fire together wire together'. This is the 'brainy' language for depicting the *recursive* nature of our minds that Siegel expressed above when claiming that, *"memory is the way past events affect future function."* What Hebb and Shatz tell us, is that behind this first-person experience in which the past becomes the present, there is a 'materialistic-mechanistic' explanation that has a substantial deterministic component to it. The brain-mind is a dynamic learning system that perceives based on its past and reacts based on it. This brings efficiency and enables real-time processing but it has a substantial downside as many have observed.

Our minds tend to get comfortable with seeing the world as they have seen it yesterday. They have a tendency toward pruning themselves out of options. Minds easily and unwittingly, create a self-justifying system. Their automated pedagogy – an internal kaleidoscopic setting – entails the positioning of past states of being as filters that yield a present moment of reality, which is dyed in the colors of a past.

McGilchirst associates this more with the left brain's functioning:

> ...its tendency to recur to what it is familiar with, tends to reinforce whatever it is already doing. There is a reflexivity to the process, as if trapped in a hall of mirrors: it only discovers more of what it already knows, and it only does more of what it already is doing. (2009, p. 86)

Returning to my students, the above amounts to this: enter a 'boring' history lesson once and then twice, and your brain-mind-body will start to form a habit. A student's mind will become primed to invoke a *state of being* that is counterproductive to the learning of history, for she will anticipate the history lesson that's coming up to be boring. Anticipating it thus is no other than priming one's brain to see things through a certain setting of one's mind-kaleidoscope – a *state of being* that sets the mind to see *now* as it saw in the past. Such mind thus makes a 'prediction' – 'history, *again*'. Unsurprisingly, coming out of the lesson a student might tell her friend: 'I told you it's going to be boring'. Perhaps true – but was there a mind there at all that was willing to permit a change of view within its own self-justifying system? Was it not a *pruned* mind, which entered the lesson governed by a past that seems to close its future? *States of being fly beneath the radar of our awareness, determining our 'education' from* in here *while we are busy with 'education'* out there.

*

EMBODIED PERCEPTION: SOME THOUGHTS ABOUT 'EDUCATIONAL' PRACTICE

When we think from the perspective of the 'social curriculum' we come to believe that we can teach 'knowing' as independent from 'being'. We come to think that *being* is there only to serve 'knowing'. As Palmer (1983) wrote, "The way we interact with the world in knowing it, becomes the way we interact with the world as we live in it" (p. 21). I suspect that, to some degree, many teachers intuitively understand this. Nevertheless, they might unwittingly enact the separation of 'knowing' from 'being', by implementing the monolithic *out there* attending meta-pedagogy that the 'system' 'educates' them to deploy.

The domain of *embodied perception* invites the balancing opposite: 'knowing' is there to serve *being*. Those objects that the 'social curriculum' positions as the subject matter, are there so that we can explore who we are *now*, and de-prune our minds out of rigidity. For educational practice, theory, and research the implications cannot be spelled out more clearly:

> If all perception is eventually the mind's perceiving itself as it attends to *out there* (or to *in here*), then the 'social curriculum' approach that has our eyes stuck only on how information travels in space from *out there* to *in here*, without questioning how it travels within our minds is no less than naïve. Real-time bead-to-bead perception does not separate the affective component of how we experience something from what that something is. As a very basic operant conditioning, a student who repetitively experiences being shouted at while studying multiplication does not learn only multiplication. He learns to avoid multiplication. At some point the thought of multiplication would be enough to make him sense terror as his body will send his mind searching for ways to disappear and avoid the situation. At that point learning to cope with terror will be superimposed over the 'social curriculum', possibly blocking any attempt to learn math. On the same token, fondness of literature may have as much to do with Virginia Wolff, as with the teacher that affected the state of being over which these 'beads of knowing' were thread. She made you or me experience love, but that love had to do primarily with loving the states of being, which we were experiencing as we learned. Our future experiences with literature may flourish over this bedrock.

This entire discussion has little to do with how *accurate* our perceptions are. While the 'social curriculum' aims to cultivate accurate perception of *out there*, *embodied perception* begins with the facticity of a perspective that precedes right vs. wrong. The *being* that undergirds 'knowing' is an experience to be attended to, not argued with. We are not in a position to change the past based on which our present has conditioned our embodied perception to prune this moment in *this* particular way. We are, however, in a position to de-prune it at the moment of perception as we come to accept this as a natural reaction to that which we perceive.

The examples of the 'shout' and my work with my curriculum design students brought above, are but two practical examples of how we can engage students in a meta-pedagogical turn that allows them to cultivate insight into *embodied perception*. They were brought in order to provide a minimal idea of how such curricular domain might become practically engaged. There are certainly methodical and rigorous ways in which to introduce students to *embodied perception*. Their common denominator would be a meta-pedagogical turn to where the 'action' of *embodied perception* takes place – *in here*. Mindfulness practice and other body-based contemplative practices (e.g., yoga, tai chi) are by all means a fruitful path in this respect.[17] This book focuses on 'curriculum' more than on pedagogy hence it has not been explaining mindfulness as much as it has been applying it toward the reconstruction of 'education'; however, as a closure I will briefly propose a pedagogical perspective that I've elaborated elsewhere (Ergas 2016a), and leave it to linger on into the next chapter:

Mindfulness, as a formal meditation practice, can be viewed as a practice that provides the mind with a *neutral* stimulus (e.g. the sensation of the breath, bodily sensations). By so doing, it provokes the mind to fill the void with its *inner curriculum*. Sitting still deliberately, one applies one's own mind to study one's own mind. The result is a pedagogy that unfolds the *inner curriculum of embodied perception* as well as the *curricula of me* and *I* that the next chapters will discuss. This view from within emerges only once we 'sacrifice' the 'social curriculum' for certain periods of time. As long as we fail to do so, we remain with the "illusion of omniscience" (Chapter 3); a two-layered blindness in 'curricular-pedagogical' practice: we do not know what we don't know, nor *that* we don't know. A reconstructed 'education' that will position the mind at the center of 'curriculum' and 'pedagogy' will have to include practices that turn the flashlight of attention to reach those blind-spots.

SUMMARY OF CHAPTER 7

- When something is perceived from *out there*, something happens *in here*. Our 'social curriculum' is focused on the former, the curriculum of embodied perception explores the latter.
- Undergirding content and 'knowing' is a *state of being* that infuses this moment with meaning.

- Real-time perception has a certain structure in which a stimulus is attended to, an embodied reaction appears, an appraisal determines my approach, and I react/respond.
- My appraisal system, and the things I will choose to attend to are shaped by my past experiences, and a brain that takes after survival, salience, and satisfaction, as well as by a present *state of being*.
- States of being are shaped by arousal, valence and that which is on our mind at that moment, which in itself emerges from the past.
- Experiences I have now, are stored in memory and affect my future encounters with reality.
- The more that which occurs *out there* evokes a high level of emotional arousal *in here*, the more we tag the experience as significant. This in and of itself, affects how it will be stored in our memory, and the extent to which it will affect our future perception of similar situations.
- The mind is a pedagogue that enacts *embodied perception* as an *inner curriculum*. It places a kaleidoscope through which we attend. The reality we get is dyed in changing colors of our state of *being*.

Any way we look at it, we have all the reasons to engage in a rigorous study of the mind as participating in the construction of the curriculum and as an active pedagogue. The fact that we do not attend to the mind as pedagogue does not make it less significant, it only makes its effects hidden.

NOTES

1. See also McGilchrist: "[T]hings change according to the stance we adopt towards them, the type of attention we give to them, the disposition we hold in relation to them" (2009, p. 4).
2. This is what Kahneman (2011) describes as our automatic and primary 'system 1' that 'thinks fast'.
3. This is a very fundamental basis of perception to which neuroscientists refer as the dual-processing that combines bottom-up sensual data, with top-down representations (Hochstein and Ahissar 2002). Basically, to make our perception far more efficient and quicker, once we've learned to read or to identify an object, our brains constantly anticipate what's coming next. One can think of it as a scientist-in-the-mind that makes a conjecture and changes it only if it doesn't work. The brain is thus an "anticipation machine" (Siegel 2012, p. 128).

4. "There is general agreement that emotion states bear two important phenomenal features, one mental and the other bodily...we will refer to these two components of emotion as valence (a subjective feeling of pleasantness or unpleasantness) and arousal (extent of bodily excitation), respectively" (Berkovich-Ohana and Glikshon 2014, pp. 11–12).

5. The term state of being parallels the term 'mental state' as applied in Siegel (2012).

6. See also Ellsworth and Scherer (2003) and Davidson et al. (2003).

7. There's no coincidence in the induction of *fear* as a way to get students' attention. It certainly gets students' attention for that moment though unfortunately, evidence shows that stress has a damaging effect on memory encoding (Elzinga et al. 2005).

8. This is especially the case in conditions such as post-traumatic stress disorder (Davidson 2012; Elzinga et al. 2005)

9. What Siegel refers to as "the first phase of emotional response" seems to be what some have analyzed as the "feeling tone" when discussing cognition from a Buddhist perspective (Grabovac et al. 2011; Varela et al. 1991, p. 67).

10. By the way, running is exactly the wrong thing to do in such case...

11. I use this "shout"-pedagogy when I teach philosophy of education, curriculum theory, social-emotional learning, and other courses.

12. See Nummenmaa et al. (2014) for an illuminating research in the domain of emotional body maps.

13. There is growing evidence from neuroscience that associates this self-other relationship with the functioning of the insula; especially in the research of compassion (Singer et al. 2009; Zaki et al. 2012).

14. There are some interesting parallels here with Kahneman's (2011) 'system 1' vs. 'system 2' though I believe the theory proposed here accredits the mind with more potential.

15. "arousal leads to enhanced encoding via increased neuronal plasticity and the creation of new synaptic connections and therefore increased likelihood of future retrieval" (Siegel 2012, p. 163). See also Phelps and Sharot (2008).

16. "emotionally arousing experiences become better remembered by a combination of direct physiological effects (perhaps on the genetic activation leading to synapses formation...) and complex cognitive effects on the encoding of memory via the retrieval, rehearsal, and reencoding process" (Siegel 2012, p. 76).

17. Kahneman's *Thinking Fast and Slow* (2011) is a book that applies various cognitive experiments, which effectively bring *embodied perception* into the reader's experience. It constitutes a 'colder' intellectual approach, nevertheless it can significantly contribute to any development of this domain of the *inner curriculum*.

CHAPTER 8

The *Curriculum of Me*

> As the material of the carpenter is wood . . . so the subject-matter of the
> art of living is each person's own life.
>
> Epictetus (2008), Discourses 1.15.2.

Embodied perception revealed the underlying 'mechanism' of bead-formation within the *inner curriculum*, and how the necklace (i.e., past, present, future) can be seen in *each* bead. The *curriculum of me* emerges from the formation of the necklace to manifest the *inner curriculum* over the horizontal time axis. The subject matter of *me* consists of all thoughts, emotions, and sensations, which I note in my brain-mind-body (and you note in yours) that make up the 'narrative self'. This narrative can appear while a student is sitting in a 'Geography lesson', yet her mind is miles away from the 'social curriculum', preoccupied with content that has little to do with it. All beads are treated here as 'knowledge', thus obviously challenging the very essence of how we have been accustomed to think of the term as we examined in Chapter 4. *Me* is who we take ourselves to be as we create ourselves actively through our thoughts and actions, or as we are created passively as we are thought into being by the mind. *Me* is that habitual, taken-for-granted sense of *agency, identity,* and *ownership* with which most of us travel throughout the day as we think, act, emote, and sense. It travels with the essential feeling that 'I am (or should be) going somewhere', 'need to do this', 'need to be that', 'get there on time'.

© The Author(s) 2017
O. Ergas, *Reconstructing 'Education' through Mindful Attention*,
DOI 10.1057/978-1-137-58782-4_8

In this chapter we are going to examine who is that *particular me*, that the 'social curriculum' treats as a *universal* unnamed 'student'. Curricular thinking as it has developed for public schooling is not about *me*. Individual difference in our 'social curriculum' is set aside in favor of learning 'shared knowledge'. It is a system that is supposedly for everyone, which means for no-one in particular. That means thinking of Sarah, John, Ruth, Ahmad, David, Morrie, Jane...as – a 'student' – collapsing many *mes* into 'society', and thus writing them out of 'education'. *Me's* idiosyncrasy as a first-person experience is left aside in favor of its *generic* ability to perceive the world *out there*. The content of this 'black box' *in here*, that's sealed from the teacher, is usually not considered to be utterly important for the process of 'education' as we have constructed it. The mind is considered to be there, ready to absorb what 'society' has planned for it, far more than to contribute content to the process itself beyond answering specific and *relevant* questions asked. In this process, idiosyncrasy, personality, subjectivity – all those 'things' that make life what it is for *you* – are set aside in favor of an idealist *objective* perspective that hovers above the plain of the sticky business of life. This 'social', third person perspective, is definitely helpful and probably inevitable when we think of mass-'education'. It maintains the order of countries and systems, but it results as the expulsion of 'self' from the curriculum, which leads to the creation of a system that can never fully succeed. Why? – for by expelling *me* from 'education', we essentially teach that the responsibility for 'education' is in the hands of the state/country/'society' – not in *my own* hands.

This expulsion of 'self' has been critiqued ferociously by numerous scholars.[1] I have been referring to it as the expulsion of mind from 'education'. Obviously we cannot expel our minds completely, for it is the mind based on which we also study the 'social curriculum'. By the expulsion of mind, I mean the expulsion of our first-person experience – the actual embodied experience of 'education' as lived. It's all those thought, sensations, and emotions to which only *you* have access. These make *here now* a living undoubted moment for you that is utterly *non-contingent*.

In order to treat *me* as a curricular domain, we must leave heavy assumptions at the door. This process of cleaning ourselves from preconceptions of 'what counts as "curriculum"/"education"', is an integral part of engaging with this *inner curriculum*. The essential argument that is to be understood is that, in tune with, or regardless of, that which goes on *out there*, we are 'educated' constantly in and by our own minds *in here*. With every thought that arises, with every reaction/response, wise or foolish, we shape and are shaped by our own brains-minds-bodies. If 'education' hopes to change us based on a conception of 'the good', all this must be incorporated in our understanding of the 'curriculum' and affect our pedagogical approach.

This follows upon the previous chapter, in which I argued that the brain-mind-body shapes and is shaped by itself; however, within *embodied perception* – much of which occurs beneath awareness – this has a far less personal flavor. Peculiar as this may sound, what I am saying here, is that *me educates me;* that all that narrative that *me* (and I mean *you*) hears throughout its day, shapes and is shaped by *me*, to create more of *me*. But I'll also say that a feature of *me* is that it will hardly think that this is the case, which makes it a peculiar domain to study. We tend to travel with the view that this is 'just who I am', hence there's really only *me* here. How can *me* study *me*, needless to say 'educate' *me?* It is here in which the *I/me* distinction described in Chapter 3 will become crucial for our methodology. You will not learn of such distinction based on our construct of the 'social curriculum' for such distinction can only arise based on a deliberate meta-pedagogical turn to *in here*. If anything, the 'social curriculum's' meta-pedagogy depletes this possibility of meaning as we saw in Chapter 5. In this chapter, based on applying a certain type of *I* to the study of *me*, we will arrive at a great paradox: *me in fact develops to work in tandem with the 'social curriculum'. It mirrors its image and comes to expel us from 'education' from within.*

The following are the themes that will be discussed in this chapter somewhat in this order:

1. A characterization of *me* based on phenomenology, neuroscience, psychological research, and self-experimentation.
2. A discussion of how *me* can be studied, and the merits of its study.
3. An analysis of the process and content of the *curriculum of me*.
4. A review of the 'educative' effects of the curricular content of *me* on our sense of *identity* and *agency* and the mind-mechanisms behind them.
5. A discussion of how *me* can become a curricular domain within 'school'.

THE CURRICULAR BOUNDARIES OF *ME* AS NARRATIVE AND ITS FOUNDATION IN *EMBODIED PERCEPTION*

Me lives and interacts with the world *out there,* which includes the 'social' domain, the environment, and by all means other *mes.* While *me's* external actions and its/his/her interactions with others are all part of 'education', the main arena on which we will focus as the *curriculum of me* is its inner manifestations – *me's* narrative experience *in here.* When referring to 'narrative', I am speaking of thinking as the vehicle of narrative. I treat thinking as a verbal process that requires language, hence it enables the creation of a narrative. Thinking can definitely be nourished by a myriad ways that are non-verbal (e.g., images, intuition, gut feelings, sense-data) and some suggest that thinking does not require language at all (McGilchrist 2009, p. 106). Here, I chose to remain as close as possible to what I believe is one's common day-to-day experience *in here,* and I suspect that many of us are mostly aware of our thinking based on the medium of language.

Our narrative, however, is *embodied.* It happens within a body that feeds it, is fed by it, and acts upon it. Despite the fact that narrative is based on the medium of words, those words have a dramatic impact on how we feel, emote, and act. No less, our emotions and sensations fuel our narrative constantly as we've learned when we examined the curriculum of embodied perception, thus do not think for a moment that *me* is some disembodied 'concept'. One does not think thought's such as 'how am I going to treat my tumor?', 'how will I pass this test?', or 'how will I get everything done on time for my wedding?' as if these are unrelated to the body within which the mind that thinks them functions. There is a thickness to present moment experience as we've already seen, and much of it has to do with the fact that the brain-mind-body is an incredibly complex and versatile dynamic system (Siegel 2012). It processes far more than the experience of which we are aware, and our stuckness on narrative tends to hide the embodied life that fuels it.

> Experience is the result of a brain-mind that has been pruned up to this moment, and prunes this moment based on its past and present condition.

As Chapter 3 depicted, what does tend to happen, however, is that we come to identify with narrative as the main source of our *identity* to the point of so-called, 'living in our minds'. In Chapter 3 I offered an operative scaffold of operative terms by which to describe this *identity* based on

Gallagher's (2000) 'narrative self', Damasio's (2010) 'autobiographical self', and James's (2007) *me*. Binding this with the previous chapter and based on neuroscience, which will come later in this chapter, I will eventually claim that,

> Whether we attend to something *out there*, or whether we attend to our narrative *in here*, our day-to-day perception works just the same. We react and respond to stimuli that seem to initiate from *out there* and from *in here*, in quite the same way. In that sense, there is no reason to believe that *out there* has a greater 'educational' influence on who we are than *in here*. We are shaped by both, yet we are not very skilled in detecting how *out there* and *in here* are perceived by the mind that colors them in the process, and is affected by them at that moment. The mind shapes present perception based on its past, and is shaped by perception. It hence projects itself into the future, with our sense of identity and experience being constantly molded in this process. However, it tends to follow habitual patterns of perception that make *me* into a rather rigid and entrenched identity. *Me* 'educates' *me* in becoming more of who it already is, and this may be a substantial 'educational' problem, if 'education' is about change for the 'better'.

Do not worry if that was too intense. We are going to break this down throughout this chapter. At this point just bear in mind that we are dealing with an incredibly complex sense of *identity* that somewhat perpetuates itself for better and for worse. Part of the agenda of this chapter is to show how this occurs, which has a lot to do with one of the biggest problems of 'education': *We are incredibly resistant to change, and usually this applies to those characteristics that we need (or hope) to change most.* 'Educational' discourse sometimes seems to focus (so as not to say *get stuck*) on a discourse of *'social'* change, but frankly I don't see how that can work until we figure out personal change. I suspect that if we take care of the latter, the rest will follow. I am not promising too much here. I am however, following the agenda of this book that is about diagnosing where and how problems arise, which in turn will assist us in finding the 'educative' path that will help ameliorate them. Following all else in this book: if a solution exists, it must be found somewhere within the matrix of mind. We can count on attention, space, and time to tell us at least part of the story.

What's the plan then? – Given the complexity of the situation, this chapter will get our hands dirty by trying something *simple* – a self-experiment (in fact a replication of a great scientific research that I will be describing later), which I introduce in many of my courses. I call it *sampling me by surprise.* It will tell you a lot about yourself, and substantially inform the reading of the rest of the book, so I really recommend trying it. Here are the instructions:

A method: Sampling me by surprise

1. Take a timer/cellphone.
2. Set its alarm-clock between eight to ten times per day for the next three days at least. Choose random times in which you know you can be bothered with three quick questions. If possible, let someone else set those times for you so that you won't know exactly when to expect the phone to buzz.
3. When the phone prompts you, all you need to do is answer the following three questions:
   a. How are you feeling? (scale between 0 (the worst ever) to 100 (couldn't be better))
   b. What are you doing? (e.g., driving, reading, talking on the phone)
   c. Are you thinking about what you are doing? – four options:
      i. Yes, thinking about what I'm doing
      ii. No, thinking a pleasant thought. (e.g., 'this is such a wonderful day')
      iii. No. thinking a neutral thought (e.g., 'got to go buy some bread/milk')
      iv. No, thinking an unpleasant thought (e.g., 'worrying about an upcoming interview')

Make yourself an empty table like Table 8.1 in which I filled a couple of samples just to give you a feel for this. Keep this table with you as you go

Table 8.1 Sampling *me* by surprise

Sample no.	How am I feeling? (0–100)	What am I doing?	Am I thinking about what I am doing?
1.	(ex. 70)	(ex. writing this book)	i (i.e. thinking about what I'm doing)
2.	55	driving	iv (i.e. worried about a deadline)
3.	65	Speaking with my child	ii
4.			

about your daily business so that you can document yourself each time the phone prompts you.

Now here's my advice: don't go on reading before you've reached at least twenty samples over the course of the next two or three days. I assure you that everything will be far clearer after you've done this, and hopefully you will even continue to collect samples as you go on reading in order to enhance the 'educative' process here.

*

OK, I hope that you have about twenty samples. Keep at it, as you read on. It will really help getting the following that will take us into neuroscience, psychology, and phenomenology. If you only have five samples (or none . . .), consider that this too, is part of your *inner curriculum*. Your decision not to go along with this, is a feature of who you are. It doesn't make you any worse or better than anyone else. It's simply the *me* that you are at this point.

*

STUDYING THE *CURRICULUM OF ME* THROUGH MINDFUL ATTENTION

As you go about your day-to-day business driving, conversing with others, reading the newspaper, eating, getting ready for work . . . you constantly have an internal life that includes embodied sensations and emotions as well as thoughts, plans, memories, 'to do' lists, hopes, dreads, and so forth. Much of this is what I call me^2 – *I mean your me not mine* (I have my own issues to deal with . . .). The main issue I want to begin with, is the problem we face when we attempt to inquire this *curriculum of me*. That in itself will teach us a lot about *me*.

If you seriously start to listen to what goes on in your mind, which is exactly what the self-experiment above asks you to do (at least when your phone prompts you), you may find that your day passes with various degrees of awareness to your thoughts, sensations, and emotions. But, there's one feature that is the hallmark of *me* – its monolithic sense of *identity* and *agency* – that sense of 'who's in charge?', 'who's calling the shots *in here*?', 'who's thinking, planning, doing, speaking, feeling?'. These are very crucial questions to ask and *me's* answer to them is unreflective. If you indeed ask *me:* 'who's in charge of your actions?' *me* will answer: 'what kind of question is that? of course I am?' – but that's the whole point. *Me* appropriates *I* and believes there's no-one around but *me*. *Me* gravitates around itself, swimming in its own narrative. It is incapable of detachment from it for you cannot detach from that with which you identify yourself. *Me is an exemplar of the pruned mind that has no clue of having been pruned.*

If you grill *me* with questions that challenge its *agency* like: 'how come you said you wanted to study for the exam, and eventually you went to have a beer with your friends?' – *me* might say: 'well I just changed my mind'. *Me* will fail to note that it is the mind that changed it... This can sound familiar or peculiar depending on your experience, but I want to make this as empirical and grounded as possible, so first, let's see how we can possibly engage in an inquiry of this *curriculum of me* given that *me* will tend to think that *it* is the one that's doing the inquiry, whereas in fact, it is *I* that is performing it.

Inquiry means studying 'something'. When that 'something' is our subjectivity a well-known problem arises concerning the validity of the 'knowledge' that emerges in such case (Varela and Shear 1999). For our purposes, what we need to have in mind, is that *me* cannot be known without both being *me* and *not* being *me*. We need to have a first-person embodied experience of that narrative that *me* is, and the sense of a narrator behind it as an *identity* – a person; a 'narrative self'. At the same time we also need some form of an objective stance against this 'narrative self', which is the object of our inquiry. This is what *I* provides us with in respect to *me*. This was developed briefly in Chapter 3 but in this chapter and the next one, we begin to probe this more deeply.

What I am getting at here, is that a deliberate and 'educative' engagement with our mind that gives rise to this phenomenon we call *me*, requires coming at this *me*-mind from a different angle. There are ways to trick *me* out of its game, and I will tell you this: if you are going along with the self-experiment above, then you have been experiencing this very shift from *me* to *I*. That is because, the one thing that *me* never considers to do is to stop its narrative and question its value. *It doesn't prompt itself eight times a day to ask the questions you were instructed to ask yourself.* That's something that *I* enables and this self-experiment invites. There are other ways to do this all of which I consider to be both research methods *and* pedagogies within the *curriculum of me*. They are an integral part of how I teach reconstructing 'education' through mindful attention at the university. In the following, I list four of these methods and describe, which ones we will be applying here:

1) *Reflective practice* – is associated with meta-cognition and positions us over the horizontal time axis. Here *I* reflects on the day-to-day experience of being *me* in the past (or perhaps the kind of person I want to be in the future). Educational literature is replete with great examples of this pedagogy (Korthagen et al. 2012; Schön 1990) and much of this chapter is written from this perspective. Day-to-day analytical problem solving belongs in this domain as well but we will not be focusing on this aspect in this book.

2) *Journaling* – Here I do not mean just any kind of writing, but rather somewhat of taking a dictation from *me* (Barbezat and Bush 2014; Brady 2007). You can think of it as externalizing the bead-to-bead narrative that's going on in your mind by putting it in writing. The less you censor the more of *me* becomes explicit. We will briefly apply this method later on in this chapter.

3) *Mindfulness practice(s)* – This will be discussed to some extent in the next chapter. Here a direct engagement with a *'contemplative I'* is invoked by which we detach ourselves from the vehicle of narrative, yet *me* will keep barging in, revealing its nature to us as we practice.

4) *Sampling me by surprise* – this is exactly what you've been doing by following the above instructions, which are taken from a brilliant experiment conducted by Matthew Killingsworth and Daniel Gilbert (2010), published in *Science*. This is a very clever research design that provides a real-time indication of what I call *me*. If we want to study *me*, we sometimes have to play this dirty trick that we're playing on it. You see, that sense of *agency*, which *me* attributes to itself is hardly plausible. If you are self-experimenting as instructed, and you roughly fall within Killingsworth and Gilbert (2010) findings, then nearly half of your samples will reveal that you were thinking of things that were unrelated to what you were doing at the moment of sampling. It is quite probable to suggest that many of those thoughts were unintentional. *They just popped up in your mind.* If you'll ask *me* 'who thought them?', he'd probably say 'well, of course I did'. We are soon going to ask some questions about this peculiar thing – this narrative that makes *me*, and with which *me*

identifies, yet without being fully in charge of its creation. For the time being, let's look more deeply at this research.

Killingsworth and Gilbert sought to examine both how much of our day is spent in a state referred to as mind-wandering that *for the time being* we shall treat as "thinking of things that are not going on around us", and what are the effects of this state on our happiness. 2250 randomly picked healthy adults, conducted the very self-experiment that you are conducting. After analyzing half a million samples, these are some of the results that Killingsworth and Gilbert reported:

a) We wander 46.9 % of our waking hours.
b) What we think, is a far more accurate indication of how we feel, than what we do.
c) Pleasant thoughts while wandering do not affect our mood, yet neutral and unpleasant thoughts lead to unhappiness.

Finally, and most importantly, as their paper title unequivocally states *A wandering mind is an unhappy mind.* "The ability to think about what is not happening is a cognitive achievement that comes at an emotional cost" (2010, p. 932).

You might not agree with these findings and I certainly do not intend to convince you that they necessarily apply to you.[3] I, in fact, encourage you to doubt these findings, but base that on continuing your sampling so that you indeed have some empirical data with which to back your claim. Eventually, our interest is in your *particular* case of *me*, so keep on going. Also, keep in mind that our exploration of *me* as part of the *inner curriculum* is not necessarily about happiness as *the* aim of education. While happiness is certainly 'good', the overall approach I described in Chapter 6 suggests that a commitment to the *inner curriculum* is more about finding *meaning now*. Within this scheme, happiness, if we agree at all about what it means, is considered as a nice 'side effect' of a deep commitment to the beads of experience. At this point I want to continue with a discussion of the actual experience of engaging in this kind of self-experimental pedagogy. This will further open *me* and *mind-wandering* as well as demonstrate the power of such pedagogical approach.

*

SAMPLING ME AS A PEDAGOGICAL PRACTICE

In the past years I've been implementing this sampling pedagogy in courses that I teach at the University, which revolve around the reconstruction of 'education', mindfulness, contemplation, and social-emotional learning. Two weeks prior to introducing Killingsworth and Gilbert's paper, I give students the exact instructions that were given to you (p. 204). Upon arriving at 30 samples they hand in a quantitative analysis of their personal outcomes, along with a reflection on the experience of monitoring their minds in this way.[4]

Pedagogically, this has proven to be brilliantly effective as a way of engaging students with a first-person inquiry of *me*. Time and again, most students are completely shocked by how un*present* they are. They never realized that so much goes on in their mind *in here* during their day-to-day, which is unrelated to what they are doing. When they get this real-life image of *me*, they become more curious about their mind and far more committed to experimenting with formal contemplative practices such as mindfulness, in which we engage in these courses.

Importantly, the self-experimentation here becomes a form of mindfulness practice in its own right. It is not a formal practice of sitting and watching one's breath for example; however, this taking *me* by surprise as we prompt it randomly by the phone, invites *I* into our day-to-day. In the midst of the automatism of *me* – of doing whatever it is that you are doing – you receive a wakeup call that asks you to attend *in here deliberately – the very meta-pedagogical turn over which the inner curriculum stands.* You are shifted from habit that usually sends you to focus on *what* you experience, to attentiveness to *how* you are experiencing. You are asked questions that:

1. Can only be answered by you.
2. Can only be answered by bringing attention *in here now* to your embodied mind (i.e., thoughts, sensations, emotions).
3. Ask you to become aware of your attention.

Several discoveries about the nature of *me* have been emerging from this pedagogical inquiry, some of which you may have noted in your own experiment. I share only some of these here, as they come up with students, and apply them toward an analytical study of *me* afterward:

1. Mindfulness – in this case defined as, paying attention to what we are doing when we are doing it – sometimes extends beyond the

sampling process: Many students report that the mere knowing in advance, that at some point the phone will prompt them, raised their alertness throughout the day, in and of itself. Some students enjoy this while others report that this is irritating.[5]

2. Assessing how I feel is tricky: Should I mark 50 as a baseline, or is it higher? Are my happiness assessments accurate? Am I assessing myself higher than I actually feel because it feels lousy to externalize my unhappiness on this chart? Some discover that their overall feeling, hardly changes from one sample to the next. Others are all over the place . . .

3. Introspection is unsettling: Sometimes I don't know what I'm thinking at all . . . I can't tell whether I am thinking about what I'm doing or not. What does thinking about the doing mean anyhow?

4. Who's behind all this: Why do I have all these thoughts, and who's generating them?

I do not promise answers to all of these questions that all touch the foundations of the *inner curriculum*, but I do wish to examine this field more analytically. The following sections of the chapter intertwine conceptual and scientific analysis of this curricular domain, which tend to be more demanding and dense, with sections that allow a little air in, in which I integrate the former with curriculum theory. Though much of what you'll read has been published in peer-reviewed journals, some of the suggestions made are by all means bold. Now that you have some raw data of your *particular me* (and by all means keep sampling yourself), you will be able to critically assess whatever I propose in the following.

*

Mind Wandering, *Self-Reflection*, and *Reflective Practice*

Reflect for a moment about your more casual thinking life in those moments when you are *not* attempting to seriously solve a problem (which as mentioned belongs in the domain of *reflective practice*). Your sampling may enable you to identify two modes of this far more casual domain of thinking. They might feel more like a spectrum that runs between:

Active deliberate thinking, and *Passive* non-deliberate/spontaneous thinking.

To begin with, this is one flaw in Killingsworth and Gilbert's experiment, which I intentionally didn't mention before. I wonder if you noticed this yourself, but the experiment doesn't quite cover the above distinction. What we are studying when sampling our narrative is not necessarily an indication of mind-*wandering* as I will be defining it here – a mode of *passive non-*deliberate thinking. We may be sampling thoughts that could have been deliberate and intentional. Think of the difference this way: you can be driving and mind-wandering without even noting *that* you are not present to the driving, or you could be driving yet *deliberately* thinking out a problem that you deemed more important than focusing on the empty highway ahead of you (I don't recommend this... but it *does* happen). There is also the option that you didn't really choose to think about this problem, but some thought came up and you felt compelled to engage in this internal problem-solving. These are sometimes subtle differences, but they open up *three* different states of mind that we must distinguish between in order to explain the varieties of the *curriculum of me*:

First, I'm going to suggest something bold: *me's* thinking life is mostly summed in two modes of thinking and their embodied effects. I call them *mind-wandering* and *self-reflection*, and they both differ substantially from what I will call *reflective practice*. Let's get this latter state out of the way first:

Reflective practice is what we are doing right *now*. We are engaged *deliberately* and *critically* with the subject matter of *me*. This entire chapter builds on this capability. This kind of thinking has a substantially different sense of *agency* behind it. It's not *me* that does it, but rather what I call a *reflective I*. This means that there is an internal split within you in which *I* detaches from a problem (in this case for example the problem of *me*), examines *it*, and can come up with a conceptual structure of *me* as a 'curriculum' just as we are doing now. We will discuss this *reflective I* as a curricular domain in and of itself in the next chapter, for this *reflective I* has its issues as well, and this is where this book will substantially transgress beyond a good share of 'educational' discourse. So think of *reflective practice* as a method by which we are now going to explain *mind-wandering* and *self-reflection* as the two modes of the *curriculum of me*:

1. *Mind-wandering*: While you sample yourself you might notice that the extent to which you are aware of what you are thinking of, varies

significantly. Sometimes you catch yourself 'spaced out' to the point in which you might not even know what you were thinking about. Eloquently put, neuroscientists Smallwood et al. (2007b) refer to this as a state in which 'the lights are on but no-one's home'. We will call the state in which you think unintentionally and you are unaware *that* you are thinking – *mind-wandering*. Wandering is defined by the lack of awareness *that* the mind is wandering. Only in retrospect you acknowledge having been wandering (and that counts as a moment of *mindfulness* in fact). So mind-wandering is *passive* unintentional thinking in which one is unaware of the *process* of thinking. However as Smallwood and Andrews-Hanna (2013) put it in the title of their paper "not all minds that wander are lost". I will interpret this to mean, that there are times at which you may not be aware *that* you are wandering, but you *can* be aware of the *content* about which you are wandering.

2. *Self-reflection* is trickier because it is confused with *reflective practice*. In *self-reflection* you are fully there *thinking* but it's *me* doing the thinking and there is no *I* in the picture. Here *me* is sure that it is running the show and it is sure that it is running the show as the show should be running. It hearkens back to Chapter 3 – here *me's illusion of omniscience* that emerges from the structure of the origin of attention, takes center stage. *Me* believes that it sees reality as such including the veridicality of its own thoughts. It is absorbed in reaffirming its *identity*. In *self-reflection* you are your thoughts and your thoughts are you. There is no detachment, but rather a full identification with whatever the mind produces and there is this energy of 'feeling that I am right' underneath it fueling the content and reasserting the validity of the 'thinker' simultaneously.

Simply put, what I am saying is, that during your day-to-day life, much of your thinking life consists of 'narrative self' (*me*) thoughts. Most (if not all) of them are based on one of two processes: mind wandering or *self-reflection*. A *reflective I* is there in our day-to-day experience only in those cases in which we can detach from the content, which can lead to a non-habitual place that can open room for novelty rather than to 'more of the same'. This latter process can be a deliberate *reflective practice* in which *I* engages with *me* and in fact seeks to 'educate' it as

Table 8.2 Agency and identity in the *inner curriculum*

Mode of thought	Mind wandering	Self-reflection	Reflective practice
Name of sensed agency	Me	Me	I
Sense of agency	Passive	Active	Active
State of being	Identified	Identified	Detached
Type of engagement with *curriculum of me*	Non-deliberate	Non-deliberate	Deliberate

we will see. However, the blindness of *me* that I will be describing in this chapter concerns *me's* belief that *self-reflection* equals *reflective practice*. Or simply put:

me thinks it's I.

Table 8.2 offers a structured way of looking at this. It depicts two modes of engagement with the *curriculum of me*, which at this point might not yet make sense to you, but I hope that by the end of this chapter and possibly the next, it will.

So we have an initial analytical structure, which must be *questioned* and *tested* by your sampling, as I flesh it out throughout this chapter. The first thing I want to do, before we explore what neuroscientists say about this, is to provide an account of *me's* curricular content.

*

THE CURRICULAR CONTENT OF *ME*

Let's look at what it feels like to mind-wander and self-reflect. I want to offer a few distinctions here that will help us understand what these states entail, and how they reflect ways in which the *inner curriculum* shapes who we are. The first distinction follows the above and has to do with the *process* of thinking versus its *content*:

(a) process – is characterized by *how* the thoughts emerge (e.g., mind-wandering, *self-reflection*). This will have to do with the sense of *agency* behind the thinking. You can think of it as the *teacher* and the pedagogy she/he/it applies. When we *mind-wander* or *self-reflect* that teacher is *me*. When we engage in *reflective practice*, the teacher is *I*.

(b) content – is characterized by *what* we think about (e.g., 'what a boring lesson', 'I need to get home early today'). This is the subject matter. If the content comes up during *mind-wandering* or *self-reflecting* that would be *me*-content.[6]

We will focus on the content for quite some time before we get to the process. We are asking: what kind of *'me curricular* subject matter' do we experience? What are the broad categories to which we can divide the content of our thoughts while *mind-wandering/self-reflecting*? To get an empirical sense of this, along with sampling *me* by surprise, in my courses I use *journaling* as well as *mindfulness practice*. Here we will focus on *journaling*. These are the instructions I give my students:

> Please write down today's date and the time, and during the next five minutes write whatever you are thinking, feeling, sensing, emoting right now. There is absolutely no right or wrong involved here. This is a personal journal. No one is going to read what you wrote, unless you wish to share it with someone. Try to write whatever comes to mind without censoring; as if you are taking dictation from someone else.

Many of my courses begin with this practice. Usually in the first lesson students are somewhat perplexed when encountering this requirement. The perplexity is an indication of the effect of our monolithic meta-pedagogy that has expelled the mind from 'education', for 'education' has been constructed in students' minds as having to do with reading others' accounts, but not their own. Right from the first lesson I cultivate an attitude by which we treat these personal journals with utter respect. These will be our main textbooks in the course and they will become the main reference for final projects in these courses. We are basically externalizing our 'narrative self', garnering data for a qualitative analysis of *me* and perhaps later of *I*.

What I recommend is that you actually do this too. After a few days of writing you will be able to examine the thought-content of *me* as the subject matter that your mind produces. It is less an indication of *mind-wandering/self-reflecting*, because there is far more awareness in this process; however, it will still be helpful and enable you to corroborate or refute my next observations.

*

I do not have access to your journal, but I can offer a number of personal reflections of famous figures who seem to have described *their* personal experience of the curricular subject matter of *me*.

Here's John Dewey: "[M]ore of our waking life than we should care to admit, even to ourselves, is likely to be whiled away in this inconsequential trifling with idle fancy and unsubstantial hope" (Dewey 1997b, p. 2). Elsewhere he claimed that our 'inner-life' is,

> [T]he home of aspirations and ideals that are noble and that may in time receive fulfillment as well as of figments and airy nothings. . . . It affords a realm in which king and court fool prince and pauper, meet as equals. It is subject-matter for the philosopher as well as for the rebuffed and wistful. (Dewey 1958, p. 228)

While some might think that both the extent of wandering and the full gamut of our inner life may be a symptom of the stresses of modern living, here is poet John Milton showing that the minds of people who lived in the seventeenth century may have functioned quite similarly:

> The mind is its own place, and in it self
> Can make a Heav'n of Hell, a Hell of Heav'n.[7]

If you care for a wrier and starker version attributed to humorist Josh Billings (a contemporary of Mark Twain): "I am a very old man and I have suffered many troubles in my life most of which never happened."

None of the above apply the terms *me, mind-wandering*, or *self-reflection*, but I think that, more or less, they capture the kind of field we are speaking of when discussing the *curriculum of me*. If you manage to recognize yourself at least in some of these, then you know what this is about. If Josh Billings' saying above made you laugh, it must be your own first-person experience that enables you to relate to it. Following the questions I posed in the beginning of this section – what kind of '*me curricular* subject matter' do we have here? – and the above examples from Dewey, Milton, and Billings, I want to make more general state-ments about this curriculum. The matrix of mind that we have been using to reconstruct 'education' will come to our aid as usual. See if this captures what you have in your journal as well:

1. In terms of time: *The 'curriculum of me' dwells in the horizontal time axis. Me* is extremely busy thinking about what is not going on *here*

and now based on the mind's incredible capacity for 'mental time traveling' (Tulving 1985) – planning ahead or remembering the past. You are driving *now* yet attending to thoughts about the meeting that will happen *then*. You're conversing with someone *now* but concerned with what you forgot to do this morning (and figuring out how you will make up for that in the future).

2. In terms of space: *The 'curriculum of me' happens in here but it is mostly preoccupied with things out there and how me relates to them* – A good share of what *me* does, is assess where it stands in the 'social' arena. *Me's* narrative will thus revolve around the kind of relationships it has with others, speculating on others' perspectives ('what are they thinking about *me*') and making statements that universalize who *me* is: 'I always say things like this . . . ', 'she always does this to me', 'life is unfair'. These can certainly be positive thoughts such as self-assessments – 'this job is awesome', 'I am such a lucky guy'.[8]

When looking at the above, if we set aside the actual 'subject matter' and 'curricular design' and focus only on the orientation of attention in space and time – the *how*, rather than the *what*, we get a peculiar picture.

> Me is the inner expression of the structure of the 'social curriculum's' dwelling in the horizontal time axis, not in *now*. Paradoxically, while me is part of an inner curriculum much of the content of that 'curriculum' revolves around the 'social' *out there*; measuring myself against the yardstick of the 'social normative map' (Chapter 4, p. 112) or against 'social norms' in general.

This leads us to say something about the reconstruction of 'education' before we move on. The above may sound peculiar to some but we mustn't be surprised by this. I have been arguing that you will find nothing in the 'social curriculum' that is not a feature of the mind. In Chapter 3 I pointed to the birth of *me* out of the 'social narrative', and here you can see how the two mirror each other. The reason why the 'social curriculum' holds as it does, and why our monolithic meta-pedagogy works so neatly to send us *out there*, is that these are features of our individual minds. Our minds willingly participate in their own expulsion from 'education'. That makes sense as well for,

> "Education is a mind-making process", but 'education' is made by minds. The mind will find itself at the end of the external endeavors it creates.

'Educational' thinking seems to be too concerned with the end of 'education'. We need to be at least as concerned with where everything begins – embodied minds.

Before we turn to examine why and how this curriculum emerges. I want to position this discourse more scientifically within neuroscience.

*

ME'S WANDERING/*SELF-REFLECTING* BRAIN

I'm not sure if saying that brain and mind are sides of one coin is appropriate or correct, but I think Daniel Siegel's (2012) treating brain and mind as 'two primes' (alongside relationships as a third prime) to the understanding of experience, is of great help. What it means is that brain and mind are linked in such a way that whatever we examine as a change in one, helps us to articulate change in the other. Very colloquially: changes in neuron firings imply changes in first-person experience and vice versa. Neither explains the exact nature of the other, but each sheds light on our overall understanding of our brain and mind. Despite the fact that it was mentioned a number of times in this book, I am repeating this because *me* is an expression of habituation and automation and you can think of this either from the perspective of the mind's phenomenology or from the neuronal brain's 'behind the scenes' picture.

For several years neuroscientists were preoccupied with studying what the brain does when given a specific task to perform (e.g., solving a problem, tracking signs on a screen to test attention and eye movements, watching images). Examining a brain that is *not* given a task did not seem like a very productive thing to do. At the same time, it was clear that there needs to be some kind of baseline activity of the brain against which changes in brain function will be studied when a subject is given a task. Furthermore, at some point neuroscientists began to detect that the brain remains incredibly active even during those times at which it is given nothing in particular to think about or to do. What we would normally think of as a 'resting state', as this is sometimes referred to in neuroscience, appears to be nothing like 'rest'. In 2001 Marcus Raichle and colleagues rigorously studied this domain and gave this 'resting state' a name I believe to be far more appropriate – *the default mode network* (DMN) (Buckner et al. 2008; Raichle 2015; Raichle et al. 2001). The DMN was described as, "an organized, baseline *default mode of brain function* that is suspended during specific goal directed behaviors" (Raichle et al. 2001, p. 676, emphasis added). It is an 'external-task-inhibited network', which means that its activity is reduced when we engage in tasks that are associated with the world *out there*. The term 'default' is highly appropriate a choice for describing at least some of the DMN's activity. Just as your computer defaults into screen-saving mode after a certain period of inactivity, our brains default into the functioning of the DMN throughout our day and especially when appraising external events as boring, or unstimulating.[9]

To a great extent the story of *me* that I tell here corresponds with some of what is known about the DMN. How so? – The default mode network's functioning has been strongly associated with *mind-wandering*, which has been given several other names like daydreaming, stimulus independent thinking, and task-unrelated thinking (Baars 2010; Mason et al. 2007; Singer 1966). Both mind-wandering and *self-reflection* are considered to be *narrative* self-related processes (Andrews-Hanna 2012; Northoff et al. 2006; Northoff and Bermpohl 2004; Qin and Northoff 2011). The latter are concerned with thoughts like: 'I need to do this or that', 'What did he just say to me?', 'I have to spend more time with the kids', 'I'm looking forward to the weekend' . . . whether it occurs passively as we walk or drive somewhere (mind wandering) or whether we are engrossed in it more deliberately (*self-reflection*) – all this is created by *me* and creates *me* at one and the same time. The research in this domain is hardly decisive, and there is more to discover than is known, but let's look at what some of the research has to say about how *mind-wandering* affects us.

*

THE EFFECTS OF MIND-WANDERING ON *ME*: A JUSTIFICATION FOR THE CURRICULUM OF *ME*

Mind-wandering and *self-reflection* are perfectly natural phenomena. On the one hand, some consider mind-wandering to be a remarkable human capability (McMillan et al. 2013; Singer 1966). It is a natural consequence of our evolution, that some view as the brain's 'proactive' way of making predictions as to what shall happen next in our life based on the past (Bar 2009), create simulations, and prepare itself for the future. It's as if the brain-mind is indeed participating in an 'education' that is a preparation for life. When your mind wanders, you maintain information, interpret, respond to, and even predict environmental demands. This may actually enhance learning, reasoning, and planning (Schacter et al. 2007), it can create cohesion between your past and future (Suddendorf and Corballis 2007), and help you construct mental models (Sood and Jones 2013). Some suggest that this facilitates creativity as if you are "zoning out" of a troubling task and you hit the "refresh" button (Schooler et al. 2011). It can help one plan the future (Baird et al. 2011) and is suggested to lead to improved problem-solving (Baird et al. 2012).[10]

On the other hand, while I certainly have not read all the research in this field, even despite the above possible advantages, much of the research points to negative effects of mind-wandering. Before I offer a brief review of these effects, I'll add that I am not quite sure that scientists themselves are careful enough in the ways in which they define this state. In fact, much of the above and the later-mentioned researches, are not rigorous enough in how they distinguish mind-wandering from *self-reflection*. Furthermore, some of the above mentioned advantages might not be the result of what I refer to as mind-wandering and *self-reflection* but rather of mindfulness and contemplative practice paradoxical as that might seem. (This is how I would interpret notions such as 'positive mind-wandering' that some view as a form of 'practice' of 'constructive daydreaming' (MacMillan et al. 2013)). I will later discuss this in more detail but I argue that mind-wandering is quite like falling asleep as far as how much control we have over it. We don't fall asleep as much as sleep falls on us when we create the right conditions for it. Mind-wandering and *self-reflection* are elaborated here as domains in which *I* as a 'core self' collapses into *me*. We are basically not really in charge of these processes because *me*, as I develop later, is not a veridical *agent*.

Simply put, knowing what you are doing when you are doing it, is a substantial component of the momentary *state of mindfulness*, and having your body do things while thinking unwittingly of other things is the opposite – it's mindlessness or mind-wandering. This sounds like a binary, but it is more of a spectrum for we have varying degrees of awareness to what we think and do. If you keep up your sampling you will find that in many cases you will have trouble determining whether you are wandering/ *self-reflecting* or perhaps you are just engaging in an activity not thinking at all. From our 'educational' perspective, the punchline is that,

you have trouble saying what your mind is up to.

Which leads me to ask:

If you – who supposedly has direct access to your mind – have trouble reporting what your mind is up to, how can 'society' that has no such privileged position, be expected to 'educate' this mind without your aid?

That said, I view the negative effects of mind-wandering, that seem to be the theme of the majority of research in this field, as a more accurate frame of reference for the way I treat mind-wandering and *self-reflection* in this chapter.[11] If indeed these effects are more pervasive, then this only adds to my above suggestion that the mind must be far more active in its own 'education'.

Broadly, the study of the negative effects of mind-wandering can be divided into three strands that shed light on *me* from different angles:

a) Mind wandering as a cognitive failure that compromises our performance – That is the case in which we try to focus on a task yet we 'space out'. This position is clearly understandable and much required, but it doesn't take us far in the task of positioning the mind at the center of curriculum and pedagogy. Consider that if this is our perspective all we are doing is expressing our bias toward the wisdom in our 'social curriculum', hence solely focusing on this perspective might exacerbate the expulsion of the mind from the 'curriculum' and its further submitting to 'society'. We're trying to understand how *me* is shaped by this wandering, and not only what we're missing *out there*. Thus far more important for our case is strand b:

b) The emotional costs of a non-present mind – While our spontaneous and undirected thoughts may serve all those positive effects mentioned above, for many people these thoughts bring along virtual catastrophic scenarios, worrying, brooding, and at times even depression (Nolen-Hoeksema et al. 2008). From the perspective examined in Chapter 7 that makes much sense. If indeed my brain 'decides' to wander and prepare itself for my future, then it may be more useful to practice possible disasters and failures rather than successes, as indeed Sood and Jones (2013) suggested. If our brains have developed as mechanisms the primary concerns of which are to survive and reproduce – then the primary theme of our wandering would be simulating threats and dangers and finding a mate. Thus much research associates mind-wandering with low mood (Smallwood et al. 2007a, Smallwood et al. 2009) rumination and depression (Berman et al. 2011; Segal et al. 2002), unhappiness (Fell 2012; Killingsworth and Gilbert 2010), and even a tendency to be less compassionate (Jazaieri et al. 2016).

c) The effects of practices that are geared to reduce mind-wandering such as mindfulness practice (Mrazek et al. 2012). Given the negative effects of mind-wandering a series of researches have been showing that mindfulness practice(s), have been found to reduce wandering time, leading to reports of reduction in depression, and greater well-being (Tang et al. 2015). This strand of research shows us that a meta-pedagogical turn that orients attention *in here* based on mindfulness (and other) practices can introduce changes in *me* some of which will be mentioned in the concluding chapter.

To sum our scientific-excursion, mind-wandering and *self-reflection* seem to affect us for the worse more than for the better. However, more importantly, these are processes that seem to shape our sense of identity, how we behave, and how we engage with the world. They 'educate' us. Quite interestingly, they do so while blinding us to the fact that this is the case. The proof of that is that we don't tend to think of them in terms of 'education'. Whichever our conception of 'education' as a process of development toward a 'good', it would make sense for us to become far more interested in the processes that are involved in this, including by all means, those that occur beneath our awareness. Our task is then to explore how do mind-wandering and *self-reflection* 'educate' us, and how come we are blind to this process? Let's return to the thread developed earlier on, to see how the *curriculum of me* mirrors 'society' from within, to yield our tendency to escape *here* and *now* and seek meaning *out there* and *then*.

*

Me, 'Society' and the 'the Insufficiency of Now': The Fuel of the *Curriculum of Me*

The question that arises is what fuels the *curriculum of me*? What sends me into mind-wandering and self-reflecting? Just imagine this possibility:

> You ride on the subway or drive to work, and you only engage in *that*. That is, you simply *are* without having the urge to fill your are-ness with a narrative at all.

That's not what normally happens does it? Usually, if we commute by subway, we will 'use' such times to text someone or surf the web *out there*, or *mind-wander/self-reflect in here*. How and why does this happen and why does this inner chatter become such a main source for our sense of *identity* and *agency*?

To be sure, I am not attempting to nullify *me*. With no narrative by which we can express some form of an identity and autobiography, we simply will not be able to function. Furthermore, this 'automated' kind of functioning is clearly necessary for day-to-day living. We also need a sense of coherency that connects who we were a moment ago, with where we are going next, which seems to be an aspect of this 'narrative self'. My interest is an 'educative' one. I am questioning whether all that goes on as this narrative *me* is conducive to the mind and to 'society'? This is about making *me* into a more explicit 'curriculum'.

> This is about taking more charge of what is happening in my life; over those things that we tend to think of as beyond our control to the point in which our minds have pruned themselves to believe that this is how the world was made, and not how they themselves make it.

I suspect that at least some of the *curriculum of me* works against our wish for meaning and thriving. To discuss this I want to reposition us in Chapter 3 in which I depicted *me* as a being that is born and develops in and from the 'social'. Its problems are hence no other then the internalization of problems of 'society', and it is back to 'society' that these problems are projected by it. The two mutually edify each other in a dance of reflections justly called, a 'hall of mirrors'.

The sense that I am 'empty of meaning' mentioned in Chapter 6 (p. 156) comes to haunt us here again, for I argue that *me* is fed by a constant sense that 'something is missing'.[12] I call this the *insufficiency of now*, that creates a constant need to escape this moment, seek the next, and view the current moment as a mere means to an end. The reason why we do not tend to realize this is because:

> *we are too busy obeying this dictum.*

Recall that our conscious awareness is utterly limited. We can't experience a void within us while we are busy filling it up. Here I'll focus on two sources of this problem that manifest the brain-mind's tendency to *default* into mind-wandering and *self-reflection*. These are two extremes that characterize the overall sense that undergirds *me's* relationship with time. I locate this within our 'educational' system; however, this reflects our overall 'social narrative'. *Me's* life tends to oscillate between: too much to do, and too little to do.

1. *Having too much to do: overstress* – A common claim of most teachers and students and a sickness of 'society' writ large (Kabat-Zinn 2005). This overstress arrives at the mind from *out there* based on the 'social curriculum' as much as it emerges from *in here* as our *self-reflection* and mind-wandering fuel it with potential thought-content.
2. *Having too little to do: boredom* – Paradoxically, within the same 'educational' system that overstresses itself, boredom is a pervasive claim of students (and perhaps teachers as well).

These two poles of a spectrum are expressions of this sense that 'something is missing' – *a perceived insufficiency of now* that spirals the co-creation of the hall of mirrors between mind and 'society'; between the *curriculum of me* and the 'social curriculum'. Either something is missing, because I have too many things that need doing, thus the results of these acts are missing from *now* (or perhaps I am missing more time to catch up with everything), or something is missing because there's nothing (interesting/meaningful) to do *now*. The 'social curriculum' fills this void by providing us with things to do, but when our attention turns *in here* spontaneously (that is, not for an intentional reflective problem-solving), *me* happily steps in to fill the void immediately.

> Much of the phenomenon of time as a horizontal time axis stems from the sense that 'something is missing', which fuels mind wandering and *self-reflection* that fill this void.

Self-reflection – more of a 'too much to do mode' – sometimes compulsively nags *me* to get things done – 'need to do that', 'need to be this'. Mind-wandering – more of a 'nothing interesting to do' mode – nags *me* into existence to fill the gaps of boredom through narrative. The consequence of this is that,

> positioned between the 'social curriculum' and the 'curriculum of me' we get no rest.

It is worth of course asking, who is the one that's not getting any rest, and who is the one that can give it rest. Whoever it is, he, she, or it, must be found in this body and this mind.

The above is one way of explaining the kind of restless 'educational' experience the results of which is the 'society-*me* hall of mirrors'. It is also an explanation of how suffering and unhappiness arise in our life based on *me's* relationship with *time*. As David Loy proposes:

> Time originates from our sense of lack and our projects to fill in that lack... Uncomfortable with our sense-of-lack today, we look forward to that day in the future when we will feel truly alive; we use that hope to rationalize the way we have to live now, a sacrifice which then increases our demands of the future. (2000, p. 29)

We fill the void either by the 'social curriculum' or through the *curriculum of me*. However, both reflect that same metaphysical error of attempting to be in the future when all we can have is *now*. We've seen this from the 'social curriculum's' side of things in Chapters 4 and 5, but here you see how this works from within our minds. Mind-wandering and *self-reflection content* express *me's* impossible wish to escape *now*. How? – during these times *me* advertently or inadvertently attempts to work out the *future* (e.g., 'When I get there I'll tell them I'm not willing to do all the hard work for them...', 'I know I'm going to do well on that job interview tomorrow') or relive (and perhaps correct) the *past* (e.g., 'I should have told them that I don't want to do this job....', 'He shouldn't have said that to me...'). Sometimes, within these states of mind, we will also encounter *me* actively creating its solid *identity* as it will make generalizations on who it has been and who it always will be (e.g., 'I always barge into conversations without checking if people actually want to hear what I have to say...', 'teachers always pick on me', 'I can't stand history lessons').

The claim I make is ambivalent. On the one hand, this mental 'time traveling' at the expense of *now* is absolutely necessary. We will find life quite impossible without connecting ourselves to the past, and having plans for the future. On the other hand,

> if our experience of future and past are bound by *me*, the tacit teaching we get is the same one we receive from the 'social curriculum': *now* is never good enough so we'd better get going to *then*.

Whether we are busy with external doing, or busy *in here* with plans to do things, *me* is a restless being. No less, it is blind to its nature because,

> Busy as we are being busy, we never quite get a chance to stop and ask why run all the time? Where too, and who is running this show of 'running'?

A clear question lurks behind: is there an alternative at all? The quick answer is that there certainly *is*. In fact, I suspect that you sometimes experience the alternative. But there's a long explanation to this that will extend in to the next chapter. It begins with thinking of this in a structured way. Basically there is a spectrum between two kinds of relationships with time that is available to us – being *here now* and wishing to be 'done with this moment' and getting to *then*. They could be framed between *doing and being* and just as equally; between the experience of the horizontal time axis and the discrete moments of *now*. Much of our lives seems to be spent in the former – *me's insufficiency of now*.

> The wish to be done with the doing of something, or its being viewed merely as a means, is basically to engage in wishful thinking that reflects our aspiration to be elsewhere on the horizontal time axis – elsewhere then *now* that is perceived as too empty or too full. This is a metaphysical error that is very much the story of *me*.

How will you identify this? – Recall Chapter 7. In every moment there is a certain *state of being* that will tell the story of how we relate to the activities in which we are engaged. No matter what we are doing (e.g., studying for an exam, driving a friend, attending a lecture, jogging, waiting in line at the bank), we always have some emotion the content of which discloses to us whether we enjoy the activity or not; whether we would like to continue engaging in it or not. The question this all comes down to is whether we view our activity as a means to an end, or is it an end in itself. Existentially, this answers to the question: 'are we *here now*, or are we constantly fueled by the wish to be at another time or another place?'. For example, I can study for an exam *so that* I'll get an A, *so that* I can get to college, *or* I can study and become absorbed in the subject matter regardless of the grade; I can give my friend a ride home, although I really wish she wouldn't burden me with this, as opposed to 'I know it's a burden but I can focus on this as an act of goodness'. I can write an academic book *so that* I will get tenure or I can write it for this is *meaningful right now*.

The above are all examples of two sides of a spectrum of relationships with time between which we oscillate. This relationship is always there if you care to examine it. The horizontal time axis is experienced whenever we are engaged in a mode of wanting to get somewhere other than where we are at; to be at a time that is not *now*, as we do things that are only a means for something better and the cash value of which we expect only in the future. *Now* is paradoxically experienced when *time is forgotten*. This begins to scratch the surface of the next chapter, for there is endless talk about 'being in the moment', 'living the *now*' etc. I suspect that much of it is misunderstood.

> *Now* should be italicized but not be romanticized. When it is romanticized it becomes a 'then' in disguise – thrust into the horizontal time axis as a new ideal for wishful thinking.[13]

I am not advocating *now* as an ideal. What I am advocating is a shift from identifying with the *content* of the bead to its bear existence. What emerges from the above, is that the horizontal time axis in which we 'dwell' as *me's* much of our lives, turns out to be a less favorable abode. If the underlying affect accompanying the activity in which I am engaged in the *present* is a wish to 'get on with it', that means that I am in the present, but would in fact prefer to be in the future. How meaningful can *that* be?

Our mind-wandering and *self-reflection* are ways in which *me* experiences itself over the horizontal time axis. Since *me* is identified with thought-content, and that content almost always points somewhere in time, *me* is essentially a constant escape from *here* and *now*. When we extrapolate many beads of *me* into a necklace of *me* we get a sense of life lived on two tracks: the one lived in practice, and the one lived in our theoretical wishful thinking. It is encapsulated in that famous John Lennon saying that 'life is that thing that passes when you make plans to do other things'. This urge to be done with things could apply to engagements that span from moments to years. It spans from the minor day-to-day acts of making sandwiches and rushing one's kids to school, to the years of sitting through high-school, BA, MA, PhD – it could actually apply to life as a bulk, as depressing as this might sound. If much of our lives are ridden with that urge to be done with what we are doing, or what awaits us tomorrow, we experience that as a life that is difficult, hard, laborious, and most problematic – meaningless. This meaninglessness is the disappointment that we have with the way things are, and our sense that they ought have been different. Where do we come up with the idea that they ought have been different? – 'society' and *me*:

> 'Narrative self' and 'social narrative' work in tandem from *in here* and *out there* respectively, 'educating' us toward *out there* and to *then*.

The problem of 'education' is *our* problem; 'society's' and *me's* problem is an attention that is stuck over the horizontal time axis and turned *out there*. It is sustained by the workings of the *curriculum of me* and the 'social curriculum'. Meta-pedagogy and meta-curriculum as described in Chapters 4 and 5, are the reflection of how 'education' is created from mind to 'society' and from 'society' to mind: a vicious cycle indeed.

Since most of what we do in 'education' has to do with thinking from the 'social' side of things, which yields some unsatisfactory results, we must examine how this mechanism works from within the mind itself. We've focused so far more on the curricular *content* of *me*. It is time to move deeper, and look at the mechanisms of the *process* in order to diagnose what sustains this unwitting 'educational' process. This may help us find the way out.

*

THE *CURRICULUM OF ME* AS THE PROCESS OF AGENCY-IDENTITY-OWNERSHIP FORMATION

Me as an 'Agent'

As I suggested earlier there seem to be two kinds of *processes* involved in the sense of *agency*, which is associated with *me*: mind-wandering, in which we do not feel ourselves to be initiating the thinking, and *self-reflection*, in which we have a strong sense that we are the ones who are thinking the thoughts. Exploring these two processes first, will assist us in further characterizing how *me's* sense of *identity* emerges based on them.

I suggest that these two modes of narrative-thinking create a similar sense of false *me-agency*, yet in two different ways:

> In *self-reflection* the sense of agency 'precedes' the thinking. *Me* feels itself to be actively generating thoughts. In mind-wandering the sense of agency follows the thoughts. Thoughts are generated passively by the mind, and *me* owns them in retrospect.

Phrased poetically:

> In *self-reflection me* creates itself through thoughts; in mind-wandering *me* is thought into being.

I realize that this is a very peculiar idea, which takes quite some getting used to. Do continue testing it as you go about sampling yourself and journaling if possible. You can add one more question to the three questions you were instructed to ask (i.e., how am I feeling? what am I doing? what am I thinking about?). If you catch yourself thinking, ask '*how* did this thought arise? did I think it *deliberately*, or did it just 'come to mind?''

I suggest that during *self-reflection me* senses itself to be the agent behind the process and the content. The agency 'comes first' so to speak. During mind wandering, however, it's the other way around. Neither the process nor the content are felt to be initiated or guided by *me*, nor is *me* always aware of the thought content. However, *me owns* the content in retrospect as *me* realizes it had been wandering, which as suggested above, may be a very brief moment of mindfulness in which one suddenly realizes that his mind was gone.[14] It is a peculiar mechanism that I later describe as the pedagogical mechanism of *me's* entrenching the mind in *me*. Importantly, remember that mind-wandering and *self-reflection* flow into each other subtly, and are not clear cut boundaries that *me* cares to distinguish between. It is only when *I* enters the picture that such discernment becomes available.

The above leads me to suggest that:

> *mind-wandering and self-reflection both reflect an illusory sense of agency.*

The case of mind-wandering, in which we do not choose to think at all, is more obvious. You do not will the wandering (at least not how I define this state). It falls on you and you awaken to find yourself having been wandering.

The case of *self-reflection* is less obvious. Here is how I would explain it: Imagine yourself right after a heated argument (or remember to check this next time you get angry). As you go on with your business with the repercussions of the event probably running in your mind. You keep reasserting how right you were to say what you said and how wrong the other party was (remember the 'illusion of omniscience' from Chapter 3?). In the midst of your reaffirming your position, the question we need to ask is this: *can you switch to thinking of an object of your choice deliberately and for long*? Furthermore, imagine someone next to you telling you to just 'calm down'. Keeping at bay the urge to slap him or her in the face, you will probably feel that 'calming down' is exactly what you shouldn't be doing because you were right and anger is the very exact emotion to be experiencing and expressing right now. Whether the anger is right or wrong is not my point. The fact of the matter is that only if you can shift your attention elsewhere upon shear will and keep at it, can you be sure that someone worthy of the term *agent*, is at play here.

Agency is more likely the domain of some form of *I* as we shall see in the next chapter. *Me* is problematic as far as agency goes. Its main problem is not that its agency is illusory, but rather that it thinks that it is real. It is that same two-layered blindness discussed in Chapter 3. Many of our habitual day-to-day actions are effectively performed with no need for special care, yet believing that there is an actual *agent* there deliberately performing them, is an illusion. If you want an indication of this then try the following:

> Think of how you brushed your teeth today. Can you recall that moment at all? Can you say what you thought about while brushing? Do you recall choosing to brush your teeth and the deliberation behind moving your hand to do so? Just for the heck of it: recall your breakfast. Do you remember the actual chewing, and the actual movements of your hands to bring food into your mouth?

I am not saying that remembering the hand-movements while brushing the teeth is necessary information. I am only saying that we are hardly the *agents* we think we are. That is part of who *me* is, (or thinks it is). It's a peculiar person that's *in here* (in some sense) that accredits itself with far more *agency* and veridicality than empirical testing should warrant. It is our manifestation as pruned minds that are blind to their pruning. We will revisit this at length in the next chapter.

Me's Identity

In his book *The Master and His Emissary*, Iain McGilchrist (2009) describes how the two hemispheres of the brain function differently to yield two entirely different worldviews; *in fact personalities*. Many neuroscientists today are very suspicious of left/right hemisphere language, so I will set this aspect aside. What I do believe, however, is that the two personalities that emerge from McGilchrist's analysis apply neatly to *me* and *I*. In the following I will focus on *me* and that will also serve to characterize *I* as its negative accent and as a preparation for Chapter 9.

Me's identity (which in McGilchrist's analysis would mean a rather left-brainish person) is formed by a story *about* the world. It is not the *embodied* present, but rather a re-presentation of experience, which is based on conceptualization, narrative, and *utility*. As such *me* results as an utterly recursive being, that is, it arrives at every moment of experience grounded in a habitual past, it lays that past over what it sees, and in many cases this unsurprisingly reaffirms the framework with which it arrived at the scene. This in turn reinforces that habit and entrenches *me* in being more *me*.

What characterizes this situation is incredible intelligence on the one hand, and incredible ignorance on the other. *Me* thrives on what Kahneman (2011) calls 'system 1': a mode of 'thinking fast' that is mostly unaware (like the functioning of implicit memory discussed in Chapter 7). It gets us through much of what we do by taking things as *they are*.[15] *Me* is your day-to-day ally based on which you pragmatically engage with the world. It is all the functions and reactions that have become automated in your personality and embodiment and thanks to many of them you are here. Much of them are probably worthwhile, and they have formed based on an incredible amount of trial and error that evolved into automated habits. This is especially true as far as our motoric actions are concerned.

> Given the limited information to which you can attend in each moment, your ability to in fact not attend to the brushing of your teeth or to the movement of your hand to bring food to your mouth this morning, is that which allows you to engage in other things that might be more important at that moment.

There is great intelligence in this, and we should accredit *me* for that. However, *me* is also blind to its own process, hence it is caught up in that 'illusion of omniscience'. It is an utterly positivistic being that likes to stick with the way *it* re-presents the world through narrative. Its problem is routinization and automation. The more *me's* functioning is enacted, whether at the motoric level or at the level of how *me* comes to interpret human interactions, the more this strata that undergirds our day-to-day functioning becomes *resistant to change*, and the more our day-to-day becomes governed by it. *Me's* habits are the ones, which Dewey referred to as fixed. They are those that have a "hold upon us, instead of our having a free hold upon things" (1957, p. 14). They become our automatic reactions and are somewhat like water – they take the most rehearsed path; the one with least resistance. There is a natural intelligence in this, *but* when it comes to the field of human interaction, and coping with LIFE, such identity can get us into trouble.

Colloquially put, in your day-to-day life, whenever you feel yourself to be absolutely *right* for being angry at someone that you feel to have wronged you in some way – that's *me self-reflecting there*. The neuronal firings that correspond with this kind of self-encouragement of your right-ness, are working to reinforce your rightness. Sure enough, if you are unaware of that, do not be surprised if indeed next time you meet that person you will 'give him a piece of your mind *and he will deserve it*'. Whenever you get the feeling that the person you are speaking with is stupid, or you cannot imagine how she or he 'just don't get it' – that's *me self-reflecting*. Whenever you feel smugly intelligent after answering correctly in the classroom (and you might add to that feeling smart*er* than those around you) that's *me*. That's where *me* see's great advantages in remaining just as it is, which entrenches it indeed further in its game. Similarly, whenever you feel dumb*er* than the rest of the class that's *me too*. *Me* thrives on the bedrock of the 'normative social map' – a life of unceasing comparison – and that's usually the place where *me* detects that there are great *dis*advantages in being *me*. When things go nice *me* is convinced that this is the way to be. When they do not, *me* starts searching for solutions. Those can go in two directions – *reflective practice*, which may invoke change, or *more of me*. As long as *me* searches within its own curriculum – *out there* and *then* – all it finds is more of *me*. With luck circumstances will change and *me* might shift to thinking that everything is cool now, and since it believes in regularities, it might think that 'finally things have settled down, and now *me* thinks that it finally got it', with utter disregard to the fact that this was never the case in the past, and there is no reason to believe that it should be the case now.

The thing is, *me* can be extremely articulate and intelligent in how it uses words and expresses itself. Its issue is, however, that it will make the most convincing case for its *own* intelligence and that closes it nicely within its own self-justifying system. *Me* itself can't change *me*. It is way too busy being *me*. Staying that way is what it does for a living.

The above tells us that we are faced with an incredibly sophisticated situation. An identity that is highly effective, quick, and automatic, which gets us by much of the time on the one hand, yet on the other hand, it is a pruned *identity* that tends to perpetuate who we are. Grounding this in reconstructing 'education' – 'education' is about creating automatic habits, yet only to the point in which those are helpful. If they are not, as Dewey (1958) argued, it becomes about overcoming them. In this case, 'education' requires that we introduce more awareness into this 'curriculum' that is enacted much of the time, to see how it is shaped by us and how we are shaped by it. What we need is some form of *I* that will be methodically introduced into this scheme. In the following I focus again on *self-reflection* and mind-wandering as *inner* manifestations of *me's* curriculum that depict its identity. I offer some suggestions as to how we can identify *me*, so that we can deliberately engage with its curriculum as the next chapter will discuss in more detail:

1. *Me* is most literally a *non-present being*. This is most apparent during wandering and less during *self-reflecting*. Mind-wandering is a state of 'decoupled attention' (Smallwood et al. 2007b). You lack meta-awareness: the capacity to be aware of the process in which your mind is engaging (Schooler 2002). Driving and attending to *out there*, yet worrying *unwittingly* about the meeting to which you are driving *in here*. Conversing with someone *out there*, yet thoughts of what you forgot to do yesterday keep barging in *in here*. In *self-reflection* you are aware that you are thinking, nevertheless your thinking has little to do with the concrete present moment.

2. *Me* is a bifurcated being that is detached from the body (Varela et al. 1991, p. 28) – *Me's* source of identity is derived directly from narrative and thoughts. It might be said that *me is* thoughts.

> Just as the 'social curriculum' ignores *me*, *me* ignores *I* as a 'core/ minimal self' that is deeply embodied.

Me clearly understands that the body is part of life, but *me's* 'body' is not *em*bodied. It is far more an object with which it negotiates in various ways; a narrative *about* the body that has to do with body-image and the way it has come to see the body through 'social' eyes ('am I thin enough?', 'am I macho enough?', 'I can't stand being sick?', 'I shouldn't eat too much' . . .); or a narrative about feeling in pain and blaming the body for stalling *me's* wish to 'advance in life'. All these are not an in-dwelling within the body but rather the representation of the body through narrative.

Me's blindness to the body is featured in a cluelessness about the *curriculum of embodied perception*. It has no idea that its process of perception is comprised of reactions to a body that perceives everything. As we soon explore, even *me's* wandering and *self-reflecting* scenarios are entangled with embodied perception to which *me* is blind.

3. *Me* lives the illusion of omniscience – As discussed in Chapter 3, it is constantly fooled by the thought that 'perception = reality'. As we soon see the possibility that I do not see all there is to it; that awareness is very limited, is not part of the experience you have as *me*. Whenever you acknowledge limitedness and humility and you do *not* view them as some kind of meaninglessness, but rather as a feature of being *only* human – these would count as contemplative insights that come from *I*. They come as we shall see, when *me* is given its appropriate place – a day-to-day habitual mode that is indispensable yet needs 'education'.

Soon we will describe the pedagogical mechanisms that sustain *me* and keep it going. Before that however, I think I owe you a brief reflection on what we're doing. At this point you might feel discouraged as *me* turns out to be such a limited being. Perhaps you feel offended given that you are somewhat 'blamed' for that. Broadly, what I am doing here is shaking the grounds over which much of human life stands – the belief that you are your thoughts.[16]

> I am arguing that *me* – that narrative/narrator – is but an aspect of who you are. It is making so much noise that it's hard to hear anything else.[17]

Nevertheless, *me* feels so real. How does this happen?

ME AS PEDAGOGUE

If you have trouble falling asleep sometimes, I suspect it's *me* that's keeping you awake. Too many problems to solve... too many problems to create-... and a body that never gets its peace of mind.

I have been constantly arguing that mind-wandering and *self-reflection* as two pervasive modes of thinking that emerge from *me* and create *me*, affect who we are substantially. I have also claimed that we are more likely to think about ourselves as simply being who we are. It is very peculiar to think of ourselves as *affecting* who we are within these non-deliberate states. What I have been working toward, is the claim that,

> *me* is a pedagogue that breeds the *curriculum of me* to yield a student that becomes unsurprisingly: *me*.

In the following I analyze, what this means and how this happens. The case of *self-reflection*'s reinforcing *me* is more obvious. *Self-reflection* is a more emotionally charged state characterized by a self-reassurance that "I am like this", "I am right", "I should never do this again". As we saw in Chapter 7 more arousal may imply the attribution of more meaning, which in turn enhances memory-encoding. Mind-wandering's ability to affect us is more peculiar. How would thoughts, formed in our own minds indiscriminately, affect us, when they have to do with things that are *not* happening right now? *Why* should they make us unhappy as Killingsworth and Gilbert (2010) suggested (if you indeed take this claim to be true)?.

In the following I want to propose a 'pedagogical' perspective that explains parts of this phenomenon in which our pruned mind entrenches itself in its pruned state of *me*. This will also demonstrate the co-dependence of the *curriculum of me* and the *curriculum of embodied perception*. I describe some of these internal pedagogical mechanisms that I am quite sure, hardly exhaust the matter. The importance of their articulation is twofold: (a) They are ways of interpreting how our mind 'educates' itself *non-deliberately*, and (b) They are the mechanisms with which a *deliberate* 'educational' engagement with *me* might have to work:

1. *The realness of virtual reality*
1a. *Lack of meta-awareness and embodied perception*

Smallwood, McSpadden, and Schooler claim that, "[T]he failure to recognize that one is off task suggests that mind wandering involves a temporary failure in meta-awareness" (2007b, p. 527). Following Schooler (2002), they refer to meta-awareness, as one's ability to reflect upon the content of one's mental state. This meta-awareness is a function of *I* that I associated with *reflective practice*. *I* is exactly what we *do not* experience neither while mind-wandering nor while self-reflecting. During these states we are immersed in the content and are blind to the process. Both processes entrench *me* in *me* based on that blindness. This is a crucial mechanism for two reasons:

a) *Me* will fully submit to the principles of *embodied perception* and allow itself to be constructed based on the mind's 'movie-making' industry. How does this work?

The 'chain of reaction' process of *embodied perception* that was explored in Chapter 7, seems to be quite similar whether the stimulus to which we attend comes from *out there* or whether it comes from *in here*. As the famous Indian story goes, one is startled when *imagining* to have seen a snake, while in fact it was a rope. But this is not saved to misperceiving things *out there* and thinking them to be real. *It applies to our minds in here*, for "[W]hen recalling an event from our past we do not simply bring to mind the incident in question. Rather, we mentally re-experience the event" (Phelps and Sharot 2008, p. 147). The bullying that a student experiences during recess may be as worse as its virtual reimagining a few minutes later as the mind represents it to itself during wandering or *self-reflection*; the stress of *self-reflecting* about tomorrow's exam, may create the very stressed embodied reactions, which will appear at the time of the exam itself. As Gilbert and Wilson (2007) argued, mental simulation to the future and the past can be actually 'experienced' in the 'here and now' both at the level of sensations and at the level of their emotional consequences.

b) Lack of meta-awareness to the *process* will establish mind-wandering and *self-reflection* as simply how and who I am. It will end outside our idea of the 'curriculum' as far as *me* is concerned, because *me* cannot have any idea about the value of the *processes* that create it. Just to demonstrate this, when I first introduce my students to these states, especially to mind-wandering, many react by saying, 'I don't get why you are making such a fuss about this.

This is just a characteristic of being human'. I agree but I also suggest that mind-wandering carries the very mechanism that makes it fly under our radar and be deemed as 'just who I am and how things are'. Indeed our minds construct it in a way that it remains outside our curricular considerations. The mind expels the mind from 'education' exacerbating our personal and 'social' blindness to the mind's place in it. *Me's* deeply seated habit will express a willingness to study everything with great sophistication but not itself. Shortly we will see that this is not merely an inability to examine thought processes, but rather a far deeper concern with *me's own death*...

1b. An evolutionary perspective on mind-wandering and the brain as a curriculum deliberator.

In Chapter 7 I offered an evolutionary perspective on the brain's selective 'curricular' deliberations. That is, I attempted to make-sense of *how* the brain determines what is the 'knowledge of most worth' at the bead-to-bead level? Here we follow by asking *what would make the brain 'deliberate' to prefer wandering-content over a literature lesson, or a university lecture?* – we can explore this from an evolutionary perspective as we did in the previous chapter. This in fact follows some neuroscientists who argued that such a pervasive phenomenon must have some adaptive functions (Smallwood and Andrews-Hanna 2013).

Seen from an 'educational' perspective, the brain-mind's *defaulting* into wandering, may be one of its ways of preparing itself for the future based on past events. The agenda of mind-wandering (and perhaps *self-reflection* as well) is *further survival*. A student's brain detecting boredom during a Literature lesson, may for example determine that it is more useful to *default* into wandering and to rehearse the events of a dissatisfying incident, so that next time it will be more prepared to meet such events, or to self-reflect on how to draw the attention of a girl in which this student is interested. If indeed this is the case, then such mechanism would only serve its evolutionary function *if the mind will take its virtual and/or invented scenarios seriously*. That means that the effects of the mind's educating itself during wandering/*self-reflection must* be based on lack of meta-awareness. The mind needs to fully identify with its thought-content, so that it will ensure the tagging of such fictitious events as 'educationally' *meaningful*, and in order to affect our future functioning. The emotional cost of mind-wandering to which some refer, is in this case the price we pay for improving our chances of survival and reproduction. Evolution is primarily about the latter more than about well-being. *Me* is teaching the mind to survive.

Whichever the case, most of us we are interested in more than survival. Can we savor the good that *me-content* might bring sometimes, without paying an emotional price for the lesser content? It doesn't seem that we can do that for at least as analyzed above, while wandering/self-reflecting *me* seems to set the stage for *drama*. We'll experience content and react to it as if it is true because that is the structure of the mechanism. We can only see the content's un-realness when we awaken into mindfulness/reflective practice; when *I* sees through *me*, in what some have termed 'decentering' (Fresco et al. 2007). Yet, such detachment is exactly what *me* lacks. We have to remember that *me* thrives on narrative. Detachment from narrative cannot emerge from *me* for if narrative is gone, *me* is gone with it and that's the one thing that *me* will not have. Detachment is a feature of the *I* that we will examine in Chapter 9. Recall:

> For the moment what we attend to is reality! During wandering or self-reflecting the thought content is as real for me as things *out there* are. The 'realness' of realities we see is predetermined by the kind of 'person' we are that attends to them and hence shapes them. Changing the validity of the reality seen, requires engaging with the attender; with the 'how' – the kaleidoscope – the pedagogy of the mind.

Reality seen through habit, which is essentially *me's* way of seeing it, yields more of the same. Sameness is comfortable and handy and can be in fact, highly evolved. It is however, always a question whether comfortability and handiness are 'good enough'. There's a rather simple twofold mechanism based on which the *curriculum of me* is taught by *me* and to *me*. It's a reverberating loop that recycles *me*. During wandering it works like this:

1. A thought comes to the wandering mind.
2. Tacitly underneath every thought there is somewhat of an argument that validates their source as *me*: If it came from *in here* then it must be *me* that's behind it. Who else could it be?
3. The mind reacts to it based on the principles of embodied perception, just as it would to any stimulus; hence its realness is reasserted.
4. *Me* embraces the thought content as true and worthwhile. Why would I think falsities and non-sense? *Me* reacts to that content.
5. Experiencing these reactions breads more reactions, for the wandering mind keeps coming up with new problems to solve based on its infinite reservoir of the past and its incredible ability to create new variations (usually of old themes).

Perhaps *me* itself follows evolution as it creates more narrative to ensure its own survival? Can it get any circular than this? *Me* thinks, gets entangled in its thoughts and owns them, and those thoughts tend not to end problems but rather to present new ones or revolve in circles, thus creating the urge to think more.

> Describing me's identity in terms of Descartes's famous cogito would probably require that it be reversed: not 'I think therefore I am', but rather 'I am therefore I think'/'I think therefore I think more'/'I am therefore I can't stop thinking'. . . .

As Sood and Jones (2013) indeed suggested, "mind wandering may predispose to the same activity" (p. 139).[18] The case of deliberately *self-reflecting* is even more acute, for in such case *me* as an agency that thinks is presupposed right at the outset, as well as the intelligence and the veridicality of the thinker. It comes down to this,

> Wandering is *me's* generating itself unwittingly. *Self-reflection* is *me's* generating itself wittingly.

2. The dependency of me's survival on me-content

To be sure, when I speak of *me* – this 'narrative self' – I am speaking of the narrative, the sense of a narrator, and the one to which it is narrated. All three are *me*; all occur in one mind and one brain. The moment there's a *me*-thought the three are created, for one creates the other two. This in fact is a psychological mechanism that invites the kind of compulsive thinking to which many of us may be addicted. Why? – for if we think of ourselves as a 'narrative self' then we must have a narrative in order to exist at all. Experience needs to be filled by our inner talk for otherwise we annihilate ourselves. Yet, there is more to it. Our narrative caters to that feeling of being *empty of meaning* described in Chapter 6:

> If we are 'educated' to believe that meaning is a consequence of 'knowledge' and 'knowledge' comes in the form of discourse alone, then we need to hear words constantly (even false ones) in order for meaning to exist as we know it. Hearing no narrative feels like a void, (or "lack" in David Loy's terms (2000)), and that feels too much like death.

Following a mindfulness session at a course I taught this year, one of my student asked: "What will I do if my thinking *stops*? What will I do without worrying about the future?" There may be another question lurking behind this: "who will I be without this narrative"? Despite this student's acknowledgement that much of her mind-wandering/self-reflecting time is spent worrying and stressing about things that are not fully relevant nor necessary, and despite confessing that she would be willing to give up at least some of these thoughts, it seems as if for her, it is safer to remain a worrying *me* than to submit to an unknown state that is empty of narrative; empty of meaning; *empty*.

> We tend to think of survival in physical terms – as a survival of the body. That level is rudimentary and fully understandable. It is survival at the level of *me* that seems to be a far more substantial 'educational' individual-'social' problem. *Me's* survival depends on *me*-content, which in turn emerges from 'social narrative'. *Me*-'society' co-create the insufficiency of now; of feeling that *now* is not the time to be at. We succumb to it as it projects through the 'social curriculum' from *out there*, and we get it internally through mind-wandering and *self-reflection* from *in here*. It results as the co-expulsion of the mind to *then* and to *there*. *A mind that expels a mind that expels a mind*....

3. *The recursive nature of our brain-mind as a generator of me-content*

> Men [sic.] have no eyes but for those aspects of things, which they have already been taught to discern. (James 1984, p. 245)

Earlier I proposed that the term *default* mode network seems highly appropriate when applied to the function of mind-wandering. Like a computer, which *defaults* into 'screen saving', at least some of our mind-wandering is somewhat of 'screen-saving' our identity as *me*. What I mean by 'screen saving' *me* is that at least part of mind-wandering / self-reflecting has to be based on indiscriminate patterns of thinking that our brain-mind has developed in the past. What can we expect of the brain-mind when it wanders inadvertently if not inertia? – if you find that much of your mind-wandering or *self-reflection* tends to revolve around similar matters – worrying about the future, attempting to reconcile with the past, think of what others think about you, tell yourself that you should do this or that – don't be surprised. From a neuroscientific perspective, these constitute the experiential aspect of repetitive neuronal firings that follow an inertia of the past. You might recall Siegel's (2012) argument from the previous chapter, "*memory is the way past events affect future function*" (p. 46). This points to the recursive nature that you probably experience when mind-wandering/self-reflecting as you recycle familiar themes. Neuroscientist Marc Lewis offers the brain's side of this,

> Because each episode of real-time cognitive-emotional activity leaves some degree of synaptic change in its wake, we can say that brains develop by elaborating and extending the outcomes of their own activities ... synaptic alterations are recursive, which means that these activities tend to repeat themselves, forming lineages of individual patterning that progressively elaborate their own emergent themes. (2005, p. 272)

Similarly, here's James:

> Every state of ideational consciousness, which is either very strong or is habitually repeated leaves an organic impression on the cerebrum; in virtue of which that same state may be reproduced at any future time, in respondence to a suggestion fitted to excite it. (2007, p. 68)

The more neurons connect to each other the greater the probability of their future firing. Probability is not certainty, but it does make sense that like water, when nothing (or no-one) intervenes with the flow, neuronal patterns may very well seek a path of least resistance. That translates in your brain, to those neuronal connections that have been firing more than others – *your most habitual thought patterns*. In the case of wandering, you're not 'there' to change the flow of thoughts thus it may very well work in this somewhat closed circle of the past. In *self-reflection*, *me* supposedly wills the thinking and intervenes in the content. What that would amount to probably follows previous patterns of willing. After all if *me* is 'doing' the willing, then it is likely that *me* will find *me-content* at the end of this willing.

If you often get a sense that you're somewhat 'sick and tired' of the thoughts that you are having, or in fact, being 'sick and tired' of being 'sick and tired' of them, this may be the reason why. What the above amounts to is that as far as we consider *me* within its own closed system, it is based on the past, and creates the future in the image of the past. Supposedly in such situation it is hard to see how something new can emerge.

Is Me Indoctrinating Me?

Integrating the above mechanisms, I'll make a bold suggestion. In 'educational terms' the pattern that emerges here can be closely related to 'indoctrination'. Broadly, it is the inculcation of ideas in a way that does not consider the student/child as a critical agent with a right to consider them and assess their worth for herself (Peters 2010). Indoctrination can take various forms, but it need not necessarily be considered negative. It can appear in Fascist regimes that set the young generation's minds to blind faith in the rightness of the country's ways, but it can also appear in a very prosaic situation in which a parent is not willing to enter into a long discussion with his five year-old, about why it's a good idea to put all the Lego back in the box after playing with them, or a discussion with his fourteen year old, about why she's not allowed to come back home from a date after midnight. Most philosophers agree that any form of 'education' will include some indoctrinatory practices.

To articulate how mind-wandering and *self-reflection* appear as *me's* indoctrinating *me*, it is helpful to follow a common categorization of indoctrination that depicts its manifestations based on four criteria: (a) Content, (e.g., presenting false facts as true (Tan 2008) (b) Method (e.g., disregard or an intentional repression of students' critical faculties (Peters 2010, p. 13), (c) Intention, (e.g., discouraging attempts to question the knowledge presented, or insisting on the truth of facts that are unwarranted in spite of critique (White 2010, p. 125). (d) Results (e.g., the student ends up committing to beliefs that are impervious to criticism) (Tan 2008, p. 2).

When we start to think in these terms, both mind-wandering and *self-reflection* tend to bear marks of self-indoctrination. In the case of mind-wandering: (a) Content – we do not choose the on-set of the *process* nor the *content*, hence the content can be unrealistic and untrue, (b) Method and intention – since wandering is defined here as being unaware *that* we are wandering, this is the equivalent of being deprived of the ability to critically reflect on the content and thus determine whether it is suitable and/or worthwhile for us in the long run. (c) Intention – if the evolution thesis presented above has something to do with this, then perhaps the brain is intentionally ensuring *me's* survival (even at the cost of unhappiness), by ensuring that *I* will not get in the way as it keeps it at bay (d) Result – If we find ourselves recycling very similar matters over the years and very committed to our habitual *me-identity* despite our wish for transforming ourselves, this may be the consequence of mind-wandering/ self-reflecting.

Self-reflection is even more obvious: (a) Content – in many cases when we self-reflect about how 'right' we are, when we shift to *reflective practice* we see things in a different light (i.e. 'what was I *thinking*?'), regret the anger and even mock ourselves for making a big deal of an incident. This exposes that sometimes the thought-content experienced while self-reflecting is dubious. (b) Method – *me* basically speaks to itself in this case. It is as if a teacher is completely ignoring the impact of his words, and he goes on unwilling to take any interruptions in his lecture. (c) Intention – since the teacher here is so right. The entire game played is one of reassuring the rightness of the views. (d) Result – as long as *self-reflection* goes on (and we don't shift to *reflective practice*) *me* results as more *me*.

It is worth noting that indoctrination can work in our favor. What if *me* comes up with positive thoughts during mind-wandering and *self-reflection*? Would it not then be better to leave it be? – perhaps, but first, in these states, we seem to lack meta-awareness, which here I interpret as a wiser *I* that provides a more synoptic view on what is indeed beneficial and what isn't. Relying on *me's* habitual and pruned perspective may not be ideal. Second, we have very little control over the kind of content that will come up during these sessions, nor are we in a position to choose *how we relate to that content*. Eventually this hearkens back to Csikszentmihalyi's (1991, p. 43) claim to which I pointed in Chapter 7 as an 'educative' agenda – changing how we experience conditions to make them fit our goals better (assuming our goals are reliable). Mind-wandering and *self-reflection* do not seem to provide us with the *agency* to practice such libertarian 'education'. They seem to hold us captive within and by our own pruned minds. What all the above points to, is a startling realization:

> Broadly, mind wandering and *self-reflection* might entail resistance to both our own and 'society's' best interests. They tend to entrench us in who we already are. Some of that can certainly work in our favor, but 'education' may be about sustaining the 'good' and changing what is not. We know how difficult it is to teach math, but changing how we act is ten times more difficult – especially if we are blind to the processes and mechanisms that sustain our unfavorable habits. If our minds default on us into a state in which they 'screen save' *me*, it may be plausible that at least part of the time we may

resolve to change our ways, move an inch forward, and then mind-wandering/self-reflecting we reinforce old patterns and we retreat back to our old ways . . .

Ever resolved to study harder but didn't? Ever tried quitting smoking, eating less, going to the gym more often? Ever promised yourself not to lose your temper next time so and so happens? – how successful were you? – It is extremely hard to change for much of our time *me* sustains its baseline on so-called automatic pilot and the *I* that had resolved to change *me*, is not there when it is needed.

We may need to engage *I* deliberately and on a regular basis, so that it slowly de-prunes *me's* habitual ways, and initiates it in a habitual 'goodness'. The discourse of *reflection* in 'education' clearly notes this, but I am speaking of something deeper. 'Education' must have something to do with a generic practice that teaches us to identify *me* and shift to *I* when *me* seems to be unhelpful. In addition, even our habits of reflection may become routinized. No less, the language we use may delimit our ways of being and knowing. It seems that we will need to familiarize ourselves with a far more open capability that is in us as we will explore in the next chapter.

*

The Wandering Mind Goes to School

The penultimate section of this chapter locates *me* back in school. It is crucial that things be contextualized within this more conventional day-to-day 'educational' setting. For this purpose I'll offer a prosaic example from my son's experience with which I'll attempt to show how the *curriculum of me* can shape us, and in fact create a reverberating loop in which the world to which we project this *me* willingly mirrors us to reassert our minds' ways as pedagogues.

In the past two years my son, a 7th grader now, has been repeatedly complaining that the teachers are singling him out. 'I'm always the one to pay the price for a class commotion', is his repetitive *me*-complaint. He does have some trouble keeping himself from getting involved in everything around him, but in his eyes that's never the problem, because others are always involved too, so how come he's the one to get thrown out of the classroom?

The question whether this narrative that he details to us is an accurate descriptor of reality or not is important to some extent, but as I suggested in Chapter 7 (p. 193) in regards to *embodied perception*, accuracy is not our issue. *Me* is fundamentally grounded in the illusion of omniscience. It intuitively takes what it sees as a reflection of reality *as such*. So the point of the matter with my son is that he believes that this is who he is. This is the way his mind has been shaped to think about himself, and that same mind goes every day to school having in mind that *me* is that kind of student that teachers like to pick on. Being so inclined,

> *me* travels in the world gazing through a *me*-kaleidoscope at the end of which it sees a *me*-world that confirms the realness of the traveler and its kaleidoscope.

If we look at this from the perspective of the *curriculum of embodied perception* described in the previous chapter, whether implicitly or explicitly, what seems to happen in the brain-mind of my son is the association between 'school', 'this teacher', and 'that teacher' along with 'being singled out', 'being thrown out of classroom' and other associations that have become consolidated. The mere circumstances of being at school and perceiving the situation, are already wired in the brain to have these associations ready to leap forward and shape present moments based on past representations. As such, they feed the narrative formed as the *curriculum of me* that appears in my son's wandering or *self-reflecting*, scenarios. What happens when he gets thrown out of class, yet again? – his mind reaffirms the narrative with which it has arrived just a few moments ago at the lesson; neuronal connections associated with these thoughts, are further enhanced. As he walks to the secretary to have his name marked, his mind tells him 'just like always...I told you...they hate me...why didn't they pick on David? He was making far more noise than I did...why *me*?'. On his way home his mind may be rehearsing this story along with envisioning our reactions. We're not the kind of parents to make a fuss about getting thrown out of the classroom, but we're certainly the kind that tries to show him that his mind is caught in a self-justifying loop (hoping that we are using language that a 7th grader will understand...).

Maybe he has something to gain out of this. Perhaps this is his way of being the class clown, or being considered 'cool'. Well, perhaps. Does that make things any easier on him? No, it only make his narrative more complicated. So he's torn between two wishes thus putting *me* at odds with *me* – in itself a great way to fuel up some more narrative there. In this chapter we focused far more on the mind *in here* as it creates its narrative and plays it out only to reaffirm its identity. Here, however, we will see that it so happens that 'society' *is almost coerced into reaffirming me's position.*

If my son arrives in the classroom with a *me* the narrative of which is to be 'that student that gets thrown a lot out of the classroom', it becomes almost a slogan written on his forehead whenever a commotion arises in the classroom. The teacher has her own *me* to deal with. It's her *me* that had thrown out that student that walks with that slogan on his forehead. It's a mind that has been pruned to see the present as the past. It's a mind that on the way home from work may be wandering/*self-reflecting*: 'Oh, that student again... why can't he just keep quiet...'. There is much likelihood that the future will look the same for the mind is primed to follow in these patterns. Do you begin to see this hall of mirrors in which teacher and student reaffirm each other's narrative?

However, there is a chance that on her way home that teacher will do something very different – *reflective practice*: 'tomorrow I have to be more careful... did I really have to throw him out?'. On the same token, my son, perhaps inspired by our talk, may wonder, 'maybe tomorrow *can* be somewhat different. Maybe I need to change my script?' These would constitute deliberate engagements with *me* that introduce the *I* there to shift *me's* kaleidoscopic setting. An insistence on this opening to change will be key to educational change, yet it depends on an *internal* resolution more than anything else – a deliberate meta-peda-gogical turn to engage directly with the *curriculum of me*, on behalf of both parties – teacher *and* student. Such responsibility applies to *both*, but it cannot be cultivated by a meta-pedagogy of attending *out there* alone, which is the ultimate responsibility-depriver, as we will explore in the next chapter.

Reflecting on the above narrative I want you to note something crucial. There was not even a word up there that indicated whether this drama took place in a math/history/literature/geography/chemistry... lesson. All these, which are usually positioned at the foreground of 'education', are not unimportant, but they must be cast to the background, in order for us to see beyond the opaqueness of 'students'. The real drama is *in here now.*

I believe most of us hope that our children will know math and history, but I do suspect that we are far more concerned with more *generic* and *universal* 'educational' aims such as learning to engage with the world in ways that work both for them and for 'society'. If we are interested in the *generic* qualities or goodness, kindness, compassion, benevolence, and altruism, then the nitty-gritty of disciplinary subject matter must not blind us to their role as means by which a *curriculum of Identity-agency* and *ownership* unfolds in the process of learning disciplines and skills.

This closure leads us nicely to summarize this chapter.

SUMMARY OF CHAPTER 8

- The inner aspects of the *curriculum of me* include the sense of *me* as the narrator (teacher), *me* as the narrative (subject matter), and *me* as the 'one' (student) hearing the narrative. All 'three' are produced by the mind wittingly and unwittingly *in here* throughout our waking hours based on mind-wandering and *self-reflection*.
- *Me* is indispensable as a mode of pragmatic automation that is part of our sane functioning within a 'social' environment.
- The *curriculum of me* is a non-deliberate 'education' in which the mind entrenches itself in more of its habitual automation. It is the cusp of a pruned mind that sees a pruned world, which makes it very efficient, usable, and comfortable in some aspects, yet limited and problematic on others.
- The *curriculum of me* is fueled from without based on the 'social curriculum' and from within the mind, based on the insufficiency of now – the sense that something is missing.
- A direct engagement with the *curriculum of me* requires an *I*, which/ who was *not* characterized here, but was somewhat practiced based on *reflective practice* as the perspective from which this chapter is written, as well as based on *sampling me by surprise*, and *journaling*.

Why should *me* be part of a reconstructed 'education'?

- Research on mind-wandering shows that this pervasive phenomenon – now associated with a substantial brain network – has a dramatic effect on common 'educational' domains such as our sense of sense of *identity* and *agency*, our well-being, and actions, as well as our performance as learners.

- Mind-wandering and *self-reflection* may be a form of self-indoctrination that yields the 'screen-saving' of our identity and a false sense of agency. This becomes the locus of resistance to both our own and 'society's' best interests, because 'education' has to do with sustaining the 'good' and *changing* for the 'better'.
- Thinking in the context of school may in fact accentuate the above arguments, given the pervasiveness of overstress and boredom as two engines that generate *self-reflection* and mind-wandering.

Schools need to teach us to live in this world, but we also need to learn to live with ourselves in this world. The two are clearly more of a one. We alternate between them from one moment to the next. Not including this *curriculum of me* in the context of 'education' that is about *changing how we think, act and are*, seems utterly misguided. Whether we think deliberately or non-deliberately, attend to *out there* or to *in here*, all are part of a 'curriculum of life' that shapes who we are. So why have we been ignoring this so far? – it's all about attention; *it all hearkens back to the matrix of mind*.

- From the 'social' perspective: Our meta-pedagogy had constructed our minds to think of this *me*-narrative as irrelevant. Our minds have been shaped to think of *me* as noise that interferes with the 'social curriculum'.
- From the mind's perspective:
  - The mind that wanders/self-reflects lives the illusion of omniscience. It is unaware that it's wandering, hence cannot assess the effects of this process on its own shaping. *Me* has no clue that it is being shaped by *me*. We will never attribute significance to that which we are unaware of.
  - Following Chapters 3, 4, and 5: The *curriculum of me* is the mirror image of the 'social curriculum'. Here's a summary of their co-dependent expulsion of mind from the 'curriculum' expressed based on *the matrix of mind* (Chapter 2, p. 47):
- In terms of *space:* The 'social curriculum' nullifies the content of *me* by orienting students' attention to *out there* (to math, history . . .) or only to think *in here* about *out there* (about math, about history . . .). *Me* expresses this very structure internally: Wandering and *self-reflection* are *me*-content that is fundamentally concerned with the 'social' domain *out there* and with assessing where *me* stands against/within

it. The 'social curriculum' ignores *me* and focuses on the 'student' as an opaque entity; *me* does the same to *I*. It is oblivious to its existence.

• In terms of *time*: The 'social curriculum' and the '*curriculum of me*' are undergirded by the *insufficiency of now*. Both send attention to the *horizontal time axis* – to constantly run toward a future 'then' that is never here and now. Practically, the 'social curriculum' does so based on the 'social normative map' taught in effect in 'educational institutions' as well as informally within 'society'. *Me* does so through wandering and *self-reflection* from within.

Can we do something about this? *Yes*.

> We've diagnosed a formidable problem. For the moment what we attend to is reality, but attention is stuck *out there* and *then*. It is stuck in a loop between *me* and 'society'. If attention is stuck, attention is the place to search for solutions.

Your sampling throughout this chapter and your *journaling* have been part of a meta-pedagogical turn that is to be incorporated in a reconstructed 'education'. The suggestion is this:

> Every bead of experience is attended to by the mind and offers a choice between two possibilities: either you will strengthen an existing pattern or you weaken it and open a new path wittingly or unwittingly. Broadly, you want to strengthen those patterns that are beneficial and weaken those that are harming you and/or others. Whether we self-reflect or mind-wander both are modes of *me* and both are ways in which *me* shapes itself in the image of its past. In wandering *me* has no clue that this is the case. When *self-reflecting* it is somewhat shouting 'we don't need no education' because *me* 'already knows everything it needs to know, thank you'.

> *Me* needs *I*. 'Society' needs *I* and WE. Only a deliberate meta-pedagogical turn will take us there. That is exactly where we are heading.

NOTES

1. This has yielded several derogatory expressions such as "weeding out the self" (Kincheloe and Steinberg 1993), treating students as a "brain on a stick" (Lewis 2007, p. 100), educating "from the neck and up" (Lelwica 2009).

2. Note that I am not saying that all thoughts are *me*. Some of them concern the *reflective I* discussed in the next chapter.

3. It is important to note that other researchers arrived at results that are similar to those of Killingsworth and Gilbert's (Kane et al. 2007; McVay and Kane 2009).

4. We then analyze the outcomes we get as a class, which as I find, has been yielding closer to 55% of wandering – more than what Killingsworth and Gilbert came up with.

5. Irritation in this sense is viewed as another thing to explore: 'who is getting irritated?', 'is it *me* that doesn't like to be bothered?'

6. If it comes up during *reflective practice* it is *I and me content* but we will not explore this.

7. *Paradise Lost, Book 1, lines 254–255*, http://www.dartmouth.edu/~mil ton/reading_room/pl/book_1/text.shtml

8. In terms of time, statements such as 'I am always like this' or 'I am such a luck guy', imply having been that way in the past, objectifying *me* and understanding it as remaining that way to eternity. They belong to the reification of the horizontal time axis – a third conception-experience of time called the 'timeless', that is not developed in this book.

9. There's only one flaw in this metaphor – *this doesn't seem to save energy as it does in the computer's case*. The brain is as active in this 'resting'-state as it is while on-task despite the counterintuitive-ness of this fact. "Much of the brain's enormous energy consumption is unaccounted for by its responses to external stimuli" (Raichle 2006, p. 1249).

10. Baars (2010) also reminds us that we need to be far more moderate concerning our ability to determine the relevance or irrelevance of the thoughts we have to the tasks in which we are involved. This suggests that the distinction between task-related/task-unrelated thoughts, which at times serves to distinguish between DMN and other brain networks, may be flawed.

11. However, the chain of beads experienced as our minds flow from mind-wandering, to *self-reflection* may very well flow into spontaneous contemplative moments of insight. Suddenly we ourselves catch one of the thoughts that our own mind had just tossed at us, and it clicks miraculously into meaning. That is certainly possible, yet it is more likely that a mind that was trained in a *curriculum of I* as we will discuss in Chapter 9, will yield more moments of this sort, than a mind that spends much of the time in a state that lacks discernment neither in regards to its content nor in regards to the kind of process that gives rise to that content.

12. This can be clearly linked to the Four Nobel Truths as the essential teaching of Buddhism; especially as analyzed by David Loy (2000) who is mentioned later.

13. *Now* can be associated with two terms: 'flow' (Csikszentmihlayi's 1991) and mindfulness. Each term implies different experiences, which some have referred to as 'altered states of mind' (Berkovich-Ohana and Glickson (2014)).

14. Those experienced with mindfulness practice will recognize such moment clearly, for returning from wandering is one of the most fundamental aspects of the practice (Ergas 2016a).

15. Kahneman (2011) coins this as WYSIATI: "what you see is all there is" (pp. 85–88), that I interpret as simply another way of describing the *illusion of omniscience*.

16. To a great extent that too, is a co-'education' we get based on the mirroring of *me*-'society'.

17. There is absolutely nothing new in this suggestion. You will find it in all wisdom traditions one way or another, and certainly in the contemporary discourse that discusses mindfulness, psychotherapy, and neuroscience (Kabat-Zinn 2005; Segal et al. 2002). 'Self', *me*, and *I* are *words*, that sum experience, reality; life. Like all words they are abstractions that dwell in somewhat of a timeless realm that hovers above the horizontal axis as we shall see in Chapter 9. They are not the beads of attention but rather a way of articulating them. Lose the words and what is left? A myriad phenomena that all seem to revolve around the origin of attention.

18. It is worth exploring the relation between such understanding of mind-wandering and the Tibetan Buddhist concept of *papancha*.

The *Curriculum of I*

Deeply attending to yourself, to another human being, to a tree or a stone, it's not me that's attending. It's I. When you attend in this way, you intervene in the natural habituating inertia of embodied perception, me, and 'society'. You turn in to de-prune your mind and change its patterns based on wisdom and virtue.

The *curriculum of I* is an ambivalent place. This chapter will not describe that place as much as it will describe the conditions required to approach it and engage with it. Those conditions can be invited and they become an integral part of the 'education' that this *curriculum of I* itself teaches along with that which unfolds based on their cultivation. Why can't I describe this *I?* – because describing it is proposing a structure to that which is responsible for giving structure. However, what we see *now*, is the result of a moment that has been pruned by an 'educated' mind that reduces its *universality* to *particularity*. What we see, how we see it, and hence who we are right now, can be different. All these aspects of our existence emerge out of the frameworks through which we see and into which we have developed wittingly or unwittingly. The circularity here is thus inevitable, the language and the task itself are problematic; the results probably limited. I don't think I can remedy these unfavorable conditions. We work with what we have and simply try to be aware of our imperfection, remaining wary of falling in love with the chain of ideas that flow from a mind that is not fully in our possession.[1]

© The Author(s) 2017   251
O. Ergas, *Reconstructing 'Education' through Mindful Attention*,
DOI 10.1057/978-1-137-58782-4_9

The subject matter of the *curriculum of I* can be negatively defined as all that precedes or is beyond day to day *me*. This includes the more prosaic domain of problem solving. That is, any situation in which our automation doesn't work and we are called to address it with far more attentiveness. But, this chapter will not discuss this aspect, which has more to do with direct engagement with *out there*.[2] Here we focus on the *inner* aspects of the *curriculum of I*. Characterized positively, it is the experience of that which inquires *me*, and the experience of the origin of attention and awareness itself. The difficulty involved in depicting this curriculum comes with the non-discursive nature of its deeper territory. While *me* is heavily grounded in the use of language and thought as its boundaries, the *curriculum of I* will rest on an awareness of language as a finger that points to the moon. Whenever we mistake the finger for the moon, we are back in *me*. What will such mistake look like? – There are no clear rules here as far as I know, but usually when we get too fond of the way we phrase our understandings and fail to recheck them when we use them again, I would count that as a warning sign that we are getting stuck again.

In this sense, the entire conception of right versus wrong, so common to the 'social curriculum' that we know from schools and often critique, is challenged by the *curriculum of I*. Dwayne Huebner expresses this idea with great eloquence:

> There is more than we know, can know, will ever know. It is a 'moreness' that takes us by surprise when we are at the edge and end of our knowing. There is a comfort in that 'moreness' that takes over in our weakness, our ignorance, at our limits or end... One knows of that presence, that 'moreness' when known resources fail and somehow we go beyond what we were and are and become something different, somehow new. There is also judgment in that 'moreness' particularly when we smugly assume that we know what 'it' is all about and end up in the dark or on our behinds. (1999, p. 403)

The fact is, we are not in a position to know where we stand, and this not-knowing is an integral part of an engagement with the *curriculum of I*.

The position of language in this curriculum is itself ambivalent. It is both indispensable *and* in many cases, a stumbling block to be overcome. It has various roles here depending on the practice in which we engage. It can be a disturbance or a byproduct, something to be seen through and/ or beyond, something to be escaped, a medium that seeks to invoke an experience, or an awe-inspiring expression of knowing and being through poetics and metaphor. The experience is the heart of the subject matter here, especially when that experience remains raw, prior to or beyond its myriad interpretations. Nevertheless, signposts are required, and those are in many cases brought by the medium of language.

Language is utterly important here, but it is not the subject matter itself, nor the aim. It is a secondary expression. It is similar to the relation between numbers and mathematical thinking. Mathematical thinking does not consist of numbers, but rather of all the processes based on which we manipulate numbers and express such thinking. Those processes are not expressed in utterances such as '7 × 7 = 49' coming from an adult for whom they are no more than a habit that requires no mathematical processing. 7 × 7 = 49 is then a *me-thing* not an *I* thing. Nevertheless, it would be impossible to express or teach mathematical thinking without the means of numbers. Language has a similar status in the *curriculum of I*, hence, this chapter and this book stand on language as its means. Nevertheless, this book points both *in here* and beyond them.

So what can be done here, in this terrain that I painstakingly depict as vague and hardly accessible? – I insisted on the above so as to locate the entire chapter within an exploratory mindset, but I do believe that it is specifically *because* of engaging with a locus of being that I suspect is far more open and boundless, that I will try to be as practical as possible. This *curriculum of I* may emerge spontaneously, but in this chapter I set aside this possibility and focus on ways in which this curriculum can be brought into view through practices that intentionally engage in stepping outside of *me-*'society'. Following our exploratory approach this chapter will include a number of important themes:

1) The exploration of *agency* and its relation to ethics as we move further *in here* to work directly with the origin of attention.
2) The importance of the body as a primary non-discursive curricular domain.
3) The essence of a meta-pedagogical turn that locates the mind at the center of 'curriculum' and 'pedagogy' based on moving *in here* and accessing the 'internal door of *active attention*'.
4) The elaboration of why moving *in here* liberates us from 'social-construction', substantiates our ethical *agency*, and strengthens our ability to 'educate' 'society' based on a mind that works toward its own de-pruning.

Our methodical approach begins here by briefly conceptualizing two kinds of *I* curricula in which we then engage practically.

*

Two Types of *I*:
The *Reflective I* and the *Contemplative I*[3]

The *I* curriculum is a dual curriculum with a clear hierarchy. It includes the discursive *reflective I* and the post-discursive *contemplative I*. I'll first say some things about their common nature. Some of this may sound somewhat enigmatic at this point:

a) Both types of *I* are contemplative *I*'s. Contemplation is a term that I will be using broadly as a way of attending deeply based on stepping away from habit. The 'outer' form of this attention is the engagement with formal practices such as meditation, yoga, taichi, philosophizing, and arts. The form is crucially important but this is an aspect that I do not develop in this book.[4] Contemplation by no means implies ignoring language, words, narrative, or pushing them away. It is simply an acknowledgement of language itself as an 'object' that needs special care. It is not that automated medium of expression that is indispensable for our day-to-day engagement that comes out of our mouth as *me* speaks. It is rather acknowledged as an extremely powerful tool that rigidifies, defines, and confines. As such, words must flow from the right place within us and at times silence is preferable.

b) Both *I*'s are always available: the thought that special conditions are required for a contemplative engagement, is a *me-thought*. *I*, in both of its forms is available at any moment in which we choose to engage with it, or it can arise spontaneously.

c) The fact that I refer to these as *I(s)*, says little about their substantiality. These are not ontological claims. The interest here is 'educational'. The question of *I*'s (in)substantiality is important, only in as much as the ethical-existential implications of inquiring into it, brings meaning into how one lives.[5]

What's the difference then between the *reflective I* and the *contemplative I*? – The *reflective I* has already been mentioned and most of this book is based on it. It is very familiar in our Western philosophical heritage and its medium is *language and discourse*. It stems from Plato and Socrates, runs through Augustine, Descartes, and Kant, and clearly leads to our times. It is an incredibly powerful tool that is applied widely in 'educational' discourse following John Dewey, Donald Schon, Robert Kegan, John Mezirow, and numerous contemporary scholars. *However*, much of the contemporary 'educational' discourse in this domain is not as interested in the *reflective I* in and of itself, as much as it is interested in the content-products of reflection and their *use*. That is, reflection is commonly *used* in order to improve teaching practice, critical thinking, and problem solving.[6] Make no mistake, I am all for that. It might however, not always reflect the realization that problems *out there* are problems *in here;* that the mind is not only a means to improve how we handle life *out there,* but rather an *inner curriculum* in its own right. If *reflective practice* is engaged solely with the intention of solving problems *out there* and in the future, then we are back within the structure of our 'social curriculum'. While this is crucially necessary, I want to focus on *reflective practice* as a means to explore ourselves *here* and *now*.[7]

The *contemplative I*, as I conceptualize it here, resists the urge to philosophize and conceptualize. I call it a 'post'-discursive *I*, because this is not to be confused with a baby's *pre*-discursive experience of the 'core self' described in Chapter 3. It is in fact only after we become so invested in our narrativic existence that the engagement with this post-discursive *I* becomes a possible journey; a 'curriculum'. Especially given our 'education' into language, many of us need to work hard to regain a capacity of seeing that is not bound by the kaleidoscopic setting of words; of either *me* or in fact, of the *reflective I*. How do I know that such journey beyond the familiar exists? I have been taking it for quite some time now. My own journey, for example, has revealed a *me* that seems to be a most hard-headed case. But, I've seen this capacity emerge in many students, and there's great difficulty yet no less reward in it. I've also come to trust regular contemplative practice as a path to its invoking. That which makes it difficult is *me* as we shall see. The more *me* is invested in itself the harder it is to see through its habit. The *reflective I* may at times suffer from similar problems. It too, is invested in the medium of discourse. This carries both advantages and disadvantages. The advantage of the *reflective I* is its ability to serve as a mediator.

First, it is a link to the study of *me*. The two share great affinities. They thrive on discourse and language, and they both tend to be *disembodied* 'beings that live in the mind'. What distinguishes the *reflective I* from *me*, is its capability of detachment from the content of thinking. It is able to say 'this is non-sense' without getting furious for having been the one who thought the non-sense. There is a risk, however. Given the affinities between *me* and the *reflective I*, we may easily get too fond of the *reflective I* and find ourselves quickly collapsing into a sophisticated *me* as I'll later mention.

Second, the discursive *reflective I* can be deployed both as a component for a transformative engagement with the *contemplative I*, and as a way of rendering insights of a *contemplative I* and contemplating them through philosophy, poetry, art, and dialogue.

We need both the *reflective I* and the *contemplative I* for exploring the breadth of an *I* curriculum, but eventually it is this *post-discursive contemplative I* that I want to get to as that which studies and that which is being studied in this 'curriculum'. So here's how we will do this. In Chapter 8 *me* was our subject matter, and the *reflective I* was in the background enabling us to depict the *curriculum of me*. Here we reverse the two. We want to make this *reflective I* into the subject matter to be studied. *Me* will come to our aid, for we learn a lot by contrasting between things, and against the background of *me*, *I* will come into view more clearly. This course of action, will enable us to draw the limits of the *reflective I's agency* and *identity*, which will call us to move beyond its boundaries and to explore the *contemplative I*. As will be developed:

> The *contemplative I* is the one that takes us beyond a socially-culturally constructed identity, whether as *me(s)* or as *reflective I(s)*. It is this embodied contemplative I that takes us beyond language and discourse to enable us to escape the self-justifying system that creates the problem of education as 'education'. It all begins with attending *in here* deliberately.

The Boundaries of *Me's* and the *Reflective I's* Agencies

One way that I suggest here for exploring the *curriculum of I*, has to do with marking the boundaries of *agency* and how it relates to the boundaries between *me* and *I*. Where does *me* end and where does *I* begin? What are the limits of this *I*? In Chapter 8 I discussed how *me's* false sense of *agency* is formed based on mind wandering and *self-reflection*. In the following we continue that thread as we further poke holes in *me's* sense of *agency* based on the *reflective I*, which as mentioned above, will hardly exhaust the matter.

Reflective I, Reflective Practice, and the Limits of Their Agency

First, consider your *me* as the content of your thoughts while *mind-wandering* and *self-reflecting* throughout your day as you engage with others, as you are calm, as you lose your temper, as you feel happy, sad, driving, watching TV, working out at the gym, buying groceries, walking with your kid to his Karate lesson, standing in line at the bank, teaching or learning.....you know – consider the script of your *life* as all those beads of attention set on the horizontal time axis. If you made a long list of all thoughts that cross your mind and looked at the content of these thoughts you would probably see just how conflictual *me* is. It may in fact be more appropriately called *mes* in plural:

'I want to be a good student, but I also want to be the clown of the class', 'I want the teacher to like me, but my friends will think I'm not cool if I show that', 'I know it's wrong to cheat on the exam, but I need to pass it', 'I hate my job, but I keep working in it?', 'I know I need to spend more time with the kids, but I don't', 'I know I need to lose weight, but I still go for that extra doughnut'... but it works the other way around as well: 'Despite my urge to eat another doughnut I manage to remember that I'm on a diet', 'Though I know my friends will think I'm a nerd, I'm not going to smoke pot'. *At the back of your mind, make a mental note of what was introduced in the latter sentences. We will soon question the agency they involve.*

Me seems to provide constant options some of them wise and others problematic. Based on these options 'someone' *in here* needs to choose wisely.[8] Why is *me* so incoherent? What makes *me* choose one possibility over the other? How is it that some *me* thoughts become actions and others don't? How is it that we can get very angry sometimes and want to slap someone in the face, but we don't do that, and if by a regretful error we do, many of us may actually know that we were wrong to do so. If *me* didn't want to do it, then who did? Or can we say that *me* lost control? Well who was it *in here* that *took* control, when *me* lost it? When challenged with two conflicting wants who's choosing in there? Or is it the case, that sometimes I am a *me* that is reasonable and at other times, I am a *me* that loses his or her temper?

Based on a rational *reflective I* that explores *me* and its agency, we are broadly faced with three tacit dispositions toward all these thoughts that go on *in here*:

(a) All of them are *me*,
(b) none of them are *me*,
(c) some of them are *me* and some are not.

Each of them proposes serious problems:

a) *All thoughts are me.* Whatever comes to my mind whether I wander or self-reflect, whether I feel like the agency behind the thought or not – *is me.* This is very intuitive but incredibly problematic. What this yields is that I am a highly self-contradictory person. My mind is quite a mess. It thinks both wise and helpful thoughts as well as horrible and unhelpful thoughts. I don't have a clue of why I have the latter, but when they come I may *self-reflect:* 'you shouldn't be thinking about these things, or like this'. Broadly, I treat such thoughts as I would treat dreams at night. When these are troubling or horrific, I get troubled 'but it's just a dream', I tell myself, so I'm not really responsible for them despite the fact that they came from *in here.* That already suggests that hardly anyone seriously holds this position. Or rather we hold it only when it seems appropriate, which means that **not all thoughts are me.**

b) *None of these thoughts are me.* You can imagine that this would be unacceptable for many, for if I am neither my deliberate thoughts, nor my non-deliberate ones – then what on earth is going on? Who's going to take responsibility for all this mess *in here?* What's it for in the first place? If none of these thoughts are *me,* then why do I follow any of them and how is it that they *do* seem to affect *me?* – so this doesn't really work either.

c) *Some thoughts are 'really' me and others are not 'really' me* – No less problematic, although this is a way of being that I suspect most people adopt in one way or another. It is a strategy of coping with the fact that we are so self-contradictory, mingled with a fair amount of denial. We simply identify ourselves only with the 'better' thoughts, and try not to publicize the lesser ones that we disavow. We do much of this inadvertently for we don't seriously begin to ponder where are all the lesser thoughts or non-deliberate ones coming from. Thoughts come and go too quickly to allow us to actually spend time contemplating such things, and our attention is required at other places. So this is probably what most of us do. That means that *in here* we tacitly travel with the understanding that *me* is quite a problematic thing to cling to, but most of our lives are spent with an attention *out there* and an existence that has its 'own' problems to take care of. So we don't tend to bring such problems to the foreground. Furthermore, there does not seem to be anyone else around *in here* that can take responsibility for our thoughts so we try to live with this and hope for the best. If we lose our temper we say things like 'that wasn't like *me*' leaving the question 'well who was it like then?' as a negative accent never quite probed.

Now what did we just do above? – This was an attempt to recruit the *reflective I* to challenge *me*. It's been somewhat successful and 'educative' in showing the dubious kind of agency that *me* carries with it that we've refuted in other ways in the previous chapter. What it also proves is that the *reflective I* grants us with a certain kind of *agency*. It is reflected in two places:

a) Agency that manifests in deliberations we take in life. Recall those sentences above that I asked you to keep in mind about resisting an extra doughnut and the smoking of pot. That may very well be a *reflective I* revealing how we can regulate our emotions, suspend instant gratification, and invest ourselves in our long-term goals.

b) Agency over the *content* of thinking. This manifests in the ability to develop an argument, like the current one, concerned with the false agency of *me*. Indeed this entire book builds on this kind of *agency*. (This says little about the quality of the arguments in and of themselves, which is for *you* to determine). Hang on to this. We'll revisit this soon.

Notwithstanding, as analytical and rational as all this might seem, such analysis remains made of the same fabric of which *me* is made – discourse, language, words – *narrative*. What about the agency behind the *reflective I* itself?

*

Demarcating the Reflective I's Limits

We need to get our hands dirtier in order to point to the need for the *contemplative I*. Two quick first-person experiments will help us further demarcate the boundaries of the *reflective I's* sense of agency. These aim to explore agency over the process and content of thinking that we may associate with it.

Self-experiment 1: *Stop Thinking*

As discussed in Chapter 3, there was a phase in your life when you were not so invested in your 'narrative self' and in thinking in words, manipulating your thoughts through *self-reflection* or being manipulated by them through *mind-wandering*. Our first experiment will explore whether we have control over the *process* of thinking. Controlling the process will begin by examining whether you are able to *stop* it. So, let's see if you can stop thinking upon demand for say ... two minutes. Success would be defined as a situation in which there will be *no verbal events* coming from your mind during this period.

> Go ahead. Set a clock for two minutes from now, and try it: Sit comfortably and all you need to do, is not think for these two minutes. Go....

I hope that you tried it. I seriously doubt whether you were successful. For most people, I doubt whether even ten word-less seconds passed *in here*. Do not get frustrated, this is all part of an 'educative' journey. You see, I know at the outset that there's about a 0.000000000001% chance that anyone will be able to stop thinking based on the instructions that were given. Note also that we are just inquiring agency here. *We're not eschewing thinking as 'bad' or anything of the sort.*

What really interests us here is *what just happened in here?* How did my mind attempt to tackle this irrational injunction 'not to think'? Most people would not know how to fathom the idea of stopping their narrative. It would almost be like asking them to die for a certain amount of time. The process of thinking, whatever the content it yields in your case, seems to have a life of its own.

What we gain by our unsuccessful attempt here, is an initial image of the limits of the *reflective I*. Why? I suspect that the following options are possible experiences that you had, if you tried the self-experiment:

a) While you were trying *not* to think you may have experienced mind-wandering or *self-reflecting*, which would locate you in *me*. That's obviously thinking....

b) You may have also experienced a *reflective I* that was trying to figure out how to get rid of itself. That won't work of course. The only means the *reflective I* is familiar with for such purpose is *reflective practice* resulting in quite a cumbersome strategy – you can't stop the process of thinking by thinking it away.

If the *reflective I* attempts to divorce itself from the medium of thinking it dies, and in that sense it may suffer from the very same predicament of *me* that was discussed in Chapter 8 (p. 238).[9] The *reflective I* can exercise incredible analytical detachment from the content over which it reflects, and Descartes' *Meditations* – a masterpiece that I admire as much as I critique – may be the exemplar of this kind of thinking. But, it has no agency over the process of thinking, which is its mode of expression. So the conclusion is that *the* reflective I *has no control over the choice whether to think or not. The process of thinking is not in its hands*, at least not if you will its stopping in this kind of way. So indeed Descartes may have gotten it backward. It's not 'I think therefore I am', but rather '(reflective) *I/me* is, therefore it thinks even when it tries not to'.[10] Again I'll say this: I am not recommending *not* thinking. All I am doing is challenging the sense of agency over the process of thinking, that *me* as well as the *reflective I* seem to attribute to themselves.

Self-experiment 2: *Think Only About the Content of Your Choice*

Now perhaps you might think that if you have no control over the *process* of thinking, you might be able to control the *content* – that is, what you think *about*. Just a few paragraphs above that's what I said that the *reflective I* is capable of doing. But let's test it more closely. Choose a theme that you are really interested in (e.g., the current baseball league, a recent novel you've read, quantum physics, a political issue). Again, set a clock for two minutes from now. Success would be defined as limiting the *content* of your thinking *only* to the theme you chose to think about.

> Sit comfortably, and let's see whether you can remain focused only on this theme without the intrusion of irrelevant thoughts into this context, for two minutes. Go . . . . . .

I'll assume that you tried this. You may have noted that it is not that simple. It is true that some people are better at it and when we have a very definite issue that we need to solve, we may be able to focus for extended periods of time. In fact, there's a chance that you felt that you actually managed to think *only* on the theme you chose to think about. I suspect, however, that if you reflect back you will find that other things were there too. Perhaps some sounds around you? One or two uncalled for thoughts that barged into your thinking; discomfort in your body? We may be far better in controlling the *content* than we are in controlling the *process*, but we are not fully in control of it. If you doubt this, try extending the experiment to five, ten, thirty minutes… All this means that even the *reflective I* that's required for such *reflective practice* is not fully in our control. There are many questions to ask here, but at least at this point, we have to admit that our 'educational' journey into the nature of agency as part of the *curriculum of I*, has been quite frustrating. Neither *me* nor the *reflective I* can be fully viewed as the agents behind the content of our thinking or its process. However, there are very important things to say that sum the above before we engage our *contemplative I*. The first two points begin with the nature of the *reflective I's agency*, but then they lead us into this book's theme – reconstructing 'education'. The *matrix of mind* will again come to our aid:

1. *The reflective I is still an agent, but its agency comes into play only based on the horizontal time axis.* One has to somehow rescue our ability to actually make sense and build arguments. After all we do seem to have such capability, so how does this emerge given our lack of agency over process and limited agency over content. The answer comes from the fact that *reflective practice* is based on the horizontal time axis. As a famous saying goes: 'it's not in the writing, it's in the re-writing'. Our ability to review our ideas, change them and correct them is how we practice our agency over the content of our thinking. Such act means looking at what we have thought in a past moment, reformulating it now, reflecting on this transformed thought again, until a satisfactory idea (at least for the time being) is formed. That is, only once the horizontal time axis comes into the picture, can the kind of agency identified with this *reflective I* come to the fore.

2. The logic of *lacking* agency over thinking as a *curriculum of I*: Maybe the whole point of thinking based on a *reflective I* is *not* having full agency over thought-content. If we did have full agency over it there is a chance that we would know in advance where our thinking is going to lead; in other words, we would have the solution in our hands right at the outset and thinking would become redundant. This is a wonderful place to contemplate again why this is not merely about thinking, but about an *inner curriculum*. As opposed to the *curriculum of me* that revolves in past patterns within similar thought-content, *reflective practice* deeply acknowledges our mind as an *inner curriculum*. It is this freshness of not-knowing where our thinking will lead that spirals us mysteriously from within

our own minds to novel territories that eject us out of circularity. This may also be part of what sends 'society' out of its routinization that Weber labeled as the 'iron cage'.

3. Discovering the lack of agency is 'education' and it follows clearly in the lines of this entire book: Distinguishing contingency from that which is non-contingent. Let us not rely on what we think is the case and examine exactly what can be relied upon as the fundamentals for a reconstructed 'education'. In this sense, exposing a false/limited agency is at least as important as discovering a true one.

4. If you feel frustrated then consider that I do not think of 'education's' aim as making life easy for us. There is something redundant in an easy path. The journey *inward* is about transforming our habitual way of seeing things. Transformation, in this sense, must have something to do with challenging that which is already known.

5. The discovery of the *reflective I's* lack of agency is a call for 'education'. Consider that this *reflective I* itself has a 'tradition' to heed if it remains grounded in the philosophical tradition with which it is identified. As you may have noticed I have less of that loyalty. As Mark Twain once said 'holy cows make great hamburgers' (apologies to vegetarians), and tradition itself tends to come with quite a baggage of holy cows. The status of tradition may at times parallel the status of *me* when it becomes part of a 'social narrative' – it can prune a mind and blind it to the contingency of the assumptions that underlie the pruning. The mind starts to follow paths for the mere reason that these paths were followed before its arrival – "in the beginning there was 'education' then the mind came along" (see Chapter 1). Tradition can entail unchecked habits. It is indispensable as a structure to begin with, but it also carries the seeds of blindness.

> If a tradition does not include practices that challenge its own frameworks, then the mind that will be initiated into it will hardly harbor the possibility that there may be something beyond the frameworks that it already knows. (This applies to science, wisdom traditions and life writ large).

Before we move in to the *contemplative I*, I'll remark that I clearly cannot tell how much you actually tried the above experiments. Reluctance to perform them is perfectly understandable. However, I do admit that without your experience my argument becomes flawed. That is because your *reflective I* might be convinced, but it is embodiment that I am after. You don't have to take *my* words for the importance of embodiment to 'education'; here's Alfred North Whitehead (1967): "I lay it down as an educational axiom that in teaching you will come to grief as soon as you forget that your pupils have bodies" (p. 78) and later, "[T]o a large extent book-learning conveys second-hand information, and as such can never rise to the importance of immediate practice" (p. 81). Both Whitehead and myself are fingers pointing to the moon. The choice to try things 'for real' remains yours *always*, but as we move on, the need to do so will become more pressing...

*

Engaging the *Contemplative I:* Back Where We Started – *Attention*

There's a more primary locus of *agency*. It's neither the *process* nor the *content* of thinking. It must precede both. It makes sense to assume that agency must somehow precede the processes that it attempts to govern and control. *Me* dwells in *content* hence cannot control it. It is rather the result of *content*. The *reflective I* takes us up one level. It grants us some control over *thinking processes*. It can't *stop* thinking but it grants us with some *agency* over *content* and leads us to some agency over *me*. What will move us beyond that?

> We are back where we started. Remember James: 'for the moment what we attend to is reality'.

The *contemplative I* moves us higher in the hierarchy to directly work with the flashlight of attention. *In here now, deliberately.* Note however again,

> just as the *reflective I* does not grant us with the possibility of stopping the process of thinking, but rather allows us some agency over its content, so the *contemplative I* does not grant us the possibility of stopping the process of attending, but rather grants us with some agency over what we attend to and how. Just as our *reflective I's* agency can be trained to improve how we think, the *contemplative I's* agency can be trained to improve how we attend.

You can try stopping attention to test this, but I'll move on.[11] We will soon test what agency we do have over attention, but first let's ground this in the reconstruction of 'education'. It is only now that I bring a frequently cited passage from James on this matter:

> The faculty of voluntarily bringing back a wandering attention, over and over again, is the very root of judgment, character, and will . . . An education which should improve this faculty would be the *education par excellence*. (2007, p. 401)

Why did James say this? – because for him attention and agency (to which he referred as *will*) were considered to be two sides of the same coin. James offered a crucially important explanation for why 'educating' attention would be the ideal 'education'. I'll elaborate it and then offer a more nuanced additional explanation:

1) The control over *what* we attend to determines reality for that moment: As we saw in Chapter 7: " . . . the whole drama of the voluntary life hinges on the amount of attention, slightly more or slightly less, which rival motor ideas may receive" (James 1984, p. 247). It's all about how proficient we are in holding fast to the thoughts that serve ourselves and others best and acting upon them. Given the limited span of awareness, by holding fast to the worthy thoughts we ban competing thoughts and actions that are not as worthy.

Prosaically, it is this ability that will enable the student studying for an exam to keep at it despite the fact that the Super Bowl is on TV and he has to give it up. It is this ability that will enable him to live with the low grade received because he deliberately chose the Super Bowl after determining that it is a more meaningful activity for him even in the long run. It is this ability that will enable me to overcome trauma, whenever I am flooded with overwhelming memories. It is this ability that will enable me to face the vicissitudes of love, death, and all that life will summon to my path. How? – my reality is eventually determined by what I focus on. From the perspective of attention, there is always the choice of mobilizing experience from one place to another. This perspective is important, but it touches upon the surface of the more dramatic one that takes us back to Chapter 7:

2) The control over *how* we attend determines reality for that moment:

> There are two main strategies we can adopt to improve the quality of life. The first is to try making external conditions match our goals. The second is

> to *change how we experience conditions* to make them fit our goals better...Neither of these practices is effective when used alone. (Csikszentmihalyi 1991, p. 43, italics mine)

A recurrent theme in this book suggests that the *how* shapes the *what* to the point that the *how* becomes more important, yet our attention tends to be lured by the *what*. Attending to *how* we attend is a variation on James's explanation, for attending to the *how* makes the *how* a *what*.

> Attending to how we attend to the content means addressing the mind as pedagogue, shifting the kaleidoscopic setting that prunes this moment based on the past – based on *me* and based even on the *reflective I* – to a de-pruned mind that accesses the place from which this moment becomes a universal one, rather than the particular one that my habitual mind makes of it.

I may very well experience suffering or meaninglessness, for example, and no-one denies their existence. Yet, if suffering or meaninglessness are the *what* of my experience, there's a mind that interpreted them as such behind this experience. If that mind is stuck in the 'illusion of its omniscience', it is stuck in the *what*. If I however, turn to examine the mind that had thus defined reality, then the kaleidoscopic setting (or perhaps its mere presence) are challenged; the framework that the mind lays over experience is dispelled; the bead of experience returns to its primary state and becomes acknowledged as a placeholder of *life*. Even my suffering and meaninglessness are then nested in meaning.

The *curriculum of I* takes us to a different kind of engagement. It is that radical meta-pedagogical turn on which I have been insisting throughout the book. Any practice that will somehow turn us to engage directly, skillfully, and deliberately, with the '*origin of attention*' would be a pedagogy that opens this curriculum. Broadly speaking, this domain opens a variety of curricular-pedagogical orientations some of which are described in the final chapter within the current discourse of the 'contemplative turn in education' (Ergas and Todd 2016). Here I only mention that this turn, which has emerged around the turn of the millennium, is shaped both by scientific research and by wisdom traditions. Each of these orientations brings different ways of depicting what I view as a meta-pedagogical turn *in here* as well as a long list of curricular and pedagogical options (e.g., mindfulness, compassion meditation, philosophical dialogue, tai chi, yoga, contemplative-based arts). My concern in this book has less to do with *which* practices to apply, but rather with the facticity of the need to view them as an integral part of a reconstructed 'education'. I view this as an *ethical* orientation that I will further elaborate toward the end of this chapter. As we progress, I will develop this both theoretically and *practically* based on curricular-pedagogical foundations of the *curriculum of I*.

*

The *Contemplative I*'s Agency

An exploration of our agency at the level of attention can take us to two initial practices that are no other than variations of mindfulness practice that you've tried in previous chapters.[12] Let's first experiment with these two, and then I'll interpret them based on this book's terminology. This will require twelve minutes of your life and hopefully will leave you with the wish to further explore this. Really try to get into it, so that what comes next will make more sense. So here's the first out of two self-experiments:

> Take five minutes and try to make a commitment to stay with this exercise. Find a quiet room in your house and set yourself comfortably on a chair. Set a clock/phone to indicate when the time is up. It would probably be best to close your eyes if you can, but you can also leave them open. Bring your attention to your abdomen and take three intentional breaths to get a feel for that area. Now let your breathing fall back to its normal pattern (slow/fast/shallow/deep, whatever it is, is fine). As best you can, in the next five minutes keep your attention on the *sensation* of the breath in the area of the abdomen. If anything else comes to mind, or if you find that your attention is wandering from your abdomen, just make a mental note of wandering once you note it, and simply bring your attention back to the *sensation* of the breath in your abdomen. That's all there is to it. Keep at it until five minutes have passed.

I'll assume you just completed your five minutes. In a moment I'm going to offer an informed guess on what happened to you while you tried this, but first – write down a few sentences that describe what you've experienced while conducting this self-experiment, so you can test the credibility of my analysis.

What you've just practiced is a version of mindfulness referred to as *focused attention*. There are numerous things to say here, but I want us to stay focused on the question of agency. Based on trying this out with nearly 500 students by now, gathering from extant literature[13] that describes others' experiences and of course based on my years of practicing on a daily basis, I present the following scenarios, one or more of which might resemble what you've described. These are not necessarily mutually exclusive. They could rather be viewed as depicting different phases within the five minute span of the self-experiment:

1. You just couldn't do it, or felt that you didn't want to despite committing to it in the beginning. After a couple of breaths you just stopped. It was either annoying, or boring, or your back bothered you, but whatever it was (and you might not even be able to articulate exactly what bothered you), it seemed useless to continue.

2. You pushed on through the five minutes but found the task quite impossible to accomplish. After a few breaths, you were taken by mind-wandering and/or *self-reflection*. Thoughts came up in your mind, and you spent your time thinking of other things. The end of the session may have taken you by surprise, somewhat as if you were awakened from a dream. Which gets us to the next possibility:

3. You fell asleep or felt it coming in a moment or two. The fact that you were tired might certainly have something to do with that. You may have a very faint idea of what went on there for five minutes and since it actually felt quite nice, you settled for that. Either the thought that we were interested in examining attention never came to mind, or it did, but you were lulled into something of: 'let's do that breathing thing some other time'.

4. After a moment or two of focus, a thought came to mind that this is a great opportunity to deliberately plan your day ahead, now that you're so focused. You touched base with your 'to do list' and spent much of the time planning the near or far future.

5. You somewhat managed to be with the breath throughout, but several other things caught your attention (e.g., thoughts, pain in the back), and from time to time you 'phased out' for indiscriminate periods of time.

6. You recruited all your might and stayed focused on the breath but it felt like quite a battle. Thoughts kept barging in and you used a lot of your energy to ward them off. At the end of the five minutes you were somewhat close to a headache, your body felt somewhat tight, and it felt as if you may be missing some oxygen.

There may be other options, but there's one scenario that is almost guaranteed *not* to reflect your experience: if you are new to this, then it is very unlikely that you simply sat there fully attentive to your breath throughout the five minutes, content and happy and experiencing this to be a worthwhile endeavor.[14]

I do hope that I am not frustrating you with these experiments. They are not futile I assure you. They mark the boundaries of agency *at this moment*. Those boundaries can change as we will later see but even as such it may serve to comfort you that what we are doing aligns well with one of Socrates's most important teachings in the *Apology* – it's better to expose our false assumptions then to live based on them. We are applying that to our sense of agency at this moment. It's painful, but following another important philosopher – this time Descartes – (at least as concerned with his method rather than with its outcomes) – reconstructing foundations may require exposing the shakiness of the current ones.

So let's try a different practice before I offer an interpretation of the above experiment. The basics are similar:

> Take five minutes and try to make a commitment to stay with this exercise. Find a quiet room in your house and set yourself comfortably on a chair. Again, set a clock/phone to indicate when the time is up. Again, best to close your eyes if you can. Now take three intentional breaths just to settle in. This time: spend the next five minutes allowing your attention to wander as it pleases. It's as if you're in the dark, and you know that the territory is huge, but someone else is holding a flashlight, and you have no control over where he or she will point the beam. Yet this guy with the flashlight never spends more than an instant on any of the objects to which he orients the beam. So it lights for a moment, and then it moves elsewhere. All you have to do is just follow that flashlight, with no preference at all as to what's being chosen by this person. Your focus here is on following anything that appears, *without getting stuck*. It could be a thought, then a sensation, then a sound from *out there* and an image *in here*. Anything. That's all there is to it. Keep at it until five minutes have passed.

Again, write a few words about what you've experienced during these moments.

This time we tried another version of mindfulness referred to as *open attention* or choice-less awareness.[15] We let our natural brain-mind's tendency to seek salience 'do its thing' so to speak, and we follow its lead without imposing any preferences that will change its ways.

Focused attention and open attention are not the same practice, and they challenge us in different ways. Again, however, staying with the question of agency, an informed guess as to what you've experienced here will take us to similar scenarios that were mentioned above. Chances are that you had a really hard time to wrap your mind around the possibility of just following attention without getting stuck or in fact, taking charge of attention and 'telling it where to go'. You thus may have wandered and/or self-reflected, planned your day ahead, fell asleep, etc. If you felt that you just followed your chain of thoughts and it amounted to an actual narrative there is all likelihood that you've been had by *me*. The instructions at least ask you to note that a thought came to mind and once you note it, let your attention move on. If you actually formed ideas in a chain then your *me-content/reflective I* lured you into getting stuck on planning/remembering etc.

If we confine ourselves to the above two experiments the conclusion should be that we have little agency over attention, and this was in fact James's position as we will see. But don't be surprised at this *at all*.

> All that you experienced is the consequence of the pruning of mind through 'education' as we constructed it! Your mind has been 'educated' by *me*-'society' as well as by its own natural curriculum of embodied perception, to behave exactly as it did.

Let's look at this analytically. Basically what we are asking from ourselves in these self-experiments is to engage in a 'curriculum' the structure of which is diametrically opposed to that of the 'social curriculum' and *me*. Both educate the mind in attending *out there* to a time that is not *now*. The structure of the *curriculum of I* as it emerges from the above experiments/pedagogies reveals this based on the matrix of mind:

In terms of space: We traded the habitual *out there* preoccupation of 'society' and *me* with *in here*. This is expressed in attending to the breath *in here* in *focused attention* as well as in the need to constantly monitor *how* we attend in both practices. While we do have the breath or the objects of attention as *content*, more importantly we need to remind ourselves to *return* to the breath (in *focused attention*), or *not* to get stuck on anything in particular (in *choiceless awareness*). This constant reminding reflects the priority of the *process* of attention over the *content* attended to. We are to take more interest in *how* our minds function in relation to *what* we experience, rather than to simply attend habitually to the *what*. This stands in stark contrast to everything that our brains-minds are used to doing. Our brains-minds are the product of years of habituation toward vigilance, survival, salience, and reward as we saw in Chapter 7. Following the breath (as in *focused attention*), or disengaging constantly from objects to which our brains-minds *naturally* take (as in *open attention*) is pretty much the opposite of what they have been 'educated' to do either based on the 'social curriculum' or based on *embodied perception* and *me*. Such activities are unlikely to be seen as contributing directly to survival and reproduction, and they are the opposite of salience, because constantly bring the feeling of 'more of the same' making our reward system scream for something else.

In terms of time: The focus on the how is a constant demand to be here now. What can be a stronger commitment to *now* than the sensation of our *embodied* breath prior to any of our conceptualizations, or the monitoring of the process of attention that shapes reality? James says this far more eloquently: "Where the body is is 'here'; when the body acts is 'now'; what the body touches is 'this'; all other things are 'there' and 'then' and 'that'" (1976, p. 33). But again, however, *me* will come back at us with vengeance:

> For a brain-mind that was habituated in *me*-'society' there is no surer way to make the *insufficiency of now* more tangible, than to propose to it to practice mindfulness.

Our narrative 'self' risks extinction here. *Me's* thriving over the horizontal time axis is menaced by the *now*. It will intervene in this attempt in an instant. Mind-wandering and *self-reflection* will thus constantly bring 'society' (*out there* content) into the practice. Since the body is stationary and it cannot be active in the world as the 'social narrative' expects, the doing will become the workings of the mind as the 'narrative self' will engage in mental time traveling – remembering, planning – 'doing within the mind'. This, as we saw in the previous chapter, is the clear *defaulting* of the brain into its habitual baseline.

> Old habits indeed die hard; especially when it comes to challenging our habitual sense of identity and agency; that locus within us that we believe to be 'in charge' of all our habits...

Me and/or the *reflective I* will fill in the void with planning, remembering, and other features discussed in Chapter 8. Sophisticated as *me is*, it will easily justify this escape from the practice: 'I have far better things to do then watch the breath. This is such a waste of time.' This is the classical *me* argument that most of my students come up with and I certainly know it from first-person. How can you identify it's *me*? – arguments of a waste of time belong in the horizontal time axis. The *contemplative I* has absolutely nothing to do with it. Its undergirding disposition is one in which the facticity of *this* bead's existence has precedence over the content of experience. *Every bead counts; even a bead of 'benign attending to the breath'.*[16]

So indeed there is a logic to all this. Our brain-mind is the product of the habituation of attention. It is the result of all beads thread up to this moment. Can this be rightly referred to as *agency*? How much *are* we in charge of our lives, if our attention cannot comply with what we've asked it to do? How is it that I've begun with the breath and then something in here took charge of my decision without any apparent deliberation? Who's governing my *inner curriculum*? Is there indeed someone *in here* that really knows that it is better to wander right now, then to observe the breath? So it seems that our exploration of agency leads to an impasse. Neither *embodied perception* as a natural process, nor *me* nor the *reflective I* nor the *contemplative I*, seem to be fully in our hands. The result is then that

> for the moment what we attend to is reality and we do not have a substantial control over the reality to which we attend.

BUT, as suggested above, perhaps expecting to be agents of our attention is comparable to expecting an adult who's never seen numbers in his life to solve a quadratic equation, or asking someone who's never learned English to explain a Shakespearean Sonnet.

> All our conclusions about our lack of agency may be valid in as far as we apply them to minds that have been 'educated' in *me*-'society', yet have never been 'educated' directly in agency. We may have PhDs in rocket science but in terms of 'educating' attention we are kindergarteners.

What I am suggesting here is a resituating of ourselves in regards to our *agency* and *identity* and no less: the core of a reconstructed 'education' based on a *deliberate meta-pedagogical balancing turn*. If *we* are not in control of agency, then *who* is the one engaged there in all those activities in the 'world' and based on what and whom is she/he/it acting? Where exactly does our 'education' stand in regards to the natural process of *embodied perception* and the *me*-'society' hall of mirrors that emerges from it? How much is our 'education' really moving us *beyond* natural tendencies? We are certainly doing a serious job in teaching sophisticated 'knowledge of most worth' that no-one can be expected to know just by natural development based on our 'social curriculum', but what are we doing in regards to the core of who we are, and how we act with each other – *agency, identity?*

> Our stuckness in 'society'-*me* sends us away from the core of what most of our 'educational' agendas hope to achieve. The problem of education is 'education' – Our curricular-pedagogical practices send us *out there*, while the problem begins *in here*. We lack agency over attention, which governs our thoughts and actions. Math, history, literature are all good, but they do not tackle the fundamental 'educational' problem.

The above pedagogies of mindfulness are known as *practices*. It only makes sense to refer to them as such, if there is some trajectory of improvement/development suggested by them. That is, *if you practice, something develops*. Science has been continuously strengthening the evidence for this:

> Educating our attention based on practices that engage us directly with it, leads to a far more grounded sense of ownership over our life, manifested in diverse ways spanning from the instrumental day-to-day awareness to what we are doing to a far more impregnated sense of meaning in life.[17]

The science follows millennia of contemplative practices that originated in wisdom traditions (e.g., Buddhism, Taoism). Both science and wisdom traditions are integrated in various ways in the 'contemplative turn in education' discussed in the next chapter. My focus, however, throughout the book, is on fundamentals. It has more to do with shifting the axis of how we understand 'education', and articulating 'curricular foundations', which explain the *inner curriculum*, and how this constitutes a way out of our conundrum. This will later lead me to radically challenge what I view as an unsubstantiated belief that governs our 'education' and confines its scope: the thought that our *identity* is necessarily 'socially culturally' constructed. We will reach this argument by methodically examining the fundamental mechanism that undergirds the *curriculum of I*: The intentional opening of an internal door within the swinging door of attention, and the inquiry into how our 'social curriculum' works *again*, to dissuade us from that possibility.

*

PASSIVE AND ACTIVE ATTENTION: THE *INTERNAL* DOOR IN *HERE*

The cusp of agency lies then in 'what we do with attention' and this is the point at which the *curriculum of me*, the *reflective I*, and the *curriculum of I* part ways. When I speak of 'doing' something with attention, I mean that broadly speaking,

> At any given moment attention is either oriented by an agency that comes from *in here*, or it is drawn by the pull (or agency) of that which comes at us from *out there*. When it comes from *in here* it can come from the limited agency of *me* or the *reflective I*, or it can come from a broader, more open locus, that is the *contemplative I*.

Allow me to first flesh this out based on a fundamental distinction that was not introduced in the first part of the book. You've actually experienced this distinction when you engaged in the above self-experiments, so it might be easier to explain it now.

The distinction of which I'm speaking, has to do with what James (1984) called passive and active attention (or sustained voluntary attention). Passive attention is that which occurs to us when we are interested in something – we watch a movie, speak with a friend, play tennis, read a good book. Passive attention is not something we *do*. It is something that is done *for* us. It is basically a state that can be characterized as a complete oblivion to one's own attention, and an absorption in the *content* experienced.

Active attention is the opposite. It is the case where we need to attend to something but have difficulty doing so. Hence, we need to actively tinker with attention, motivate ourselves, and reapply ourselves in some way to sustain attention over an object. It is an act of will that when required during day to day life, is usually an indication of a problem as we will soon see. However, I will argue that *it is where the mind reclaims itself in 'education'*. First, let's connect some dots here.

Long ago, in Chapter 2, I described our experience as the result of attention that is like a door that swings between *in here* and *out there*.

What I am saying now, is that the movement between passive attention and active attention constitutes a second *internal* swinging door that distinguishes between the *curriculum of me* and the *curriculum of I.* I am basically making three claims here that will be elaborated afterward:

a) You have been practicing this all your life without knowing it.
b) The majority of people open that internal door only for a fraction of a second, applying the *I* for an instant, and shutting the door back on it as soon as *me* or the *reflective I* are back passively attending to whatever it is that they are recruited to attend to.
c) This internal door is where we can articulate more clearly how the 'social curriculum' (and *me*) expelled the mind from 'education'.

When we function as *me(s)*, or even based on the *reflective I,* we can be very active both externally as we engage in actions and internally when we are absorbed in mind-wandering and *self-reflection.* But all of this activity is either conducted in a *passive* attentional mode, or with brief interventions of active attention that are intended to shift back to the passive mode. *Me can't stand active attention.* The need to activate our attention voluntarily; to reapply ourselves to what we are doing, is an experience that arises in situations that we perceive as negative by definition. Where does it happen to us? – in cases in which we are bored, yet have to remain attentive: when we have to stay focused on our driving yet find ourselves wandering, or when we have a million things on our mind, but we still want to respect the friend that's telling us of how bad her day went, so we at least have to try to appear as if we are listening. This happens in school all the time as well as we will soon see. Ideally, when we enjoy what we are doing, we never need to reapply ourselves to it. Only when something goes wrong, or interferes with our activity do we need to engage our attention actively.

Passive attention by all means applies to mind-wandering *and self-reflection.* Even if wandering thought-content leads to intense worrying, we are still absorbed in it through passive attention. If we switch to *self-reflection* we may be actively manipulating *me*-thoughts, but we don't have to make an effort to actually attend to them. At times we are in fact so taken by these processes that anyone who interferes with these witting or unwitting activities that are passively attended to, will be considered an intruder as in 'leave me alone, *can't you see I'm thinking?*'

Whenever we make an effort to attend to something voluntarily, it implies working with the origin of attention. Normally we do so only for an instant (e.g., we suddenly steer the wheel to avoid the car that just crossed our lane while we were off wandering; we suddenly remember that we need to listen to the lecturer as we notice we've been self-reflecting on other things). We never quite imagine a possibility of making this switch itself into something of a *subject matter*. The *curriculum of I* opens once we make the opening and closing of *this* internal door into an intentional pedagogy; once we begin to open that door for extended periods of time, and based on diverse informed intentions.

Active Attention in Mindfulness Practice

Active attention is where the *contemplative I's* agency comes into the image of 'education' and is in fact practiced.

Mindfulness practices are fundamental practices hence I chose to explore them here, but contemplative practices like yoga, compassion meditation, journaling, and other are all based on the *contemplative I's* practice of active attention. The two types of practices you've tried allow us to demonstrate two different engagements with the agency of the *contemplative I*:

a) In focused attention, when bringing attention to the breath, our agency is expressed in an ability to sustain attention over an object of our choice. The sense of agency here is thus suggestive of control, governing, monitoring.

b) Open awareness is seemingly the opposite. It engages an agency that renounces control, yields, and accepts. Here we are literally allowing the beads of experience to arise in their discreteness and spontaneity. We practice an ability of giving precedence to a reality the facticity of which is *change* that is *not* in our control.[18]

Anyone who will engage in either one of these practices for extended periods of time will see, however, that each type of practice here includes aspects of the other. Focused attention, while supposedly more controlling, requires a yielding to the fact that we have very poor control over our voluntary attention. We thus need to learn to accept the frustration of our untrained mind as *me* keeps hijacking its attention. Open awareness, as an accepting agency, is challenged by the fact that we constantly get stuck. Our wish to control expresses itself in an attempt to manipulate the content experienced based on preferences of 'someone' *in here* that resists the instruction *not* to get stuck.

The practice of mindfulness is one in which *me* and the *contemplative I* (and at times the *reflective I*) reveal themselves based on the internal swinging door that alternates between passivity and activity of attention. It requires much experience to start detecting this and as I mentioned in the beginning of this chapter, my words only take us part of the way. The rest, and might we add – the most important part – comes with *your* practice. To advance further, here's what I recommend: follow the instructions of either open or focused attention above and start practicing it twice a day for five minutes each time. Bear in mind that this is by no means a guide to mindfulness practice.[19] Here it is only proposed as a necessary means to enhance your understanding and to further build your competence for testing my claims. The point I am making reiterates the above,

> Attention can be 'educated'. 'Educating' attention and that which unfolds based on it is as close as I suspect we get to 'educating' agency and identity. That is the place in which anything that happens to us is determined. It is there that it becomes what we call, experience; life as we know it.

But, let us not fall prey to our own predicament. The latter idea may be my own pruned mind speaking. Don't follow that. There may certainly be something more primary than attention as our agency; something with which we are all connected and from which *ethics* emerge as wisdom traditions propose; something such as a Source, a God, A Dharmic law, Tao, Brahman (call it what you will). Of that I cannot speak. What I do believe however, is that we stand better chances of approaching *that*, through active attention. If our excavation will reveal that we need to and can go deeper, then deeper we will have to go in order to discover that which lies beyond a *contemplative I*. The places from which contemplative practices emerge certainly point in that direction, but the *ethics* I propose in the following section leave room for such option without relying on it.

The Ethics of the *Curriculum of I*

This section will not offer a full-fledged ethical treatise.[20] My aim is to describe these points: the ethical stance involved in the choice to engage with *I*, the specific ethics that this 'curriculum' cultivates based on its 'curricular-pedagogical' approach, the nature of the 'good' in this 'curriculum' and its clear embodied sense that leads to 'social' good. The discussion proposed here, is based on a view that I will attempt to defend. Namely that the *contemplative I* is less prone to harm others and *it is beyond social-cultural construction.*

The Choice to Engage in the Curriculum of I as an Ethical Stance

Following the previous chapters, the orientation of attention toward *in here* leads to two paths. Only one of these goes to the heart of matter and reflects an explicit ethical stance:

a) The *curriculum of me* does *not* reflect an ethical deliberation. An unwitting turn *in here* that does not involve at least the *reflective I* does not reflect the ethics of the *curriculum of I. Me* may very well act ethically, but that act is based on automation and embodies the assumption that the act performed is the only one possible. It may be a wonderful deed, but it is *unreflective.*[21] Theoretically we might prefer *mes* that act ethically based on automation rather than *reflecting I's* that do wrong based on reflection, but later I will advocate a naïve view: a deep engagement with the *contemplative I* educates the *reflective I* and *me* in an embodied ethical 'good'.

b) The curriculum of 'I' – The choice to step away from *me* is an ethical choice for when practiced it embodies the understanding that *me* – as who we know ourselves to be in our day-to-day living is in some way limited, problematic, self-centered etc. The ethics emerge here from the presupposition that there must be something beyond this *me* that we are experiencing ourselves to be. Not just other, but *better.* However, that something is *here* and it is my responsibility to seek it *now.*

The ethical transition that is occurring here is one in which something in us reflects the acknowledgement that change is needed *and contrary to our habit, that change is to be sought in changing ourselves and not just in changing the world out there.* It is an ethical stance in which *I* embrace whatever agency *I* can find *in here* and take full responsibility for my life. This is not a renunciation of 'education' in *out there*, nor an escapist or egocentric view that does not care for the world. Quite the contrary, it is rather an understanding that no problems, of any kind, exist without the mind *in here* that views them as such, and hence is an integral part of them.

> The shift between *me* and *I* is a shift in attention. Agency begins there, and that is where *me* ends and *I* begin(s).

Choices based on *me* are the product of past habitual thinking. They appear as real choices, but they smack of determinism. This is extremely useful and is a necessity of life. However, it does not reflect a deliberate questioning of our ways from a place within us that can see our current condition as the result of contingency and the pruning of the mind; a mind which could have followed other paths. Such de-pruned or unpruned place becomes known based on the *curriculum of I*. Alongside learning history, math, sciences, and humanities, our core 'educational' practice should reside there for that is the gateway to how you and I will share lives grounded in wisdom, virtue, and ethics.

The point made so far then, is that the mere choice to engage with the *curriculum of I* is an ethical choice that is reflected in our understanding that what we see is limited. I want to move us forward by explaining how the actual curricular-pedagogical practice of *I* that follows this choice cultivates a specific orientation toward a 'good'.

The Embodiment of Ethics Within the Curricular-Pedagogical Practice of I

What is the key here to this transition from *me* to the *contemplative I*; from *passive attention* to *active attention*? What kind of ethics does it embody and how does it embody such ethics?

As we engage directly in practices such as mindfulness and other forms of contemplative practices, the interior domain of *I/me* opens an arena of curricular-pedagogical orientations. There are diverse components to consider here that are inherent in the different perspective we cultivate toward our encounter with the beads of experience. They interweave curriculum with pedagogy; 'what is experienced' with 'how it is experienced'. The terms I will use to describe them are always approximations and simplifications that I articulate as clearly as possible, yet constantly work to re-blur, so that we do not get too caught up in them. Again, the following is by no means a 'how to practice' guide. This is far more a drawing of some co-ordinates within a possible meta-pedagogical turn the scope of which is far beyond my capability to describe or even know. It is more of sketching ideas that examine *how* we can tread this 'educational' terrain, far more than pinning down *what* we ought to encounter there. This *how* is most basically an ethical stance. For this purpose, I propose two intertwined aspects that are concerned with the cognitive-affective disposition of the *contemplative I* as we engage with it. This cognitive-affective disposition is a *state of being* (a concept discussed in Chapter 7). It draws on the curriculum of embodied perception and binds it with the *curriculum of I*. The two intertwined aspects work directly with the internal door of *active/ passive attention*. They are:

a) The 'cold cognitive' shifting of attention with *detachment* and *discipline*.
b) The 'warm affective' space of *acceptance* and *compassion* that we open to enable *detachment*.[22]

The two reciprocally reinforce each other. They are somewhat of two poles between which an engagement in contemplative practices can run. They are always available, but during *deliberate* practice, given our limited span of attention, we focus on one, while the other lurks in the background. I'll define each component and then use the self-experiments proposed above to exemplify them.

1) *Detachment and discipline*[23]: detachment can somewhat be understood as an internalization of the *me/not-me* Jamesean separation discussed in Chapter 2 and its transposing into the *I/me* split. How so? – When my attention is *out there* I tacitly sense a separation between myself *in here* and the bird/table/text/wall *out there*. Detachment introduces the possibility of observing 'things' *in here* (e.g., thoughts, sensations) in the same way. I am neither my bodily sensations nor my thoughts as discussed in Chapter 3 (p. 62) when I described the *center/periphery* spatial experience of the origin of attention in relation to that over which the flashlight of attention shines. While this sounds peculiar, it is in fact something we do all the time in a subtle sense. For example, *self-reflecting* about a pain in our body, and wishing it would go away, somewhat reflects that we disown this pain as something that doesn't really belong *in here*. Similarly, mindwandering we may emerge with the wish to disown some of the thoughts we had just experienced. When we do this we reflect both the possibility of

detachment, and the entanglement with these thoughts and sensations that were treated as part of us in the first place (that is, had we not viewed them as 'belonging to us', there would be no need to disown them).

In the former examples however, detachment is not *practiced*, it is more imagined in an unwitting way. Practicing focused attention as you did above, you had to simply observe your breath. The detachment aspect there suggested that you observe it *as if the breath is not really yours*. You're not 'doing' the breathing; breathing happens. Clearly, you can affect its pace, hold it for a while etc. but most of your day your body takes care of the breath just fine without your deliberate assistance. The practice here brings this breath to the foreground as your subject matter at this point. You're engaged in a communicative act with it, as you would with that which the teacher writes on a board, or as you are engaging now with *this word*.

Overall I characterize this detachment as somewhat of a 'cold' pedagogical aspect of active attention within the *curriculum of I*. Its 'cold-ness' is expressed in two ways:

a) It *separates*, poses borders, places a distance between observer and observed.

b) It involves the *disciplining* aspect of calling us back to attend to the breath (or another object), whenever we note that we had wandered away.[24]

When you follow your breath, or that beam of the flashlight (during open awareness) it is highly probable that 'something' will lure your attention elsewhere. You may resist it for a while, as you actively reapply yourself to the breath but at some point you may be conquered. By whom? – Well at least in the terminology developed in this book there are not many candidates. If the content you experience as an alternative to your breaths has something to do with plans for tomorrow, memories, self-referential thinking, etc. by now you will know that *me* has arrived. If you found yourself thinking 'how stupid this practice is', 'this is such a waste of time ... I've got so many things to do', 'this might be good when I retire' – those kind of things – you can be quite sure that the *contemplative I* has been fully hijacked by *me*.

It may so happen that during such practice you will find yourself contemplating loftier questions of meaning as you develop some thought that came from nowhere. This can actually yield lovely insights.

Strictly speaking, however, at the level of agency this might be a case of being hijacked by the *reflective I* that likes to intercept as it identifies food for building ontologies and fancy arguments. It's certainly not a bad thing to do. But it is what it is – a transformation of mindfulness practice, into *reflective practice*. The only thing I am saying is that only when you've made a deliberate choice to do that, and your choice seems to be emerging from a deeper knowing, can you say that agency has not been hijacked. Whether it is *me* or the *reflective I* that show up in the practice, both indicate that the *contemplative I* had collapsed; in the former case, completely, and in the latter perhaps partially.[25]

When you suddenly 'catch yourself' wandering it is the 'cold' disciplining aspect here that comes to your aid as you call yourself back to *practice* – to re-establish detachment, which actually leads us right in to acceptance . . .

2) *Acceptance and compassion* – detachment becomes a struggle when you are overwhelmed with stressed thoughts and worries. If you discipline yourself harshly you risk paying a price of exacerbating an internal antagonism that may eventually lead you astray from practice. Disciplining here is a *friendly nurturing internal* act directly linked with the 'warm' affective qualities of *acceptance, non*-judgmentalism, kindness, compassion, empathy (the list can be extended).

The heart, core, and embodiment of ethics of the *curriculum of I* lie here. It is your mustering the best in yourself toward that which you encounter within yourself. If in the midst of your seventh attempt to 'recover' from wandering away from the breath, you get sickly annoyed with your mind – the idea is to note 'annoyance'. You feel your body's itching to move, to open the eyes, to stop. You *accept* all these as the possible content of beads of experience of 'annoyance', 'body itching to move', 'wish to open the eyes', yet you observe them as such from the non-contingent level, which proposes that each of these, is a placeholder for life.

You may even find that your eyes opened inadvertently, perhaps you even stood up without any recollection of giving your body 'permission' to do so. You may get annoyed at that too. You note that, accept it, live with it now. Your ability to note it non-judgmentally is the expression of having detached yourself from it; of having accepted it. Whenever you can't accept, you practice accepting your unacceptance, you get annoyed; perhaps shout. You did what you could. You'll come around . . . detach . . . *accept*.

This is the place where the horizontal time axis becomes embodied in *now*. The only way you can compassionately address this untamed mind is a certain belief – in itself something that is gradually cultivated – that this mind is not hopeless. That it can learn to bring itself to the moment. The *future* thus appears in the affective disposition of kindness toward oneself *now* that is based on the faith that there is a point in this. But the point is made *now* as *I* unfolds in this curriculum. It is not 'wishful thinking'. It is only the undercurrent of courage and minimal faith to face oneself *now*.

The Body as a Gateway to the Contemplative I

There are diverse ways by which we can engage with the *contemplative I*. Many of them are in fact becoming more known and practiced in educational settings within the contemplative turn that will be discussed in Chapter 10. They include arts such as music, dance, calligraphy, martial arts, as well as meditation, contemplative reading, and several others. My own experience allows me to speak more about the body as a gateway to this curricular locus, since it has been central to my personal quest both in academic writing and in life (if one cares to distinguish between these two at all).

My aim here is not a general elaboration of the place of the body in the curriculum; a theme that several scholars have addressed in an attempt to remedy some of the maladies of the 'social curriculum'.[26] My intention is to very briefly elaborate why *sensations* must be engaged as an integral part of a *curriculum of I*, how this relates to active and passive attention as well as to the cold and warm curricular-pedagogical aspects discussed above.

As I mentioned when discussing the *curriculum of me* (p. 203), in order to examine habitual ways, we must come at our habit from a different angle. We need to transcend the ballpark within which that habit plays its game, for a habit's power lies in the inertia it has gained by automated practice and by its relentless life within that very ballpark. As Dewey claimed, "[H]abits may be profitably compared to physiological functions like breathing, digesting" (1957, p. 14). I view being *me* as a nexus of habits that create somewhat of a closed system that becomes quite resistant to change. Such habits as Dewey would define them have a "fixed hold upon us, instead of our having a free hold upon things" (ibid.). However they are not merely, "passive tools waiting to be called into action from without" (1958, p. 54) such as walking, typing, or driving. They cease opportunities toward enactment and rule our thoughts and our actions (1958, p. 25).

When we discussed the *curriculum of me* one of the methods proposed for coming at it from a different angle was *sampling me by surprise*. Engaging the *curriculum of I* requires a more dedicated and deliberate practice, especially if we wish to move beyond the *reflective I*. A *reflective I* is already characterized by the capacity of detachment and distance from *me*. Our engagement in *reflective practice*, is already a stepping away from *me*. This *reflective I's* capacity is its great virtue, but in many cases it also comes with the price of an alienation from the body and an entrenchment in the fortress of discourse – even when that discourse is remarkably wise. Although phenomenologists such as Merleau-Ponty (1965) have offered insightful accounts that expressed our embodiment in philosophical discourse, you cannot transcend philosophy by more philosophy.[27] To put this in other words – here Wittgenstein's (1961), tractatus 7: 'whereof one cannot speak, thereof one must be silent' is not interpreted as an end but as a beginning. Clearly this spells out an agenda: that we *need* to transcend philosophy in as far as it is understood based on its hegemonic traditional 'Western' rationalistic school of thought. Why this agenda? – for without knowing *all aspects and manifestations* of *who* is it *in here* that governs our actions, it is not clear what is 'education' working with (or against) and what can it hope to change, nor can we expect to 'educate' anyone to become a moral *agent*.

> Let us then indeed 'not speak' and by all means remain silent, and once we do so long enough, dwelling in embodiment – there will be far more to speak *about* based on a *reflective I*, and a *me* that will grow closer to adopt a *contemplative I's* way of being.

This has been my own experience, as well as the experience of many students, whom I have been teaching at universities and colleges in the past years.

Body-based contemplative practices are those in which bringing awareness to our sensed body is a substantial part of the practice. In that sense, words like 'yoga', or 'meditation', explain very little. I argue that,

> It's what we do with attention and what attention does with us, that defines the reality of practice. Saying 'I practice yoga' means very little unless the intention behind the form of the practice is explained.

The *inner* pedagogical practice in this case is an active orienting of attention to bodily sensations based on the two curricular-pedagogical orientations of detachment and *acceptance/compassion*. The outer form of this practice can be mindfulness of the body (e.g., of the breath as practiced above), a yogic posture, a tai chi form, a Feldenkrais lesson, or simply standing, sitting, walking. All these are possible structures within which, with time, one can learn to mobilize oneself from 'living in the mind' within *me* and even within the *reflective I*, to a stepping *in* to the *contemplative I*, which is grounded in inhabiting the body in its *own* right.[28] This tells us something about the integration of all three *inner curricula*: Whereas math and literature, history, and physics are very different disciplines that we are accustomed to teach separately, the three domains of the *inner curriculum* can be (and usually *are*) integrated within one activity. Once one attends *in here* deliberately, one works directly with *I*, encounters *me*, and may very well in some practices begin to see *embodied perception* at work, as one witnesses how any stimulus that is noted is responded/reacted to *in here*.

One of the fundamentals of the pedagogy involved in the *curriculum of I* is the shift of active attention that returns a mind lured by narrative to a body that is usually silenced by it. Yet, this body feeds that narrative and lives and flows beneath it, as an ever present undercurrent. A mind that has been engaged most of its life in *me* narrative, is always happy to barge in with interpretations, but it can learn novel ways of engagement, if those are pursued with intention and perseverance. These novel ways require the movement from passive attention to active attention; from our fondness of words that are such 'handy' habitual tools for communication, to the unlabeled, pre-pruned world of sensations. The practice of active attention, as in the bringing back of a wandering mind to sensations in mindfulness practice, is a befriending of the body. It is an acknowledgment of new forms of *meaning*. *It challenges our views about what is worth attending; what is 'knowledge'; what is meaning.* It is *this* movement that opens the *curriculum of I*.

> Every incidence in which *me* (or even the *reflective I*) appears in the midst of mindfulness practice or a tai chi form by suggesting a wandering thought, a complaint about the dullness of the breath or the practice, or even an insightful comment, and a *contemplative I* sees that happening and returns to the sensed body, reflects an acknowledgement of *me's* limited and limiting agency and an opening to a more authentic and primary agency.

Why do I consider this to be more authentic? – because with no words there's no articulation of judgment and interpretation. There is less of a chance that how I see things is shaped by a very certain preconfigured kaleidoscopic setting of an 'educated' mind. The pruned mined is stepped away from to a mind that is open to new possibilities. There is just being that is a knowing of *now*.

"Where the 'body' is is *now*" James (1976, p. 33) tells us. It is embodiment that is far more *universal*, because it is wordless; because there's no *me* that narrates it and prunes it into *my particular* body, *particular* self. With no *me* the border-line with *not-me* begins to dissolve and two things happen: (1) the urge to be at a place that is not here in a time that is not now loses much of its grip. The 'curriculum' as a 'running somewhere' becomes a choice that is determined by the agency of an attention that can be mobilized from *out there* and *then* to *in here* and *now*. But also (2) I become far closer to the *universality* that binds me with you as we will soon see.

The above sounds far more sophisticated and cumbersome when articulated based on words. But frankly, it is as advanced or simple as taking a breath *right now*.

> *Breathe*
>> *Breathe.*
> Do that for a while.
>>> Be with the breath.
>>> Be the breath.
>>>> *Be*

If there is anything advanced here, it's not the breath, but *me* or the sophisticated *reflective I*, which translates being into words and seeks and finds meaning *only* when it follows the 'social-*me*' narrative form of *meaning*. The *contemplative I* has no need to do so. It can value this wordless experience, as it dwells in this *knowing of being; being of knowing*.

What I am speaking of here is a vision of 'good', which is *not* some Platonic ideal. It is by all means an embodied, lived and felt experience. It is an available possibility *here* and *now* at the level of a *contemplative I*, which means that its core is left unexplained and non-discursive. It can be articulated and philosophized based on *that* experience. Such statements, however, immediately beg the question – how can we know that this 'Good' that I advocate here, is 'Good' and what exactly does such experience offer to a reconstructed 'education'?

There is something utterly cumbersome in discussing the kind of embodied ethics that I describe here. It is almost like asking one to prove that his or her right hand exists. *Embodied ethics* is a very basic feeling. It is unlikely to appear when you feel threatened or angry, for example. Simply put, if your embodied feel (and usually its outer manifestation) tends toward closure, the rejection of others or of yourself, leads to pessimism and a sense of meaninglessness, to a diminished wish to live and engage in this world, to a sense of limitedness, or a lack of confidence in your abilities, then it is likely that you are moving in the wrong direction. Chances are that all these descriptions are *me's* shapings of the kaleidoscopic settings of your mind. Conversely, if you experience a zest for life, a will to engage with the world and with yourself, to know more, do more, be more not just for yourself *but also for others*, and you find meaning *now*, then you are probably in the right direction. No less, 'goodness' is found also in being fully taken by one of our lesser moods that want to drown us in muddy waters, yet still seeing the H_2O-ness of this mood and knowing it to be *contingent; pruned*.

I am well aware that such statement might sound simplistic and naïve and will soon address this with far more sophistication, but not before I insist that at some point our need for academic conceptualization may well impede on our ability to experience, and in fact, enjoy and celebrate life. If we had somehow gotten ourselves stuck in a conception of meaning that is only acceptable if it arrives based on 'academic' discourse, this only reasserts the need to take a serious look at the minds that have been pruned to see things in such way. If this is what our 'educative' frameworks have yielded, then 'education' becomes alienation; a practice of bifurcating mind from body-heart rather than a practice of *integration*. Intellectualism and discursive meaning *have their place*, but we ought to resist the equation of the non-discursive and non-intellectualized with meaninglessness, shallowness, or non-sense-ness. In the way I am speaking of this locus of being, it might in fact be the place from which all meaning flows, which must be a place that is more open, more liberated, and in fact *more* meaningful – a place that cannot be pruned.

So this 'good' of which I speak, is embodied, accessible *here* and *now*, but most importantly we need to understand it's 'social' implications. Very briefly, as I stated in the beginning of this chapter, I know that this place exists for my daily practice leads me to it, but far more important for us is that teaching contemplative education at the university, I've seen students get in touch with this place and suddenly find that there is worth in *this* moment *now*, and not just in the future in which 'I will finally become someone that *I* am not already'.

The 'Good' as a Tangible – Socially Engaged Practice

The 'good' of which I speak needs less discourse and philosophy. It needs practice that brings its tacit presence. The practice itself is the practice of getting in touch with the place that is pre and post-discursive, embodied, and felt. My own stubborn case is here to attest that *I* needs incessant care. Much of the time I am just *me* that chases 'goodness' in the wrong places – *there, then* – that are eventually no other than acting out my sleepiness. James's words apply in this case:

> Most of us feel as if we lived habitually with a sort of cloud weighing on us, below our highest notch of clear-ness in discernment, sureness in reasoning, or firmness in deciding. *Compared with what we ought to be, we are only half-awake.* (1907, p. 3, *emphasis added*)

I do think though that practice has been both informing my *me* and introducing more moments of *I* in there (*reflective*, and *contemplative*). The practice however, embodies the ethical knowing that this 'good' experienced *here* and *now* can evaporate in an instant and that which replaces it is this half-awakeness of *me* that James described, or in better cases a *reflective I*. Unlike a car that needs to see a garage every now and then, here we are speaking of maintenance from one moment to the next.

This 'goodness' that I describe as *embodied* is not the feeling one gets when eating a sugary cake, or the rush of blood following a complement that sends our egos flying out of our ears. It is a feeling that we need to buy our way into by stepping outside of *me*, after years of entrenching ourselves in it. How will we recognize it in our day-to-day living?

> It comes to us when in the midst of an interaction with another human being we catch ourselves about to respond in our automated defensive me-way, and we shift skillfully to *I*, as we do something that we've hardly ever done before – we actually attend and listen deeply to the needs of another human being rather than act blindly based on our own. When that happens, we *know: This is Good*, and I suspect that the other with which we are interacting knows as well and affirms our knowing.

The *curriculum of I* is ethical to its core and active attention is its pedagogical tool. The very choice to engage in it, is an acknowledgement that there is something *in here* that is *better* and accessible *now*. At the same time once I choose to engage with this curriculum, I practice this 'goodness', for what must be realized is that as we work directly with active attention – with *agency* – we constantly teach ourselves 'goodness'. Every incidence in which we awaken to return to the breath with acceptance of the reality of our *me*-mind that had been seen through, we simultaneously strengthen the habit of forgiveness and kindness. We practice giving this forgiveness and acceptance to ourselves and become utterly familiar with what it is that we are giving. It is only based on this familiarity that we will be able to give this to another human being.

> Expecting that we become compassionate or kind to others without knowing the subject matter of 'compassion' and 'kindness' within embodiment is wishful thinking. The *curriculum of I* teaches this subject matter. Daily practice is both life *and* our constant study for its tests.

The route for a compassionate 'society' will come from the mind, because the mind is the source of our lack of compassion. The mind that gets too entrenched in the illusion of omniscience, is a mind habituated in a *me* that places itself as a Kaleidoscopic setting that hides the possibility of compassion. Speaking about compassion may help; so may role modeling, but the root cause is within. Mindfulness that is grounded in acceptance and compassion constitutes one orientation of practices among many others that I will not elaborate here.

If you and I choose to engage this *I* with perseverance, we will become familiar with what it's like to feel compassion, and to offer it. We will become far more articulate in discerning what kind of curriculum is enacted in us, as we engage with each other: Is it *me*? Is it *I*? Who is the agent here? Attending *in here* based on *active attention* that will have become the feature of a more open and less pruned 'educated' mind, as we engage with each other, I believe the answers we shall receive from within, stand far better chance of being authentic and 'good'-oriented than any other.

*

Some, however, might not at all 'buy' the above, and view it as rhetoric of the worst kind. The philosopher's *reflective I* is thus required for its defense. In the following, I will attempt to open this route to your mind as well.

THE *CONTEMPLATIVE I* VERSUS
THE 'SOCIALLY'-CONSTRUCTED SUBJECT

I am well aware of the difficulties involved in attributing *authenticity* and *primary-ness* – in fact – Truthfulness, 'good'-ness and even agency to the *contemplative I*. It seems to reflect Universality, Absolutism, Essentialism and all those constructs that are deemed naïve from diverse perspectives that either reflect post-modernist worldviews and/or argue that all human experience is culture-bound, culturally determined, and/or 'socially' constructed. It is thus important that I position myself in relation to these views.

For the sake of clarity, it need be mentioned that the term 'social-construction' as Hacking (1999) analyzed, can mean various things and leads to diverse strands of thinking. I treat it here as a conception of *you* as *completely*-dependent on 'social narrative' as was discussed in Chapter 3, as opposed to a possibility that our internal life can stem from an internal non-discursive 'core self' or even a source that is beyond (and/or within) our brain-mind-body (e.g., God, Tao, Dharma). 'Social-construction' stands, as Hacking discusses, against the possibility of a self-construction of some kind, that is, a more existentialist Sartrean-Nietzschean possibility of overcoming this 'social-construction' as a practice of liberation. As far as we think of it this way, I fully agree that developmentally our brains-minds-bodies are by all means 'socially-constructed' as Chapter 3 fully acknowledges. This is also a feature of the very fundamentals of perception as I've shown when discussing the *curriculum of embodied perception* in Chapter 7. Almost all that happens during our first years of life seems to be a submission of our attention to our situated-ness within a social-cultural context. Setting aside survival and physical necessity (e.g. avoiding fire, refraining from jumping from high places), the social-cultural context brings a heavy load of contingent priorities, preferences, things to avoid or approach (e.g., wearing certain kinds of cloths and not others, teaching reading at a young age). The latter have everything to do with the historical and cultural *contingent* norms that have so-happened-to-develop as the circumstances into which we were born. In other words, these early years reflect the birth of *me* in and from the 'social'.

From the moment in which we are able to construct a narrative-*me*, that narrative will already be fully loaded with opinions and behaviors that are undergirded by taken for granted premises, which we are by no mean capable of seeing. Our bodies are perhaps the most obvious locus based on which to demonstrate this, as Lelwica (1999) shows in her analysis of the culture of thinness, as Lorber (1994) demonstrates in discussing conventions of masculinity and child rearing, and most famously, as Clark and Clark (1940) studied in regards to preferences of skin color.

In the face of these robust claims then, my arguments about authenticity, a place of Truth and 'good', and in fact, a contemplative *I*, may indeed seem naive. A number of claims can be made to defend such ideas. Most of them, however, require that those that reject the possibility of authenticity will dive *in here* based on contemplative practices for a reasonable period of time in order to corroborate the validity of the orientation I propose. Paradoxically, however, the more someone is entrenched in the belief that subjectivity is culturally constructed the less likelihood there is, that he or she would be willing to corroborate a view that seems to require a mode of inquiry that stands in stark opposition to their argument (you probably remember that *the problem of education is 'education'*...). Unless we are willing to step outside of the frameworks with which we come to inquire ourselves, abandon concepts and words, and invoke a *contemplative I*, we are likely to indeed identify ourselves with *me* that is by all means 'socially constructed'. The *reflective I* is only a tad more liberated. Its game is played in and by language; *the medium* over which 'social' and cultural construction stands. The way out from *this* worldview, if it is possible through language, lies only within poetry (McGilchris 2009); yet another form of *contemplative practice*.

> We are socially and culturally constructed as long as our language stems from *me* or depends on the *reflective I*. Liberation is to be sought within embodiment and the *contemplative I*.

It is only the *contemplative I* that allows us to break-down culture and 'society' into finer elements in order for them to lose their grip on us, and to enable liberation to an identity that is far more open and free. In this sense, the examples I brought above in regards to the body as the most obvious locus of 'social construction', need some refining. It is only if that body is experienced based on *me* that treats it as narrative, that this body can be seen as 'socially constructed'. It is only *me* that is concerned with color, thinness, masculinity, race etc. If, however, the body is sensed from *in here* based on the *contemplative I*, 'social' construction disappears at least for that moment. The *contemplative I* pulls the rug of language from underneath *me*-'society', hence 'social construction' loses its foundation.

Following this book from the beginning, it becomes clear that in our brains-minds there is certainly a possibility of confining ourselves to the limiting constructs of 'culture' and 'society'. That option emerges 'happily' from *me* that is gordically knotted with 'society' and 'culture'. It is further justified by the *reflective I* when we take it to be the agency that runs our show.[29] That is where post-modernist ideas of our being culturally bound dwell. Very paradoxically, it annihilates the subject, yet remains utterly bound by a *me*-perspective, or a more sophisticated one within a *reflective I*. This, however, is exactly the place from which Chapter 1 began; the same place from which this book hopes to liberate us:

> The problem of 'education' disguises itself as a 'social' problem, but it emerges from a mind that had stuck itself in a position from which it fails to see its own role within the creation of 'education' itself. Blind to its role it participates in a 'society' that spreads the word around and the word earns a life of its own.

It's a 'society' that is a BIG MIND that could be accused of the flipside of navel-gazing. It gazes at its own belief system, engaging in an escapism not from the world, but from the mind that has created it. Such a mind refuses to see through the ways into which it had been 'educated', that reproduce a world *out there* that is molded in those very ways. Stuck *out there* with its eyes wide open and somewhat attentive, it supposedly sees a world, but not itself as responsible for its shape.

I thus sum my argument by saying that I have no quarrel with claims of 'social-construction', as long as we understand where they begin and where they end. The limits of 'social-construction' are the very same limits of agency that run between *me* and the *contemplative I*. In fact, I would add that this book explicitly claims that 'social'-construction *is* our problem as long as we do not see its boundaries. Our embedded-ness in it has yielded an 'educational' construct that further entrenches us in the problem. Contrary, however, to those that propose that there is no way out, I suggest that there most definitely *is*. The way out begins with separating ourselves from the makings of concepts. The sensed body is one of the gateways to that place. Only in so doing can we return with a difference infused by a perspective that empowers us to see 'society' *out there* as a possible content *in here* that has its merits, as well as its problems. Only based on such perspective will we not only see *this*, but in fact work to transform this 'society' based on an understanding that its problems are the external manifestations of *this* mind's problems – *which are my own*. This path then is perhaps the opposite of ideation. It takes *you* to be the most concrete aspect of existence and begins *there, which is here now*. I believe Andrew Olendzki's words capture the idea I am proposing:

> The goal of becoming a better person is within the reach of us all, at every moment. The tool for emerging from the primitive yoke of conditioned responses to the tangible freedom of the conscious life lies just behind our brow. We need only invoke the power of mindful awareness in any action of body, speech or mind to elevate that action from the unconscious reflex of a trained creature to the awakened choice of a human being who is guided to a higher life by wisdom. (2010, p. 158)

The *Curriculum of I* Goes to School

Similarly to the way I ended Chapter 8, I want to bring the current chapter to a closure by locating the *curriculum of I* in 'school' and by demonstrating its principles more practically. This will somewhat continue in to the next chapter, which will show that current 'educational' practice is already beginning to work to incorporate the *curriculum of I*.

Reconstructing 'Education' Through Passive and Active Attention[30]

In Chapter 2 we constructed 'education' from the fundamental of attention. We concluded that the foundation of any 'education' is its translation into actions that work with attention. Based on that we came up with three spatial options of orienting attention *in here, out there,* or both. These options reflect our meta-pedagogical deliberation in regards to: *where we orient students' attention.* When including active and passive attention in this analysis we get an additional perspective that yields three more options. These answer to: *who will be the agent of attention in 'education'?*:

1. 'Education' can work with *passive* attention. This means that wittingly or unwittingly we will seek to ensure that students will *not* have to reapply their attention to the subject matter, for the teachers will present it in such engaging and interesting ways, that it will be as if students were watching an action movie.

2. 'Education' can work with *active* attention. That is, 'education' will be based on practices that intentionally require that students reapply themselves to the 'curriculum' based on their internal work with *their* agency. This will mean working with contemplative practices like those you've tried throughout the book.

As usual, these two give rise to a third option:

3. 'Education' can work with both *passive* and *active* attention.

When we take a look at our *public* 'educational' construct, it is quite obvious that option two and three have very little to do with it, set aside the relatively recent 'contemplative turn' that I will discuss in the next chapter. The idea of *active attention* somewhat jars against our construct of 'education' and the way in which we think of good teaching practice. Paradoxically, one of the heroes of this book, William James, expressed this best, as he advocated *passive attention* as the ideal form of teaching: " . . . the more the passive attention is relied on, by keeping the material interesting; and the less the kind of attention requiring effort is appealed to; the more smoothly and pleasantly the class-room work goes on" (1983, p. 101). Ellen Langer can be viewed as continuing this orientation in more contemporary times. Langer's (1997) *Mindful Learning* is no other than an insightful attempt to show how *passive* attention can be ensured in teaching and how this pedagogical approach can work to enhance students' learning.

James and Langer are absolutely right. Indeed, when teaching subject matter concerned with the world *out there*, ensuring *passive attention* is probably the best strategy. This by no means implies *passive learners* but rather the opposite. When students do not need to reapply themselves constantly to learning that's a sign of ideal learning because the teaching is superb and the students are engaged. In the context of studying *out there*, the need for *active attention* is in fact an indication of poor curricular deliberations in terms of subject matter and/or poor teaching practice. Both James and Langer identified the natural tendency of the mind to seek novelty and salience hence curricular-pedagogical practice according to them, is about the teachers' taking full charge of the students' attention. This pretty much sums the premises undergirding almost the entire field of 'educational' practice, theory, and research. Almost all research on curriculum and pedagogy is no other than a guide to how to ensure that students will *not* be required to apply active attention.

"Where is the problem", we ask? – the problem of education is 'education' . . .

> Passive attention is probably the best strategy for teaching subject matter as far as that subject matter is not *in here*. If it comes without an 'education' in active attention, it may be the ultimate depriver of agency. The great paradox is that the more we focus on improving teaching without considering the *inner curriculum*, the more we teach students that 'education' is not their responsibility.

Again and again, it is not what is explicit that should be probed, but rather its negative accent – the *null curriculum*. In this case, it appears in the premise that 'education' must obey the dictum of the wandering mind rather than directly work with this strata over which any kind of subject matter will be learned. A mind that has been 'educated' in agency and *responsibility* for its attention, which are grounded in the ethics described above, is probably a mind that can engage in the learning of anything it or 'society' will deem worthy. It is a mind that has also turned to explore its own individuality thus it might be far wiser in the kinds of deliberations it will make in what to study and why study it.

> Working with the tendency of the mind toward salience and feeding it by curricular-pedagogical practice that relies solely on passive attention is at the same time teaching that mind that its wandering nature is hopeless; that it needs to be fully dependent on *out there* to sustain itself. Conversely, incorporating practices that deliberately engage active attention send a clear message to that mind – 'knowledge of most worth' emerges by engaging *in here now* deliberately. The power to 'educate' exists *in here* just as much as it exists *out there*. 'Education' is your responsibility. Are you going to take it?

So, yes, in order to study math, history, and chemistry, we will certainly have to rely on a good share of passive attention, but learning this 'social curriculum', important as it is, might not be our biggest problem. How do we overcome our inherent illusion of omniscience that keeps us apart? How do we cultivate insight into the way in which our *embodied perception* shapes our experience? How do we govern that reptilian brain in us that seeks survival and instant gratification rather than love, compassion, and connectedness? How do we learn to regulate our emotions and to establish ourselves in a kind *state of being* in spite of emotional turmoil? How do we manage ourselves in this digital age that only seems to exacerbate alienation? How do we learn to live with pain, sickness, boredom, fatigue, stress...? How do we find *meaning*? Who am I and why am I here?

We need math and history, but they will not teach us these lessons in any direct way. These lessons are learned through actively engaging *in here*. The only ones who can engage *in here* are us; each one of us within his or her mind-body-heart. *Here now*.

SUMMARY: THE VARIETIES OF THE *CURRICULUM OF I*

The *curriculum of I* includes two modalities: the *reflective I* and the *contemplative I*.

- The *reflective I:* is familiar within educational discourse and follows the philosophical tradition.
  - It is language and thinking based.
  - It is 'socially constructed'.
  - It is an agent of the *content* of thinking but not of attention.
- The *contemplative I:* is less familiar in educational discourse.
  - It is *post*-discursive.
  - It moves beyond 'social construction'.
  - It is an agent of *what* we attend to and *how* we attend to it, but cannot decide *to stop attending*.
- Both agencies can be trained.
  - The *reflective I* can be taught to think better, problem-solve better, and intervene when *me* gets us in trouble.
  - The *contemplative I* can improve its ability to control *what* we attend to and *how* we attend to it.
- The shift between the *curriculum of me* and the *curriculum of I* is:
  - A shift from a non-deliberate engagement with *in here* (mind-wandering/*self-reflection*) to a deliberate engagement with *in here* (contemplative practice/reflective practice).
  - A shift from an automated habituated way of being to an ethical stance.
- The agency over attention can be external or internal.
  - When it is external, it is called *passive attention:* I do not need to make any effort to attend. I am entertained either from

within (e.g., mind-wandering) or from without (e.g., movie, school-lesson).

- When it is internal, it is called *active attention:* I need to attend to how I attend and reapply myself to an object of choice (*in here* or *out there*)
- Contemplative practices are fundamentally grounded in active attention.
- The shift from *me* and the *reflective I* to a *contemplative I* is the opening of the *internal* door that takes us from passive attention to active attention.
- 'Educational' research, theory, and practice advocate an entrenchment in *passive* attention that is perfectly understandable if what we teach is the 'social curriculum' *out there.*

- The *curriculum of I* is embedded in ethics:
  - At the level of the *deliberate* choice to engage in it that expresses the belief that *me* is limited.
  - At the level of the 'curricular-pedagogical' approach over which it is based:
    - Detachment and discipline.
    - Acceptance and compassion.
  - At the level of its embodied 'goodness'.
  - At the level of its 'social'-engagement.
- The *curriculum of I* means a reconstruction of 'education' in which *active attention* becomes part of 'curriculum' and 'pedagogy', because:
  - It is the last resort of *agency.*
  - It positions 'education' in *my* hands and in *my* responsibility.
  - It works to make us aware of 'education' as pruning and re-opens the mind to de-prune *me* and 'society' based on ethics.

The *curriculum of I* involves getting in touch with the place from which *personal* meaning is made. It has to remain open rather than neatly 'defined' in order for it to serve its purpose of de-pruning 'education' and de-pruning the mind. Just as we like to think of the 'world' *out there* as inexhaustible; as a locus that we can perhaps explore with ever-growing levels of sophistication through our science, yet never quite exhaust, so too, the *other half of the 'curriculum'* – the terrain of the mind that studies itself and the world, ought to be seen as open ended. This chapter focused more on the ways to engage with this open ended terrain. It had less to do with the results of this activity. At the same time, as many have acknowledged: epistemology and ethics are two sides of one and the same coin. Thus,

> How we engage in studying (*both out there and in here*), is what we become. 'How we engage' and 'how we study' are simply different ways of saying: *how we attend; how we 'educate'.*

That said, the deep teachings of the *curriculum of I* are:

> The reclaiming of the last resort of agency; the granting us with choice in the face of the push and pull of *me* and 'society'; the cultivation of kindness toward ourselves and others; the appreciation of our minds and bodies as loci of knowledge; the celebration of this moment *here and now* that might not always be ideal but will remain that which *is*; the realization that 'education' is my responsibility and I manifest this responsibility by my own attending to this mind and this body from which all my actions, thoughts, emotions and sensations emerge; The realization that in so doing I take care of you as best I can.

This is hardly as clear as learning multiplication, reading, or the chemical formula of salt, but it certainly does not exclude them, and it does seem to me like an 'education' I would wish for myself and for my own children.

NOTES

1. As opposed to Chapters 7 and 8, which relied on neuroscience and psychological research, the grounding for much of what you will read in this chapter is my readings in philosophy and wisdom traditions, teaching the reconstruction of 'education' in higher education courses, and mostly, my own practice of yoga, tai chi, and mindfulness in the past twenty years. I am not saying that these settle my position as a knowledge authority. I say this because there is always the balance between making claims and justifying claims. This chapter leans toward the former. As reiterated in this book, you'll have to test these ideas, and see if they are helpful. Eventually, this is about *you*.
2. Most notably this concerns Donald Schon's work.
3. There are more than these two *I*s. For example, the 'reflective *I*' can be split into an *I* that engages in intimate reflective *discursive* practice over the nature of oneself with an acknowledgement of embodiment, as well as a 'philosopher's *I*' that is a more disembodied creature that follows the

substantial strand of Western philosophy and works within the *timeless* domain as a third conception-experience of time mentioned briefly in a footnote in Chapter 2. Here I collapsed these two *I's* into the 'reflective *I'*.

4. I *will* say that the importance of form lies in the extent to which it invokes a stepping away from *me* both as our sense of *identity-agency* and as a habitual narrative. Shunryu Suzuki (1999) and B.K.S. Iyengar (2005) are two prominent practitioners who point to the crucial role of form in practice.

5. This clearly follows the Buddha's pragmatic approach (see especially Malunkyaputta Sutta) and to some extent reflects Socratic ideals as well (see Hadot 1995).

6. With the exception of important work concerned with the exploration of the "teaching self" (see for example, Kelchtermans et al. (2009); Palmer (1998)).

7. The more profound 'educational' exploration of this domain is clearly found in Socratic dialogues, and in the intention of exercising philosophy 'as a way of life' (Foucault 1988; Hadot 1995).

8. The neuroscientific perspective is most telling. As many have argued the brain is a 'vetoing organ' far more than a choosing one. At any given moment numerous options are indeed available, but they are inhibited leaving but the enactment of one with perhaps an embodied experience of great turmoil expressing all those that were not taken (Libet et al. 1999; McGilchrist 2009).

9. Philosophers are sometimes married to their *reflective I* as somewhat of a substitute for *me*, yet to the point in which the two are less distinguishable. Wittgenstein positioned the limits of philosophy and in fact the world, within the limits of the ability to state them in language. That's exactly what I move beyond. This is an 'educational' matter to me, and the argument is only debating philosophy as a byproduct of this, but I see no reason why philosophy needs to end where words end. I also see no reason why the Wittgensteinean world of language cannot be nourished by the *world that exists beyond it*. Those who are inexperienced in contemplative practices may very well not understand what this is about. If they practice intently and with the right guidance I assure them that they will come to understand what I am speaking of.

10. See Raveh (2012) who offers an interesting comparison between Descartes and Patanjali (ch. 1).

11. Falling asleep, for example, does not count for two reasons: a) you can't fall asleep upon demand. You create the conditions for it, and sleep falls on you. b) It's only deep sleep that may possibly be viewed as 'stopping attention'; however, if you wake up and know *that* you slept deeply, could it be said that no-one was there noting that?

12. The distinction between these two strands is found both in contemporary scientific literature (Slagter et al. 2011; Tang et al. 2015) and in the

Buddhist tradition from which both are derived (Rāhula 1974; Wallace 2006).

13. See for example: Kabat-Zinn (2005), Wallace (2006) and Young (2013).

14. If this *does* reflect your experience, then try teaching your skill to us mortals that are less advanced.

15. See Slagter et al. (2011) and Young (2013).

16. Conversely, the *reflective I* can go either way. It is an intermediary that can be harnessed to the horizontal time axis for the purpose of day-to-day problem solving, which Kahneman (2011) associates with 'system 2' or it can serve the *here* and *now contemplative* orientation.

17. See Dahl et al. (2015), Garland et al. (2015), Jha et al. (2007), Schonert-Reichl and Roeser (2016), Segal et al. (2002), and Tang et al. (2015).

18. An apt metaphor for this is the Daoist conception of *yang* and *yin* associated respectively with *focused attention* and *choiceless awareness*. This is further strengthened in the next paragraph as I point to the interplay between these two kinds of agencies.

19. There are excellent books to consult in this domain. The list is probably endless but here are some: Goldstein and Kornfield (1987), Suzuki (1999), Wallace (2006), and Young (2013).

20. I believe broader ethical discussions such as Gyatso (1999) and Palmer (1983) align well with the view described here.

21. The standards that I embrace here are somewhat Kantian. I say 'somewhat' for by no means am I speaking of 'reason' here as some mind-enclave that enables moral judgment. I do, however, maintain that only when one is aware of his thoughts and actions can one be considered to be a moral agent. At the same time I add that we should hope that moral action will come to us spontaneously *but not automatically;* the former being associated with some-thing that one does almost naturally and with awareness, while the latter signifying an unaware reaction. One needs to acknowledge his acts as moral, feel them as such in an embodied sense, be able to justify them in some way in retrospect, and be convinced (as Kant's *categorical imperative* proposes) that he or she would prefer a world in which all would act this way.

22. I do not develop this here, but broadly, this divide is a simplification of a traditional Buddhist one, between *shamatha* on the one hand, and *vipassana* and *Brahma Vihara* on the other. There is a very thick contemporary debate concerned with mindfulness as ethics-laden vs. mindfulness as ethics-neutral to which this alludes, which is not developed here (Purser 2015).

23. Classical yoga's terms for these are *abhyasa* (yogasutra 1.13) as disciplined practice and *vairagya* (yogasutra 1.15) as detachment. See Iyengar (1993) for an analysis of these concepts.

24. This can clearly be linked to 'remembering', as one of the meanings of the term *sati* from which the term 'mindfulness' has evolved (Gethin 2011).

During practice this translates as: remembering to practice, remembering to attend to the breath, remembering to not get annoyed when we catch ourselves wandering (Chaskalson 2014).

25. The kind of detachment that the *contemplative I* and the *reflective I* are capable of, is similar; however, the *reflective I* practices it toward the *content* of thinking, while the *contemplative I* practices it toward the *process* (as well as toward thoughts, sensations, and emotions).

26. See Eisner (1998) and O'Loughlin's (2006) concerning body and arts, and Ergas (2013, 2014) for an exploration of yoga as embodied pedagogy.

27. See Damasio (2005) and Lakoff and Johnson (1999). There is a lot to say here that I will not develop. Merleau-Ponty drew us far closer to the body through the language of the *reflective I*. He offered an impressive account *of* the body and embodiment, yet the medium of language leaves us there, unless we come up with some pedagogy that will lead us from *his* words to our first-person experience. The *reflective I* in this sense remains a finger that points to the moon as long as the words are not tranformed into an injunction to experience our sensed *embodiment*.

   Furthermore, contemporary philosophers such as Richard Shusterman (2008) need to be underscored; especially given the clear influence of his experience as a Feldenkrais technique teacher on his philosophy. His 'somaesthetics' draws us even closer to an understanding of the body as a starting point, rather than as a vehicle that moves the mind from one classroom/lecture-hall to another. I say 'closer' for again, there is still a step further to take there in order to render his writings in the language of teaching, learning, and curriculum theory.

28. For excellent accounts refer to Feldenkrais (2010), Iyengar (2005), and Yuasa (1993).

29. Roth (2008) calls this position 'cognitive imperialism' and provides a cogent argument that strongly supports my position from the perspective of wisdom traditions.

30. This discussion is elaborated with more nuance in Ergas (2016b).

CHAPTER 10

Conclusion: The Reconstruction of 'Education' and the 'Contemplative Turn'

The mind is not only a means for 'education'. It is also 'education's' end.

I am aware of the fact that the theory-practice developed and demonstrated in this book are way beyond the understanding of the current construct of 'education' as we know it. The point of this book has been to escape the vicious circularity of this construct, in which minds create 'education' – a mind-making process – implement it, diagnose its problems, and attempt to address them after having been shaped by the process itself. As anyone who spends years writing a book I hope that it will be read by many, but I also suspect that if it *will* be read there will be several critical responses to its ideas. Why am I so sure of that? – because when one starts moving foundations the entire structure is affected. Being the *mes* that we are, that tend to be fond of stability and certitude, we usually become very uneasy when someone starts annoying us with such endeavors...However, I am hardly alone in this. I hinted to this sporadically throughout the book, but contrary to common academic conventions, I chose *not* to begin this book with a literature review that would have pointed directly to scholars and discourses that share at least some of the ideas proposed here. There are several reasons for why I've chosen to take this non-conventional path, but mostly it is because I sought a path to *your mindful attention* – to a mind that is willing to take a novel path of

© The Author(s) 2017
O. Ergas, *Reconstructing 'Education' through Mindful Attention*,
DOI 10.1057/978-1-137-58782-4_10

inquiry, which is not constantly defined by comparison and negation. Had I begun with the 'literature review' convention, this would have resulted in two problems that I hoped to avoid:

a) Given the span of discourses and methods that were incorporated in this book, I suspect that we would have gotten side tracked by discussing what this book is *not* rather than what it *is*; and with endless debates with *this* philosopher, *that* curriculum theorist, *this* psychologist, or other. Such discussions are by all means necessary, but I decided to 'get things out there' and leave them for future books.

b) The aspiration of this book to 'reconstruct education' based on an unpruned mindful attention would have been compromised. Locating us within specific discourses can sometimes prune the mind to work within rigid boundaries, whereas it was your *un*pruned mind that this book sought to evoke, based on the limits of my own pruned mind...

Only *you* will be the judge of whether my strategy has been successful. As I mentioned elsewhere, if you do not agree with much of what has been written here, but you're still reading and you have been encouraged to engage your mind, I consider that to be a success on my behalf.

This concluding chapter hopes to serve a number of aims. After spending quite some time opening the mind, it is now safe to narrow things down a little, and indeed locate this book within and against the discourse that seems closest to its ideas: 'the contemplative turn in education'. I will not offer a broad review of this movement, but rather point to a number of aspects in it, that are most relevant to the understanding and further location of this book's ideas. These will include:

a) The understanding of the contemplative turn in education as a meta-pedagogical turn, focusing on its manifestations within mindfulness-based curricular 'interventions'.

b) A review of some evidence that warrant the feasibility of educating in active attention, and the mentioning of some results of this approach.

c) A positioning of this book's justification for the *inner curriculum* in relation to the scientific and the wisdom traditions' justifications.

d) Concluding comments on 'education'.

THE 'CONTEMPLATIVE TURN IN "EDUCATION"'

The 'contemplative turn in "education"' has been depicted by several scholars in recent years (Barbezat and Bush 2014; Ergas and Todd 2016; Gunnlaugson et al. 2014; Lin et al. 2013; MLERN 2012; Palmer and Zajonc 2010; Schonert-Reichl and Roeser 2016; Zenner et al. 2014). It is the movement that has become growingly noticeable since around the turn of the millennium, when 'educational' institutions across America and Europe have begun to incorporate contemplative practices in their curricular, pedagogical, and institutional agendas (Ergas 2014). This phenomenon has diverse manifestations in terms of its intensity. More commonly it is reflected in the proliferation of contemplative (or mindfulness)-based 'interventions' in which students across ages are taught to practice mindfulness and other forms of meditation based on structured and usually short-termed programs, that are geared toward specific aims (e.g., stress-reduction, concentration improvement, social-emotional learning) (Schonert-Reichl and Roeser 2016). However, in higher education there are now also several examples of more robust curricula at the core of which lies an interdisciplinary study and practice of contemplation (Barbezat and Bush 2014; Roth 2006).

The growing number of educational institutions involved in this movement, does not in itself imply, that there is a clear consensus as to the place of contemplative practices in 'education'. Critical accounts of this movement propose diverse perspectives (Ergas 2015). These include for example, disquietude in respect to the possibility that a religion is proselytized to students given the origins of many of these practices within wisdom traditions. Conversely, there are those who are disconcerted by the way in which these practices have been extracted from these very wisdom traditions and instrumentalized to suit a contemporary capitalist society. Others might raise economic concerns with the value of time spent 'meditating rather than studying'. My aim here is *not* to offer a full review of this movement and the diverse voices within it, but rather to articulate how this book relates to this movement. For this purpose, I will focus more on the overall orientation of the contemplative turn and what seems to be its most pervasive strand within the above mentioned mindfulness-based curricular 'interventions'.

The first argument I want to propose follows our long journey to reconstruct 'education'. This book argues that:

> the mind needs to be positioned at the center of our 'curriculum' and 'pedagogy' by balancing our meta-pedagogy. We need to become as

interested in how the mind shapes itself deliberately and non-deliberately based on engaging the *inner curriculum*, just as much as we are interested in how 'society' shapes the mind based on the 'social curriculum'. In practice this means embracing a meta-pedagogical turn, which implies the incorporation of practices that engage students directly with active attention.

When we focus on the *practical* aspects of the 'contemplative turn in "education"' the above is certainly reflected in its manifestations in the field. Once mindfulness, yoga, tai chi, compassion meditation, or other forms of contemplation become more widely *practiced* (with reasonable integrity) across 'educational' settings, I count that as a meta-pedagogical turn. It reflects an engagement with active attention, which means a deliberate engagement with the *inner curriculum*, and a growing acknowledgement of the centrality of *mind* to 'curriculum' and 'pedagogy'. We can call this a 'turn' because until around the turn of the millennium, the idea that school-time will be utilized for instructing students to scan their bodies and attend to their minds rather than learn more natural/social science, or humanities, would either sound out of place, or perhaps be saved for alternative schools (e.g., Waldorf) and unique higher education institutions (e.g., Naropa University).

This book then clearly aligns with this movement judged by its practical orientation. The question I ask however, concerns the deep agenda of this book that is concerned with reconstructing the idea of 'education' in our minds? This book aimed to,

> reconstruct our understanding of 'education', as it has been 'socially-constructed' in our minds based on 'what we do in schools' – i.e., our curricular-pedagogical approach. The aim was to arrive at a point at which attending to our *inner curriculum* will not be considered as an extra-curricular activity, but would rather become commonplace as the study of math, reading, and history are in our contemporary 'educational institutions'.

I may have aimed too high, but this is what I meant by reconstructing 'education' and positioning the mind at the center of curriculum and pedagogy. Why? – hearkening back to Chapter 1, I believe one of the biggest problems of education is 'education', if the term has come to be constructed in our minds as an activity that 'society' *does* to the individual, which in turn implies that the individual is not responsible for it. Becoming responsible for our own 'education' means becoming fully responsible for *these minds-bodies* that each of us *is* (in his or her own version), from which we perceive and based on which we act, react, respond to ourselves and to each other. The 'social curriculum' that sends us to attend *out there* clearly *must* be part of 'education', but only a serious engagement with the *inner curriculum* can truly drive the lesson of responsibility home, for without it, one will never quite realize that one's entire life is determined from within just as much as it is affected from *without*. The question then is, to what extent does the contemplative turn in 'education' bring us closer to *this* agenda?

The short answer is, yes. I believe that overall we are heading in the right direction, especially in the cases of the more robust higher education programs that are dedicated to the study, research, and practice of contemplation (Barbezat and Bush 2014; Gunnlaugson et al. 2014; Palmer and Zajon 2010; Roth 2006). I will set this strand aside and focus on the way in which contemplation is moving into the mainstream of 'education' within mindfulness-based 'interventions' (MBIs) that are implemented in schools (Schonert-Reichl and Roeser 2016; Zenner et al. 2014). I focus on this strand both because it is far more widespread (and constantly growing), and because it is a discourse that will enable me to further articulate the position of this book.

I'll point first, to the great advantage of this strand as a way of supporting the 'contemplative turn' and the reconstruction of 'education' as a turn to *active attention*. If science shows that this is a feasible agenda that yields results, which lead to our highest visions of 'education' in ways that are more productive than the ones to which we are accustomed to apply in 'schools', this should make a strong case for the reconstruction of 'education'. This I believe to be the case; however, I will then suggest that, if this becomes our *only* path for justifying a meta-pedagogical turn in 'education', we may fall back into our own predicament of being unaware of the pruning of 'education' and mind.

In the following, I briefly present research from mindfulness-based 'interventions'. Again, this is hardly a review of the field. I focus specifically on the possibility of cultivating *active attention* that supports the argument of the previous chapter, and then I conclude with prospective statements that are based on meta-analytical studies in this field. This brief review will point to the feasibility of the meta-pedagogical turn of which I speak as well as to some of its results; however, it will also lead me to argue why this still leaves something to be desired in terms of how this book views the reconstruction of 'education'. The ideal of *here* and *now* suggests that there needs to be a justification for the engagement in the *inner curriculum* that is less results-dependent. 'Results' can easily send us back to *then* and *there*.

Evidence of the Feasibility of a Meta-pedagogical Turn and Its Effects

Various studies demonstrate that *active attention* can be cultivated and that deliberately engaging with its cultivation yields important results.[1] The following review only scratches the surface of the wealth of research in this field and points only to few notable examples.

Jha and colleagues found that participants in an 8-week mindfulness-based stress reduction course improved the function of orienting attention compared to controls. They concluded that, "concentrative meditation may indeed alter functioning of the dorsal attention system to improve voluntary response and input-level selection processes" (2007, p. 116).[2] Tang and colleagues (2007) showed that even 20-minutes per day for 5 consecutive days of integrative meditation and mind-body training, yield improvement in attention in an experiment group of 40 participants compared to a control group who was taught a relaxation technique. They claimed that, "attention, and the quality of moment to moment awareness are flexible skills that can be trained" (p. 17155). Another short-term intervention compared the effects of four sessions of mindfulness with four sessions of listening to a book reading (note the difference between active and passive attention here), in terms of cognitive processing, sustained attention, and mood. While both groups (approx. 25 adults in each) showed improved mood, only the mindfulness group showed improvements in cognitive processing and sustained attention (Zeidan et al. 2010). In another experiment, Napoli et al. (2005) implemented a program called 'attention academy' geared toward teaching first, second, and third grade students, "to focus and pay attention" (p. 99). Approximately 250 students participated in this program, which included 24 weeks of bi-monthly mindfulness practice sessions based on breath-work, bodyscan, and other techniques. The most significant finding was "an increase in . . . the ability to choose what to pay attention to" (p. 113). Some researchers have also made headway in the important domain of attention deficits (ADD/ADHD) that was not discussed in this book. Zylowska and colleagues (2008) found that mindfulness improves attentional capacities in cases of ADHD in a feasibility study conducted with 24 adults and 8 adolescents, and Tarrasch and colleagues (2016) found that a two-month mindfulness workshop given to 24 adults suffering from ADHD and/or dyslexia, "reduced impulsivity and improved sustained attention, and this, in turn, improved reading of adults with developmental dyslexia and ADHD" (p. 2).

Some of the above findings consist of small sample groups. Furthermore, the results do not always point to direct 'educational' implications of engaging active attention, and certainly not to the deeper aspects concerned with *agency* and *identity* to which I pointed in Chapter 9; however, they do point to the feasibility of cultivating active attention and they do warrant the further development of mindfulness-based curricular 'interventions' introduced in schools. Several studies have been demonstrating the broader results of these interventions. Here I only bring summaries from two robust meta analytical reviews. One comes from the Mind and Life Educational Research Network, including some of the leading scientists studying contemplation:

> Ideas drawn from contemplative practices that promise to improve the regulation of attention, emotion, motivation, social cognition, and behavior are one potential strategy for reducing the risks children face and improving both social and academic outcomes through schools today. A growing body of evidence in adults highlights the benefits of these practices in the regulation of attention and emotion, in cultivating empathy, and in altering brain function and structure to support these behavioral changes. (MLERN 2012, p. 151)

In another meta-analysis Zenner and colleagues (2014) argued that:

> Mindfulness can be understood as the foundation and basic pre-condition for education … Mindfulness practice enhances the very qualities and goals of education in the twenty first century. These qualities include not only attentional and emotional self-regulation, but also prosocial dispositions such as empathy and compassion, self-representations, ethical sensitivity, creativity, and problem solving skills. (p. 2)

Here we find statements that point clearly toward this book's claims in regards to *identity* and *agency*.[3] Scholars are certainly careful to acknowledge that this is still a nascent field with a paucity of evidence (MLERN 2012). There are still various methodological problems involved in the study of this domain (e.g., lack of longitudinal studies, difficulty in isolating the components that yield the positive effects) and to some these do not warrant the enthusiasm that seems to prevail in the current advocacy of these 'interventions' (Greenberg and Harris 2012).[4] The proliferation of these interventions in schools and the research that accompanies them, does say something about the feasibility of the implementation, the validity of the claim that active attention can be cultivated, and about the 'educational' results of practice. This brings us however, to discuss where this book aligns with *this* strand of the 'contemplative turn' and where it may be pointing beyond it. Broadly a discourse of *results* and 'interventions' risks pruning the mind and 'education' yet again, if we miss the 'educational' essence and succumb to the problem of 'education' yet in a more sophisticated form. Presenting analysis of this argument requires, again, the *matrix of mind* and a shift in our attention from the *what* to the *how*.

Two paths of justification for the inner curriculum:

1. Results: Out there and then
Before proposing some critical arguments, let me reiterate that the above 'interventions' involve practices, which reflect the meta-pedagogical turn of which this book speaks. These are practices of *active attention*. Anyone engaging with them seriously, will sooner or later face *me*, invoke *I*, and will, with the right guidance, encounter *embodied perception*. The extent and seriousness of the engagement surely bear directly on the effects, yet the buds and manifestations of a meta-pedagogical turn are there. Where can problems arise?

> When minds 'educated' in *then* and *there* appropriate practices that essentially orient attention to *here* and *now*.

My claim is that scientific findings as to the effects of mindfulness or other contemplative practices, ought not to be confused as *the* or *the only* reason to engage with the *inner curriculum*. There is clear logic in engaging in an activity, *because* it yields certain results; especially when we are speaking of a 'social' operation that is funded by a government, which needs to know that things are 'working'; however, this is exactly the perspective out of which this book sought to draw us.

Mindfulness-based curricular interventions may be moving us in the right direction, but there are risks and problems involved. The research in this field (and writ large) is bound by the contemporary discourse of 'education' and its clear links to economical thinking and policy making. One can see this at least in two domains of *how*:

1) The way these researches are structured, which is the reverse of how this book was structured to reconstruct 'education'.
2) The construct of an 'intervention' as it corresponds with the construct of 'education'.

Contemporary 'educational' discourse is governed by 'economic' constructs such as accountability, assessment/evaluation and standardization (Gilead 2012). In other words, the position from which research in 'education' (including that of interventions) begins, is that 'educational aims' are somewhat of a 'known'. The studies ask whether certain practices improve the ways to achieve them. This hearkens back to:

in the beginning there was 'society'; there was 'education', then comes the mind that has little to contribute to 'educational' practice-theory.

This is a justification that works from existing conceptions of 'education'; from *out there* to *in here*. Throughout the first and second part of the book I attempted to show what kind of problems emerge when this is the *only* position from which we work. The problem lies not in the 'interventions' nor in the 'science'. It is, as usual, *in the mind*. It can be stated this way:

minds that have been 'educated' in 'education' as an endeavor of attending *out there*, require the appeal of science that speaks to this *out there* inclination, in order to justify the idea that attending *in here* makes 'educational' sense.

How would you ever convince someone that attending to the breath or to bodily sensations is an activity that is not only more than 'navel-gazing', but in fact contributes to 'education'? The uncanny idea that attending *in here* belongs in school as an 'educational' agenda cannot but ride over the means of a rhetoric based on which our current 'education' stands. What language is that? – standardization, accountability, academic achievements, all of which are 'economic' constructs. This economic framework may very well stand in opposition to the geist of the *inner curriculum* that I described in the third part of this book. It reflects the *me-*'social' far more than it reflects the *curriculum of I – the contemplative I,* which is the aspect that is most missing from the construct of 'education'.

We need to be aware of the risk involved in transforming a meta-pedagogical turn *in here* as a meritorious process in its own right, into a process that becomes a means to serve a 'social' ethos in which again meaning-making will be appropriated by *out there.* How can this happen? – If mindfulness is advocated for its *results* rather than as a novel way of engaging with ourselves and others, then it becomes a new 'social normative map', yet one that is far more difficult to see through. If students are encouraged to practice this meta-pedagogical turn, *because* it is an 'effective strategy' to reduce stress, feel better, perform better academically, improve their job-market skills, that is by all means 'good', but it substantially attenuates what I have in mind as a reconstructed 'education'.

> A reconstructed 'education' has to do with viewing the mind as an end not only as a means. *In here* needs to become a meaningful locus *now*, not only an instrument, which serves aims that 'society' had deemed desirable. This is about finding one's agency in 'education' and becoming fully responsible for it.

The overall narrative of 'schooling' in our times is substantially shaped by 'economic' thinking. We might find ourselves easily tempted to measure the *outcomes* of a mindfulness intervention by examining whether students' academic achievements have improved, or determine that six sessions of mindfulness rather than eight yield similar *outcomes.* The latter would make perfect sense from the position of the 'social curriculum' as we know it, yet this will also be framing the *inner curriculum* as a mere means for its service. The more radical Neo-Marxist critique of this possibility, suggests that mindfulness may become a 'pathology'-proofing technology that increases our performativity, while eventually serving a Capitalist agenda (Reveley 2016). It may shape a 'false consciousness' that is far more difficult to become liberated from.

The very conception of what an 'intervention' means in the context of 'education' can further demonstrate this. Such framing cannot but propose that what we normally call 'education' is being 'intervened' by something that is not yet considered within the construct. The 'social curriculum' is being suspended by something 'else', which is either a scaffold for 'education' or some extra-'curricular' activity. Clearly, if we think of 'school' as an opportunity to open the minds of students to additional ways of growth, such aim may be served in this way; however, the reconstruction of 'education' that I proposed here does not fully emerge.

It must be clear that my argument has little to do neither with 'science' nor with the endeavor of mindfulness-based curricular interventions itself. I believe enough has been written in this book to show my deep appreciation of science both as a way of thinking and as a wealth of human knowledge. The problems are never in the 'tools' we apply but rather in *how* our minds frame them. If we remain stuck in the *what* we become blind to the *how*. The rhetoric of mindfulness-based curricular 'interventions' tends to speak the language of *me*, for that is where 'society' stands at this moment. It is a 'society' that is 'educated' in the ethos of *me* – 'getting somewhere' and 'being someone'.

There are many more consideration relevant to the above but as a closure of these points it is important to suggest a few counterarguments:

First, the above claims do not acknowledge that interventions are as poor or worthy as their implementations. This applies in the teaching of physics just as much as it applies to teaching mindfulness. Some of those implementing mindfulness or other contemplative practices in schools are well-suited to overcome some of the problems that I mention, and others might not. It is clear however, that the more we are aware of these issues, the better the chance we have of addressing them.

Second, based on personal acquaintance I know that some of the scientists who are involved in the study of these interventions, are not only aware of the problems described (as well as others), but also seek to ameliorate them. Nevertheless, they cannot but do so from within the limits that the scientific discourse allows, which means more nuanced research.

Third, between the choice of *not* introducing these intervention or introducing them, I most obviously prefer the latter. This also has to do with something utterly paradoxical. The very orientation of mindfulness-based curricular interventions may carry the seeds of liberation from the predicament of the economic-scientific rhetoric over which it currently stands.

The very practices that are embraced based on these 'interventions', which lure the *me*-mind, are at the same time those that are designed to dispel its false agency over our lives. Could science be leading 'education' into a non-instrumental embrace of the *inner curriculum*? We may recall the illusion of omniscience and acknowledge that we might know far less about what we are doing then we think.

The more we engage with the *contemplative I* and identify it as a far more authentic source of *identity* and *agency*, the more aware we become of the *me-*'society' agency that works within us through automation; the more we become capable of infusing it with wisdom and virtue from *within*; the more we reconstruct 'education'.

2. In here and now

The kind of justification for the *inner curriculum,* which this book sought, avoided the path of *results out there.* It was far more about *in here now.* To demonstrate this I'll very briefly point to an additional discourse that is crucial to the understanding of the 'contemplative turn'. Very peculiarly (or not), I intentionally avoided grounding this book in this discourse – the origins of contemplative practices within wisdom traditions...

Mindfulness is a word that was translated in the nineteenth century from the Pali language, to describe a set of practices as well as a part of the Buddhist eightfold path. This orientation and discourse was attenuated in this book despite the fact that I would not be who I am without studying and teaching it throughout my academic career, and without practicing diverse contemplative practices on a daily basis. Here too, I will not elaborate how the contemplative turn is rooted in this discourse, although it is crucial to highlight that many of the above mentioned scientific studies, literally point to Buddhism as the source of mindfulness (e.g., MLERN 2012; Schonert-Reichl and Roeser 2016; Slagter et al. 2011; Zenner et al. 2014). More importantly, I will say *why I haven't relied neither on Buddhism nor on other wisdom traditions directly.* It would seem only natural to rely on these robust traditions and the wealth of interpretations of Buddhist, Taoist, Yogic or other texts, yet you will find very little of that in this book.

By now you may be able to answer this question on your own. The reason is that 'wisdom traditions' too, can easily send the mind *out there* and to *then.*[5] The path I sought was into *your* non-conceptualizing mind from which I hoped that, together, we will reconstruct 'education'. At the outset I stated that 'educational' research, theory, and practice have been focusing almost entirely on the 'social' side *out there* and on where we are going. What I believe we are missing is a better diagnosis of the problems that the mind brings to 'education' before we go about conceptualizing this mind-making process.[6] Ideation as we find in different wisdom traditions (and as we sometimes read it into them), is crucial for the development of 'educational' visions, but this book stemmed from the belief that we have little shortage of that kind of thinking. Our minds have become lost in ideals whereas 'education' happens *here* and *now* where our bodies are. What we need then is a grounding; not another grand narrative or tradition(s) developed by others. Had I relied too heavily on the words of the Buddha, Socrates, and their interpreters, eventually I would have cut the branch over which this book stands. That branch is your brain-mind-body-heart, and the call to engage with it and appreciate this engagement in the reconstructed understanding and practice of 'education'.

A Reconstructed 'Education'

'Education' as I envision it, is the meta-discourse of all discourses and its practice in embodied living. It is the most complex of human endeavors, because it entails all the difficult questions for which we do not have an answer. Given this incertitude it ought to be fed by all we do know, which includes the best of science, the best of wisdom traditions, and the best of human experience past, present, and future.[7] When the best of humanities, natural, and social sciences as well as wisdom traditions are explored through first, second, and third person methods of inquiry, we stand a far better chance of informing ourselves as to the 'good' toward which we hope to develop when we say 'education'; as to what is possible and which curricular-pedagogical approaches can enable us to reach that place, which we will always call *here* and *now*.

I do not view 'education' as having to do with loyalty to one tradition or another, nor to specific findings of empirical science. It is the individual-'social' locus in which all knowledge is tested in the laboratory of life; within this mind-body that is 'educated' moment-by-moment based on beads arriving from *out there* as well as from *in here*. This mind is like a pivot. Whether its beam of attention turns *in* or *out*, infinity awaits everywhere. It is to *this* mind that 'education' is to be tailored; a mind that sees beyond its contingent pruning, and by so doing returns to the 'social' with a difference.

My experience with students at universities and colleges with whom I explore the themes discussed in this book, gives me hope. Those who are willing to take this journey discover that the mind is an open-ended territory. It awaits those who are willing to engage *in here* deliberately as they open the internal door of attention with growing *acceptance*.

There is absolutely *nothing* simple in what this book suggests. The only obstacles that stand in our way are our own minds. Eventually, this is about facing ourselves, and being willing to take a leap beyond habitual 'education'. 'Societies' have been teaching us to play by the rules of 'social' games, yet in most cases they do not mention that the game we play is one out of many. Playing a 'social' game without getting to know the minds that had made it and are engaged in its playing, results in playing the game with a blindfold on our eyes. It can certainly be played, but chances are that the players will run in to each other far more often. Paradoxically, we need to blindfold our eyes to the 'social' game, engage *in here* and probe the mind with eyes shut in order to learn to see more.

A substantial part of the problem of 'education' is the wishful thinking of expecting that 'society' will change without engaging with the mind *directly*. The greatest task of 'education' is to overcome the thought that 'education' is a process that is 'done *to*' the mind by 'society' and that it is confined to certain ages, certain institutions, and/or certain times of day. A mind that has come to think of 'education' in this way, has been pruned by 'education' in the negative sense of the term. The task of 'education' is to shape a mind that is willing to challenge its own ways of seeing and being, based on taking responsibility for working with its own attentive powers. A mind that has been shaped to question its own ways through a *reflective I* as well as a *contemplative I*, is a mind that acknowledges the dangers of pruning and works to ameliorate them. It is a mind that attunes *in* to constantly be in touch with the way it perceives, the motivations underlying its actions, and the results of its inner workings as they affect others.

Some might argue that this kind of reliance on our individual minds raises the risk of anarchy and a loss of the 'social' glue that binds us. I do not think so. A mind that seriously engages in questioning *its own* ways, is not necessarily a mind that will become anti-social. If indeed 'we are "social" beings' and there is no contingency in *that*, then the mind will choose 'society' time and again, yet that choice will be an aware, deliberate, and wisdom-based one. Based on this choice, this mind will come to care for that 'society' for it will indeed come to see itself as an extension of its own embodiment.

The invitation to engage in the *inner curriculum* is a reclaiming of a mind that is far beyond our understanding. Existence in five hundred years is going to be very different. What hides in this mind *now* to allow for that? I believe the answers and the questions exist *in here now* as they emerge from a mind that attends to what *is*.

Notes

1. To be sure, attention is by no means a uniform phenomenon. Scientists usually divide attention into different functions such as alerting, orienting, and conflict monitoring, or sustained versus selective attention (Petersen and Posner 2012). As Tang and colleague's (2015) meta-analysis reports, the improvements of active attention that I describe apply diversely to these different aspects of attention, and differ in relation to the kind of practice applied. The neural mechanisms involved are not fully clear and scholars are working to refine methods that will enable their further study (2015, p. 217).

2. Another experiment found that three months of intensive mindfulness meditation improves our attentiveness to stimuli that are presented in a stream, reducing the effects of what is called 'attentional blink' (Slagter et al. 2011).

3. See Roeser and Peck (2009) for a compelling specific discussion of the relation between agency and contemplative education.

4. Furthermore, some raise questions about the possibility of adverse effects of meditational practice (see Willouby Britton's (Brown University) work).

5. Monotheistic religions (e.g. Christianity, Judaism) may tend to do so more than core teachings of Buddhism, given their conceptions of God, and life after death.

6. I am not a Buddhism expert, but I think this would be a reasonable description of the Buddha's approach to diagnosing the problems of existence.

7. I do believe that the integrative theories that have been developing in recent years, are moving us substantially forward in this direction. There are numerous examples but to mention a few: Daniel Siegel's (2012) interpersonal neurobilogy, Richard Davidson's (2012) emotional styles of the brain, Varela et al's. (1991) integration of phenomenology, cognition, and first-person methods of inquiry, Roth's (2006) conception of contemplative studies, McGilchrist's (2009) analysis of brain and culture, Austin's (1998) analysis of Zen and the brain. Most of the above mentioned, are unsurprisingly, theories that were developed by scholars who have invested themselves in a rigorous study of their scientific discipline but no less of their own minds, based on contemplative practices.

Epilogue

We've reached the end of our journey. I suspect that I may have lost you here and there. Speaking philosophy, neuroscience, psychology, sociology, and other 'languages', methods, and discourses may have been my own wishful thinking, expressed in the hope to appeal to diverse readers' inclinations and tastes, while perhaps risking losing them all. 'Education', however, hides there as a deliberate message too – in the *how* of this book that lurks behind the *what*. Changing the language and the discourse about every second chapter in this book sought to address the unpruned mind that is there in you. It is a mind that can potentially speak all languages and discourses. I can only speak a few of those and in a limited way. My limitations have no doubt yielded mistakes to which my own pruned mind may be blind. If you find that this is the case, it is up to you to 'educate' me and others about them. I can only hope that the grounding for your claims will stem from the *contemplative I* within you, which will teach them to the *reflective I*, then transform *me*, and from there will enlighten our 'society' through 'education'.

> *The door of attention swings in and out.*
> *Engage thy mind.*
> *Engage thy body.*
> *I await(s) there for you to discover.*
> *'Society' awaits your wisdom and virtue.*
>
> Oren Ergas, Modi'in.

© The Author(s) 2017
O. Ergas, *Reconstructing 'Education' through Mindful Attention*,
DOI 10.1057/978-1-137-58782-4

REFERENCES

Ainsworth, M. S. (1979). Infant–mother attachment. *American Psychologist, 34*(10), 932–937.

Alexander, H. (2001). *Reclaiming goodness: Education and the spiritual quest.* Notre Dame, IN: University of Notre Dame Press.

Andrews-Hanna, J. R. (2012). The brain's default network and its adaptive role in internal mentation. *The Neuroscientist: A Review Journal Bringing Neurobiology, Neurology and Psychiatry, 18*(3), 251–270.

Apple, M. W. (2013). *Knowledge, power, and education: The selected works of Michael W. Apple.* London; New York, NY: Routledge, Taylor and Francis Group.

Ataria, Y., Dor-Ziderman, Y., & Berkovich-Ohana, A. (2015). How does it feel to lack a sense of boundaries? A case study of a long-term mindfulness meditator. *Consciousness and Cognition, 37*, 133–147.

Austin, J. H. (1998). *Zen and the brain: Toward an understanding of meditation and consciousness.* Cambridge, MA: MIT Press.

Baars, B. J. (2010). Spontaneous repetitive thoughts can be adaptive: Postscript on "mind wandering." *Psychological Bulletin, 136*(2), 208–210.

Baird, B., Smallwood, J., & Schooler, J. W. (2011). Back to the future: Autobiographical planning and the functionality of mind-wandering. *Consciousness and Cognition, 20*(4), 1604–1611.

Baird, B., Smallwood, J., Mrazek, M. D., Kam, J. W. Y., Franklin, M. S., & Schooler, J. W. (2012). Inspired by distraction: Mind wandering facilitates creative incubation. *Psychological Science, 23*(10), 1117–1122.

Bar, M. (2009). The proactive brain: Memory for predictions. *Philosophical Transactions of the Royal Society B: Biological Sciences, 364*(1521), 1235–1243.

Barak, D. (2015). Educational authenticity. In S. Tadmor & A. Freiman (Eds.), *Education – The human questions* (pp. 173–182). Tel Aviv: Mofet.

© The Author(s) 2017   321
O. Ergas, *Reconstructing 'Education' through Mindful Attention*,
DOI 10.1057/978-1-137-58782-4

Barbezat, D., & Bush, M. (2014). *Contemplative practices in higher education: Powerful methods to transform teaching and learning.* San Francisco, CA: Jossey-Bass.

Barbezat, D. P., & Bergman, C. J. (2014). Introduction to the first issue. *The Journal of Contemplative Inquiry, 1*(1), vii–viii.

Berkovich-Ohana, A., & Glicksohn, J. (2014). The consciousness state space (CSS)—A unifying model for consciousness and self. *Frontiers in Psychology, 5*(341), 1–19.

Berman, M. G., Peltier, S., Nee, D. E., Kross, E., Deldin, P. J., & Jonides, J. (2011). Depression, rumination and the default network. *Social Cognitive and Affective Neuroscience, 6*(5), 548–555.

Bernstein, B. (1971). On the classification and framing of educational knowledge. In M. Young (Ed.), *Knowledge and control* (pp. 47–69). London: Collier-Macmillan.

Bloom, A. (1987). *The closing of the American mind: How higher education has failed democracy and impoverished the souls of today's students.* New York: Simon and Schuster.

Brady, R. (2007). Learning to stop, stopping to learn discovering the contemplative dimension in education. *Journal of Transformative Education, 5*(4), 372–394.

Buckner, R. L., Andrews-Hanna, J. R., & Schacter, D. L. (2008). The brain's default network. *Annals of the New York Academy of Sciences, 1124*(1), 1–38.

Cassidy, J., & Shaver, P. R. (1999). *Handbook of attachment: Theory, research, and clinical applications.* New York: Guilford Press.

Chabris, C. F., & Simons, D. J. (2010). *The invisible gorilla: And other ways our intuitions deceive us.* New York: Crown.

Chalmers, D. J. (1996). *The conscious mind: In search of a fundamental theory.* New York: Oxford University Press.

Chaskalson, M. (2014). *Mindfulness in eight weeks: The revolutionary eight-week plan to clear your mind and calm your life.* Hammersmith, London: HarperThorsons.

Clark, K. B., & Clark, M. K. (1940). Skin color as a factor in racial identification of negro preschool children. *The Journal of Social Psychology, 11*(1), 159–169.

Craik, F., & Bialystok, E. (2006). Cognition through the lifespan: Mechanisms of change. *Trends in Cognitive Sciences, 10*(3), 131–138.

Csikszentmihalyi, M. (1991). *Flow: The psychology of optimal experience.* New York: HarperPerennial.

Dahl, C. J., Lutz, A., & Davidson, R. J. (2015). Reconstructing and deconstructing the self: Cognitive mechanisms in meditation practice. *Trends in Cognitive Sciences, 19*(9), 515–523.

Damasio, A. (2005). *Descartes' error: Emotion, reason, and the human brain.* London: Penguin.

Damasio, A. R. (2010). *Self comes to mind: Constructing the conscious brain.* New York: Pantheon Books.

Davidson, R. J., with Begley, S. (2012). *The emotional life of your brain*. New York: Plume.

Davidson, R. J., Scherer, K. R., & Hill, H. (Eds.). (2003). *Handbook of affective sciences* (Vol. xvii). New York, NY: Oxford University Press.

Deresiewicz, W. (2014). *Excellent sheep: The miseducation of the American elite and the way to a meaningful life*. New York, NY: Free Press.

Dewey, J. (1957). *Human nature and conduct*. New York, NY: The Modern library.

Dewey, J. (1958). *Experience and nature* (2nd ed.). Chicago: Open Court Publishing Company.

Dewey, J. (1997a). *Democracy and education: An introduction to the philosophy of education*. New York: Free Press.

Dewey, J. (1997b). *How we think*. Mineola, NY: Dover Publications.

Durlak, J. A., Domitovich, C. E., Weissberg, R. P., & Gullotta, T. P. (2015). *Handbook of social and emotional learning: Research and practice*. New York, NY: Guilford Press.

Dweck, C. S. (2006). *Mindset: The new psychology of success*. New York: Random House.

Eisner, E. (1996). *Cognition and curriculum reconsidered*. London: Paul Chaoman Publishing Ltd.

Eisner, E. W. (1988). The primacy of experience and the politics of method. *Educational Researcher, 17*(5), 15–20.

Eisner, E. W. (1993). Forms of understanding and the future of educational research. *Educational Researcher, 22*(7), 5–11.

Eisner, E. W. (1994). *The educational imagination: On the design and evaluation of school programs* (3rd ed.). New York: Macmillan.

Eisner, E. W. (1998). *The kind of schools we need: Personal essays*. Portsmouth, NH: Heinemann.

Elzinga, B. M., Bakker, A., & Bremner, J. D. (2005). Stress-induced cortisol elevations are associated with impaired delayed, but not immediate recall. *Psychiatry Research, 134*(3), 211–223.

Epictetus. (2008). *Discourses and selected writings: Epictetus*. (R. Dobin, Trans.). New York, NY: Penguin.

Ergas, O. (2013). Descartes in a headstand: Introducing body-oriented pedagogy. *Philosophical Inquiry in Education, 21*(1), 4–12.

Ergas, O. (2014). Overcoming the philosophy/life, body/mind rift. *Educational Philosophy and Theory, 46*(1), 74–86.

Ergas, O. (2015). The rhetoric of contemplative practice in the curriculum. In P. Wexler & Y. Hotam (Eds.), *New sociological foundations: Education in post-secular society* (pp. 107–128). New York: Peter Lang.

Ergas, O. (2016a). Educating the wandering mind: Pedagogical mechanisms of mindfulness practice for a curricular blind spot. *Journal of Transformative Education, 14*(2), 98–119.

Ergas, O. (2016b). Attention please: Positioning attention at the center of curriculum and pedagogy. *Journal of Curriculum Theorizing*, *31*(2), 66–81.

Ergas, O., & Todd, S. (2016). *Philosophy east-west: Exploring intersections between educational and contemplative practices*. West Sussex: Wiley-Blackwell.

Feldenkrais, M. & Beringer, E. (2010). *Embodied wisdom: The collected papers of Moshé Feldenkrais*. San Diego, CA; Berkeley, CA: Somatic Resources; North Atlantic Books.

Fell, J. (2012). I think, therefore I am (unhappy). *Frontiers in Human Neuroscience*, *6*, 1–2.

Fishbane, M. A. (2008). *Sacred attunement: a Jewish theology*. Chicago: University of Chicago Press.

Foucault, M. (1988). *Technologies of the self: A seminar with Michel Foucault*. Amherst: University of Massachusetts Press.

Freire, P. (2007). *Pedagogy of the oppressed*. New York, NY: Continuum.

Fresco, D. M., Segal, Z. V., Buis, T., & Kennedy, S. (2007). Relationship of posttreatment decentering and cognitive reactivity to relapse in major depression. *Journal of Consulting and Clinical Psychology*, *75*(3), 447–455.

Gallagher, S. (2000). Philosophical conceptions of the self: Implications for cognitive science. *Trends in Cognitive Sciences*, *4*(1), 14–21.

Garland, E. L., Farb, N. A., Goldin, P. R., & Fredrickson, B. L. (2015). Mindfulness broadens awareness and builds eudaimonic meaning: A process model of mindful positive emotion regulation. *Psychological Inquiry*, *26*(4), 293–314.

Gethin, R. (2011). On some definitions of mindfulness. *Contemporary Buddhism*, *12*(1), 263–279.

Gilbert, D. T., & Wilson, T. D. (2007). Prospection: Experiencing the Future. *Science*, *317*(5843), 1351–1354.

Gilead, T. (2012). Education and the logic of economic progress. *Journal of Philosophy of Education*, *46*(1), 113–131.

Giroux, H. A. (2011). *On critical pedagogy*. New York, NY: Continuum.

Goldstein, J., & Kornfield, J. (1987). *Seeking the heart of wisdom: The path of insight meditation*. Boston: Shambhala.

Golland, Y., Bentin, S., Gelbard, H., Benjamini, Y., Heller, R., Nir, Y., Hasson, U., & Malach, R. (2007) Extrinsic and intrinsic systems in the posterior cortex of the human brain revealed during natural sensory stimulation. *Cerebral Cortex*, *17*(4), 766–777.

Goodrick, M. (1987). *The advancing guitarist: Applying guitar concepts & techniques*. Milwaukee, WI: Distributed by Hal Leonard Publishing.

Grabovac, A. D., Lau, M. A., & Willett, B. R. (2011). Mechanisms of mindfulness: A Buddhist psychological model. *Mindfulness*, *2*(3), 154–166.

Greenberg, M. T., & Harris, A. R. (2012). Nurturing mindfulness in children and youth: Current state of research. *Child Development Perspectives*, *6*(2), 161–166.

Gunnlaugson, O., Sarath, E., Scott, C., & Heesoon, B. (2014). *Contemplative learning and inquiry across disciplines.* Albany, NY: State University of New York Press.

Gyatso, T. (1999). *Ancient wisdom, modern world: Ethics for a new millennium.* London: Little, Brown.

Hacking, I. (1999). *The social construction of what?* Cambridge, MA: Harvard University Press.

Hadot, P. (1995). *Philosophy as a way of life: Spiritual exercises from Socrates to Foucault.* Malden, MA: Blackwell.

Hans, J. S. (1993). *The mysteries of attention.* Albany, NY: State University of New York Press.

Hanson, R., & Mendius, R. (2009). *Buddha's brain: The practical neuroscience of happiness, love & wisdom.* Oakland, CA: New Harbinger Publications.

Hargreaves, A. (2003). *Teaching in the knowledge society: Education in the age of insecurity.* New York: Teachers College Press.

Hebb, D. O. (1949). *The organization of behavior: A neuropsychological theory.* New York, NY: John Wiley and Sons Inc.

Hochstein, S., & Ahissar, M. (2002). View from the top: Hierarchies and reverse hierarchies in the visual system. *Neuron, 36*(5), 791–804.

Hoffman, D. (2008). Conscious realism and the mind-body problem. *Mind and Matter, 6*(1), 87–121.

Holt, J. (1995). *How children fail* (Rev. ed.). Reading, MA: Perseua Books.

Huebner, D. E. (1999). *The lure of the transcendent: Collected essays by Dwayne E. Huebner.* Mahwah, NJ: Lawrence Erlbaum Associates.

Iyengar, B. K. S. (1993). *Light on the yoga sūtras of Patañjali.* London: Aquarian/Thorsons.

Iyengar, B. K. S. (2005). *Light on life: The yoga journey to wholeness, inner peace, and ultimate freedom.* Emmaus, PA: Rodale.

James, W. (1907). The energies of men. *The Philosophical Review, 16*(1), 1–20.

James, W. (1976). *Essays in radical empiricism.* Cambridge, MA: Harvard University Press.

James, W. (1983). *Talks to teachers on psychology and to students on some of life's ideals.* Cambridge, MA: Harvard University Press.

James, W. (1984). *Psychology, briefer course.* Cambridge, MA: Harvard University Press.

James, W. (2007). *The principles of psychology.* New York, NY: Cosimo.

Jaynes, J. (1976). *The origin of consciousness in the breakdown of the bicameral mind.* Boston: Houghton Mifflin.

Jazaieri, H., Lee, I. A., McGonigal, K., Jinpa, T., Doty, J. R., Gross, J. J., & Goldin, P. R. (2016). A wandering mind is a less caring mind: Daily experience sampling during compassion meditation training. *The Journal of Positive Psychology, 11*(1), 37–50.

Jha, A. P., Krompinger, J., & Baime, M. J. (2007). Mindfulness training modifies subsystems of attention. *Cognitive, Affective & Behavioral Neuroscience, 7*(2), 109–119.

Kabat-Zinn, J. (1994). *Wherever you go, there you are: Mindfulness meditation in everyday life.* New York: Hyperion.

Kabat-Zinn, J. (2005). *Full catastrophe living: Using the wisdom of your body and mind to face stress, pain, and illness.* New York, NY: Delta Trade Paperbacks.

Kahneman, D. (2011). *Thinking fast and slow.* New York: Farrar, Straus & Giroux.

Kane, M. J., Brown, L. H., McVay, J. C., Silvia, P. J., Myin-Germeys, I., & Kwapil, T. R. (2007). For whom the mind wanders and when. An experience-sampling study of working memory and executive control in daily life. *Psychological Science, 18*(7), 614–621.

Kaufer, D., & Francis, D. (2011). Nurture, nature, and the stress that is life. In M. Brockman (Ed.), *Future Science: Cutting-edge essays form the new generation of scientists* (pp. 56–71). New York: Oxford University Press.

Kegan, R. (1982). *The evolving self: Problem and process in human development.* Cambridge, MA: Harvard University Press.

Kelchtermans, G. (2009). Who I am in how I teach is the message: Self-understanding, vulnerability and reflection. *Teachers and Teaching: Theory and Practice, 15*(2), 257–272.

Killingsworth, M. A., & Gilbert, D. T. (2010). A wandering mind is an unhappy mind. *Science, 330*(6006), 932–932.

Kincheloe, J., & Steinberg, S. (1993). A tentative description of post-formal thinking: The critical confrontation with cognitive theory. *Harvard Educational Review, 63*(3), 296–321.

Korthagen, F. A. J., Kim, Y. M., & Greene, W. L. (Eds.). (2012). *Teaching and learning from within: A core reflection approach to quality and inspiration in education.* New York: Routledge.

Kuhn, T. S. (1970). *The structure of scientific revolutions.* Chicago: University of Chicago Press.

Lakoff, G., & Johnson, M. (1999). *Philosophy in the flesh: The embodied mind & its challenge to western thought.* New York: Basic Books.

Langer, E. J. (1997). *The power of mindful learning.* Reading, MA: Addison-Wesley/Addison Wesley Longman.

Lelwica, M. M. (1999). *Starving for salvation: The spiritual dimensions of eating problems among American girls and women.* New York: Oxford University Press.

Lelwica, M. M. (2009). Embodying learning: Post-cartesian pedagogy and the academic study of religion. *Teaching Theology & Religion, 12*(2), 123–136.

Lewin, D. (2014). Behold: Silence and attention in education. *Journal of Philosophy of Education, 48*(3), 355–369.

Lewis, H. (2007). *Excellence without a soul: Does liberal education have a future?* New York: PublicAffairs.

Lewis, M. D. (2005). Self-organizing individual differences in brain development. *Developmental Review, 25*(3–4), 252–277.

Libet, B., Freeman, A., & Sutherland, K. (Eds.). (1999). *The volitional brain: Towards a neuroscience of free will.* Thorverton: Imprint Academic.

Lin, J., Oxford, R. L., & Brantmeier, E. J. (2013). *Re-envisioning higher education: Embodied pathways to wisdom and social transformation.* Toronto: Information Age Publishing.

Lorber, J. (1994). *Paradoxes of gender.* New Haven: Yale University Press.

Loy, D. (1988). *Nonduality: A study in comparative philosophy.* New Haven: Yale University Press.

Loy, D. (2000). *Lack and transcendence: The problem of death and life in psychotherapy, existentialism, and Buddhism.* Amherst, NY: Prometheus Books/Humanity Books.

MacLean, P. D. (1990). *The triune brain in evolution: Role in paleocerebral functions.* New York: Springer.

Mason, M. F., Norton, M. I., Van Horn, J. D., Wegner, D. M., Grafton, S. T., & Macrae, C. N. (2007). Wandering minds: The default network and stimulus-independent thought. *Science, 315*(5810), 393–395.

McGilchrist, I. (2009). *The master and his emissary: The divided brain and the making of the Western world.* New Haven: Yale University Press.

McMillan, R., Kaufman, S. B., & Singer, J. L. (2013). Ode to positive constructive daydreaming. *Frontiers in Psychology, 4*(626), 1–9.

McVay, J. C., & Kane, M. J. (2009). Conducting the train of thought: Working memory capacity, goal neglect, and mind wandering in an executive-control task. *Journal of Experimental Psychology. Learning, Memory, and Cognition, 35*(1), 196–204.

Menon, V. (2015). Salience network. In A. W. Toga (Ed.), *Brain mapping: An encyclopedic reference* (Vol. 2, pp. 597–611). Los Angeles, CA: Elsevier.

Merleau-Ponty, M. (1965). *Phenomenology of perception.* London: Routledge & Kegan Paul.

Miller, J. P. (2013). *The contemplative practitioner: Meditation in education and the workplace* (2nd ed.). Toronto: University of Toronto Press.

Mind and Life Education Research Network (MLERN), J. Davidson, R., Dunne, J., Eccles, J. S., Engle, A., Greenberg, M., . . . Vago, D. (2012). Contemplative practices and mental training: Prospects for American education. *Child Development Perspectives, 6*(2), 146–153.

Mrazek, M. D., Smallwood, J., & Schooler, J. W. (2012). Mindfulness and mind-wandering: Finding convergence through opposing constructs. *Emotion, 12*(3), 442–448.

Nagel, T. (1986). *The view from nowhere.* New York: Oxford University Press.

Napoli, D. M., Krech, P. R., & Holley, L. C. (2005). Mindfulness training for elementary school students. *Journal of Applied School Psychology, 21*(1), 99–125.

Neill, A. S. (1960). *Summerhill: A radical approach to child rearing*. New York: Hart Pub. Co.

Nietzsche, F. (2014). *Schopenhauer as educator: Nietzsche's third untimely meditation*. (D. Pellerin, Trans.). Create Space Independent Publishing Platform. https://www.amazon.com/Schopenhauer-Educator-Nietzsches-Untimely-Meditation/dp/1503386317

Nolen-Hoeksema, S., Wisco, B. E., & Lyubomirsky, S. (2008). Rethinking rumination. *Perspectives on Psychological Science, 3*(5), 400–424.

Nørretranders, T. (1998). *The user illusion: Cutting consciousness down to size*. New York: Viking Penguin.

Northoff, G., & Bermpohl, F. (2004). Cortical midline structures and the self. *Trends in Cognitive Sciences, 8*(3), 102–107.

Northoff, G., Heinzel, A., de Greck, M., Bermpohl, F., Dobrowolny, H., & Panksepp, J. (2006). Self-referential processing in our brain – A meta-analysis of imaging studies on the self. *NeuroImage, 31*(1), 440–457.

Nummenmaa, L., Glerean, E., Hari, R., & Hietanen, J. K. (2014). Bodily maps of emotions. *Proceedings of the National Academy of Sciences, 111*(2), 646–651.

Olendzki, A. (2010). *Unlimiting mind: The radically experiential psychology of Buddhism*. Boston, MA: Wisdom Publications.

O'Loughlin, M. (2006). *Embodiment and education: Exploring creatural existence*. Dordrecht: Springer.

Palmer, P. (1983). *To know as we are known: A spirituality of education*. San Francisco, CA: Harper & Row.

Palmer, P. (1998). *The courage to teach: Exploring the inner landscape of a teacher's life*. San Francisco, CA: Jossey-Bass.

Palmer, P., & Zajonc, A. (2010). *The heart of higher education: A call to renewal: transforming the academy through collegial conversations*. San Francisco, CA: Jossey-Bass.

Peters, R. (1967). *The concept of education*. London: Routledge & Kegan Paul.

Peters, R. S. (2010). What is an educational process? In R. S. Peters (Ed.), *The concept of education* (pp. 1–16). London: Routledge.

Petersen, S. E., & Posner, M. I. (2012). The attention system of the human brain: 20 years after. *Annual Review of Neuroscience, 35*, 73–89.

Phelps, E. A., & Sharot, T. (2008). How (and why) emotion enhances the subjective sense of recollection. *Current Directions in Psychological Science, 17*(2), 147–152.

Philips, D. C. (2014). Research in the hard sciences, and in very hard "softer" domains. *Educational Researcher, 43*(1), 9–11.

Pinar, W., & Grumet, M. R. (2014). *Toward a poor curriculum* (3rd ed.). Kingston, NY: Educator's International Press, Inc.

Polanyi, M. (1958). *Personal knowledge; towards a post-critical philosophy*. Chicago: University of Chicago Press.

Postman, N. (1995). *The end of education: Redefining the value of school.* New York: Knopf.

Purser, R. E. (2015). Clearing the muddled path of traditional and contemporary mindfulness. *Mindfulness, 6*(1), 23–45.

Qin, P., & Northoff, G. (2011). How is our self-related to midline regions and the default-mode network? *NeuroImage, 57*(3), 1221–1233.

Rāhula, W. (1974). *What the Buddha taught.* New York: Grove Press. Distributed by Random House.

Raichle, M. E. (2006). The brain's dark energy. *Science, 314*(5803), 1249–1250.

Raichle, M. E. (2015). The brain's default mode network. *Annual Review of Neuroscience, 38*(1), 433–447.

Raichle, M. E., MacLeod, A. M., Snyder, A. Z., Powers, W. J., Gusnard, D. A., & Shulman, G. L. (2001). A default mode of brain function. *Proceedings of the National Academy of Sciences, 98*(2), 676–682.

Raveh, D. (2012). *Exploring the yogasutra. Philosophy and translation.* London: Continuum International Pub.

Reveley, J. (2016). Neoliberal meditations: How mindfulness training medicalizes education and responsibilizes young people. (ahead of print) *Policy Futures in Education.*

Robinson, K., with Aronica, L. (2009). *The element: How finding your passion changes everything.* New York: Viking.

Roderick, L., & Merculieff, I. (2013). *Stop talking: Indigenous ways of teaching and learning and difficult dialogues in higher education.* Anchorage, Alaska: University of Alaska Anchorage.

Roeser, R. W., & Peck, S. C. (2009). An education in awareness: Self, motivation, and self-regulated learning in contemplative perspective. *Educational Psychologist, 44*(2), 119–136.

Roth, H. D. (2006). Contemplative studies: Prospects for a new field. *Teachers College Record, 108*(9), 1787–1815.

Roth, H. D. (2008). Against cognitive imperialism. *Religion East & West, 8*, 1–26.

Saxe, R., & Baron-Cohen, S. (2007). *Theory of mind.* Hove: Psychology Press.

Schacter, D. (1987). Implicit memory: History and current status. *Journal of Experimental Psychology: Learning, Memory, and Cognition, 13*, 501–518.

Schacter, D., Addis, D. R., & Buckner, R. L. (2007). Remembering the past to imagine the future: The prospective brain. *Nature Reviews Neuroscience, 8*(9), 657–661.

Schön, D. (1990). *Educating the reflective practitioner.* San Francisco: Jossey-Bass.

Schonert-Reichl, K. A., & Roeser, R. W. (Eds.). (2016). *Handbook of mindfulness in education: Integrating theory and research into practice.* New York, NY: Springer.

Schooler, J. W. (2002). Re-representing consciousness: Dissociations between experience and meta-consciousness. *Trends in Cognitive Sciences, 6*(8), 339–344.

Schooler, J. W., Smallwood, J., Christoff, K., Handy, T. C., Reichle, E. D., & Sayette, M. A. (2011). Meta-awareness, perceptual decoupling and the wandering mind. *Trends in Cognitive Sciences*, *15*(7), 319–326.

Schopenhauer, A. (1966). *The world as will and representation* (Vol. 1). (E. F. J. Payne, Trans.) (Reprint Edition edition). New York: Dover Publications.

Schwab, J. J. (1969). The practical: A language for curriculum. *The School Review*, *78*(1), 1–23.

Searle, J. R. (2015). *Seeing things as they are; a theory of perception*. New York: Oxford University Press.

Segal, Z., Teasdale, J. D., & Williams, J. M. G. (2002). *Mindfulness-based cognitive therapy for depression: A new approach to preventing relapse*. New York: Guilford Press.

Shatz, C. (1992). The developing brain. *Scientific American*, *267*(3), 60–67.

Shusterman, R. (2008). *Body consciousness: A philosophy of mindfulness and somaesthetics*. Cambridge; New York: Cambridge University Press.

Siegel, D. (2010). *Mindsight: The new science of personal transformation*. New York: Bantam Books.

Siegel, D. (2012). *The developing mind: How relationships and the brain interact to shape who we are* (2nd ed.). New York: Guilford Press.

Singer, J. (1966). *Daydreaming; an introduction to the experimental study of inner experience*. New York, NY: Random House.

Singer, T., Critchley, H. D., & Preuschoff, K. (2009). A common role of insula in feelings, empathy and uncertainty. *Trends in Cognitive Sciences*, *13*(8), 334–340.

Slagter, H. A., Davidson, R. J., & Lutz, A. (2011). Mental training as a tool in the neuroscientific study of brain and cognitive plasticity. *Frontiers in Human Neuroscience*, *5*(17), 1–12.

Smallwood, J., & Andrews-Hanna, J. (2013). Not all minds that wander are lost: The importance of a balanced perspective on the mind-wandering state. *Frontiers in Psychology*, *4*(441), 1–6.

Smallwood, J., Fishman, D. J., & Schooler, J. W. (2007a). Counting the cost of an absent mind: Mind wandering as an under recognized influence on educational performance. *Psychonomic Bulletin & Review*, *14*(2), 230–236.

Smallwood, J., McSpadden, M., & Schooler, J. W. (2007b). The lights are on but no one's home: Meta-awareness and the decoupling of attention when the mind wanders. *Psychonomic Bulletin & Review*, *14*(3), 527–533.

Smallwood, J., Fitzgerald, A., Miles, L. K., & Phillips, L. H. (2009). Shifting moods, wandering minds: Negative moods lead the mind to wander. *Emotion*, *9*(2), 271–276.

Sood, A., & Jones, D. T. (2013). On mind wandering, attention, brain networks, and meditation. *Explore*, *9*(3), 136–141.

Spencer, H. (1860). *Education: Intellectual, moral, and physical*. New York, NY: D Appleton & Company.

Suddendorf, T., & Corballis, M. C. (2007). The evolution of foresight: What is mental time travel, and is it unique to humans?. *The Behavioral and Brain Sciences*, 30(3), 299–313.

Suzuki, S. (1999). *Zen mind, beginner's mind* (1st rev. ed.). New York: Weatherhill.

Tan, C. (2008). *Teaching without indoctrination: Implications for values education*. Rotterdam/Taipei: Sense Publishers.

Tang, Y. Y., Hölzel, B. K., & Posner, M. I. (2015). The neuroscience of mindfulness meditation. *Nature Reviews Neuroscience*, 16(4), 213–225.

Tang, Y.-Y., Ma, Y., Wang, J., Fan, Y., Feng, S., Lu, Q.,…Posner, M. I. (2007). Short-term meditation training improves attention and self-regulation. *Proceedings of the National Academy of Sciences*, 104(43), 17152–17156.

Tarrasch, R., Berman, Z., & Friedmann, N. (2016). Mindful reading: Mindfulness meditation helps keep readers with Dyslexia and ADHD on the lexical track. *Frontiers in Psychology*, 7(578), 1–18.

Tulving, E. (1985). *Elements of episodic memory*. Oxford: Oxford University Press.

Turkle, S. (2012). *Alone together*. New York: Basic Books.

Tustin, K., & Hayne, H. (2010). Defining the boundary: Age-related changes in childhood amnesia. *Developmental Psychology*, 46(5), 1049–1061.

Varela, F. J., & Shear, J. (1999). *The view from within: First-person approaches to the study of consciousness*. Thoverton: Imprint Academic.

Varela, F., Thompson, E., & Rosch, E. (1991). *The embodied mind: Cognitive science and human experience*. Cambridge, MA: MIT Press.

Wallace, A. B. (1999). The Buddhist tradition of Samatha: Methods of refining and examining consciousness. *Journal of Consciousness Studies*, 6(2–3), 175–187.

Wallace, A. B. (2006). *The attention revolution: Unlocking the power of the focused mind*. Boston: Wisdom Publications.

Weil, S. (1986). *Simone Weil, an anthology*. New York: Weidenfeld & Nicolson. https://www.amazon.com/Simone-Weil-Anthology/dp/0802137296.

Werner, K. (1996). *Effortless mastery: Liberating the master musician within*. Albany, NY: Jamey Aebersold Jazz, Inc.

White, J. P. (2010). Indoctrination. In R. S. Peters (ed.), *The concept of education* (pp. 123–133). London: Routledge.

Whitehead, A. (1967). *The aims of education and other essays*. New York: Free Press.

Wilber, K. (1981). *No boundary: Eastern and Western approaches to personal growth*. Boulder, CO: Shambhala.

Wittgenstein, L. (1953). *Philosophical investigations*. (trans. G. E. M. Anscombe). Oxford: Basil Blackwell Ltd.

Wittgenstein, L. (1961). *Tractatus logico-philosophicus*. New York: Humanities Press.

Wood, N., & Cowan, N. (1995). The cocktail party phenomenon revisited: How frequent are attention shifts to one's name in an irrelevant auditory channel? *Journal of Experimental Psychology. Learning, Memory, and Cognition, 21*(1), 255–260.

Young, S. (2013). Five Ways to Know Yourself. Self published.

Yuasa, Y. (1993). *The body, self-cultivation, and ki-energy*. Albany, NY: State University of New York Press.

Zajonc, A. (2009). *Meditation as contemplative inquiry: When knowing becomes love*. Great Barrington, MA: Lindisfarne.

Zaki, J., Davis, J. I., & Ochsner, K. N. (2012). Overlapping activity in anterior insula during interception and emotional experience. *NeuroImage, 62*(1), 493–499.

Zeidan, F., Johnson, S. K., Diamond, B. J., David, Z., & Goolkasian, P. (2010). Mindfulness meditation improves cognition: Evidence of brief mental training. *Consciousness and Cognition, 19*(2), 597–605.

Zenner, C., Herrnleben-Kurz, S., & Walach, H. (2014). Mindfulness-based interventions in schools—A systematic review and meta-analysis. *Frontiers in Psychology, 5*(603), 1–20.

Zylowska, L., Ackerman, D. L., Yang, M. H., Futrell, J. L., Horton, N. L., Hale, T. S., . . . Smalley, S. L. (2008). Mindfulness meditation training in adults and adolescents with ADHD a feasibility study. *Journal of Attention Disorders, 11*(6), 737–746.

INDEX

Note: Page references with letter 'n' refer to notes.